A Social History of

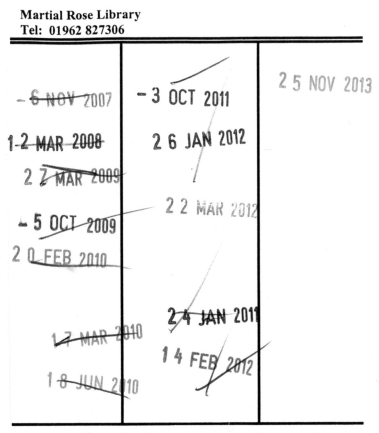

THE UNIVERSITY OF
WINCHESTER

A Social History of the Media

From Gutenberg to the Internet

Second edition

ASA BRIGGS AND PETER BURKE

polity

First published in 2005 by Polity Press

Reprinted 2006 (twice), 2007

Polity Press
65 Bridge Street
Cambridge CB2 1UR, UK

Polity Press
350 Main Street
Malden, MA 02148, USA

ISBN: 978-0-7456-3511-8
ISBN: 978-0-7456-3512-5 (pb)

A catalogue record for this book is available from the British Library and has been applied for from the Library of Congress.

Typeset in 9.5 on 12 pt Utopia
by SNP Best-set Typesetter Ltd, Hong Kong
Printed and bound in Great Britain by TJ International Ltd, Padstow, Cornwall

For further information on Polity, visit our website: www.polity.co.uk

Contents

List of Illustrations   *vi*
Preface   *viii*

1   Introduction   *1*
2   The Print Revolution in Context   *13*
3   The Media and the Public Sphere in Early Modern Europe   *61*
4   From Steam to Electricity   *88*
5   Processes and Patterns   *100*
6   Information, Education, Entertainment   *151*
7   Convergence   *216*
8   Multimedia   *254*

Chronology   *269*
Further Reading   *281*
Index   *295*

Illustrations

1 Anon, *The Vision of St Bernard*, Book of Hours, *c.*1470 (Utrecht, Museum het Catherineconvent, ABM hs. 19) *2*

2 Tintoretto, *St Mark Rescuing a Slave*, 1548. Venice, Galleria dell'Accademia (photo AKG London/Cameraphoto) *3*

3 Anon tapestry, *Apocalypse*, 14th century (Angers, Musée des Tapisseries/photo Lauros-Giraudon) *8*

4 Ramist table of contents from Robert Burton's *Anatomy of Melancholy*, 1st edition, 1621 (Cambridge University Library) *17*

5 John Ogilby, road map from his *Britannia*, 1675, showing Cambridge (British Library) *20*

6 Register of household literacy examination in Sweden *27*

7 *The Repeal, or the Funerary Procession of Miss Americ-Stamp*, 1765 (© British Museum) *32*

8 Marguerite Gérard and Jean-Honoré Fragonard, *The Reader* (Cambridge, Fitzwilliam Museum/photo Bridgeman Art Library) *52*

9 Lucas Cranach, woodcuts of *Passional Christi and Antichristi*, 1521 (British Library) *66*

10 Hans Baldung Grien, woodcut of Martin Luther with halo, *c.*1523 (British Library) *67*

11 The seventeen provinces and principal cities for iconoclasm in 1566 (from S. Deyon and A. Lottin, *Les Casseurs de L'été 1566*, Paris, Hachette, 1981) *71*

12 Richard Overton, *Canterbury, his Change of Diet*, title page, 1644 (Oxford, Bodleian Library) *75*

13 Political plate, *c.*1790 (Nevers, Musée Municipale) *83*

14 King Steam and King Coal watch anxiously the Infant Electricity. A *Punch* cartoon of 1881 (Mary Evans Picture Library) *98*

15 *The Laying of the Transatlantic Cable*, 1865. (Mary Evans Picture Library) *105*

16 Thomas Edison at work. Both his laboratory and his study were workplaces. (Hulton Getty) *116*

17 'Weavers of Speech'. A telephone advertisement for the Bell Telephone Company, (Property of AT&T Archives. Reprinted with permission of AT&T) *119*

18 The young Guglielmo Marconi. (Hulton Getty) *125*

19 *The Jazz Singer*. A Warner Brothers film, 1927. (© Bettmann/Corbis) *139*

20 Alfred Harmsworth, first Viscount Northcliffe, seen here in 1911 with members of the Astor family. (Hulton Getty) *148*

21 In the stadium. Hitler addresses a huge rally. (AKG London) *175*

22 At the fireside. Franklin D. Roosevelt uses radio to chat to his fellow citizens. (© Hulton Archive) *176*

23 A cartoon of John Reith shows him outside the new Broadcasting House. (Reproduced with permission of Punch Ltd) *179*

24 Transistor radios transformed life on the beach and in the desert. Transistors had a bigger history, a key invention in the development of the lap-top computer. (Advertising Archives)   *184*

25 The moon landing, 1969. The Americans tell the world they are in space. (NASA)   *205*

26 The press retains its power: police and photographers at May Day protests, London, 2001. (Geoff Caddick/National Pictures)   *213*

27 The Second World War Colossus electronic code-breaker at Bletchley Park, Buckinghamshire. (Bletchley Park Trust/Science and Society Picture Library)   *222*

28 Education and communications technology: *a.* Pupils from Wembley School listening to a radio broadcast in 1933; *b.* Walter Perry, first Vice-Chancellor of the Open University, at the opening of its first (BBC) production studio at Alexandra Palace, 1970. (© BBC Worldwide)   *250, 251*

29 The founders of Yahoo!, the Internet search engine. Jerry Yang and David Filo. (Frank Spooner Pictures)   *265*

Preface

The aim of this book – on a vast and ever-expanding theme – is to show the relevance of the past to the present by bringing history into media studies and the media into history. Our own choice of medium reflects a qualified optimism in the future of the book, which we believe will continue to exist alongside newer forms of communication as manuscripts did in the age of print. There will be a new division of labour between media.

So far as our own division of labour is concerned, Peter Burke is primarily responsible for Chapters 1–3, Asa Briggs for Chapters 4–8, but the two authors joined forces to revise the text, meeting regularly in different locales, from King's Cross Station to Claridge's, as well as keeping in touch by telephone. Historians of the twenty-first century may like to note that the text was written partly in longhand and partly on a personal computer by two academics whose resistance to driving cars and using e-mail is in no way incompatible with an interest in technological and social change in the present and the future as well as in the past.

We should like to thank Amleto Lorenzini for first yoking us together in a project on the history of communication, and John Thompson for commissioning the volume. We are indebted to Pat Spencer for her help in getting both the first edition and this new thoroughly revised edition into the hands of the printers and Peter Burke is grateful to Joad Raymond for his comments on a draft of Chapter 3.

1 Introduction

It was only in the 1920s – according to the *Oxford English Dictionary* – that people began to speak of 'the media', and a generation later, in the 1950s, of a 'communication revolution', but a concern with the means of communication is very much older than that. Rhetoric, the study of the art of oral and written communication, was taken very seriously in ancient Greece and Rome. It was studied in the Middle Ages, and with greater enthusiasm in the Renaissance.

Rhetoric was still taken seriously in the eighteenth and nineteenth centuries, when other key ideas were emerging. The concept 'public opinion' appeared in the late eighteenth century, while a concern with the 'masses' is visible from the early nineteenth century onwards, at the time when newspapers, the history of which is charted in each chapter, were helping to fashion national consciousness by making people aware of their fellow readers.

In the first half of the twentieth century, especially in the wake of two world wars, scholarly interest shifted towards the study of propaganda. More recently, some ambitious theorists, from the French anthropologist Claude Lévi-Strauss to the German sociologist Niklas Luhmann, have extended the concept of 'communication' still more widely. Lévi-Strauss wrote about the exchange of goods and women, Luhmann about power, money and love as so many *Kommunikationsmedien*. If this is the case, as readers may already be asking themselves, what in the world does not count as communication? This history will restrict itself to the communication of information, ideas and entertainment in words and images by means of speech, writing, print, radio, television and most recently by the Internet.

Significantly, it was in the age of radio that scholars began to recognize the importance of oral communication in ancient Greece and in the Middle Ages. The beginning of the television age in the 1950s brought in visual communication as well and stimulated the rise of an interdisciplinary theory of the media. Contributions were made from economics, history, literature, art, political science, psychology, sociology and anthropology, and led to the emergence of academic departments of communication and cultural studies. Striking phrases encapsulating new ideas were coined by Harold Innis (1894–1952), who wrote of the 'bias of communications'; by Marshall McLuhan (1911–80) who spoke of the 'global village'; by Jack Goody, who traced the 'domestication of the savage mind'; and by Jürgen Habermas, the German sociologist who identified the 'public sphere', a zone for 'discourse' in which ideas are explored and 'a public view' can be expressed.

This book argues that, whatever the starting-point, it is necessary for people working in communication and cultural studies – a still growing number – to take

Fig. 1 Anon, *The Vision of St Bernard*, Book of Hours, c.1470.

history seriously, as well as for historians – whatever their period and preoccupations – to take serious account of communication, including both communication theory and communications technology.

Students of communication should realize that some phenomena in the media are older than is generally recognized, as two examples may suggest. Today's television serials follow the model of radio serials, which in turn follow the model of the stories serialized in nineteenth-century magazines (novelists from Dickens to Dostoevsky originally published their work in this way). Again, some of the conventions of twentieth-century comic books draw directly or indirectly on an even longer visual tradition. Speech balloons can be found in eighteenth-century prints, which are in turn an adaptation of the 'text scrolls' coming from the mouths of the Virgin and other figures in medieval religious art (see Figure 1). St Mark, in the painting by Jacopo Tintoretto (1518–94) known as *St Mark rescuing a slave*, is presented like Superman in the comics four hundred years later, diving head first from Heaven to rescue a Christian captive (Figure 2).

Denunciations of new media follow a similar pattern, whether the object of these denunciations is television or the Internet, and they take us back to debates about the unfortunate effects of romances on their readers and of plays on their audiences as early as the sixteenth century, stressing the stimulation of the passions. San Carlo Borromeo (1538–84), archbishop of Milan, described

Fig. 2 Tintoretto, *St Mark Rescuing a Slave*, 1548. Venice, Galleria dell'Accademia.

plays as the 'liturgy of the devil'. The first chapter of Dennis and Merrill's *Four Arguments for the Elimination of Television* was entitled 'The Belly of the Beast'. The role of the press, and of the journalists who earn their living from it, has always been controversial: the unreliability of the 'gazetteers' was already a commonplace in the seventeenth century. The charge of 'muck-raking' is also an old one.

Despite all such continuities, this book will concentrate on changes in the media; in presenting them, an attempt will be made to avoid two dangers, that of asserting that everything has got worse or that of assuming that there has been continuous improvement. Either way, the implication that trends have moved in a single direction must be rejected, although writers trusting in it have often been eloquent and distinguished in their own fields. Thus, the Italian historian Carlo Cipolla, in his study of *Literacy and Development in the West* (1969), stressed the contribution of literacy to industrialization and more generally to 'progress' and to 'civilization', suggesting that 'widespread literacy meant . . . a more rational and more receptive approach to life'. In this respect, Cipolla's work is representative of a mid-twentieth-century faith in 'modernization', a faith which underlay the literacy campaigns organized by UNESCO and by the governments of Third World countries such as Cuba.

The problems raised by this kind of approach demand discussion (see p. 207). So, too, do statements about the Internet and its potential as an agency of 'democratization'. It is not possible at this point in its history to conclude that through the widening of access and its transformation 'from below' it will in the long run fulfil that role. Already some critics fear that it undermines all forms of 'authority', affects behaviour adversely, and jeopardizes individual and collective security. Rightly, therefore, a number of specialists in media studies have focused on what they call 'media debates'. They concern both topical issues and long-term processes.

A relatively short history like this must be extremely selective and must privilege certain themes, like the role of the public sphere, the supply and diffusion of information, the growth of networks and the rise of mediated entertainment. It must also concentrate on change rather than continuity, although readers will be reminded from time to time that, as new media were introduced, older ones were not abandoned but coexisted and interacted with the new arrivals. Manuscripts remained important in the age of print, as books and radio did in the age of television. The media need to be viewed as a system, a system in perpetual change in which different elements play greater or smaller roles.

What follows is essentially a social and cultural history with the politics, the economics and – not least – the technology put in, yet it rejects technological determinism, which rests on misleading simplifications (see pp. 11–12, 14). We have been influenced at the outset by the simple but deservedly famous classic formula of the American political scientist Harold Lasswell (1902–78), describing communication in terms of who says what to whom in which channel and with what effect. The 'what' (content), the 'who' (control) and the 'whom' (audience) matter equally. So, too, does the 'where'. The responses of different groups of people to what they hear, view or read always demand study. How big the different groups are – and whether they constitute a 'mass' – is also relevant. The language of the masses emerged in the course of the nineteenth century and reminds us to consider Lasswell's 'whom' in terms of 'how many?'

The immediate intentions, strategies and tactics of communicators need at every point in the story to be related to the context in which they are operating – along with the messages that they are communicating. The long-term effects, especially the unintended and sometimes surprising consequences of the use of one means of communication rather than another, are more difficult to separate, even with the gift of hindsight. Indeed, whether 'effects' is the right term, implying as it does a one-way cause–effect relationship, is itself a subject of controversy. The words 'network' and 'web' were already in use in the nineteenth century.

This book concentrates on the modern West, from the late fifteenth century onwards. The narrative begins with printing (*c*.1450 AD) rather than with the alphabet (*c*.2000 BC), with writing (*c*.5000 BC) or with speech, but despite the importance often attributed to Johann Gutenberg (*c*.1400–68), whom readers of one British newspaper voted 'man of the millennium' (*Sunday Times*, 28 November 1999), there is no clean break or zero point at which the story begins, and it will sometimes be necessary to refer back briefly to the ancient and medieval worlds. In those days, communications were not immediate, but they already reached to all the corners of the known world.

The twentieth-century Canadian Harold Innis was one of several scholars who noted the importance of the media in the ancient world. Trained as an economist, he made his reputation with the so-called 'staple theory' of Canadian development, noting the successive dominance of the trade in furs, fish and paper, and the effects of these cycles on Canadian society. 'Each staple in turn left its stamp, and the shift to new staples invariably produced periods of crisis.' The study of paper led him into the history of journalism, and the study of Canada, where communications mattered profoundly for economic and political development, colonial and postcolonial, drew him to the comparative history of empires and their media of communication, from ancient Assyria and Egypt to the present. In his *Empire and Communications* (1950), Innis argued, for instance, that the Assyrian Empire was a pioneer in the construction of highways: it was claimed that a message could be sent from any point to the centre and an answer received within a week.

As a good economic historian, when he wrote of 'media', Innis meant the materials used for communication, contrasting relatively durable substances such as parchment, clay and stone with relatively ephemeral products such as papyrus and paper (the sections on the so-called 'ages' of steam and electricity later in this book will underline his point about the material media of communication). Innis went on to suggest that the use of the heavier materials, as in the case of Assyria, led to a cultural bias towards time and towards religious organizations, while the lighter ones, which may be moved quickly over long distances, led to a bias towards space and political organizations. Some of his earlier history is weak and some of his concepts are ill-defined, but the ideas of Innis as well as his broad comparative approach remain a stimulus as well as an inspiration to later workers in the field. It is to be hoped that future historians will analyse the consequences of using plastic and wire in the way in which Innis approached stone and papyrus.

Another central concept in Innis's pioneering theory was the idea that each medium of communication tended to create a dangerous monopoly of knowledge. Before Innis decided to become an economist, he thought seriously about becoming a Baptist minister. The economist's interest in competition, in this case competition between media, was linked to the radical Protestant's critique of 'priestcraft'. Thus, he argued that the intellectual monopoly of medieval monks, based on parchment, was undermined by paper and print, just as the 'monopoly power over writing' exercised by Egyptian priests in the age of hieroglyphs had been subverted by the Greeks and their alphabet.

In the case of ancient Greece, however, Innis emphasized speech more than the alphabet. 'Greek civilization', he wrote, 'was a reflection of the power of the spoken word.' In this respect he followed a Toronto colleague, Eric Havelock (1903–88), whose *Preface to Plato* (1963) focused on the oral culture of the early Greeks. The speeches in the Assembly at Athens and the plays recited in the open-air amphitheatres were important elements of ancient Greek civilization. In this, as in other oral cultures, songs and stories came in fluid rather than fixed forms, and creation was collective in the sense that singers and storytellers continually adopted and adapted themes and phrases from one another. So do scholars today, although plagiarism is denounced and our conceptions of intellectual property require that the source of borrowed material be acknowledged, at least in a footnote.

Clarifying the process of creation, the Harvard professor Milman Parry (1900–35) argued that the *Iliad* and the *Odyssey* – although they have survived into our own time only because they were written down – were essentially improvised oral poems. To test his theory, Parry carried out fieldwork in the 1930s in rural Yugoslavia (as it then was), recording performances by narrative poets on a wire-recorder (the predecessor of the tape recorder). He went on to analyse the recurrent formulae (set phrases such as 'wine-dark sea') and recurrent themes (such as a council of war or the arming of a warrior), prefabricated elements which enabled the singers to improvise their stories for hours at a time.

In Parry's work, developed by his former assistant Albert Lord in *The Singer of Tales* (1960), Yugoslavia, and by analogy Homeric Greece, illustrated the positive aspects of oral cultures which had too often been dismissed – as they sometimes still are – as merely 'illiterate'. That ancient Greek culture was shaped by the dominance of oral communication is a view which is now widely shared by classical scholars.

Yet Alexander the Great carried Homer's *Iliad* with him on his expeditions in a precious casket, while a great library of about half a million rolls was founded in the city named after him, Alexandria. It is no accident that it was in association with this vast library of manuscripts, which allowed information and ideas from different individuals, places and times to be juxtaposed and compared, that a school of critics developed, taking advantage of the library's resources to develop practices which would only spread in the age of print (see p. 18). The balance between media is discussed in Rosalind Thomas's *Literacy and Orality in Ancient Greece* (1992).

Images, especially statues, were another important form of communication, indeed of propaganda, in the ancient world, notably in Rome in the age of Augustus. This Roman official art was to influence the iconography of the early Church: the image of Christ 'in Majesty', for example, was an adaptation of the image of the emperor. For Christians, images were both a means of conveying information and a means of persuasion. As the Greek theologian Basil of Caesarea (*c.*330–79) put it, 'artists do as much for religion with their pictures as orators do by their eloquence'. In similar fashion, Pope Gregory the Great (*c.*540–604) described images as doing for those who could not read, the great majority, what writing did for those who could. The tactile aspect of images also deserves to be noted. Kissing a painting or a statue was a common way of expressing devotion, and one still to be seen in the Catholic and Orthodox worlds today.

It was the Byzantine Church which stayed close to ancient models. Christ as Pantocrator ('ruler of all') figured in the mosaics decorating the interior of the domes of Byzantine churches. In a part of Europe where literacy was at its lowest, Byzantine culture was a culture of painted icons of Christ, the Virgin and the saints. As an eighth-century abbot declared: 'The gospels were written in words, but icons are written in gold.' The term 'iconography' would pass into high culture and later, in the twentieth century, into popular culture, where 'icon' refers to a secular celebrity such as – appropriately enough – Madonna, the pop singer.

Byzantine icons could be seen in homes and streets as well as in churches, where they were displayed on the iconostasis, the doors screening the sanctuary from the laity. There was no such separation in the Roman Catholic churches. In both faiths symbolism was a feature of religious art and the messages it conveyed, but in Byzantium, unlike the West until the Reformation, teaching through visual culture was sometimes under assault, and images were intermittently attacked as idols and destroyed by iconoclasts (image-smashers), a movement which reached its climax in the year 726.

Islam banned the use of the human figure in religious art, as did Judaism, so that mosques and synagogues looked very different from churches. Nonetheless, in Persia from the fourteenth century, human figures along with birds and animals were prominent in illuminated manuscripts which went on to flourish in the Ottoman Empire and Mogul India. They were illustrating history or fable. The most famous western example of such illustration was in needlework, the *Bayeux Tapestry* (*c.*1100), which vividly depicted the Norman Conquest of England in 1066. A strip 232 feet long presented a visual narrative which has sometimes been compared to a film in respect of its techniques and effects.

In medieval cathedrals, images carved in wood, stone or bronze and figuring in stained-glass windows formed a powerful system of communication. In his novel *Notre Dame de Paris* (1831–2), Victor Hugo portrayed the cathedral and the book as two rival systems: 'this will kill that'. In fact, the two systems coexisted and interacted for a long time, like manuscript and print later. 'To the Middle Ages', according to the French art historian Emile Mâle (1862–1954), 'art was didactic'. People learned from images 'all that it was necessary that they should know – the history of the world from the creation, the dogmas of religion, the examples of the saints, the hierarchy of the virtues, the range of the sciences, arts

Fig. 3 Anon tapestry, *Apocalypse*, 14th century.

and crafts: all this was taught them by the windows of the church or by the statues in the porch'.

Ritual was another important medieval medium which remained significant in later contexts. The importance of public rituals in Europe, including the rituals of festival, during the thousand years 500–1500 has been explained (perceptively if inadequately) by the low rate of literacy at that time. What could not be recorded needed to be remembered, and what needed to be remembered had to be presented in a memorable way. Elaborate and dramatic rituals such as the coronation of kings and the homage of kneeling vassals to their seated lords demonstrated to the beholders that an important event had occurred. Transfers of land might be accompanied by gifts of symbolic objects such as a piece of turf or a sword. Ritual, with its strong visual component, was a major form of publicity, as it would be once more in the age of televised events such as the coronation of Queen Elizabeth II. The word 'spectacle', commonly used in the seventeenth century, was revived in the twentieth century. (See below, p. 201.)

Nonetheless, medieval Europe, like ancient Greece, has been viewed as an essentially oral culture. Preaching was an important means of spreading information. In the words of a pioneering student of the subject, the Cambridge don H. J. Chaytor, what we now call medieval literature was produced for 'a hearing not a reading public'. In his book *From Script to Print* (1945), he explained that if the reading room of (say) the British Library were to be filled with medieval readers, 'the buzz of whispering and muttering would be intolerable'. Medieval accounts were 'audited' in the literal sense of someone listening to them being read aloud. So were poems of all kinds, monastic or secular. The Icelandic saga, stretching back into a non-Graeco-Roman past, takes its name from the fact that it was read aloud, in other words spoken or 'said'.

It was only very gradually, from the eleventh century onwards, that writing began to be employed for a variety of practical purposes by popes and kings, and a trust in writing (as Michael Clanchy showed in *From Memory to Written Record*, 1979) developed still more slowly. In England in 1101, for example, some people preferred to rely on the word of three bishops rather than on a papal document which they described contemptuously as 'the skins of wethers blackened with ink'. Yet, despite such examples of resistance, the gradual penetration of writing into everyday life in the later Middle Ages had important consequences, including the replacement of traditional customs by written laws, the rise of forgery, the control of administration by clerks (literate clerics) and, as Brian Stock has pointed out in *The Implications of Literacy* (1972), the emergence of heretics who justified their unorthodox opinions by appealing to biblical texts, thus threatening what Innis called the 'monopoly' of knowledge of the medieval clergy. For these and other reasons, scholars speak of the rise of written culture in the twelfth and thirteenth centuries.

Manuscripts, including illuminated manuscripts, were being produced in increasing numbers in the two centuries before the invention of printing, a new technology introduced in order to satisfy a rising demand for reading matter. And in the two centuries before printing, visual art was also developing what in retrospect came to be regarded as portraiture. The poet Dante and the artist Giotto (1266–1330) were contemporaries. Both were fascinated by fame, as was Petrarch (1304–74) a generation later, and all three achieved it in their own lifetime. So, too, did Boccaccio (1317–75) and Chaucer (?1340–1400) in England. The latter wrote a remarkable poem, 'The House of Fame', which through the images of dream drew on the treasury of his brain to contemplate what fame meant. Petrarch wrote a 'Letter to Posterity' in which he gave personal details, including details of his personal appearance, and proudly proclaimed that 'the glorious will be glorious to all eternity'. The emphasis on permanence would be still stronger in the age of print.

Following the development of electrical communication, beginning with the telegraph in the nineteenth century (see pp. 20–1), a sense of imminent as well as immediate change developed, and the media debates of the second half of the twentieth century have encouraged re-evaluation both of the invention of printing and of all the other technologies that were treated at their beginning as wonders. That changes in the media have had important social and cultural consequences is generally accepted. It is the nature and scope of these consequences which is more controversial. Are they primarily political or psychological? On the political side, do they favour democracy or dictatorship? The 'age of radio' was not only the age of Roosevelt and Churchill but also that of Hitler, Mussolini and Stalin. On the psychological side, does reading, listening or viewing encourage empathy with others or do they encourage withdrawal into a private world? Does television or 'the Net' destroy communities or create new kinds of community in which spatial proximity is less important?

Again, are the consequences of literacy, or of television, more or less the same in every society or do they vary according to the social or cultural context? Is it possible to distinguish cultures of the eye, in which what is seen outweighs what is heard, and cultures of the ear, more attuned to soundscapes? Chronologically, is there a 'Great Divide' between oral and literate cultures, or between societies pre- and post-television? How do the steam engine and industrialization relate to this division? With its invention, adoption and development, locomotives and steamships could reduce travel times and extend markets. And electronics, a word not used in the nineteenth century, brought immediacy nearer, as nineteenth-century commentators already anticipated.

Some of the people who initiated media debates gave positive answers, not only Cipolla (see p. 4), but theorists from quite different academic backgrounds, such as Marshall McLuhan and his student Walter Ong, best known for his *Orality and Literacy* (1982). The former quickly established his own fame while the latter was content to be a priest and scholar. In *The Gutenberg Galaxy* (1962), written in experimental form, *Understanding Media* (1964) and other works, McLuhan, following in the wake of his Toronto colleagues Innis and Havelock, asserted the centrality of the media, identifying and tracing their specific characteristics irrespective of the people who use them, the organizational structures within which their providers operate and the purposes for which they are used.

For McLuhan, who had been trained as a literary critic, what was important was not the content of communication so much as the form that it took. He encapsulated his interpretation in memorable phrases like 'the medium is the message' and the distinction between 'hot' media such as radio and cinema and 'cool' media such as television and the telephone. More recently, the psychologist David Olson, another Canadian, in *The World on Paper* (1994), coined the phrase 'the literate mind' to sum up the changes which the practices of reading and writing have made – so he argues – to the ways in which we think about language, the mind and the world, from the rise of subjectivity to the image of the world as a book. Ong, more interested in context, acknowledged his debt to this Toronto school of media theory (the name, like that of the Frankfurt school (see pp. 200–1), is a reminder of the continuing importance of cities in academic communication). He emphasized the differences in mentality between oral cultures and writing cultures, noting, for example, the role of writing in 'decontextualizing' ideas, in other words, taking them out of the face-to-face situations in which they were originally formulated in order to apply them elsewhere.

The anthropologist Jack Goody discussed both the social and the psychological consequences of literacy in ways which run parallel to Ong's. In *The Domestication of the Savage Mind* (1977), on the basis of an analysis of written lists in the ancient Middle East, for example, Goody emphasized the reorganizing or reclassification of information, another form of decontextualization made possible by writing. Drawing on his own fieldwork in West Africa, he noted the tendency of oral cultures to acquire what he calls 'structural amnesia', in other words forgetting the past, or more exactly remembering the past as if it were like the present. The permanence of written records, on the other hand, acts as an obstacle to this kind of amnesia and so encourages an awareness of the difference between past and present. The oral system is more fluid and flexible, the written system more fixed. Other analysts have made more sweeping claims about the consequences of literacy as a condition for the rise of abstract and critical thought (not to mention empathy and rationality).

These claims about the consequences of literacy have been challenged, notably by another British anthropologist, Brian Street. In *Literacy in Theory and Practice* (1984), Street criticized not only the concept of the 'Great Divide' but also what he calls the 'autonomous model' of literacy as 'a neutral technology that can be detached from specific social contexts'. In its place he proposed a model of literacies in the plural which focused on the social context of practices such as reading and writing and the active role of the ordinary people who make use of literacy. Taking examples from his fieldwork in Iran in the 1970s, he made a contrast between two literacies, the art of reading taught in the Koranic school and the art of keeping accounts taught in the commercial school in the same village.

A similar point might be made about modern Turkey, where the country's leader Kemal Atatürk ordered a change from Arabic script to the western alphabet in 1929, declaring that 'our nation will show with its script and with its mind that its place is with the civilized world'. The change vividly illustrates the symbolic importance of the media of communication. It is also related to the question of memory, since Atatürk wanted to modernize his country and by changing the script he cut the younger generation off from access to written tradition. However, in the Koranic schools in Turkey, as in Iran, the traditional Arabic script is still taught.

The exchange between Goody and Street, together with the more recent debate on virtual reality and cyberspace, offers vivid and always pertinent illustrations of both the insights and the limitations associated with disciplinary biases. In the course of their fieldwork, anthropologists, for example, have more opportunities than historians for investigating social context in depth, but fewer opportunities for observing changes over the centuries. From the 1990s onwards, the media analyses of both anthropologists and historians were pushed aside by writers (including novelists and film-makers). Meanwhile, economists, when they confronted the issues raised under the heading 'globalization' (see p. 256), tended to concentrate on what was statistically measurable. Some producers and scriptwriters, bypassing the problem of the relation of science to technology, reduced 'all the things in the world to blips, to data, to the message units contained within the brain and its adjunct the computer'. Others dwell on complexity and the way in which the computer has altered 'the architectonic of the sciences [and arts] and the picture we have of material reality'.

For historians and specialists in social studies, there is a continuing division between those who emphasize structure and those who emphasize agency. On one side, there are those who claim that there are no consequences of computers as such, any more than there are consequences of literacy (including visual literacy and computer literacy). There are only consequences for individuals using these tools. On the other hand, there are those who suggest that using a new medium of communication inevitably changes people's views of the world, in the long term if not earlier. One side accuses the other of treating ordinary people as passive, as objects undergoing the impact of literacy or computerization. The reverse accusation is that of treating the media, including the press, as passive, as mirrors of culture and society rather than as agencies transforming culture and society.

This is not the place to attempt to close such debate. On the contrary, readers are asked to keep alternative viewpoints in mind while reading the pages which follow. No single theory provides a complete guide to the contemporary realm of 'high-definition, inter-drive, mutually convergent technologies of communication', where relationships, individual and social, local and global, are in continuous flux.

2 The Print Revolution in Context

This chapter and the chapter which follows are concerned with Europe in what historians call the 'early modern' period, running from about 1450 to about 1789 – in other words from the 'print revolution' to the French and Industrial Revolutions. The year 1450 is the approximate date for the invention in Europe, probably by Johann Gutenberg of Mainz, of a printing press – perhaps inspired by the wine presses of his native Rhineland – which used movable metal type.

In China and Japan, printing had been practised for a long time – from the eighth century, if not before – but the method generally used was what is known as 'block printing', the carved woodblock being used to print a single page of a specific text. This method was appropriate for cultures which used thousands of ideograms rather than an alphabet of twenty to thirty letters. It was probably for this reason that the Chinese invention of movable type in the eleventh century had few consequences. In the early fifteenth century, however, the Koreans invented a form of movable type with what has been described by the French scholar Henri-Jean Martin as 'an almost hallucinatory similarity to Gutenberg's'. The western invention may have been stimulated by news of what had happened in the East.

The practice of printing spread through Europe via a diaspora of German printers. By 1500, presses had been established in more than 250 places in Europe – 80 of them in Italy, 52 in Germany and 43 in France. Printers had reached Basel by 1466, Rome by 1467, Paris and Pilsen by 1468, Venice by 1469, Leuven, Valencia, Cracow and Buda by 1473, Westminster (distinct from the city of London) by 1476, and Prague by 1477. Between them, these presses produced about 27,000 editions by the year 1500, which means that – assuming an average print run of 500 copies per edition – about thirteen million books were circulating by that date in a Europe of 100 million people. About two million of these books were produced in Venice alone, while Paris was another important centre of printing, with 181 workshops in 1500.

In contrast, print was slow to penetrate Russia and the Orthodox Christian world more generally, a region (including modern Serbia, Romania and Bulgaria) where the alphabet was usually Cyrillic and literacy was virtually confined to the clergy. In 1564, a White Russian trained in Poland brought a press to Moscow, but his workshop was soon destroyed by a mob. This situation changed in the early eighteenth century thanks to the efforts of Tsar Peter the Great (ruled 1686–1725), who founded a press at St Petersburg in 1711, followed by the Senate Presses (1719) in Petersburg and Moscow, the Naval Academy Press (1721) and the Academy of Sciences Press (1727). The location of these presses suggests that the Tsar was interested in literacy and education primarily in order to make Russians familiar with modern science and technology, especially military technology. The fact that printing arrived so late in Russia suggests that print was not an independent agent, and that the print revolution did not depend on technology alone. Printing required favourable social and cultural conditions in order to spread, and Russia's lack of a literate laity was a serious obstacle to the rise of print culture.

In the Muslim world, resistance to print remained strong throughout the early modern period. Indeed, the Muslim countries have been regarded as a barrier to the passage of printing from China to the West. According to an imperial ambassador to Istanbul in the middle of the sixteenth century, the Turks thought it a sin to print religious books. The fear of heresy underlay the opposition to printing and western learning. In 1515, Sultan Selim I (ruled 1512–20) issued a decree punishing the practice of printing with the death penalty. At the end of the century, Sultan Murad III (ruled 1574–95) allowed the sale of non-religious printed books in Arabic characters, but these were probably imports from Italy.

Some Europeans were proud of their technical superiority in this respect. Henry Oldenburg (1618–77), the first secretary of the Royal Society of London, and a man professionally concerned with scientific communication, linked the absence of print with despotism, claiming in a letter of 1659 that 'ye Great Turk is an enemy to learning in regard of his subjects, because he finds it his advantage to have such a people on whose ignorance he may impose. Whence it is, that he will endure no printing, being of this opinion, that printing and learning, especially such as is found in universities, are the chief fuel of division among christians.'

The chequered history of printing in the Ottoman Empire reveals the strength of the obstacles to this form of communication, as also to visual representations. The first Turkish press was established only in the eighteenth century, more than 200 years after the first Hebrew press (1494) and more than 150 years after the first Armenian press (1567). A Hungarian convert to Islam (formerly a Protestant clergyman) sent a memorandum to the sultan on the importance of the press, and in 1726 he was given permission to print secular books. However, there was opposition from scribes and religious leaders. The new press printed only a handful of books and it did not last long. The official Ottoman gazette was not founded until 1831, while the first unofficial newspaper in Turkish (launched by an Englishman) appeared in 1840.

The idea that the invention of printing was epoch-making is an old one, whether the new technique was discussed on its own, coupled with the invention of gunpowder, or taken as part of a trio of print, gunpowder and the compass. For the English philosopher Francis Bacon (1561–1626), this was a trio which had 'changed the whole state and face of things throughout the world', though the French essayist Michel de Montaigne (1533–92), writing a generation earlier, had reminded his readers that the Chinese had already enjoyed the benefits of printing for 'a thousand years'. Samuel Hartlib, an East European exile in Britain who supported many schemes of social and cultural reform, wrote in 1641 that 'the art of printing will so spread knowledge that the common people, knowing their own rights and liberties, will not be governed by way of oppression'.

The bicentenary of the invention of printing was celebrated – about ten years too early, according to modern scholars – in 1640 and its tercentenary in 1740, and in the famous outline of world history by the Marquis de Condorcet (1743–94), published in 1795, printing, like writing, was identified as one of the milestones in what the author called 'the progress of the human mind'. The unveiling of the statue of Gutenberg at Mainz in 1837 was accompanied by enthusiastic celebrations. 'Among salvoes of artillery the veil was removed from the statue and a hymn was sung by a thousand voices. Then came orations; then dinners, balls, oratorios, boat races, processions by torchlight . . . Gutenberg! was toasted in many a bumper of Rhenish wine.'

All the same, some commentators wished the new epoch had never arrived. The triumphalist accounts of the new invention were matched by what we might call catastrophist narratives. Scribes, whose business was threatened by the new technology, deplored the arrival of the press from the beginning. For churchmen, the basic problem was that print allowed readers who had a low position in the social and cultural hierarchy to study religious texts for themselves, rather than relying on what the authorities told them. For governments, the consequences of print to which Hartlib referred were no reason for celebration.

The rise of newspapers in the seventeenth century increased anxieties about the effects of print. In England in the 1660s, the chief censor of books (see p. 76), Sir Roger L'Estrange, was still asking the old question 'whether more mischief than advantage were not occasion'd to the christian world by the invention of typography'. 'O Printing! How thou hast disturbed the peace of Mankind!', wrote the English poet Andrew Marvell (1621–78) in 1672.

Scholars, or more generally anyone in search of knowledge, had other problems. Let us look from this point of view at the so-called information 'explosion' – a metaphor uncomfortably reminiscent of gunpowder – which followed the invention of printing. The most serious problems were those of information retrieval and, linked to this, the selection and criticism of books and authors. There was a need for new methods of information management, just as there is today, in the early days of the Internet.

In the early Middle Ages the problem had been the lack of books, their paucity. By the sixteenth century, the problem had become one of superfluity. An Italian writer was already complaining in 1550 that there were 'so many books that we do not even have time to read the titles'. Books were a forest in which readers could lose themselves, according to the reformer Jean Calvin (1509–64). They were an ocean in which readers had to navigate, or a flood of printed matter in which it was hard to escape drowning.

As books multiplied, libraries had to become larger, and as they became larger, it was more difficult to find any given book on the shelves, and catalogues became more necessary. Compilers of catalogues had to decide whether to arrange information by subject or in the alphabetical order of authors. From the mid-sixteenth century, printed bibliographies offered information about what had been written, but as these compilations increased in size, subject bibliographies became increasingly necessary.

Librarians also faced the problems of keeping catalogues up to date and of learning about new publications. Scholarly journals provided information about new books, but as the numbers of these journals multiplied it was necessary to look elsewhere for information about them. Since so many more books existed than could be read in a lifetime, readers had to be helped to discriminate by means of select bibliographies and, from the later seventeenth century, reviews of new publications.

The coexistence of triumphalist and catastrophist accounts of printing suggests the need for precision in any discussion of its consequences. The Victorian historian Lord Acton (1834–1902) was more precise than his predecessors, emphasizing both what might be called the lateral effects of print – making knowledge accessible to a wider audience – and its vertical or cumulative effects – enabling later generations to build on the intellectual work of earlier ones. Print, according to Acton in his lecture 'On the Study of History' (1895), 'gave assurance that the work of the Renaissance would last, that what was written would be accessible to all, that such an occultation of knowledge and ideas as had depressed the Middle Ages would never recur, that not an idea would be lost.'

This was a one-sided and bookish assessment of the Middle Ages, ignoring oral tradition and leaving out much that would now be considered essential. More recent studies, particularly those associated with media debates, have sometimes rejected older insights as well as developing and occasionally exaggerating them. Social historians, for example, have pointed out that the invention of printing changed the occupational structure of European cities. The printers themselves were a new kind of group, artisans for whom literacy was essential. Proof-correcting was a new occupation which print called into existence, while a rise in the number of booksellers and librarians naturally followed the explosion in the numbers of books.

More adventurous and more speculative than the historians, Marshall McLuhan emphasized the shift from auditory to visual punctuation, on occasion going so far as to speak of 'the print-made split between head and heart'. Both the strength and the weakness of his approach is summed up in one of the many concepts he did much to launch, that of 'print culture', which suggested links between the new invention and the cultural changes of the period, without always specifying what these links might be. Ong was more cautious, but he too believed in the long-term psychological consequences of print. 'While the invention of printing has been discussed conventionally in terms of its value for spreading ideas, its even greater contribution is its furthering of the long-developing shift in the relationship between space and discourse.' Ong also emphasized the rise of diagrams and the visual or spatial organization of sixteenth-century academic books with their dichotomized tables of contents 'which mean everything to the eye and nothing to the ear', because they are impossible to read aloud. The contents of the first edition of Robert Burton's *Anatomy of Melancholy* (1621) were summarized in this way (see Figure 4). The same point about information designed for the eye might be made about timetables and astronomical tables (from the sixteenth century onwards) and tables of logarithms (first printed in the seventeenth century).

Such books were too expensive and too technical to appeal to more than a tiny minority of the population, and printed matter also came in cheaper and simpler

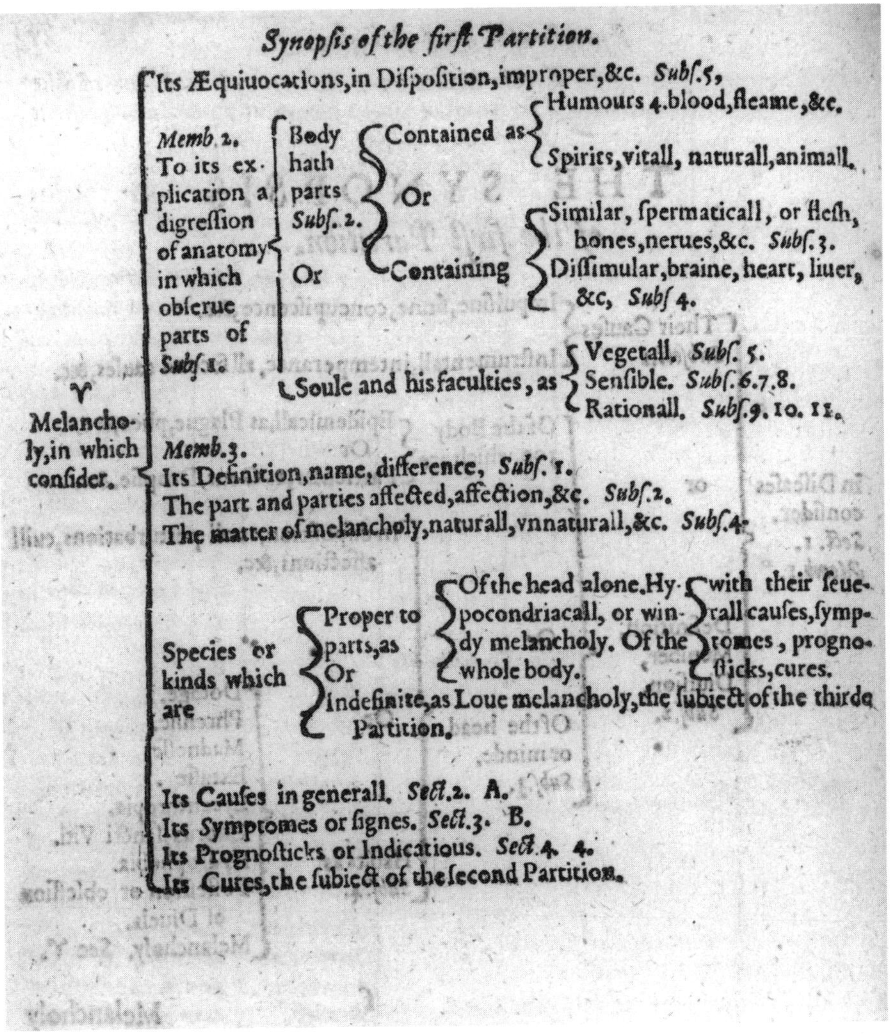

Synopsis of the first Partition.

Melancho-ly, in which confider.

Its Æquiuocations, in Difpofition, improper, &c. *Subf.5,*

Memb. 2. To its ex-plication a digreffion of anatomy in which obferue parts of *Subf.1.*

Body hath parts *Subf.2.*

Contained as — Humours 4. blood, fleame, &c.
Spirits, vitall, naturall, animall.

Or

Containing — Similar, fpermaticall, or flefh, bones, nerues, &c. *Subf.3.*
Diffimular, braine, heart, liuer, &c, *Subf.4.*

Soule and his faculties, as — Vegetall, *Subf.5.*
Senfible. *Subf.6.7.8.*
Rationall. *Subf.9.10.11.*

Memb. 3. Its Definition, name, difference, *Subf.1.*
The part and parties affected, affection, &c. *Subf.2.*
The matter of melancholy, naturall, vnnaturall, &c. *Subf.4.*

Species or kinds which are

Proper to parts, as

Or

Of the head alone. Hy-pocondriacall, or win-dy melancholy. Of the whole body.

with their feue-rall caufes, fymp-tomes, progno-fticks, cures.

Indefinite, as Loue melancholy, the fubiect of the thirde Partition.

Its Caufes in generall. *Sect.2.* A.
Its Symptomes or fignes. *Sect.3.* B.
Its Prognofticks or Indications. *Sect.4.* 4.
Its Cures, the fubiect of the fecond Partition.

Fig. 4 Ramist table of contents from Robert Burton's *Anatomy of Melancholy*, 1st edition, 1621.

forms such as 'chap-books', often illustrated, though the illustrations were some-times taken over from earlier books and had little to do with the text. Chap-books were booklets which were sold by 'chapmen' or pedlars in most parts of early modern Europe, and in some regions in the nineteenth and even twentieth cen-turies as well. Since the 1960s, historians have been studying French chap-books, the 'Blue Library' (Bibliothèque Bleue), as they are called, referring to the fact that the booklets were bound in the coarse blue paper used for wrapping sugar. The major centre of production was Troyes, in north-east France, but thanks to the pedlar network the booklets were widely distributed in the countryside as well as the towns. The most common subjects of these booklets were lives of the saints and romances of chivalry, leading some historians to the conclusion that the literature was escapist, or even a form of tranquillizer, and also that it represented the diffusion downwards to artisans and peasants of cultural models created by and for the clergy and the nobility.

This conclusion is too simple to be accepted without qualification. In the first place, the books were not bought by ordinary people alone. Noblewomen are known to have read them. In the second place, the Bibliothèque Bleue did not represent the whole culture of its readers. Their oral culture was probably more important. In any case, we do not know how readers or listeners reacted to the stories; whether, for example, they identified themselves with Charlemagne or with the rebels against him. Despite the problems raised by this case-study, it is clear that in France and other European countries, including Italy, England and the Netherlands, printed matter had become an important part of popular culture by the seventeenth century, if not before.

Summing up the work of a generation on the subject, an American historian, Elizabeth Eisenstein, made the claim, in an ambitious study first published in 1979, that printing was 'the unacknowledged revolution' and that its role as an 'agent of change' had been underestimated in traditional accounts of the Renaissance, the Reformation and the scientific revolution. Drawing on the ideas of both McLuhan and Ong, Eisenstein domesticated them by translating them into terms which would be acceptable to her own professional community, that of historians and librarians. While she was cautious in drawing general conclusions, she emphasized two long-term consequences of the invention of printing. In the first place, print standardized and preserved knowledge which had been much more fluid in the age of oral or manuscript circulation. In the second place, the critique of authority was encouraged by print, which made incompatible views of the same subject more widely available. To illustrate this point, Eisenstein took the example of Montaigne, whose scepticism she accounted for as the fruit of his wide reading. 'In explaining why Montaigne perceived greater "conflict and diversity" in the works he consulted than had medieval commentators in an earlier age', she argued, 'something should be said about the increased number of texts he had at hand.' More should be said, however, about his distinction between 'private' and 'public', the result of his experience.

The Print Revolution Reconsidered

Eisenstein's book remains a valuable synthesis. Nonetheless, in the years since its publication the author's claims for revolutionary changes following the invention of printing have come to look somewhat exaggerated. In the first place, the changes she outlined took place in the course of at least three centuries, from Gutenberg's Bible to Diderot's *Encyclopédie* (to be discussed below, see p. 80). Adaptation to the new medium was gradual, therefore, whether in the case of styles of presentation or habits of reading (see p. 50). In other words, as in the case of the Industrial Revolution – in the eyes of some of its recent historians – what we see is what the British critic Raymond Williams (1921–88) called a 'Long Revolution'. It is an intriguing question, whether a revolution which is not rapid can be regarded as a revolution at all.

A second problem is the problem of agency. To speak of print as the agent of change is surely to place too much emphasis on the medium of communication at the expense of the writers, printers and readers who used the new technology for their own different purposes. It might be more realistic to view print, like new media in later centuries (television, for example), as a catalyst, assisting social changes rather than originating them.

In the third place, Eisenstein views print in relative isolation. Yet, in order to assess the social and cultural consequences of the invention of printing it is necessary to look at the media as a whole, to view all the different means of communication as interdependent, treating them as a package, a repertoire, a system, or what the French call a 'regime', whether authoritarian, democratic, bureaucratic or capitalist.

The system, it must be stressed, was in perpetual change, even if some of the changes became visible only in the perspective of the long term. For example, print technology did not stand still after Gutenberg. The Dutch printer Willem Blaeu improved the design of the wooden press in the seventeenth century. Large presses were introduced in order to print maps. The Stanhope iron hand-press (1804) doubled the normal rate of production, while Koenig's steam press (1814) quadrupled the productivity of the Stanhope (see pp. 91–2).

To think in terms of a media system means emphasizing the division of labour between the different means of communication available in a given place and at a given time, without forgetting that old and new media can and do coexist and that different media may compete with or echo one another as well as complement one another. Changes in the media system also need to be related to changes in the transportation system, the movement of goods and people in space, whether by land or water (river, canal and sea). The communication of messages is a part of the system of physical communication.

Physical Communication

It was, of course, traditional for information flows to follow trade flows, since merchants operating by sea and land brought news along with their merchandise. Printing itself had spread across Europe via the Rhine, from Gutenberg's Mainz to Frankfurt, Strasbourg and Basel. In the sixteenth, seventeenth and eighteenth centuries, messages on paper followed the silver route from Mexico or Peru to the Old World, or the sugar route from the Caribbean to London. What is new in the sixteenth and seventeenth centuries is the evidence of increasing awareness of the problems of physical communication. The enthusiasm of Renaissance humanists for ancient Rome included an interest in Roman roads, discussed, for instance, in Andrea Palladio's famous treatise, *Four Books of Architecture* (1570). Guides to the roads of particular countries were published, notably Henri Estienne's *Guide des chemins de France* (1553) and John Ogilby's *Britannia* (1675; see Figure 5), the first English road atlas, the roads being displayed on what the author called 'imaginary scrolls'. An up-to-date version of these maps in reduced format was produced in 1719 and reached its twenty-second edition in 1785, ample testimony of travellers' need for such a book.

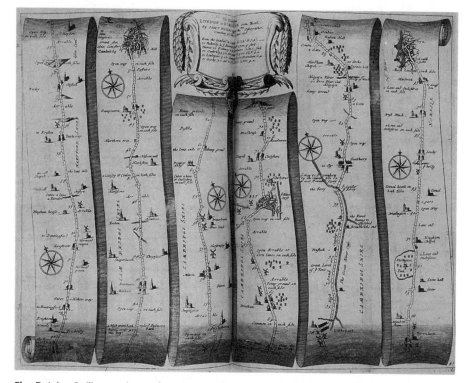

Fig. 5 John Ogilby, road map from his *Britannia*, 1675, showing Cambridge.

Governments also concerned themselves more with the roads, even if major improvements in the European system are difficult to discern before the middle of the eighteenth century. In France, a new post was created around 1600, that of *Grand Voyer*, in order to oversee the system. One reason for this concern with roads was the increasing need, in an age when European states were becoming more centralized, to transmit commands more rapidly from the capital to the provinces. The interest in communication on the part of governments was a major reason for the rapid expansion of the postal system in the early modern period, although merchants and other private individuals also took advantage of it.

In early modern Europe, transport by water was usually much cheaper than transport by land. An Italian printer calculated in 1550 that to send a load of books from Rome to Lyons would cost eighteen *scudi* by land compared with four by sea. Letters were normally carried overland, but a system of transporting letters and newspapers, as well as people, by canal barge developed in the Dutch Republic in the seventeenth century. The average speed of the barges was a little over four miles an hour, slow compared to a courier on horseback. On the other hand the service was regular, frequent and cheap, and allowed communication not only between Amsterdam and the smaller towns, but also between one small town and another, thus equalizing accessibility to information. It was only in 1837, with the invention of the electric telegraph (see p. 109), that the tra-ditional link between transport and the communication of messages was broken.

Empire and Communication

Communications, as the American political scientist Karl Deutsch puts it, are 'the nerves of government', especially important in large states, above all in far-flung empires. Charles V (ruled 1519–58), whose dominions included Spain, the Netherlands, Germany and much of Italy as well as Mexico and Peru, tried to solve the problem of communication by travelling incessantly throughout Europe. Charles's abdication speech noted that in the course of four decades as emperor he had made forty journeys: ten visits to the Low Countries, nine to Germany, seven to Italy, six to Spain, four to France, two to England and two to North Africa. Yet the traditional medieval style of nomadic kingship was no longer sufficient for Charles's needs. The age of the 'paper empire' had arrived, together with a regular system for the transmission of messages: the postal system, so-called because it involved the establishment of posts with men and horses stationed along certain routes or post-roads.

In the sixteenth century, one family dominated the European postal system, that of the Tassis or Taxis (the term 'taxi', now in international currency, is derived from their name). It was this family, postmasters to the Habsburg emperors from 1490 onwards, who developed the system of ordinary couriers, operating accord-ing to a fixed timetable (available in print from 1563). Brussels – now the centre of so much else – was the hub of their system. One route went via Augsburg and Innsbruck to Bologna, Florence, Rome and Naples. Another went to Paris and through France to Toledo and Granada.

Special couriers, changing horses at frequent intervals, were able to travel up to 125 miles a day and so to bring the news of important events relatively rapidly. In 1572, for example, the news of the massacre of Protestants in Paris (known as the Massacre of St Bartholomew) arrived in Madrid in three days. To travel 'post haste' was a common expression of the period. However, the time normally taken for messages to arrive was considerably longer, since ordinary couriers averaged from six to eight miles per hour. From Rome to Milan an ordinary courier took from two to three days, according to the season; from Rome to Vienna, twelve to fifteen days; from Rome to Paris, about twenty; while it required from twenty-five to thirty days for the courier from Rome to reach London or Cracow. Ordi-nary couriers took about eleven days from Madrid (which was Spain's capital from 1556 onwards) to Paris, and twelve or thirteen days from Madrid to Naples (which was part of the Spanish Empire).

The Spanish Empire in the age of Charles V's son and successor Philip II (ruled 1556–98), although smaller in extent, has been well described by the great French historian Fernand Braudel (1902–85) in his famous study, *The Mediterranean and the Mediterranean World in the Age of Philip II* (1949), as 'a colossal enterprise of sea and land transport' requiring 'the daily dispatch of hundreds of orders and reports'. Philip's strategy was the opposite of his father's. It was to remain as far as possible in one place, in or near Madrid, and to sit at his desk for many hours a day, reading and annotating the documents which reached him from all over his dominions. No wonder that his subjects gave him the mocking nickname of 'the king of paper' (*el rey papelero*).

The great problem was the length of time the documents took to reach Philip, or conversely, the time his orders took to reach their recipients. The obsession of sixteenth-century statesmen and ambassadors with the arrival of the mail was emphasized by Braudel. The delays of the Spanish government were notorious, leading one official to wish that Death would arrive from Spain. These delays cannot, or not always, be explained by the indecisiveness of King Philip II, but rather by the communication problems of an empire which stretched across the Mediterranean from Spain to Sicily, across the Atlantic to Mexico and Peru, and across the Pacific to the Philippines (named after Philip because they became a Spanish possession in his time). At this time it would normally take a ship one or two weeks, according to the winds, to cross the Mediterranean from north to south, and two or three months from east to west, so that Braudel called the Mediterranean world of the period 'sixty days long'.

Nevertheless, communication by sea was usually swifter than communication over land. In Mexico, for example, the Spaniards had to construct what they called 'royal roads', like the famous 'silver road' from the mines in Zacatecas to Mexico City. The names of these roads also survive in modern California and New Mexico. In Eastern Europe, where the population was less dense and cities smaller and fewer than in the west, communication was correspondingly slower. In the Russian Empire in the age of Catherine the Great (ruled 1762–96), for example, it might take eighteen months for an imperial order sent from St Petersburg to reach Kamchatka in Siberia, and another eighteen months for the reply to be received in the capital. Communication problems help to explain why the empires of early modern Europe, Russia excepted, were seaborne empires. They included the Portuguese, Spanish, Dutch, French and British intercontinental empires and also the Swedish empire in Europe, constructed around the Baltic sea.

Transatlantic Communications

In order to communicate with his viceroys in Mexico and Peru, Philip II and his successors were dependent on the annual departures and returns of the ships which transported the silver of the New World to the port of Seville and for safety's sake sailed in convoy. The convoy to Mexico, for example, sailed in the summer and began the return voyage from the New World in the autumn. Letters from Spain to Mexico might take as little as four months to arrive, but to Lima they normally took six to nine months and they might take up to two years to the Philippines. Communications between England and New England were much more rapid, but letters might be lost or at least delayed. A letter relating the execution of Charles I, written in March 1649, only arrived in New England in June. It was common practice to make copies of letters and to send them by different ships in order to minimize the risk of loss.

Only in the eighteenth century did improvements in communications shrink the Atlantic, at least as far as the British Empire was concerned. Sea traffic between England and North America doubled between the 1680s and the 1730s. In 1702, a system of ships (known as 'packet boats'), carrying letters from London to Barbados or Jamaica, was set up, with monthly sailings, a hundred-day schedule and some 8,500 letters carried in each ship. As a result, from the point of view of communications, the Atlantic had been shrunk to the size of the Mediterranean in the age of Philip II.

The ships crossing the Atlantic carried not only letters but also books and newspapers. Since books were heavy physical objects, the majority of copies tended to remain fairly near the place in which they had been manufactured. However, there is evidence of long-distance distribution. In the sixteenth century, for example, romances of chivalry were exported to Mexico and Peru in considerable numbers, despite the disapproval of the clergy. In 1540, a single printer had 446 copies of the popular romance *Amadis de Gaula* in stock in his shop in Mexico City. The same book was one of the favourites in Lima in 1583. In 1600, no fewer than 10,000 copies of another romance, *Pierres y Magalona*, arrived in Mexico City. In Puritan New England, by contrast, there seems to have been more demand for printed sermons. Individuals such as the clergyman Increase Mather (1639–1723) received regular shipments of barrels of books from London. News-sheets were sent to Boston during the English Civil War, and by the early eighteenth century the regular arrival of news encouraged the foundation of local news-sheets such as the *Boston Newsletter* (1704). What the Australian historian Geoffrey Blainey describes as the 'tyranny of distance' was gradually being undermined.

Oral Communication

It is sometimes claimed that the invention of the printing press did not alter the fundamentally oral nature of European culture. As this book attempts to show, the claim is exaggerated (and the attempt to characterize European culture in terms of a single medium misguided), but behind the exaggeration lurks an important point. Despite the huge scholarly literature on the importance of oral communication and especially what is often called 'oral literature', the place of the oral medium in the history of early modern Europe – and its relation to changes in visual culture – has received less attention than it deserves.

In the Middle Ages the altar rather than the pulpit was at the centre of Christian churches. Yet preaching was already an accepted priestly duty, and friars preached in the streets and squares of cities as well as in churches. Distinctions were drawn between *sermones dominicales* for Sundays and *sermones festivi* for the many days of festival, and the style of preaching (plain or flowery, serious or entertaining, restrained or histrionic) was consciously adapted to the audience, whether it was urban or rural, clerical or lay. In short, the possibilities of the oral medium were consciously exploited by the masters of what was known in the sixteenth century as 'ecclesiastical rhetoric'. No wonder that the sociologist Zygmunt Bauman has described the pulpits of the Catholic Church as a 'mass medium'.

After the Reformation, Sunday preaching became an increasingly important part of religious instruction for Protestants and Catholics alike. Although Martin

Luther (1483–1546) hailed the new printing press as 'God's highest gift of grace', he still considered the church as 'a mouth house and not a pen house'. Some preachers drew crowds, among them the poet John Donne (c.1572–1631), who was dean of St Paul's in London. The public role of the sermon was acknowledged by Roman Catholics too, especially after the Council of Trent, and there were great Catholic preachers such as Jacques Bossuet (1627–1704) at the court of Louis XIV. The enthusiasm of some members of the public for sermons which lasted two or three hours would be difficult to believe today were it not attested in the diaries of the time.

Governments were well aware of the value of the pulpit for communicating information, especially in rural areas, and also for encouraging obedience. Queen Elizabeth I spoke of the need to 'tune the pulpits', and Charles I agreed, declaring that 'people are governed by the pulpit more than the sword in times of peace', a classic early statement of the idea of cultural hegemony.

Another kind of oral communication was academic. Instruction in universities took place through lectures, formal debates or disputations (testing the logical skills of the students), and formal speeches or declamations (testing their powers of rhetoric). The art of speaking (and gesturing) was considered by rhetoricians to be just as important as the art of writing. By contrast, the written essay, like the written examination, was virtually unknown in academic circles at this time. In the grammar schools, great emphasis was placed on speaking Latin, and dialogues and plays were composed by the teachers in order to give the students practice in speaking well.

Yet another important domain of oral communication was the song, especially the ballad, the song which told a story. The theories of Parry and Lord discussed above (p. 6) are highly relevant to the ballads which circulated in early modern Europe. In the case of the famous border ballads of northern England and the Lowlands of Scotland, for instance, as in their equivalents in Scandinavia or Spain, it is not difficult to identify both formulae and themes. 'Blood-red wine', for example, or 'milk-white steed' are epithets as formulaic as Homer's 'wine-dark sea'. Recurrent themes of British ballads include sending a letter, sitting in a bower and galloping on a horse; plants grow out of the graves of tragic lovers and join them at last. The survival in different versions of a given ballad, *The Bonny Earl of Murray*, for example, or *Barbara Allen*, in manuscript or in print, different in length and in phrasing, suggests that, as in Parry's Yugoslavia, individual minstrels developed their own style of recitation which was probably semi-improvised.

Rumour has been described as an 'oral postal service' which operates with remarkable speed. The messages transmitted were not always spontaneous: they were sometimes disseminated for political reasons, and in times of conflict one side would regularly accuse the other of spreading rumours. Three famous examples of rumour and its effects in early modern Europe, whether spontaneous or not, are the movement of iconoclasm of 1566 in Northern France and the Netherlands (see p. 70); the English 'Popish Plot' in the 1680s (see p. 76); and the so-called 'Great Fear' in the French countryside in 1789, studied in depth in the 1930s by the French historian of the Revolution, Georges Lefebvre (1874–1959). In this last case, news circulated among French peasants to the effect that brigands were coming to massacre them or to attack their harvests, perhaps at the orders of the British or the aristocracy. Rather than dismissing these rumours or believing them, Lefebvre studied their chronology and geography with care and used them as evidence of social tensions.

Oral culture in this period should not be thought of purely in terms of survival or of what Ong has called 'oral residue'. New institutions which structured oral communication developed in this period, including such more or less formal discussion groups as academies, scientific societies, salons, clubs and coffee-houses. To judge from the treatises on the subject, the art of conversation was cultivated with particular intensity at this time. Bookshops, too, functioned as social centres, and James Boswell met Samuel Johnson for the first time in the back parlour of a bookshop owned by Tom Davies.

The development of commerce had important consequences for oral communication, notably the rise of exchanges or bourses, including Bruges (1409), Antwerp (1460), Lyons (1462), Amsterdam (1530), London (1554), Hamburg (1558) and Copenhagen (1624). A vivid description of one of them, Amsterdam, was given by the Sephardic Jewish merchant Joseph Penso de la Vega in a dialogue in Spanish entitled *The Confusion of Confusions* (1688), which shows that the habit of speculation in company shares and even the categories of 'bulls' and 'bears' had already become standard practice at this time. So was the deliberate spreading of rumour in order to force prices up and down. The volatile behaviour of stock exchanges, their liability to mood swings from manic to depressive, most obvious in this period in the rapid rise and collapse of the South Sea Bubble (in other words, speculation in the stock of the South Sea Company of London in 1720), should be explained in part at least in terms of the oral medium. The phenomenon is still to be seen and heard on stock exchanges in our own time.

Centres of oral communication included taverns, public baths and coffee-houses, an innovation in this period. Istanbul was famous in the late sixteenth century for its coffee-houses, some 600 of them. Storytellers performed there, as they still did in Yugoslavia in the 1930s, when Parry and Lord visited the *kafanas*, as they were called, with their tape-recorders. There were at least 500 coffee-houses in London in the age of Queen Anne (reigned 1702–14). They prepared the way for 'clubland' for the wide range of establishments that catered for different kinds of customer and different topics of conversation. Discussions of scientific subjects might be heard in Child's coffee-house, or Garraway's, or the Grecian coffee-house, where one might see and hear Sir Isaac Newton (1642–1727). Insurance was discussed at Lloyd's, which was a coffee-house in the late seventeenth century before it developed into an independent institution. In the mid-eighteenth century, Slaughter's coffee-house was the locale for a club of artists which included William Hogarth (1697–1764). In Paris in the eighteenth century, the leading café included the Café de Maugis, a centre for attacks on religion, and Procope's, founded in 1689 (and still open), which was frequented by leading intellectuals of the Enlightenment. The authorities in most cities, concerned with coffee-houses as places which encouraged subversive comments about the government, kept them under surveillance more or less effectively.

Clubs and coffee-houses inspired the creation of imagined communities of oral communication. The best English example is the imaginary Spectator Club, composed of a variety of characters including a country gentleman, a merchant, a clergyman and an army officer, which functioned as a framework for *The Spectator*, edited by Joseph Addison (1672–1719) and Joseph Steele (1672–1729), published 1711–12, discussed below (p. 59). A journal founded in Leipzig in 1698 took the title *The Curious Coffeehouse at Venice*. The Milanese journal *Il Caffè* (1764–6) played an important role in the Italian Enlightenment (see p. 59). In several countries plays also were set in coffee-houses, culminating in Voltaire's comedy *Le café ou l'Ecossaise* (1760) in which the customers are shown in the act of making critical remarks about other plays.

In similar fashion, some eighteenth-century newspapers, from the *Bristol Postboy* to the *Hamburgische Patriot*, helped create imagined local communities, in the same way that, as Benedict Anderson argued in *Imagined Communities* (1983), the nineteenth-century newspaper contributed to the formation of national consciousness by treating its readers as a community, a national public.

Written Communication

The importance of the contexts in which writing is learned or utilized was already plain in early modern Europe, where reading and writing were often taught separately. For the commercial context of literacy and the business demand for writing and numeracy, we may turn to Florence in the fourteenth and fifteen centuries, where specialized abacus-schools taught writing and arithmetic, based on commercial examples, to boys who were going to become merchants or book-keepers. Like other cities in the Mediterranean world, Florence might be described as a notarial culture, in which written documents had an indispensable function, especially to record transfers of property on the occasion of marriages and deaths. Lay literacy was relatively high in Florence, and the practice of keeping diaries or chronicles was relatively widespread. Examples of this kind of personal document can also be found in other towns, among them Augsburg, Barcelona, Bologna, London, Nuremberg and Paris. These 'autobiographies' usually focused on the family or the city rather than the individual, and they sometimes circulated in manuscript form within an urban neighbourhood.

The religious context of literacy is particularly visible in Protestant Europe in the seventeenth and eighteenth centuries. A classic example is that of Lutheran Sweden, in which the Church conducted annual examinations of every household to see how well each member of the family could read, how well they knew their catechism, and so on. The results were recorded systematically, distinguishing levels of ability such as 'beginning to read', 'reads a little', and so on. The records were preserved with care and remain a uniquely rich source for the study of early modern literacy (Figure 6). Among other things, they reveal that the widespread ability to read, which extended as far as women and children in rural areas, was the result of a massive campaign between 1670 and 1720. On the whole, however, early modern Europe was a society of restricted literacy in which only a minority of the population (especially males, townspeople and Protestants) could read and fewer still could write.

Fig. 6 Register of household literacy examination in Sweden.

Hence the importance of what has been called 'mediated literacy', in other words, using literacy for the benefit of the illiterate. In cities of the period, a not uncommon occupation – as in Mexico City and Istanbul today, or at least until recently – was that of public writer, a man with an 'office' in the street, composing as well as writing letters for people who lacked these skills. In Paris, for example, some of these writers operated in the Cemetery of the Innocents. The English traveller John Evelyn (1620–1706) described them as 'inditing letters for poor maids and other ignorant people who come to them for advice and write for them into the country, both to their sweethearts, parents and friends, every large grave stone a little elevated serving them for a table'. In eighteenth-century Finland, illiterate peasants needed to communicate with the government in writing to avoid recruitment into the Swedish army. In their case, the local clergy-man serving as a scribe was the crucial intermediary.

For a dramatic illustration of mediated literacy and its unintended conse-quences, one might take a case that came before the Tribunal of the Governor of Rome in 1602, involving a love letter written by a certain Giovanantonio to his 16-year-old neighbour Margarita. Unfortunately, Margarita could not read, so she needed to pass the letter to another neighbour to have it read to her, thus increasing the chances of detection by her parents, who did indeed discover the affair and take the case to court.

The consequences of the spread of literacy and its increasing penetration into everyday life were many and various. There was a rise in the number of people in occupations connected with writing, for example, clerks, book-keepers, scriveners, notaries, public writers and postmen. Some of these occupations had a relatively high social status, among them that of private secretary in the service of important people who did not have the time to write their own letters. Liter-acy, an obstacle to the traditional process of 'structural amnesia' (see p. 10), encouraged a sense of distance between past and present. A sense of historical anachronism, for instance, seems to have become increasingly sharp from the fourteenth and fifteenth centuries onwards.

The political consequences of literacy included the spread of written records – noticeable by the thirteenth century, if not before – and with it great depen-dence on the processing of 'information', a term which was to figure prominently in future theories of communication, for example, in the late twentieth-century identification of an 'information society' (see p. 210). The information might relate to numbers (what came to be called 'statistics') as well as to facts. Given access to it, the style of government moved closer to the model of administra-tion by paperwork, or bureaucracy as the German sociologist Max Weber (1864–1920) called it. In his discussion of what he called 'legal-rational author-ity', Weber emphasized the relationship between the increasing use of writing to formulate and record decisions and a more impersonal kind of administration, characterized by the imposition of formal rules for the appointment of officials, for their respective spheres of responsibility and for their place within a hierar-chy. Weber's arguments have since been extended from politics to the domains of religion, business and the law.

Philip II, whose problems of communication have already been discussed, was not the only paper king in early modern Europe. Great nobles, who saw their par-ticipation in decision-making eroded, frequently complained about what they called the 'rule of the secretaries'. The increasing use of writing in the process of administration was a necessary condition for control at a distance, for the rise of the centralized state. Yet the increase in the number of documents to be read and signed was too much even for conscientious monarchs such as Philip II or, in the seventeenth century, Louis XIV of France. Secretaries had to be authorized to forge the king's signature on documents he had not seen, the point being that orders would not be obeyed if they did not appear to come directly from the king. As so often happens, social practices lagged behind technical innovations.

The political uses of literacy for ordinary people should not be forgotten. Rebellions were accompanied by the formulation of grievances in writing, during the German Peasant War of 1525, for example, or in *cahiers* at the beginning of the French Revolution, to mention only two of the most profound upheavals. The signing of petitions by a wide range of people was a practice which entered English politics in the seventeenth century. Fifteen thousand citizens of London signed the Root and Branch Petition in 1640 at the beginning of the Civil War, and later petitions displayed as many as 30,000 signatures. In the nineteenth century, they were claimed to have reached millions.

The medium of writing is not synonymous with handwriting, still less with pen and ink. In the early modern period, painted and chiselled inscriptions were a distinct form of communication. The epitaphs on gravestones and church monuments were chosen with care, and foreign visitors often made a point of reading them, a practice facilitated by the fact that before the eighteenth century most of these epitaphs were in Latin. A history of communication cannot afford to neglect the linguistic media through which communication took place.

Languages of Communication

The rise of a print society is often associated with the rise of the vernacular languages of Europe, in contrast to a medieval pre-print society in which written communication was predominantly in Latin and oral communication in local dialect. The increasing employment of the vernaculars for literary purposes was accompanied by their standardization and codification, a process aided by print. Martin Luther's translation of the Bible into German is often cited as an example of the new trend, important in itself and also as a model for other translations such as Tyndale's Bible (see p. 69), the Czech Bible of 1579–94 (the Kralice Bible) and the English Bible of 1611 (the Authorized Version).

Yet Dante and Chaucer had written their poems in Italian and English, and concerned as he was with the status of Latin, Petrarch, too, employed Italian for his introspective poetry and his praise of his muse, Laura. Outside Italy, the Frenchman Joachim Du Bellay (1522–60) and the German Martin Opitz (1597–1639) were among the writers who sang the praises of the vernacular as a medium for poetry.

In the field of politics, a date often cited is that of 1539, when King Francis I of France ordered legal documents to be drawn up in French instead of the traditional Latin. In the academic domain, the German physician Theophrastus von Hohenheim, known as Paracelsus (1493–1541), broke with tradition by lecturing in the vernacular at the University of Basel, although most of his colleagues resisted this innovation and it was only in the eighteenth century that German, English or Italian could regularly be heard in the lecture rooms of universities. At around the same time, French replaced Latin as the main language of international diplomacy.

Nevertheless, as the last two examples suggest, the decline of Latin must not be dated too early. Translations from the vernaculars into Latin were common, especially translations from Italian and French, made for a northern European public. At least 1,200 such translations were made between the late fifteenth and the late eighteenth centuries, reaching their peak in the first half of the seventeenth century. To take only English examples, the essays of Francis Bacon, the philosophy of John Locke, Robert Boyle's *Sceptical Chemist* and other works, Newton's *Optics*, and even Milton's *Paradise Lost* and Gray's *Elegy in a Country Churchyard* were most familiar on the Continent in Latin versions, since the English language was not well known in other countries until the second half of the eighteenth century.

Visual Communication

The language of gesture, taken seriously in early modern Europe, was taught in schools as part of the discipline of rhetoric, and it was the subject of a number of treatises, from *The Art of Gesture* (1616) by the Italian jurist Giovanni Bonifacio to the *Chirologia* (1644) of the English physician John Bulwer, concerned with 'manual rhetoric', in other words 'the natural language of the hands'.

As for visual communication in a broader sense, Renaissance humanists would have had little to learn from the French critic Roland Barthes (1915–80) about what he called 'the rhetoric of the image' – as Barthes himself, who analysed modern advertisements with the help of Aristotle's *Rhetoric*, would probably have been the first to recognize.

Despite their remarkable innovations in style, what are commonly and somewhat anachronistically called the 'works of art' of the Renaissance should be seen as images or even what the sociolinguists call 'communicative events'. For example, *The Punishment of Corah*, a fresco by the Florentine painter Sandro Botticelli (1445–1510) in the Sistine Chapel in Rome, represents the earth opening to swallow a man who had dared to rebel against the authority of Moses. Commissioned by Pope Sixtus IV at a time, the late fifteenth century, when there was talk of summoning a council of the Church to limit the power of the Pope, the fresco makes a firm statement to the effect that the Pope is the new Moses and that rebellion does not pay. The famous religious paintings of the Renaissance, such as Michelangelo's *Last Judgement* or Tintoretto's *St Mark rescuing a slave* (see Figure 2), were not innovative in this respect, although the new three-dimensionality may have made them more effective as religious communication. The uses of the image in arousing the emotions of its viewers were already well known.

Secular paintings, increasingly identified with individual painters from the years around 1500 onwards, communicated a greater variety of messages to smaller audiences. Whereas a large number of religious paintings were displayed in churches where anyone could see them, most secular paintings of the Renaissance were bought by private individuals to hang in their own houses. Botticelli's *Spring*, for instance, may be well known today, thanks to exhibitions and reproductions, but in the Renaissance itself the painting was invisible to most people because it hung on the walls of a private villa.

Both religious and secular works were generally made on commission, for particular clients and according to their specifications, which were sometimes extremely precise, as surviving contracts show. Literary works, too, were often created for specific patrons and dedicated to them. It was only in the course of the early modern period (in the sixteenth century in the Netherlands, in the eighteenth century in France and England) that artists and writers (see p. 48) began to work for the market, producing first and selling afterwards rather than the other way round.

Printed Images

The rise of the market was associated with the rise of the mechanically reproduced image, and in particular of the 'print', a general term for printed images, whether the medium employed was a block of wood or a copper or steel plate, whether the image was incised on the plate (an engraving) or eaten away by acid (as in the case of the etching).

The first known woodcut dates from the late fourteenth century, and was probably inspired by the stamping of patterns on textiles. In fact, collections of woodcut images of religious scenes were already being produced a generation before Gutenberg's Bible. The etching developed in the sixteenth and seventeenth centuries (Rembrandt's etchings are particularly famous). The advantage of this method, in which a metal plate is covered with wax on which lines are drawn before the plate is submerged in a bath of acid, is that gradations of tone can be achieved by immersing the plate more than once, adding new lines and making the old ones deeper and so darker. In the eighteenth century, the invention of the mezzotint, with tiny holes of different depths replacing the lines on the plate with still more subtle gradations, made it possible to make realistic reproductions of oil paintings in black and white. In 1796, the lithograph was invented by Aloys Senefelder (1771–1834). Produced by drawing on stone with grease pencils, the new medium allowed cheap coloured images to be produced for the first time.

The rise of the print was the most profound change in visual communication in this whole period, since it made images so much more widely available than before. Print-making quickly involved leading artists of the Renaissance, such as Botticelli, who produced a series of woodcut illustrations for Dante's *Divine Comedy.*

Prints were relatively cheap to make and transport, thus enabling the work of their designers to reach relatively large numbers of people fairly quickly. It is likely, for instance, that the most vivid and memorable images of the New World were not those conveyed in words by Christopher Columbus or later explorers but by the woodcuts of Indians wearing feathered head-dresses and cooking and eating human flesh. Popular piety was encouraged by woodcuts of saints distributed on their feast-days, and similar images of Luther helped to spread the ideas of the reformers of the Church in the 1520s. The paintings of Leonardo, Raphael and Michelangelo were reproduced in the form of woodcuts and engravings and so introduced to a wider audience, like the paintings of Rubens in the seventeenth century. Prints also introduced Western European images to other cultures. They were used as models by painters of religious images in the Russian Orthodox world from the middle of the seventeenth century onwards, and they also influenced styles of representation as far afield as Persia, India, China, Mexico and Peru.

Popular political consciousness, to be discussed in more detail in the next chapter, was encouraged by the spread of satirical prints, especially in

Fig. 7 *The Repeal, or the Funerary Procession of Miss Americ-Stamp*, 1765.

seventeenth- and eighteenth-century England and in revolutionary France (see pp. 74, 79). Some of these images are known to have sold extremely well. For example, a print celebrating the repeal of the Stamp Act, to which the American colonies strongly objected, in 1765, sold 2,000 copies at a shilling each in only four days, and it is said that another 16,000 copies were sold in illegal versions (see Figure 7). In the course of the period the conventions of representation changed, with the allegorical print, such as the mock-funeral, being replaced by the more direct political caricature of, for instance, Sir Robert Walpole, Charles James Fox, or the Prince of Wales, the main target of the artist James Gillray (1756–1815) in the 1780s, before he turned to satirizing the French Revolution.

In the world of scholarship, systematic discussions of the significance of the printed image as a medium of communication parallel the detailed investigations of printed texts. Nineteenth- and twentieth-century bibliographers concerned themselves with the appearance, the dating and the printing history of books, while art historians considered prints in similar fashion. Both groups of scholars were supposed to pay attention to reproduction and to the number of copies in circulation, although they did not always do so. According to the German Marxist critic Walter Benjamin (1892–1940), the work of art changed its character following the Industrial Revolution. 'That which withers in the age of mechanical reproduction is the aura of the work of art.' The machine 'substitutes a plurality of copies for a unique existence' and in so doing produces a shift from the 'cult value' of the image to its 'exhibition value'. Whether or not the aura of the image is lost is a difficult hypothesis to test, and it might even be argued that familiarity with a reproduction sharpens rather than sates the desire to see the original.

Benjamin was thinking of nineteenth-century media such as lithography and photography (see p. 133), but William M. Ivins Jr (1881–1961), a curator of prints at the Metropolitan Museum of Art in New York, made a case for the importance of sixteenth-century prints as 'exactly repeatable pictorial statements'. Ivins argued that prints were 'among the most important and powerful tools of modern life and thought'. He pointed out that the ancient Greeks, for instance, had abandoned the practice of illustrating botanical treatises because of the impossibility of producing identical images of the same plant in different man-uscript copies of the same work. From the late fifteenth century, on the other hand, herbals were regularly illustrated with woodcuts.

Maps, which began to be printed in 1472, offer another example of the way in which the communication of information by images was facilitated by the repeatability associated with the press. In a more literal sense than that meant by David Olson (see p. 10), they offered readers 'the world on paper' and made it easier than ever before for groups armed with these documents to control parts of the earth, whether their control was primarily military, political, economic or ideological. Generals and governments, merchants and missionaries encour-aged the making of manuscript maps of the world beyond Europe. They often hoped to keep this information to themselves, but it was gradually leaked into print and into the public domain.

The transfer of the two-dimensional map to the three-dimensional globe, of which the oldest surviving example is Martin Behaim's of 1492, made it easier to think of the earth as a whole. When maps were collected into atlases, beginning with the *Theatre of the World* by Abraham Ortelius (first published at Antwerp in 1570), they allowed viewers to see the world both as a whole and in detail. Although the ideal of cosmopolitanism goes back as far as the Stoic philosophers in the age of the Roman Empire, the spread of these globes and printed maps must have encouraged global consciousness.

Another development of this period was the narrative strip or picture story, the ancestor of the twentieth-century comic strip. The visual narrative in which the viewer 'reads' the episodes, usually from left to right and from top to bottom, was already known in the Middle Ages, but its importance increased with the rise of the woodcut in the Renaissance. Woodcuts in particularly long strips were pro-duced to record events such as processions through the streets. These strips, the printed equivalents of medieval rolls, gave their viewers the impression of watch-ing the procession pass. The true 'moving pictures' of the early modern period, however, were the processions themselves.

Multimedia Communication

It is likely that the most effective forms of communication at this time were – as they are today – those which appealed simultaneously to the eye and to the ear and combined verbal with non-verbal messages, musical as well as visual, from the drums and trumpets of military parades to the violins accompanying indoor performances. In early modern Europe these forms included rituals, spectacles, masques, plays, ballets and operas.

Rituals were messages, but they were both more and less than a way of communicating information. They were less, because it is unlikely that very much of the information encoded in the action was actually assimilated by a majority of the spectators, because they failed to understand allusions to ancient history or classical mythology, for example, or because they were literally in no position to see what was going on. On the other hand, rituals were more than a means of transmitting information in the sense that they created solidarity, whether between the priest and his congregation, the ruler and his subjects, or the members of a guild or corporation marching together in procession. It should be added that it was commonly believed at this time that rituals were a means to make changes happen in the world. The consecration of the Host transformed it into the body and blood of Christ, while the ceremony of coronation turned a person into a king. The touch of the kings of France and England was supposed to heal the sick, at least those suffering from the skin disease known as scrofula, and sufferers arrived at the royal palaces in their thousands on certain days of the year.

'Ritual' is not always the best term to describe many of these multimedia events. It might be better to follow seventeenth-century usage and to describe some of them at least as spectacles. The main form of public spectacle at this time was the procession (generally religious but sometimes secular, as in the case of royal entries into cities). Mock-battles, such as medieval jousts and tournaments, might also be described as a form of outdoor spectacle, and one which continued to be important in this period too, but there was nothing 'mock' about executions, another common form of spectacle at this time. They were staged in public precisely to impress spectators and to communicate the message that it was hopeless to try to resist the authorities and that evil-doers would come to a bad end. Another kind of spectacle might be described as the 'theatre' of the everyday life of the ruler, who often took meals in public and might even turn his getting up in the morning and going to bed at night into rituals, as in the famous case of Louis XIV of France (reigned 1643–1715). Again, Queen Elizabeth I, who declared that princes were 'set on stages', was skilful in exploiting this situation for political purposes, turning herself into a goddess or a myth, as effectively as Eva Perón in the very different media system of Argentina in the middle of the twentieth century.

These examples suggest that students of the media should try to place in historical perspective the claim of Roger-Gérard Schwartzenberg that the rise of the 'spectacle state' and the 'star system' in politics was a consequence of the rise of television, or the assertion of Guy Debord (below, p. 201) that twentieth-century society is a 'society of the spectacle', in which the 'ruling order discourses endlessly upon itself in an uninterrupted monologue of self-praise'. Television may be responsible for a revival of political theatre, and has certainly given it new forms (by allowing so many people to observe political leaders in close-up), but the public dramatization and personalization of politics, like the official monologue of self-praise, goes back a very long way.

As a case-study of spectacle as communication, the Florentine festival of St John the Baptist in the late fifteenth century is of interest because it was a celebration of the wealth and power of the city of Florence and especially of its government. Florence was a large city for the period (with about 40,000 inhabitants) as well as a city-state controlling a substantial part of Tuscany. St John the Baptist was the principal patron and protector of the city and his feast, on 24 June, was a particularly splendid occasion. One of the main festive events was a procession from the cathedral to the river Arno and back, a procession in which monks, friars, secular clergy, choirboys and religious confraternities took part. They walked through streets decorated with rich cloths and filled with spectators, accompanied by music, carrying relics and followed by floats representing religious scenes such as the birth of St John and his baptism of Christ.

The secular part of the celebrations in Florence included an exhibition of luxury goods produced by the craftsmen of the city, notably cloth, jewels and goldsmiths' work, displayed outside the workshops, and also a race (*palio*), not unlike the race which still takes place in Siena twice a year, with colourful costumes for the horses and their riders. The civic aspect of the festival was marked by a banquet for the *Signoria* (the local equivalent of the mayor and aldermen), by the part played in the organization of the day's events by the different wards of the city, and by the arrival of deputations from Tuscan towns subject to Florence – among them Pisa, Arezzo, Pistoia, Volterra and Cortona – to offer tribute to the saint, and thus to the city of which he was the patron. Hence the rituals may be described as an expression of the collective identity of the Florentines.

The idiom of European ritual changed in the sixteenth and seventeenth centuries. Two of these changes deserve particular emphasis: the restructuring of ritual along ancient Roman lines and the rise of the theatre, which culminated in one of the most famous 'slogans' associated with communications, 'All the world's a stage'. Renaissance humanists, in the process of reviving classical antiquity, classicized ritual, as in the case of the mock naval battle which was waged, in the style of the ancient Romans, in the courtyard of the Palazzo Pitti in Florence, which had been filled with water for the occasion. In a number of other cities, scattered in different countries, a recurring version of classical spectacle was provided by the ritual entry of a prince. Following the ancient Roman precedent, the prince rode in a chariot, passing through triumphal arches and attended by figures personifying Fame, Victory or Justice. Famous examples were the entry of the emperor Charles V into Bologna for his coronation in 1530, the entry of King Henri II into Rouen in 1550, and the entry of King Charles IX into Paris in 1571. The practice became widely taken up and was not limited to rulers. In London in the seventeenth century, the new Lord Mayor passed through triumphal arches of this kind in his inauguration ritual, the annual Lord Mayor's Show.

How intelligible were these spectacles? To help spectators understand what was happening at the time of the performance, an interpreter might be introduced, like St George in the Lord Mayor's Show in London in 1609. Alternatively, written notices might be attached to particular figures, a procedure mocked by the playwright Ben Jonson (1572–1637), who preferred a learned to a popular audience, with his satirical examples 'This is a dog, or This is a hare'. The spectacles were also frequently described in printed and illustrated books which might be available on the day itself, or shortly afterwards, precisely in order that the spectators, or some of them, would know what to expect and how to understand what they were seeing, or discover the meaning of what they had just seen.

Who was saying what to whom through these rituals? In the case of state visits to cities the obvious answer is that the city was demonstrating its loyalty to the prince. This answer is not incorrect but it is incomplete. Communication was a two-way process, a form of dialogue, and princes demonstrated their good will towards their subjects as well as receiving applause. Moreover, the rituals were sometimes performed for the benefit of foreign princes, to whom the expression of loyalty was inappropriate. Bologna was part of the states of the Church when it welcomed Charles V in 1529, and Venice an independent republic when King Henri III of France made a formal entry into it in 1574. Finally, it is possible to find occasions when cities used rituals to send another kind of message to the prince, not so much a panegyric as a petition. When Charles V entered Bruges in 1515, the pageants drew attention to the economic decline of the city, which was being displaced as a centre of commerce by the port of Antwerp. One of the scenes shown to Charles was a wheel of fortune, with Bruges sitting at the bottom. The message was clear. It was an appeal to the prince to restore the lost prosperity of the city.

Major festivals were the traditional time for the performance of plays, religious plays on the feast of Corpus Christi, for example, or secular plays during carnival. These performances usually took place either in the street, at the royal court, or in private houses. A major new development, from the later sixteenth century onwards, was the rise of the public theatre in London, Madrid, Paris and elsewhere. Plays began to be performed by professional actors in inns or in purpose-built playhouses, such as the Hôtel de Bourgogne in Paris (1548) or the Theatre (1576) or the Globe (1598) in London, open to all on payment of a reasonably low fee. Admission cost a penny in Shakespeare's London, a price which apprentices as well as merchants and gentlemen could afford. The commercial opera began a little later, in Venice, where the first public theatre was opened in 1637.

The rise of the commercial theatre at much the same time in different countries suggests that – apart from the imitation of new foreign models – a crucial factor in its development was the rise in the population of cities above a threshold of 100,000 people or so. With a potential audience of this size, professional actors were able to settle down in one place instead of wandering the country in search of new spectators and perform the same play to different people night after night, or more often, perform the same two or three plays over a few weeks.

Interactions between Media

Multimedia events are not the only examples from this period of the interaction between different means of communication – the interface between media. Another is that of the so-called iconotext, an image which depends for its interpretation on texts incorporated into it – the names of saints, for example, speech scrolls coming from the mouths of the characters or captions over or under the image. For example, the prints of William Hogarth, such as *Gin Lane, The Harlot's Progress* or *The Industrious Apprentice*, depend for their elucidation on textual material tucked away in corners of the image. Hogarth was also commissioned to produce paintings illustrating scenes from an extremely successful musical of his day, John Gay's *Beggar's Opera*.

Another kind of interaction may be illustrated by the function of manuscripts in early modern Europe. It is a recurrent theme in cultural history that when a new genre or medium (in this case, print) makes its appearance, earlier genres or media do not disappear altogether. The old and the new – the cinema and television, for instance – coexist and compete until eventually some division of labour or function is established. That manuscripts continued to be used for private communications, such as family or commercial letters, is obvious enough, although it may be worth pointing out that the manuscript letter was influenced by print in this period, via the many treatises on the art of letter-writing published in large numbers in Italy and elsewhere from the sixteenth century onwards. These printed treatises offered useful models for letters of con-gratulation or condolence, love-letters, apologies, or letters requesting money.

What requires more extended examination here is the survival into the early modern period of the manuscript as a major channel for the public circulation of messages. To be more precise, manuscripts were still used to transmit mes-sages in a semi-public manner. In Russia as late as 1700, secular literature was still circulating in manuscript form as well as orally because the few existing presses were located in monasteries and used for the production of religious books. Even in Western Europe, which was full of presses, as we have seen, cir-culation in manuscript continued to perform some useful functions.

In the sixteenth and seventeenth centuries, men of high status (and women even more so) were often unhappy with the idea of publishing books, on the grounds that the books would be sold to the general public and so make the authors look like tradespeople. As a result of this prejudice, coterie poets and other writers preferred to circulate their work in manuscript copies to their friends and acquaintances. It was in this form that the poems of Sir Philip Sidney (1554–86), for example, the sonnet sequence *Astrophel and Stella*, circulated in Elizabethan England. Again, the love lyrics of John Donne, written in the 1590s, were not published until 1633, two years after the author's death. Donne was probably unwilling to publish poems on love because he had entered the Church and become a deservedly famous preacher.

This form of manuscript circulation differed from printed circulation in a number of ways. It was a means of social bonding between the individuals involved, often a group of friends. The calligraphy of the manuscripts sometimes made them into works of art in their own right. The texts were less fixed and more malleable than printed ones because transcribers often felt free to add to or sub-tract from the verses they copied, or to change names in order to adapt what was written to their own situation. Manuscript was what we would now call an 'inter-active' medium.

A second and still more important reason for manuscript circulation was to evade religious, moral and political censorship. In other words, to adopt a term widely current a few years ago, manuscript was the samizdat of the early modern period, the equivalent of the 'publish-it-yourself' typescripts and xeroxes criticizing communist regimes which circulated unofficially in the USSR, Poland and elsewhere before 1989. For example, the *Letter to the Grand Duchess* by Galileo Galilei (1564–1642), a discussion of the delicate issue of the relationship between religion and science, circulated widely in manuscript before it was finally published in 1636. In France, towards the end of the reign of Louis XIV (ruled 1661–1715), a great variety of manuscripts satirizing the king, his family and his ministers were in circulation. Books attacking Christianity also circulated in this underground fashion. In some cases, printed books were copied for clandestine distribution in a region in which their publication was banned. In early eighteenth-century Paris, for example, the trade in manuscript copies of unorthodox books was highly organized, with professional copyists working for entrepreneurs who sold their wares near cafés. More than a hundred unorthodox texts circulated in this way in the first half of the eighteenth century.

In between the two kinds of manuscript discussed above came the manuscript newsletters, letters sent in multiple copies to a limited number of subscribers, especially from 1550 to 1640, in other words in the generation or two before the rise of newspapers. The flexibility of the manuscript form permitted variations in the news sent to individual subscribers, according to their interests and needs. This personalized news service was available only to wealthy people, but it allowed the circulation of information which governments might have preferred to remain secret. Hence there was still a market for manuscript newsletters after 1650 despite the rise of the printed news-sheet (see p. 48). In France, for example, the Comte de Lionne was the centre of a manuscript news network in Paris around the year 1671. His employees followed the French armies abroad and sent reports back to him which he put into wider circulation.

Another example of the interaction between manuscript and print takes us back to the letter. The editors of printed journals of different kinds, from the *Transactions of the Royal Society* to the *Spectator*, often solicited and received correspondence from their readers. Some of these letters were printed, while others influenced the topics chosen for discussion and the opinions expressed in the journal.

For a final example of the interfaces between media we may turn to the relation between orality and print. Printed texts often reproduced what Ong has called 'oral residue', turns of phrase or grammatical constructions more appropriate to speech than to writing, to the ear than to the eye. Books in dialogue form, popular throughout the early modern period, from Castiglione's *Courtier* (1528) to Diderot's *Rameau's Nephew* (written in the 1760s, though not published until 1830), were fuelled by oral exchanges in courts, academies or salons. Preachers were often inspired by texts, from the Bible to the sermon outlines which were already available in print in the fifteenth century, so that clergymen did not need to lie awake on Saturday night thinking what to say to their congregations the next day. Preachers also sent their own texts to the printer, or if they did not do so others acted for them, taking down their words in shorthand and transcribing them afterwards.

The uses of printed books in this period also reveal the interaction between speech and print. For example, one of the most famous devotional books of the sixteenth century was the *Spiritual Exercises* (1548), written by the founder of the Jesuit order, Ignatius Loyola, a guide to meditation and to the examination of conscience. Published in Latin, the *Exercises* were not intended to be read by the Catholic laity. The text was an instruction manual for a priest or spiritual director, who would pass the message on to the laity by word of mouth. In similar fashion, the drill manuals which began to appear in print in the seventeenth and eighteenth centuries were intended for officers or sergeants rather than the rank and file.

In early seventeenth-century England printed ballads were sometimes used as aids to oral performance, the equivalent of today's karaoke. The texts were pasted onto the walls of taverns so that people who did not know or could not remember the words of a particular ballad could sing along with the rest. There was still such a lively oral culture, however, that many people exercised more creativity, composing ballads of their own about their neighbours or enemies. These home-made ballads might adapt verses from a printed text – in a manner similar to the writers of the manuscripts discussed above – and they were often sung to tunes which broadside ballads had made familiar.

The art of conversation was influenced, if not transformed, by the spread in print of books on the subject, beginning in sixteenth-century Italy with Baldassare Castiglione's *Courtier* (1528), Giovanni Della Casa's *Galateo* (1558) and Stefano Guazzo's *Civil Conversation* (1574), and continuing through a series of French, Spanish and German treatises and the reflections on the subject of Swift, Fielding and Lord Chesterfield. These treatises offered instruction to men and women of different ages and social groups, advising them when to speak or keep silent, to whom, about what, and in what style. The number of editions through which they passed, together with the underlinings and annotations in some surviving copies, suggest that this advice was taken seriously. In other words, print was contributing to what the authors of the treatises would have called the refinement of speech, and also to its increasing uniformity, a process which was also encouraged by the publication of grammars of different European languages. Indeed, language is one of the domains which best illustrates Eisenstein's point about the connections between printing and standardization.

The interactions between orality and print may be studied in more detail by examining some Italian versions of what English scholars generally call chapbooks (see pp. 17–18). An examination of some of these booklets, published in Italy in the late fifteenth and early sixteenth centuries, reveals the continuing importance of romances of chivalry – as in France more than a century later. An account-book recording the expenses of a printing shop near Florence between 1476 and 1486 reveals that nearly 500 copies of one romance of chivalry were sold wholesale to a man described as Bernardino 'who sings on a bench'. It therefore seems plausible to suggest that what Bernardino did was what is still done in remote parts of Brazil and elsewhere in the Third World – to recite the poem and then to sell printed copies of it. The performance was a form of marketing. It drew an audience of potential readers, and gave them a chance to test the quality of the product. Buying the text allowed listeners to repeat the performance to their families and friends. If they were illiterate, they could always ask someone else to read or recite the poem to them.

Many other texts published in Florence or Venice at this time open or close with formulae suggesting that a singer is performing in public, with the openings often calling on God to help and on bystanders to pay attention. 'Pay attention to me, for I can recite a new poem in rhyme.' Or: 'If you pay attention I will make you enjoy yourselves.' Or again: 'Lords and good people I can tell you many stories which I know by heart.' The closing formulae express the hope that the listeners have enjoyed the story, presumably passing the hat around for money at the same time. 'This story is told in your honour.' 'Think about my needs, prudent listener.' 'Elegant beautiful and gracious ladies, I thank you for the attention you have given my poor eloquence.' Such openings and closings recall passages, usually in verse, at the beginning and end of stage plays (and later of operas), where the playwright (or composer) directly addresses the audience.

In these texts it is not difficult to identify formulae and themes of the kind discussed by Milman Parry and Albert Lord (see p. 6). They include some of the very themes used by the twentieth-century Yugoslav poets, such as the holding of a council or the sending of a letter (reminding us of the importance of writing in a semi-oral culture). Examples of the formulae include 'with sweet speech', 'threw him to the ground', 'like a cat', 'appeared to be a dragon', and so on. The texts also offer frequent examples of the redundancy typical of oral performance: 'Crying and weeping with sorrow' (*Lagrimando e piangendo con dolore*) for instance, or 'That day was one of great heat and it was burning hot' (*Era quel dì gran caldo e grande ardore*). Redundancy of this kind should not be interpreted as a weakness on the part of the poet. It is a device that makes it easier for the audience to follow the story.

In short, oral and printed media coexisted and interacted in fifteenth- and sixteenth-century Italy, as they did on the Anglo-Scottish borders in the eighteenth century. In his famous study of oral poetry, Lord argued that literacy and print necessarily destroy traditional oral culture. He went so far as to speak of the 'death' of oral tradition. These Italian examples, on the other hand, suggest that oral culture and print culture were able to coexist for a considerable period. It is of course thanks to this kind of coexistence that the traditional ballads of Scotland, England and Scandinavia, which were written down and printed from the sixteenth century onwards, have survived.

Censorship

As the remarks in the last section about clandestine communication by manuscript have already suggested, censorship of the media was a major preoccupation of the authorities in European states and churches, Protestant and Catholic alike, in the early modern period, whether they were principally concerned with heresy, sedition or immorality.

In a society in which only a minority were literate, repression could not be confined to books alone. Plays, for instance, were often subject to censorship. In London, they had to be licensed by the Master of the Revels before they could be performed. Texts were carefully scrutinized for references to important people, at home and abroad, as well as for comments on topical religious or political issues. The censor's problem was that although the text of the play might be submitted in advance, it was difficult to prevent actors from improvising subversive remarks in the course of performance. It was for this reason that some plays running in London, such as Thomas Middleton's notorious *Game at Chess* (1625), which satirized the court of Spain, were brought to an abrupt end by order of the Bishop or the Privy Council.

A reforming archbishop of Bologna spoke of drawing up an index of prohibited images. It never happened, perhaps because it was too difficult to organize such an enterprise, but specific images were not infrequently criticized, destroyed or expurgated by repainting. In the case of Michelangelo's *Last Judgement*, for instance, the naked bodies were ordered to be furnished with fig-leaves. The painter Paolo Veronese (1528–88) was summoned before the Venetian Inquisition because his painting of the Last Supper included what the inquisitors called 'buffoons, drunkards, Germans, dwarves and similar vulgarities'. Some Protestants smashed images, considering them idolatrous, while Catholics buried the images they were coming to view as unseemly – naked St Sebastians, for example, or representations of St Martin as a soldier and of St Eloy as a goldsmith.

The most famous and widespread censorship system of the period was that of the Catholic Church, with its 'Index of Prohibited Books'. The Index was a printed catalogue – perhaps better described as an 'anti-catalogue' – of printed books which the faithful were forbidden to read. There were many local indexes too, beginning with the one published in 1544 by the Sorbonne (the Faculty of Theology of the University of Paris), but the important ones were those issued by papal authority and binding on the whole Church, from the mid-sixteenth century to the mid-twentieth century.

The Index might be said to have been invented as an antidote to Protestantism and printing. It was an attempt to fight print with print. The model index, issued in 1564, began with a set of general rules forbidding three main types of book: the heretical, the immoral and the magical. Then came an alphabetical list of authors and titles, the authors divided into first class (all their writings being prohibited) and second class (in which case the ban extended only to specific works). Most of the books on the Church's list were devoted to Protestant theology in Latin, but some literary works which later became classics can also be found on it, among them the satires written by the humanist Erasmus and the *Gargantua and Pantagruel* of Rabelais (not for the obscenity which worried some eighteenth- and nineteenth-century readers, but for the author's criticisms of the Church). Machiavelli's *Prince* was also there, as were Dante's treatise *On Monarchy* (thanks to its exaltation of the emperor over the Pope), Petrarch's sonnets against the papacy and Boccaccio's *Decameron*.

There was disagreement among censors as to how far to go. A hard line was taken by the Italian Jesuit Antonio Possevino (1534–1611), who attacked romances of chivalry as 'stratagems of Satan' (perhaps for their emphasis on love, perhaps for their magic). On the other hand, another Italian Jesuit, Roberto Bellarmino (1542–1621), defended the great trio of Tuscan writers, Dante, Petrarch and Boccaccio, on the grounds that they were all good Catholics.

Two examples of censorship at work may show more clearly what the inquisitors were looking for. When Montaigne visited Italy he submitted his recently published *Essays* to a papal censor, who suggested a few alterations – references to fortune should be changed to providence, for instance, while references to heretical poets should be deleted altogether. A Calvinist pastor expurgated the *Essays* before their publication in Geneva was permitted, removing a favourable reference to the Roman emperor Julian 'the Apostate', who was converted from Christianity to paganism.

The second example is that of Boccaccio's *Decameron*, which had long been a target for clerical critics. Its condemnation was discussed at the Council of Trent, which met in the middle of the sixteenth century to discuss the reform of the Church. The Duke of Florence sent an ambassador to the Council to beg for the reprieve of the book, since his own prestige depended on the cultural capital represented by the local writers Dante, Petrarch and Boccaccio. Thanks to this diplomatic lobbying, the book's condemnation was commuted to expurgation. The Inquisition was always hypersensitive to its own reputation, and in the expurgated edition, one story (dealing with the hypocrisy of an inquisitor) completely disappeared. Elsewhere in the text, the names of saints and clerics were removed, at the price of making some stories virtually unintelligible. As in the case of Rabelais, what worried the inquisitors was not the frequent obscenity of Boccaccio's stories, but their anti-clericalism.

The campaign of repression had its absurd side but it may have been a reasonable success in its own terms. From the point of view of the orthodox, books were dangerous. The example of Menocchio, the Italian miller who was encouraged by books to think for himself (see p. 53), suggests they had a point. It is difficult to measure the effectiveness of the repression, but the Inquisition records themselves reveal the continuing importance of the trade in contraband books, such as the copies of Erasmus and Machiavelli which were still being smuggled into Venice in the 1570s and 1580s.

Protestant censorship was less effective than Catholic censorship not because the Protestants were more tolerant but because they were more divided, fragmented into different churches with different administrative structures like the Lutheran and the Calvinist. In Calvinist Geneva, manuscripts were submitted by the printer, in advance of publication, to be read by experts in theology, law, medicine and so on, before written permission to print was given. To ensure that the orders were obeyed, the printing houses were regularly inspected and forbidden books were confiscated and might be burned by the public executioner. Secular censorship in France, England, the Dutch Republic, the Habsburg Empire and elsewhere was organized on similar lines.

In England, printing was restricted to London, Oxford and Cambridge and was controlled through the Stationer's Company, founded in 1557, which registered new publications. The manuscripts of books were also inspected before publication. According to the English Licensing Act of 1662, law books had to be inspected by the Lord Chancellor, history books by a secretary of state, and most other kinds of book by the Archbishop of Canterbury and the Bishop of London or their deputies. The system was brought to an end in 1695 when the Licensing Act was allowed to lapse.

Clandestine Communication ▓▓▓▓▓▓▓▓▓▓▓▓▓▓▓▓▓

The efficacy of the censorship system should not be overestimated. One of its unintended consequences was to awaken interest in banned titles which some readers might not otherwise have known about. Another reaction to formal censorship was to organize or reorganize clandestine communication. A considerable variety of messages was communicated underground, from the secrets of governments to commercial or technical secrets, and from unorthodox religious ideas to pornography.

'Pornography' – a term that was coined in the nineteenth century – is not easy to define. If it is used to refer to texts which are not only intended to arouse lust but also to sell for this very reason, the term was applicable to a number of early modern works. *120 Days of Sodom* by the Marquis de Sade (1740–1814) was among the most notorious examples, but far from the first. A century earlier, the anonymous *Venus in the Cloister* (1683) had been equally notorious. In the early sixteenth century, images of different sexual postures drawn by Giulio Romano (1499–1546) and engraved by Marcantonio Raimondi (d. 1534), with accompanying verses by Pietro Aretino, circulated in Rome before they were discovered and suppressed.

It is not easy to draw the line between public and private communication. The passing on of secrets by word of mouth, however safe it might have seemed, could be vulnerable to eavesdropping, in one case at least in the literal sense of the term. In 1478, some Venetians made a hole in the roof of the Doge's Palace in order to discover the latest news from Istanbul, news which was of obvious commercial value. It is no wonder that secrecy within a given group was sometimes maintained by the use of a private language, as in the case of the jargon of professional beggars and thieves.

Occult and alchemical works as well as heretical or subversive ones often circulated in manuscript copies. In other cases, what was transcribed was a confidential letter or report, such as a report by an ambassador to the Venetian Senate on his return from a mission abroad. Unofficial copies of these reports were sold openly in Rome in the seventeenth century. Again, in eighteenth-century Paris, police reports sometimes circulated among members of the public.

To prevent leaks of this kind, codes and ciphers of various kinds were often used by merchants, by governments and even by scientists (or as they were called in the seventeenth century, 'natural philosophers'), who wanted to ensure that their rivals did not steal their ideas. A famous example from astronomy is that of the Dutchman Christiaan Huygens (1629–95), who discovered in 1655 that the planet Saturn was surrounded by a ring. In order to claim priority and at the same time avoid plagiarism, he first announced his discovery by means of a Latin anagram: AAAAAA CCCCC D EEEEE G H IIIIIII LLLL MM NNNNNNNNN OOOO PP Q RR S TTTTT UUUUU, which stood for '*Annulo cingitur, tenui, plano, nusquam cohaerente, ad eclipticam inclinato*' (It is girdled with a ring, which is thin, flat, in no way coherent and inclined to the ecliptic). Governments made considerable use of cipher, and the ciphers, thanks to the aid of leading mathematicians, code-makers and code-breakers, became more and more sophisticated in the early modern period. Private individuals also used ciphers, and the diarist Samuel Pepys was not alone in using foreign languages to conceal some of the activities he recorded from possible readers, including his wife.

In the third place, there were clandestine publications. Raids on printers suspected of trading in forbidden books were not uncommon, but presses were sometimes set up in private houses and moved around the country in order to avoid detection. In Elizabethan England, for example, pamphlets attacking the episcopate were originally printed in a country house in Surrey, and later in Northampton and Warwick. The *Lettres Provinciales* (1657), a famous attack on the Jesuits by the polymath Blaise Pascal (1623–62), were printed in secret. Again, a critique of serfdom, censorship and autocracy, the *Journey from Petersburg to Moscow* (1790), was published by the author, Aleksandr Nikolaevich Radishchev (1749–1802), on a private press on his estate in the country. He was immediately imprisoned and later exiled to Siberia.

The authors of such publications usually wrapped themselves in a cloak of anonymity, referring to themselves only by pseudonyms. The attacks on the Elizabethan bishops were signed 'Martin Marprelate': Pascal's attacks on the Jesuits were signed 'Louis de Montalte'. The printers likewise disguised their identities, while the place of publication, if it was mentioned at all, was generally false, often imaginary and sometimes extremely imaginative. As two early seventeenth-century Italian cardinals complained, 'to deceive the Catholics more easily', Protestant propaganda arrived with the names of Catholic cities on the title page, and some printers even imitated the typography of the Catholic printers of Paris, Lyons or Antwerp. A favourite imaginary place of publication was 'Freetown' or its equivalent in other languages (Villefranche, Vrijstadt, Eleutheropolis). Another, for some reason, was Cologne, where for 150 years books were attributed to a non-existent printer, Pierre de Marteau, presumably so-called because he hammered his victims. The printer of the Marprelate pamphlets claimed to work 'overseas, in Europe, within two furlongs of a bouncing priest'. Some late eighteenth-century French pornographic works claimed to be published 'at the press of the odalisques' in Istanbul or even at the Vatican itself.

Another possibility in the early modern period – as for so many East European writers in the age of the Cold War – was actually to print abroad rather than simply claim to do so. A famous seventeenth-century example is that of the anti-papal *History of the Council of Trent*, written by a Venetian friar, Paolo Sarpi (1552–1623). The book was first published in London, in Italian, in 1619. The manuscript was brought in secret from Venice to London via the British Embassy, in instalments described in the correspondence by the code-name of 'songs'.

Printed books were also frequently smuggled across frontiers. By the early 1550s, there were regular clandestine routes from Switzerland to Venice along which heretical books travelled. Again, in the early seventeenth century, prohibited books, usually unbound, were being smuggled into Spain, the large bibles hidden in bolts of cloth and the small catechisms disguised as packs of playing cards. Books which were critical of King Louis XIV and his court were published in French in Amsterdam and then smuggled into France.

Finally, it was of course possible to publish in the normal way but to communicate messages on two levels, the manifest and the latent. In Poland under the Communist regime, for example, critics of the government used what they called the 'method of Aesop', after the ancient Greek writer of fables about animals, which could easily be applied to the human world. In the early modern period, writers also followed Aesop. One of the most famous examples is the *Fables* of Jean de Lafontaine (1621–95). They are now treated as stories for children, but the fact that Lafontaine refused to serve Louis XIV, remaining loyal to a patron who had fallen into political disgrace, suggests that the figure of the tyrannical lion, for instance, should be read in a political manner.

Alternatively, a message about a topical subject might be disguised as a history of similar events in the past. For example, the deposition of King Richard II by Henry of Bolingbroke (the future King Henry IV) had considerable political resonance towards the end of the reign of Queen Elizabeth, with the Earl of Essex cast in the role of Henry. No wonder then that in 1599, when Sir John Hayward published a history of the *Life and Reign of King Henry IV*, the queen asked Francis Bacon whether there was treason in the book. Again, when the Earl of Essex (1566–1601) rebelled against the queen, his followers gave money to actors to play Shakespeare's *Richard II*; Elizabeth was said to have remarked at the time, 'I am Richard II, know you not that?' Similar allegorical techniques were in use in late seventeenth-century England during the so-called 'Exclusion Crisis' (discussed on p. 77).

This allegorical method is still employed on occasion, for example by Arthur Miller, whose *The Crucible* (1953) presented a critique of the 'witch-hunting' of Communists by Senator Joe McCarthy (1909–57), in the form of a play about a trial for witchcraft in New England in the seventeenth century.

The Rise of the Market

Printing might be dangerous, but it was also profitable. Some printers (though not all) were mercenaries, working for Catholics and Protestant alike during the wars of religion (see p. 64). One important consequence of the invention of printing was to involve entrepreneurs more closely in the process of spreading knowledge. Bestsellers go back to the early days of printing. The *Imitation of Christ*, a devotional work attributed to the fourteenth-century Netherlander Thomas Kempis, had appeared in no fewer than ninety-nine editions by 1500. The Scriptures, too, sold well at this time, especially the New Testament and the Psalms, although the Catholic Church prohibited vernacular bibles in the later sixteenth century on the grounds that they encouraged heresy. Print runs of books were normally small by later standards, averaging from 500 to 1,000 copies, but as many as three or four million copies of almanacs were printed in seventeenth-century England.

In order to sell more books, printers, whose range of products might involve far more than what is now known as 'literature', published catalogues and engaged in other forms of advertising. In Italy, the first known catalogue of books with prices goes back to 1541. In the sixteenth century, like today, the Frankfurt Book Fair and its equivalent in Leipzig made particular titles known internationally. Pages at the front or back of books advertised other works sold by the same printer or bookseller (the modern distinctions between printer, publisher and bookseller were not yet the norm in this period).

Advertising in print also developed in the seventeenth century. In London around 1650, a newspaper would carry about six advertisements on the average; a hundred years later, it would carry about fifty. Among the goods and services advertised in England at this time were plays, race-meetings, quack doctors and 'Holman's Ink Powder', perhaps the first brand name, for a product which was patented in 1688.

News was itself a commodity and was viewed as such at the time, at least by satirists such as Ben Jonson in his play *The Staple of News* (1626), imagining an attempt to monopolize the trade. As the sociologist Colin Campbell has argued, eighteenth-century novels, like television serials today, allowed readers the vicarious enjoyment of expensive consumer goods and also encouraged them to buy, thus acting as midwives in what has been called 'the birth of consumer society' (see below, p. 50).

The rise of the idea of intellectual property was a response both to the emergence of consumer society and to the spread of printing. Some sense of literary ownership goes back to the fifteenth century, if not before. Thus, humanists accused one another of theft or plagiarism, while themselves claiming to practise creative imitation. A famous Spanish example of plagiarism is fairly typical of the period. The second part of *Don Quixote*, published in 1614, was not written by Cervantes but by a certain 'Avellaneda'. This was a slightly unusual form of plagiarism, since it involved stealing a character rather than a text, or stealing someone else's name for one's own work in order to cash in on their reputation. All the same, the original author resented it. In order to drive out the work of his competitor, Cervantes had to produce a second part of his own.

In this way, market forces encouraged the idea of individual authorship, an idea reinforced by new practices such as printing the portrait of the author as a frontispiece to the work, or introducing an edition of someone's collected works by a biography of the author. By 1711, the first issue of *The Spectator* could poke gentle fun at the reader unable to enjoy a book 'till he knows whether the writer of it be a black or a fair man, of a mild or choleric disposition, married or a bachelor'. Writing was even more of a path to individual fame than it had been in the Middle Ages (see p. 9).

During the eighteenth century, legal regulation also reinforced the idea of literary or intellectual property. In Britain, for example, an Act was passed in 1709 which granted authors or their assignees the sole right to print their work for fourteen years. William Hogarth (1697–1764), who suffered from piracies of his popular series of engravings of *The Harlot's Progress* (1732), campaigned with success for a new copyright Act (1735), which gave graphic artists like himself similar rights to those enjoyed by authors. The meaning of the 1709 act was clarified in the courts in cases such as *Millar* v. *Taylor* (1769) and *Donaldson* v. *Beckett* (1774), when the term 'copyright' was by then in general use. For international copyright, on the other hand, it was necessary to wait until the Berne Convention of 1887.

For a view in close-up of the market in the media, it may be illuminating to examine in chronological sequence three of the main centres of the book trade in early modern Europe: sixteenth-century Venice, seventeenth-century Amsterdam and eighteenth-century London.

In the fifteenth century, more books were printed in Venice than in any other city in Europe (about 4,500 editions, equivalent to something like two million copies, or 20 per cent of the European market). The Venetian book industry had a capitalist organization, with a small group in control and the financial backing of merchants whose economic interests ranged much more widely than books. In the sixteenth century, it has been estimated that about 500 printers and publishers produced from 15,000 to 17,500 titles and possibly eighteen million copies. The most famous of these printers, Aldo Manuzio (*c.*1450–1515), made his reputation and possibly his fortune by publishing editions of the Greek and Latin classics in a small format which allowed scholars and students to carry them about with ease (a correspondent praised his 'handy' volumes which could even be read when walking). There was cut-throat competition between print-ers, who regularly ignored one another's privileges and published the same books as their rivals, claiming that their editions were more correct or included new material, even if this was not the case. The large number of printers and publishers in Venice was one of the attractions of the city for men of letters, since it allowed them to make a living independent of patrons, even if it did not make them rich.

A group of these men of letters were nicknamed the *poligrafi* because they wrote so much and on such a wide variety of topics in order to survive. They were what would be known in eighteenth-century English as 'hacks', in other words, writers who were for hire, like hackney carriages. Their works included verse as well as prose and original compositions as well as translations, adaptations and plagiarisms from other writers. A genre in which they specialized was that of works offering practical information, including conduct books, a treatise explaining how to write letters on different topics, and a guide to Venice for foreign visitors which was still being reprinted in the seventeenth century. Some of these writers served particular printers (notably Gabriel Giolito, who pub-lished some 850 books in his long career) as editors and proof-readers as well as authors. In a sense, the *poligrafi* were on the frontier between two worlds. They were essentially compilers working in the medieval tradition, recycling the work of others. Living in the age of print, however, they were treated as individual authors with their names on the title page. Consequently, they were criticized by their rivals for plagiarism, an accusation from which medieval writers had been free.

The economic and political position of Venice was skilfully exploited by the printers. For example, Venetians, drawing on the skills of different groups of immigrants in the city, printed books in Spanish, in Croat, in demotic Greek, in Old Church Slavonic, in Hebrew, in Arabic, in Armenian. They also looked beyond Europe, as the city of Venice did more generally. Among their special-ities were accounts of the discovery of distant new lands. In the sixteenth century, Venice was second only to Paris in publishing books about the Americas, including various editions of the letters of Christopher Columbus (1451–1506) and Hernán Cortés (1485–1547). The products of sixteenth-century Venetian presses might be described as multicultural as well as polyglot.

The distinctive Venetian contribution to the book trade, associated with the city's tradition of tolerance for other cultures and other religions, the practical live-and-let-live attitude of merchants, was undermined by the spread of the Counter-Reformation. The Inquisition was established in Venice in 1547, books were burned on the Piazza San Marco and near the Rialto in 1548, a Venetian Index of Prohibited Books was produced in 1549 (fifteen years before the Index binding on the whole Church), and a ban on printing in Hebrew was issued in 1554. Booksellers began to be interrogated on charges of smuggling heretical or otherwise pernicious books from abroad. Some printers migrated to other cities such as Turin, Rome and Naples. Others, such as Gabriel Giolito, shifted their investments towards the publication of devotional books in Italian for a geographically more limited market.

In the seventeenth century, the Dutch republic replaced Venice as an island of relative tolerance of religious diversity and also as a major centre and market of information. The export of printed matter in Latin, French, English and German made an important contribution to the prosperity of this new nation. One of the leading printers in the republic, the Elzevir family, followed the example of Aldo Manuzio in publishing editions of the classics in small format. Elzevir also launched what may have been the first series of books ever to have an academic editor, Caspar Barlaeus, who was in charge of a range of compendia of information about the organization and resources of different states of the world, from France to India.

Barlaeus may be described as a Dutch equivalent of the *poligrafi*. Other hack writers included French Calvinist pastors who came to the Dutch Republic after Louis XIV had forced them to choose, in 1685, between conversion to Catholicism or emigration. There were too many pastors for the needs of the French Protestant churches in exile, so some of these well-educated men turned to writing for a living. Pierre Bayle (1647–1706), for example, who had left France for Rotterdam, edited a literary journal, the *News of the Republic of Letters*, which appeared monthly from 1684 onwards, as well as compiling his famous *Historical and Critical Dictionary* (1696).

The centre of Dutch publishing, as of much else in European industry and finance, was the city of Amsterdam. In the early seventeenth century Amsterdam was already Europe's major centre of newspapers, a new literary genre which probably illustrates the commercialization of information better than any other. The papers, which appeared once, twice or three times a week in Latin, French and English as well as in Dutch, included the first newspapers printed in English and French, *The Corrant out of Italy, Germany etc*, and the *Courant d'Italie*, both of which began publication in 1620. From 1662 onwards, a weekly paper in French, the *Gazette d'Amsterdam*, offered not only information about European affairs but also criticisms of the Catholic Church and of the policies of the French government.

By the second half of the seventeenth century Amsterdam had become the most important centre of book production in Europe, as Venice had once been. More than 270 booksellers and printers were active there in the twenty-five years 1675–99. A substantial proportion of them were, like the professional writers, Protestant refugees from France.

As in Venice, maps and accounts of voyages to exotic places formed an important part of the printers' repertoire. The most important printing establishment in Amsterdam, that of Joan Blaeu (*c.*1598–1673) – with nine presses for type and six more for engravings, an enterprise so large that it was one of the sights of the city for foreign visitors – belonged to a firm which specialized in atlases. The Blaeu family advertised in a newspaper in 1634 that they were about to produce a world atlas in four languages: Latin, Dutch, French and German. The two-volume atlas duly appeared in 1635 and contained 207 maps. A few years later, a rival Amsterdam publisher published a still more comprehensive atlas, only to be overtaken in his turn by the second version of the Blaeu atlas, in six volumes this time, published in 1655.

As in Venice, and once again drawing on the skills of different groups of immigrants, books were printed in Amsterdam in a variety of languages, including Russian, Yiddish, Armenian and Georgian. In 1678, an English visitor to the city found a Dutch printing-house producing bibles in English, and commented that 'you may buy books cheaper at Amsterdam in all languages than at the places where they are first printed'. French books were acquired by German readers through the mediation of Dutch entrepreneurs. Protestant printers produced Latin missals (with 'Cologne' on the title page) to sell in the Catholic world. The printers did not worry too much about infringing the rights of their competitors.

During the eighteenth century the primacy of Amsterdam passed to London. London booksellers, like those of Venice and Amsterdam before them, were already notorious by the late seventeenth century for the theft of their rivals' literary property, a practice known as 'counterfeiting' or as 'piracy' (in the twentieth century the term was extended to unofficial radio stations). As a protection against piracy, printers began to form alliances and to share their expenses and profits. Pooling their resources in this way allowed them to finance large and expensive works such as atlases and encyclopaedias which required considerable investment. Works of this kind were not infrequently published by subscription, often with a printed list of subscribers prefacing the book. The system of partnership has been compared to that of joint-stock companies, and the shares in printed editions were bought and sold by booksellers meeting in private. Sharing costs and risks enabled publishers (a new group emerging between printers and booksellers) to dispense with subscriptions.

A few authors began to receive substantial payments from their publishers, large enough for them to begin to think of abandoning patrons and living from the proceeds of their writing. Dr Johnson (1709–84), for instance, whose hatred of patronage was notorious, received £1,575 in advance for his *Dictionary* from a group of five booksellers, including Thomas Longman and Andrew Millar. Millar gave the philosopher-historian David Hume (1711–76) an advance of £1,400 for the third volume of his *History of Britain,* and William Robertson (1721–93) an advance of £3,400 for his *History of Charles V.* The poet Alexander Pope (1688–1744) had received a still higher sum, £5,300, for his translation of Homer's *Iliad.* Millar's successors, the partners William Strahan and Thomas Cadell, offered £6,000 for the copyright of Captain Cook's discoveries.

We should not be too hasty in idealizing the situation of writers in eighteenth-century London. A group of them, known collectively as 'Grub Street' after the place in London where they lived, were struggling to make ends meet, like earlier groups in Amsterdam and Venice. As in Amsterdam, this group included a number of French Protestant émigrés who were particularly active in journalism. Even for the more successful, the new freedom had its price. Johnson would probably have preferred to write his own books rather than compile a dictionary, and Pope to work on his own poems rather than translate Homer's. Hume wrote history because it sold better than philosophy, and if he were able to return to earth and consult the catalogue of the British Library, it is unlikely that he would be pleased to find himself listed as 'David Hume, historian'. All the same, some eighteenth-century men of letters enjoyed a greater degree of independence than their sixteenth-century predecessors, the *poligrafi*, had done.

The wider context for these developments in publishing is what historians have come to call 'the birth of a consumer society' in the eighteenth century, a shift particularly visible in England but extending to other parts of Europe and even beyond. English examples of the commercialization of leisure at this period included horse-racing at Newmarket, concerts in London (from the 1670s onwards) and some provincial cities, operas at the Royal Academy of Music (founded in 1718) and its rivals, exhibitions of paintings at the Royal Academy of Art (founded in 1768), lectures on science in coffee-houses, and balls and masquerades in newly constructed public assembly rooms in London, Bath and elsewhere. Like the plays presented in the Globe and other public theatres from the late sixteenth century onwards, these events were open to anyone who could afford the price of a ticket.

The History of Reading

The commercialization of leisure included reading. In considering the practice of reading books and newspapers, or indeed viewing prints, we move from supply to demand. At first sight, the idea of the history of reading may appear odd, since reading is an activity most of us take for granted. In what sense can it be said to change over time? And suppose that it did so, given that the movement of the eye produces no traces on the page, how can historians possibly say anything reliable about the changes? The last generation of historians have been addressing themselves to these problems. Arguing from the evidence of the physical format of books, from marginal notes written in books and from descriptions or pictures of readers, they have concluded that styles of reading did indeed alter between 1500 and 1800.

Five kinds of reading deserve separate attention here: critical reading, dangerous reading, creative reading, extensive reading, and private reading.

1.   Traditional accounts of the effects of print, as we have seen (p. 9), emphasize the rise of critical reading, thanks to increasing opportunities for comparing the diverse opinions propounded in different books on the same subject. The change in habits must not be exaggerated, since reading was not always critical. There is ample evidence of respect or even reverence for books in early modern times. Satirists made fun of people who believed everything they saw in print. The Bible, not yet subjected to critical scrutiny by scholars, with the exception of a few unorthodox individuals such as the Jewish philosopher Baruch Spinoza (1632–77), was a particular object of reverence. San Carlo Borromeo, archbishop

of Milan, was said to read Scripture on his knees. The Bible was sometimes used as a form of medicine and placed under the pillow of the sufferer. Its pages might be opened at random and the passages coming into view treated as heavenly guidance directed towards the problems of the reader.

2.   The dangers of private reading were frequently discussed. Whether or not it acted as a tranquillizer (see p. 18), contemporaries sometimes viewed the activity as dangerous, especially when practised by subordinate groups such as women and by 'the common people'. Analogies with twentieth-century debates about 'mass culture' and the dangers of television are clear enough, and they were pointed out more than a generation ago by the sociologist Leo Lowenthal. Today, the rise of the Internet has initiated another debate of this kind.

If we define the issues more broadly, these debates may be placed in a longer perspective. The decline after 1520 of images of the Blessed Virgin reading, images which had been relatively common in the late Middle Ages, appears to have been an early response to what might be called the demonization of reading by the Catholic Church. In late sixteenth-century Venice, for instance, a silk-worker was denounced to the Inquisition because 'he reads all the time' and a swordsmith because he 'stays up all night reading'. In similar fashion, both then and later, secular authorities considered unsupervised reading to be subversive. The reading of newspapers in particular was seen as encouraging ordinary people to criticize the government.

The dangers of reading fiction, especially for women, were regularly discussed by male writers from the early sixteenth century onwards. As in the case of the theatre, novels were feared for their power to arouse dangerous emotions such as love. Some men thought that women should not learn to read at all in case they received love-letters, although, as we have already seen (p. 28), illiteracy was not an impregnable defence. Others thought that women might be permitted to read a little, but only the Bible or devotional books. A few brave people argued that upper-class women could or even should read the classics.

Several sources suggest that, in practice, more kinds of women read more kinds of book than the critics allowed. In Spain, for instance, St Teresa of Ávila (1512–82) described her youthful enthusiasm for romances of chivalry. Some of the evidence comes not from autobiographies but from portraits, in which women are sometimes represented with books of poetry in their hands. The evidence of fiction points in the same direction. The heroine of an Italian story by the priest Matteo Bandello (*c*.1485–1561) is described as reading Boccaccio's *Decameron* and Ariosto's *Orlando Furioso* in bed. In the France of Louis XIV, the most important novelists were women, notably Madame de Lafayette (1634–93), writing primarily for other women. Opportunities for women to read increased in the eighteenth century, when novels and some historical writings, including histories of women published in Britain and Germany, were deliberately aimed at the female market. Lillian Lov described books in 1726 as 'closet companions', and a number of eighteenth-century paintings of women show them with books in their hands (see Figure 8). By this time some women were also reading newspapers. A 23-year-old French girl, working as a cook in 1791, claimed to read four newspapers regularly.

Fig. 8 Marguerite Gérard and Jean-Honoré Fragonard, *The Reader*.

3.   The extent of creative reading requires a different kind of examination. The meaning of texts has been a major topic of debate within literary studies in the 1990s. From a historian's perspective, it has long been clear that texts can and have often been read in ways quite contrary to the author's intentions. The *Utopia* of Thomas More (1478–1535), for instance, has been treated not only as a satire on the England of his day, but also as a blueprint for an ideal society, a 'utopia' in the modern sense of the term. *The Courtier*, by Baldassare Castiglione (1478–1529), an open dialogue in which appropriate behaviour in different social

situations is debated inconclusively, was presented by sixteenth-century printers and treated by some readers (as we know from their marginal annotations) as an unproblematic guide to good conduct. The ironies of Daniel Defoe (1660–1731) and Jonathan Swift (1667–1745) escaped some literal-minded readers, who believed that Defoe's *Shortest Way with the Dissenters* was really recommending the persecution of Nonconformists and that Swift's *Modest Proposal* was arguing in favour of cannibalism.

The sixteenth-century Italian miller Menocchio, rescued from obscurity by the Italian historian Carlo Ginzburg, offers a fascinating example of unorthodox reading in more than one sense of that term. Menocchio, interrogated by the Inquisition on a heresy charge, was asked about the books he had read, which included the Bible, Boccaccio's *Decameron*, the imaginary *Travels* of a certain Sir John Mandeville (a well-known book in the fifteenth and sixteenth centuries), and possibly the Koran as well. What Menocchio read was less surprising to the inquisitors than the way he read it, the interpretations he gave the texts. From Boccaccio's story of the three rings, for example, he derived the conclusion that if he had been born a Muslim, he should have remained one.

4.   Menocchio offers a good example of an intensive reader, rereading a few texts and brooding over them, a style of reading apparently typical of the first centuries of print as it was of the manuscript age which had preceded it. However, it has been argued that the later eighteenth century witnessed a 'reading revolution' in the sense of a shift towards the practices of skimming, browsing and chapter-hopping in the course of consulting books for information on a particular topic. In the period before 1750, there were fewer books and print was often treated as sacred. The period after 1750, on the other hand, has been described as a period of extensive reading, marked by the proliferation and the consequent desacralization of books.

The shift must not be exaggerated, because it is perfectly possible to practise the intensive and extensive styles alternately according to need. On one side, there is evidence of reading for reference in the late Middle Ages, especially in academic circles. On the other, there are the examples of the absorbed readers of the later eighteenth century, buried in one of the tear-jerking romances popular at that time, from the *New Héloise* of Jean-Jacques Rousseau (1712–78) to *The Sorrows of Werther* by Johann Wolfgang von Goethe (1749–1832).

5.   All the same, a shift in the relative importance of the two styles of reading is likely to have occurred, linked to the trend towards the privatization of reading. In any case, the format of books changed in ways which facilitated skimming or browsing. Texts were increasingly divided into chapters and within chapters into paragraphs. Printed notes in the margin summarized the message of each section. Detailed tables of contents and indexes organized in alphabetical order helped readers who were in a hurry to find particular items of information.

The privatization of reading has often been viewed as part of the rise of individualism and also of empathy or 'psychic mobility', as the media sociologist Daniel Lerner called it in his book on *The Passing of Traditional Society* (1958).

The basic idea behind the phrases is well captured in images, relatively common from the eighteenth century onwards, of a man or woman alone, reading a book, sitting or sprawled on the floor and oblivious to the outer world. The long-term trend towards 'privatization' from the fourteenth century to the twentieth is reflected in evidence from the format of books. Fifteenth-century books were often folios in large print which needed to be read on stands or lecterns. In the sixteenth and seventeenth centuries, small books became popular, the octavo, for instance, or the still smaller 12mo or 16mo format, which the famous Venetian printer Aldo Manuzio used for his editions of the classics.

In his brief life of Thomas Hobbes (1588–1679), the biographer John Aubrey (1626–97) told the story that when the philosopher was employed as a page to the earl of Devonshire, he bought himself 'books of an Amsterdam print that he might carry in his pocket (particularly Caesar's *Commentaries*) which he did read in the lobby or anti-chamber, whilst his Lord was making his visits'. This passage gives us the reader's view of the uses of the Elzevir classics in small format which were discussed above (p. 48). Books of poetry in particular were often printed in this format, which encouraged reading in bed, especially in the eighteenth century, when bedrooms in upper- or middle-class houses were gradually becoming private places.

Nevertheless, to view the history of reading in terms of a transition from public to private is as much of an oversimplification as viewing it in terms of a simple shift from the intensive to the extensive mode. Silent reading had sometimes been practised in the Middle Ages. Conversely, reading aloud in public persisted in the early modern period, as it was to do in working-class circles in the nineteenth century. The German Reformation offers some vivid examples of reading as a public activity (see p. 68).

It may be possible to make a distinction between reading habits according to social class – the middle classes tended to read privately while the working classes listened publicly. It is also necessary to make distinctions by situation. For example, the medieval practice of reading aloud at meals, whether in monastic refectories or royal courts, persisted into the sixteenth and seventeenth centuries. Reading aloud at home in the family circle persisted into the nineteenth century, at least as an ideal, as many images attest. It is likely that the texts of the Bibliothèque Bleue, discussed above (p. 17), which circulated in regions where literacy rates were low, were read aloud during the *veillées*, occasions when neighbours met to spend the evening working and listening. The rise of newspapers also encouraged reading aloud at breakfast or at work, while the fact that so many people were reading the same news at more or less the same time helped to create a community of readers.

Instruction and Entertainment

The uses of reading in early modern Europe were as varied as they are today, although these uses were not described in quite the same way then as now. The main categories were information and moral instruction, and it was only very slowly that a third kind of book, oriented solely towards entertainment, was admitted to be a legitimate use of readers' time. The increasing importance, between 1450 and 1800, of reading to acquire information is revealed by the proliferation of what we call 'reference books' of various kinds – dictionaries, encyclopaedias, chronological tables, gazetteers, and a range of 'how-to-do-it' books on subjects as varied as agriculture, good manners, cooking and calligraphy. The importance of moral instruction is revealed by the number of sermons which appeared in print as well as by treatises on the virtues requisite for particular roles in society (noble, wife, tradesman and so on).

On the other hand, the history of the words 'entertainment' and 'entertaining' tells us something about the obstacles to the emergence of this category of book or pamphlet. In the early seventeenth century, entertainment was associated with the hospitality shown to visitors. It was only around 1650 that the term acquired the additional meaning of something interesting or amusing, and only in the early eighteenth century that performances, such as plays, could be described as 'entertainments'. (For the later history of the media as entertainment, see Chapter 6.)

Books which we might describe as entertaining, from jest-books to romances, were already in print as early as the fifteenth century, but they were often provided with a moralizing framework or packaging, presumably in order to weaken the resistance of clerics, fathers of families and other 'gatekeepers' to these kinds of text. Pamphlets and single-sheet broadsides, retailing the exploits of criminals (a new sixteenth-century genre which may have been designed to appeal to a new group of readers), were presented in a similar fashion, emphasizing the punishment and if possible the 'hearty repentance' of the criminal.

However, this moralizing approach was undercut by a rhetoric of sensationalism, with title pages, like modern headlines, referring to 'terrible', 'wonderful' or 'dreadful' events, 'bloody' atrocities, 'strange and inhuman murders', and so on. Over the long term, and especially in the eighteenth century, the literature of entertainment broke out of its moralizing framework, to become part of the commercialization of leisure, alongside concerts, horse-races and circuses.

The Print Revolution Revisited

After this survey of the early modern media it may be illuminating to return to the discussion of the print revolution (see p. 18). There is an obvious parallel between the controversy over the logic of writing and that regarding the logic of print, as there is between debates over the consequences of printing and the consequences of literacy (see p. 11), down to such details as the rise of the fixed text and the problems of trusting a new medium. The critics of the revolution thesis often argue that print is not an agent, but a technology employed by individuals or groups for different purposes in different locales. For this reason, they recommend the study of the uses of print in different social or cultural contexts. The defenders of the revolution thesis, on the other hand, see print, like writing, as an aid to decontextualization. We seem to have returned to the conflict between an autonomous model and a contextual model, a problem discussed above (p. 11). Should we speak of print culture in the singular, or of cultures of print in the plural?

It is not necessary, of course, to take up an extreme position in this contro-versy. It is more rewarding to ask what insights each group of scholars has to offer, and to consider whether, by making the appropriate distinctions and qual-ifications, it may be possible to combine them. One might begin by rejecting the stronger formulations on both sides, both the determinism implicit in the revo-lutionary position and the voluntarism of the contextualists. It is probably more useful to speak, as Innis did (see pp. 1, 5), of a built-in bias to be found in each medium of communication. From the geographical point of view, it is prudent to think in terms of similar effects of print in different places, rather than effects which were either identical everywhere or completely different in each locale. From the chronological point of view, it is helpful to distinguish between the immediate and the long-term consequences of the introduction of print. The contextualists deal more satisfactorily with the short term, with the intentions, tactics and strategies of individuals. The revolutionaries, on the other hand, grapple more closely with the long-term and with the unintended consequences of change.

In early modern Europe, as in other places and periods, cultural change was often additive rather than substitutive, especially in the early stages of innova-tion. As has been shown, the old media of oral and manuscript communication coexisted and interacted with the new medium of print, just as print, now an old medium, coexists with television and the Internet in the early twenty-first century.

At this point we may return to the arguments about permanence and fixity dis-cussed earlier (p. 16), adding the necessary qualifications. It is true that writing encouraged the fixing of texts long before print was known. It is true that many printed works were treated by contemporaries as ephemeral. Divergences between copies of early printed books are quite common, because proofs were corrected in the workshop during the process of production. Print, especially in the hands of 'pirates' (see p. 49), often put inaccurate texts into circulation. For these reasons, scholars have recently been placing increasing emphasis on the instability of print. However, these qualifications do not overturn the moderate argument that the press favoured the relative fixity of texts.

A similar answer may be given to the larger question of the stability of knowl-edge. Print facilitated the accumulation of knowledge by making discoveries more widely known as well as by making it more difficult for information to be lost. On the other hand, as was pointed out above (p. 16), print destabilized knowledge, or what had been thought to be knowledge, by making readers more conscious of the existence of conflicting stories and interpretations. As in the case of texts, therefore, the fixity of knowledge encouraged by print was relative rather than absolute. The changes which took place, however important, were changes in degree rather than in kind.

One of these changes was a relatively new concept of writing which we now call 'literature', together with the concept of an 'author', linked to the idea of a correct or authorized version of a 'text'. As it was remarked earlier, oral culture is fluid, and oral creation a co-operative enterprise. In manuscript culture, there was already a tendency to fixity, but this was countered by the inaccuracy and also, as we have seen (p. 37), by the creativity of scribes. What we call plagiarism, like the intellectual property it threatens (see p. 46), is essentially a product of the print revolution.

Another important consequence of the invention of printing was to involve entrepreneurs more closely in the process of spreading knowledge. The use of the new medium encouraged increasing awareness of the importance of publicity, whether economic ('advertising', see p. 45), or political (what we call 'propaganda', a term which came into use at the end of the eighteenth century). The reputation of Louis XIV, for example, his 'glory' as he called it, owed more than a little to print. Several hundred engraved portraits of the king were put into circulation during his reign.

Another form of mechanical reproduction was the bronze medal. Following classical precedents, the medal was revived in fifteenth-century Italy and was soon adopted by rulers as a means of spreading a favourable image of themselves and their policies. The number of copies struck was relatively low, perhaps no more than a hundred, but these copies would be distributed to foreign ambassadors or foreign heads of state in order to make an impression where it mattered most. Persuasion by medals became increasingly important in the seventeenth century. Earlier rulers had contented themselves with thirty or forty different medals, but three hundred-odd medals were struck to commemorate the major events of the reign of Louis XIV. They could be viewed in cabinets, but the volumes which displayed engravings of the medals together with explanatory and glorificatory comments reached a much wider public. Official poets sang the praises of Louis – and other monarchs of his day – in print, and official historians published accounts of his marvellous deeds for contemporaries and posterity alike. The major court festivals, expensive but ephemeral events, were fixed in the memory by printed and illustrated descriptions.

Among the events which were captured in this way were some which never happened. According to the American historian Daniel Boorstin, in *The Image* (1962), the creation of 'pseudo-events' was the result of what he calls the 'Graphic Revolution' of the nineteenth and twentieth centuries, the age of photography and television. Yet examples of such events are not difficult to find in the age of woodcuts and engravings. The last dying speeches of criminals who were executed at Newgate in London in the eighteenth century, complete with illustrations, were sold on the day of the execution, and, in cases in which the criminal was reprieved at the last moment, he was in a position to read about his own death. An engraving of Louis XIV being shown around the Royal Academy of Sciences in Paris was published in 1671, at a time when the king had not yet visited the newly founded academy.

Reliable or unreliable, printed matter became an increasingly important part of everyday life. This pervasiveness deserves to be emphasized. The spread of books, pamphlets and journals was only part of a story which also included the rise of two genres normally associated only with the nineteenth and twentieth centuries – the poster and the official form. Official notices multiplied on street corners and on church doors. In Florence in 1558, for example, the new Index of Prohibited Books was displayed on the church doors of the city. In London from *c.*1660 onwards, for example, plays were advertised on placards posted in the street. A Swiss visitor to London in 1782 was struck by the prevalence of shop names rather than signs. Street names were increasingly written on walls. For the inhabitants of Europe's major cities, illiteracy was becoming more and more of a disadvantage. A western visitor to Tokyo today may be in a good position to appreciate the anxiety of someone who is aware that many messages are displayed in the street (possibly important ones), but is completely unable to decode them.

As for printed forms, they were already being used in the early modern period for leases, tax declarations, receipts and censuses. In sixteenth-century Venice, for instance, all the census-takers had to do was to fill in the appropriate boxes, classifying households as nobles, citizens or artisans, and counting the numbers of servants and gondolas. The Church as well as the State made use of forms. Parish priests filled in forms in order to certify that female orphans who were about to marry were good Catholics. By the seventeenth century, cardinals were using printed forms in Conclave to vote for a new pope, with blank spaces in which they wrote, in Latin, both their own name and the name of the candidate they were supporting.

It was thanks above all to the daily newspaper, a piece of ephemera that was to become increasingly valuable for social historians, that print became part of daily life in the eighteenth century, at least in some parts of Europe (when Goethe visited the city of Caltanissetta in Sicily in 1787, he discovered that the inhabitants had not yet heard of the death of Frederick the Great the year before). In England alone, it has been estimated that fifteen million newspapers were sold during the year 1792. And the daily or weekly or bi-weekly paper was supplemented by monthly or quarterly publications, by what came to be called 'periodicals' and 'magazines'. There were also scholarly journals like *The Transactions of the Royal Society of London* (1665–) or the *News of the Republic of Letters* (1684–) which spread information about new discoveries, the deaths of scholars and, not least, about new books. The book review was an invention of the late seventeenth century. In this way, one form of print advertised and reinforced another.

Other journals, like the French periodical the *Mercure Galant*, founded in 1672, were aimed at a less scholarly public. Written (mainly, at least) by a man, the playwright Jean Donneau de Visé (1638–1710), but aimed at female readers in particular, the journal, which was illustrated, took the form of a letter written by a lady in Paris to a lady in the country. The letter naturally gave news of the court and the city, recent plays and the latest fashions in clothes and interior decoration, but *Mercure Galant* also carried short stories, mainly concerned with love. Readers were invited to send in verses and solve puzzles, and the names and addresses of those who succeeded were printed in the journal along with the winners of poetry-writing competitions. The *Mercure Galant* also included accounts, generally flattering, of the actions of Louis XIV and the victories won by his armies, a form of propaganda for which the editor received a substantial pension from the government.

By contrast, the English periodical *The Spectator*, which began publication in 1711, two years after *The Tatler*, prided itself on its independence. The point of the journal's title was to emphasize its detachment from party politics and the desire of the editors to watch the fray rather than to join it. Its declared aim was to bring philosophy out of academic institutions 'to dwell in clubs and assemblies, at tea-tables and in coffee-houses'. Its coverage ranged from deep moral and aesthetic questions to the latest fashion in gloves. Like Donneau de Visé, its editors (Joseph Addison and Richard Steele, hiding behind the mask of 'Mr Spectator' and the 'Spectator Club') encouraged their readers to participate in the journal, placing an advertisement in the first issue advising 'those who have a mind to correspond with me' to direct their letters to the printer. Many people did so, and some letters were published. In similar fashion, a few years before Addison and Steele, the London bookseller John Dunton (1659–1733) had founded a journal, *The Athenian Mercury*, 'resolving all the most nice [precise] and curious questions proposed by the ingenious'. In its six-year existence, the journal offered answers to about 6,000 questions from its readers. The idea of an interactive medium, so often discussed today, clearly has its roots in the past. Dunton was a genuine pioneer.

The success of the Addison–Steele formula may be measured partly by the number of collected editions of *The Spectator* which continued to appear in book form for the rest of the century, partly by its translation into foreign languages, and, above all, by the many 'moral weeklies' which imitated its style and approach, in England, France, Holland, Germany, Italy, Spain and elsewhere.

The effects of the rise of newspapers and other journals have been discussed from that day to this. From the start they had their critics, some complaining that they were bringing into the open what should have been kept secret, others accusing them of triviality. Yet they had their admirers too. Thus, the Milan journal, *Il Caffè*, claimed that they broadened the mind and, more exactly, that they turned Romans and Florentines into Europeans. The rise of new kinds of reference book such as the 'newspaper dictionary' (*Zeitungslexikon*) or the 'gazetteer' (originally a dictionary of the names of places mentioned in gazettes) suggests that such papers widened their readers' horizons, not least by making people conscious of what they did not know.

Two concrete examples of the way in which they may have helped to shape the attitudes of their readers concern suicide and scepticism. In *Sleepless Souls* (1990) Michael MacDonald and Terence Murphy argued that 'the style and tone of newspaper stories about suicides promoted an increasingly secular and sympathetic attitude towards self-killing' in eighteenth-century England. The impression was being created through the frequency of the reports that suicide was a commonplace event. Suicide notes were printed in the papers, allowing readers to see the event from the actor's point of view, and these printed letters in turn influenced the style of the notes left by later suicides.

Newspapers may be said to have encouraged scepticism, too. The discrepancies between reports of the same events in different newspapers, which offer a more extreme case of the discrepancies between books noted by Eisenstein (see p. 18), generated a distrust of print. Even if people read only one paper, they could hardly fail to be impressed by the regularity with which later reports of an event contradicted the statements made in earlier issues. By the late seventeenth century, discussions of the trustworthiness of historical writing commonly cite the gazettes as a paradigm case of unreliable accounts of events. For those who had participated in them – or simply witnessed them – the accounts of these events printed in the papers often seemed blatantly untrue, at least in detail.

Those were the negative consequences. More generally, newspapers contributed to the rise of public opinion, a term which is first recorded in French
around 1750, in English in 1781 and in German in 1793. This development has
been redefined in the last generation as the rise of the 'public sphere', thanks to
an influential book by Jürgen Habermas, *The Structural Transformation of the
Public Sphere*, first published in 1962. To be more exact, the phrase has spread
thanks to the translation of Habermas's term *Öffentlichkeit* (literally 'publicity'
in the general sense of 'making public') into a more explicitly spatial phrase, a
transformation which itself tells us something about the process of communication between cultures.

As in the case of Eisenstein on the print revolution, what Habermas has given
us is not so much a new argument as the reformulation of a traditional one.
Instead of speaking about public opinion, which seems to assume a consensus,
he speaks about an arena in which debate took place and offers an argument
about argument. Habermas claims that the eighteenth century (a long eighteenth century beginning in the 1690s) was a crucial period in the rise of rational and critical argument, presented within a liberal bourgeois 'public sphere'
which – at least in principle – was open to everyone's participation. Habermas's
study is especially important for its view of the media as a system (including
newspapers, coffee-houses, clubs and salons) in which the different elements
worked together: he emphasizes the structural transformation of this sphere in
the later eighteenth century in England and France, its 'non-instrumentality' (in
other words, its freedom from manipulation), and its contribution to the rise
of rational and critical attitudes to what would be known – after the French
Revolution – as the 'old regime'.

The views of Habermas on public debate have themselves led to a public
debate, in which he has been criticized for offering a 'utopian' account of that
century, for failing to notice the manipulation, even at that time, of the public
by the media, for placing too little stress on people who were in practice excluded
from the discussion (ordinary men and women), and for placing too much stress
on what he calls the 'model case' of Britain in the late eighteenth century at the
expense of other places and periods. It has also been argued that there was more
than one public sphere in early modern Europe, including that of the royal
courts, where political information was available in abundance and avidly discussed. Rulers such as Louis XIV (as we have seen earlier in this chapter) were
well aware of the need to have themselves presented in a favourable light to this
court public via a wide range of media from poems and plays to paintings,
engravings, tapestries and medals.

One purpose of the following chapter will be to test the ideas of Habermas by
examining in more detail a number of public discussions of religion and politics
in Europe from the Renaissance and Reformation to the French Revolution.
Twentieth-century developments, beginning with radio and television and the
growth of advertising, totally change the context of the Habermas thesis, as he
himself has clearly recognized. These developments are discussed in Chapters 3,
4 and 5 of this book. Chapter 6 returns to instruction (education) and entertainment which, along with information, came to constitute a media trinity.

3 The Media and the Public Sphere in Early Modern Europe

This chapter offers a narrative of change in the media, analysing the sequence of communicated events from the 1450s to the 1790s, and focusing on events or clusters of events to which labels have been attached – the Reformation, the Wars of Religion, the English Civil War, the Glorious Revolution of 1688 and the French Revolution of 1789. It concentrates on a single theme, introduced at the end of the last chapter: the rise of the public sphere, and of what has come to be called political culture – the information, attitudes and values shared in particular European societies or in particular social groups within a society. We will examine how the different media contributed to these events, and how the events themselves contributed to the evolution and modification of the media system.

A recent study of early newsbooks, Joad Raymond's *The Invention of the Newspaper* (1996), warned readers against the traditional linear account 'of an expansion of political franchise being reflected in increasingly wide access to news; of the breakdown of censorship and the evolution of political liberty; in short of the movement from an ancient regime to a democratic one'. By contrast, the story to be told in these pages might be described as a zigzag one, moving from region to region and noting particular moments in which access to information became narrower rather than wider. All the same, certain long-term changes are visible between the 1520s and the 1790s.

As in the case of the print revolution, there is no single landmark date at which to start this story, no clean break with what had gone before. Before the Reformation, in the Italian city-states, especially Florence in the thirteenth, fourteenth and fifteenth centuries, constant reference was made to 'the people' (*il popolo*, the members of trade and craft guilds). A relatively high proportion of the population participated in Florentine political life, 4,000–5,000 adult males in a city of fewer than 100,000 people. Important political offices were filled by drawing names out of a bag and might be held for as little as two months. Florentine political culture, like that of classical Athens (see p. 6), was essentially oral and visual. The squares of the city, especially Piazza della Signoria, were a kind of public sphere in which speeches were given and politics discussed. Fluent speech was highly appreciated in this culture because it was crucial to what the Italians of the time called the *vita civile*, the politically active life of a citizen.

Urban chroniclers sometimes recorded the political posters displayed and the graffiti written on the walls, and the public relations of the city were conducted not only orally, by sending ambassadors to other states, but also in writing. The Florentine chancery, in which official letters were written in the name of the government, was staffed by humanists, students of the culture of classical antiquity who were able to write letters in an elegant and persuasive Latin. The Duke of Milan, a leading enemy of the Florentine republic, was said to have remarked that he feared the pen of the humanist chancellor Coluccio Salutati (1331–1406) more than he feared a troop of horsemen. On a smaller scale than Florence or Venice, some cities in the Netherlands, Germany and Switzerland, such as Antwerp, Nuremberg and Basel, developed a similar civic culture.

The Reformation

If the Italian city-state was the milieu in which the Renaissance developed, the German city-state or 'free city', such as Nuremberg or Strasbourg (not yet incorporated into France), was the milieu of the Reformation, the first major ideological conflict in which printed matter played a major role. The Reformation, at least in its first generation, was a social movement, a conscious collective enterprise, even if its conscious aim was to reform the old Church rather than, as actually happened, to found new ones. Martin Luther, born in 1483, a friar turned heretic, was a professor at Wittenberg University in eastern Germany, who deeply resented what he saw as the Italian dominance of the Church, the 'magic' within it and its commercialization. In favour of more direct involvement of the laity in religious activities, Luther encouraged reading of the Bible in the vernacular – this involved new translations – and using a vernacular liturgy. He justified this involvement by what he called the 'priesthood of all believers', the idea that everyone had direct access to God without the need for clerical mediation.

Habermas has stressed what he calls the 'privatizing' effects of the Reformation, a withdrawal of believers into the interior realm, a withdrawal which was supported by Luther's belief that obedience to the ruler was the duty of a good Christian. (It should be pointed out that Luther did not live in a free, self-governing city but was a subject of the Elector of Saxony.) So far as the long-term consequences of the Reformation are concerned, Habermas may well be right. In the early years of the movement, however, the vigorous debates which took place, first in Germany and then in other parts of Europe, about the functions and powers of the Pope and the Church and the nature of religion, all made an important contribution to the rise of critical thought and of public opinion.

These events followed a recurrent pattern which may be described as a 'sorcerer's apprentice' model of political change in early modern Europe. Again and again, disputes within elites led to their appealing for support to a wider group, often described as 'the people'. In order to reach this wider group, the elites could not rely on face-to-face communication and so they turned to public debates and to pamphlets. The appeal to the people was often successful. Indeed, it was sometimes more successful than those initiating it expected or even wanted. On a number of occasions, frightened by what they had started, the elite tried to damp down debate, only to discover that they were too late and that the forest fire was out of control.

Although the term 'public opinion' was not yet in use in the early sixteenth century, the views of the people mattered to governments at this time for practical reasons, whether they tried to suppress these views, mould them or – much more rarely – to follow them (as in a few towns in Germany in the 1520s, in which citizens were asked by the council to vote whether the city should remain Catholic or turn Protestant). The involvement of the people in the Reformation was both a cause and a consequence of the involvement of the media. The invention of printing undermined what has been described, with some exaggeration, as the information monopoly of the medieval Church (see p. 6), and some people were aware of this point at the time. The English Protestant John Foxe, for instance, claimed that 'either the pope must abolish knowledge and printing, or printing must at length root him out'. As we have seen, the popes seem to have agreed with Foxe, and it was for this very reason that the Index of Prohibited Books was established (see p. 41).

After the Protestant churches – Lutheran, Calvinist and Zwinglian – had become established, they were able to pass on their traditions through the education of children. Plays, paintings and prints were now rejected in favour of the word, whether written or spoken, Bible or sermon. In the first generation, on the other hand (a fairly short period, essentially the 1520s and 1530s), the Protestants relied on what might be called a 'media offensive', not only to communicate their own messages but also to weaken the Catholic Church by ridiculing it, drawing on the traditional repertoire of popular humour in order to destroy their enemy through laughter. This was a period when, in contrast to their later behaviour, Protestant zealots were often satirical, irreverent and subversive.

A major aim of the reformers was to communicate with all Christians. Where the great humanist Erasmus (*c.*1466–1536), who also wanted to reform the Church, wrote in Latin so that he would be read in academic circles all over Europe, Luther usually followed the opposite strategy. He wrote in the vernacular so that his message could be understood by ordinary people, at the price of restricting it in the first instance to the German-speaking world.

Thanks to the new medium, Luther could not be silenced in the way that earlier heretics such as the Czech reformer Jan Hus (1369–1415), whose ideas resemble Luther's in a number of respects, had been silenced by being burnt at the stake. In this sense, print converted the Reformation into a permanent revolution. It would indeed have helped the Catholic Church very little to burn Luther as a heretic once his writings were available in large numbers at a fairly low price. Four thousand copies of his address 'To the Christian Nobility of the German Nation' (*An der christlichen Adel Deutscher Nation*) were sold within a few days of its publication in 1520 by the printer Melchior Lotter of Wittenberg, who was a friend of the author.

Luther's translation of the Bible was even more important than his pamphlets for the development of Protestantism in the long run. He was not altogether pleased with the printed text of his *New Testament* of 1522, which included some errors, but any printed version in the vernacular allowed far more people to read the Bible than before. A single printer in Wittenberg, Hans Lufft, sold 100,000 copies of the Bible in the forty years from 1534 to 1574. Luther's *Small Catechism* (1529) probably reached an even wider public.

This achievement should not be taken too lightly. There was no standard vernacular German language at this time, partly because there was little popular printed literature, and one reason for there being little popular printed literature was that there was no standard vernacular language. Somehow or other, Luther managed to break out of this vicious circle, writing not in his own Saxon dialect but in a kind of lowest common denominator of dialects, modelled on the style of the imperial chancery and intelligible from east to west, from Saxony to the Rhineland. In this way, the potential readership of Luther's writings was multiplied, making their printing a commercial proposition, while over the longer term Luther's translation of the Bible helped standardize written German. It was not print alone or Luther alone but their combination which made this achievement possible.

Some printers in Strasbourg and elsewhere were prepared to print both Luther's writings and those of his Catholic opponents, as if they were mercenaries simply interested in what would sell (see p. 45), but others, like Lufft and Lotter, printers who were committed to the ideas which Luther and his followers helped put into circulation, confined themselves to Protestant works. They were not alone. A letter to the Swiss reformer Ulrich Zwingli (1484–1531) mentions a pedlar who sold Luther's writings, and nothing else, from door to door.

Despite its small size, the university city of Wittenberg, where Luther lived and taught, was the communications centre of Lutheranism. One reason for the spread of Luther's ideas in north-east Germany – in contrast to the south-west, where the ideas of Zwingli prevailed – was the ease with which preachers and printed matter from Wittenberg could reach this region. In both cases, pamphlets addressing ordinary people in the vernacular were of crucial importance to the success of the Reformation. More than 80 per cent of the books in German published in the year 1523 – to be exact, 418 titles out of 498 – dealt with the reform of the Church. In 1525, 25,000 copies of the Twelve Articles of the rebel peasants were printed. Between 1520 and 1529, 296 polemical pamphlets appeared in the city of Strasbourg alone. By 1550, about 10,000 pamphlets in German had been printed.

These pamphlets have been described, with some exaggeration, as a 'mass medium'. The exaggeration lies in the fact that only a minority of the German-speaking population could afford to buy pamphlets and only a minority were able to read. The texts were probably read in public more often than in private and their message heard by more people than were able to read it. Another claim which now seems exaggerated is the assertion that without the book there would have been no Reformation.

Such claims ignore the important role at the time of both oral and visual propaganda. To understand the spread of the Reformation it is necessary to look not at print alone but at the media system as a whole. Since only a minority of the population could read, let alone write, it follows that oral communication must have continued to predominate in the so-called age of the printing-press. It took many different forms in different settings, ranging from sermons and lectures in churches and universities to rumour and gossip in the marketplace and the tavern. Preaching was of particular importance in the early years of the Reformation, while hymns in the vernacular allowed the audience to participate in religious services more actively than in the days when they simply 'heard Mass'. Luther himself wrote hymns for this purpose, the most notable, still sung, being 'A Mighty Fortress is Our Lord' ('*Ein Feste Burg ist Unser Gott*').

Judicial archives, recording attempts to repress heresy, have much to tell us about the reception of the new ideas via different media. For example, they reveal the frequency of the singing of printed ballads dealing with topical religious and political events, yet another example of the interaction between media discussed in the previous chapter (p. 36). Many of these records shine a searchlight on the tavern in particular, revealing it as an important centre for the exchange of ideas and rumours. This communicative function of inns may well have been a traditional one, but it is not often recorded in the Middle Ages. In the divided Germany of the 1520s, however, a number of individuals are caught in the beam of the searchlight, in the act of criticizing the clergy, discussing pamphlets or raising doubts about Catholic doctrines such as transubstantiation or the Immaculate Conception.

The records reveal both the importance of public discussions of heretical ideas and the role of the book or pamphlet in provoking such discussions. The heresy trials thus support the so-called 'two-step' theory of communication, developed out of a study of the American presidential election of 1940. According to this theory, put forward by Elihu Katz and Paul Lazarsfeld in their *Personal Influence* (1955), voters who changed their mind were not directly influenced by the messages which reached them from newspapers and the radio. What they felt was the 'personal influence' of local 'opinion leaders'. These leaders follow events in the media (in our case, the Protestant pamphlets) with more attention than their fellows, but then influence their followers primarily through face-to-face contact.

Images, too, were enlisted in the religious struggle. Luther, unlike Calvin, did not disapprove of them – he displayed a picture of the Virgin Mary in his study. What he opposed was superstition, what he called idolatry – the veneration of the signifier at the expense of what it signified. In Lutheran churches a few religious paintings continued to be displayed, mainly paintings of Christ, with the Resurrection as a particularly popular subject.

Images in print as a form of communication with the illiterate were a still more important means for the diffusion of Protestant ideas, as Luther himself was well aware when he appealed to the 'simple folk', as he called them. His friend Lucas Cranach (1472–1553) produced not only paintings of Luther and his wife but many polemical prints, like the famous *Passional Christi und Antichristi*, which contrasted the simple life of Christ with the magnificence and pride of his 'Vicar', the Pope. Thus one pair of woodcuts shows Christ fleeing from the Jews because they are trying to make him their king, while the Pope, on the other hand, defends with the sword his claim to temporal rule over the states of the Church (an obvious reference to the belligerent Pope Julius II, who had died in 1513). Christ was crowned with thorns, the Pope with the triple crown or tiara. Christ washed the feet of his disciples, but the Pope presents his foot for Christians to kiss. Christ travelled on foot while the Pope is carried in a litter (see Figure 9).

Many paintings of Luther were produced in the workshop of the Cranach family in Wittenberg, doubtless to hang in private houses as a symbol of loyalty to the Reformation. Some of these images, notably a woodcut made in 1521, present the reformer as a kind of saint, complete with a halo and a dove hovering over his head to signify his inspiration by the Holy Ghost (Figure 10). Such a

Fig. 9 Lucas Cranach, woodcuts of *Passional Christi and Antichristi*, 1521.

use of conventions facilitated communication with ordinary people with traditional mentalities. The price of the facility, however – a price which has been paid many times in the history of communication – was that it diluted the Protestant message by adopting the very practices which it was supposed to replace.

Ritual was also a means as well as an object of debate at this time. Catholic rituals were parodied by a Protestant procession in Saxony in the 1520s carrying horses' bones as mock-relics, in protest against the recent canonization of a local saint, Benno of Saxony. In the early years of the Reformation, the Protestants also resorted to street theatre to turn the people against the Church. For example, in 1521 the Swiss printer Pamphilus Gengenbach of Basel (*c.*1480–1524) staged an attack on the profits the clergy made from the doctrine of Purgatory. The play was called 'The Eaters of the Dead' (*Die Totenfresser*) and it showed a bishop, a monk and other clerics sitting around a table carving up a corpse. Again, in 1528, the Swiss painter Nikolas Manuel of Bern (*c.*1484–1530) staged a play entitled 'The Seller of Indulgences' (*Der Ablasskrämer*) in which he mocked the Catholic commercialization of religion, as Luther had done before him.

As for the Catholics, they did not respond to the Protestant challenge in the same media, at least not on the same scale or for the same wide public. Nor did they produce as many pamphlets to defend the Church as the Protestants

Fig. 10 Hans Baldung Grien, woodcut of Martin Luther with halo, c.1523.

did to attack it. They did not produce their own translations of the Bible, which the Church thought dangerous. When they did produce religious plays, these were generally directed at an elite audience such as the parents of the noble pupils at Jesuit colleges in France, Italy and Central Europe, rather than a popular one.

This point illustrates a general feature of communication which might be called the conservative dilemma, common to authoritarian regimes – at least in societies of restricted literacy – whenever they are under attack. In the sixteenth-century case, if the Church did not reply to Luther, people might be led to think that the heretic was in the right. On the other hand, if the Church did reply, this might encourage the laity, in the manner discussed above (p. 62), to compare the two sides, think for themselves, and choose between alternatives instead of doing as they were told. For defenders of old regimes, who rely on habits of obedience, the right response at the level of message might therefore be the wrong response at the level of medium.

For their part, the Catholics continued to put a good deal of effort into the production of religious images, particularly after iconoclastic Protestants had destroyed them inside and outside churches, in the process transforming the appearance of 'holy places'. Catholics paid great attention to the rhetoric of the image, making sacred paintings and statues a more dramatic and, so they believed, an even more effective means of persuasion than they had been before the so-called 'Counter-Reformation' following the Council of Trent (1545–63). The iconography often referred to the doctrines which the Protestants had attacked. Scenes of the repentance of St Peter or St Mary Magdalen, for example, were selected specifically because they were considered to justify the sacrament of confession. Saints, too, were given back their haloes, some of which (despite Luther's halo) had been swept away.

The development of the opposed – but in retrospect, complementary – institutions of propaganda and censorship may have been inevitable consequences of the invention of printing, but they were the immediate result of the religious wars of the sixteenth century. Propaganda and censorship were religious before they became political. Just as printing helped guarantee the survival of the Protestant Reformation, making it impossible to suppress the ideas of Luther as the ideas of medieval heretics had been suppressed, so in turn the Reformation was an economic boon for printers, whether in the form of bestselling pamphlets or, in the longer term, vernacular bibles.

Contrary to Habermas's thesis, it may be argued that the German Reformation contributed to the rise of a 'public sphere', at least for a time. The writers of pamphlets used self-conscious strategies of persuasion, they tried to appeal to a wide public, they encouraged criticism of the Church and, after the new ideas had been widely debated in public during the first years of the movement, they drew some Catholics into the open. There are important similarities between what happened in the German-speaking world in the early sixteenth century and what is happening in the Muslim world of our own day: the rise of a public sphere that is largely religious and linked to the emergence of new media (print in the sixteenth century, videos and websites today).

As for the secular authorities, they too discovered that the new medium was a powerful force which might serve political ends. The conflict between the Emperor Charles V and his rival King Francis I of France was conducted through pamphlets as well as on battlefields from the mid-1520s onwards, and the timing of this paper campaign suggests that both rulers had learned a lesson from Luther.

The Religious Wars and the Revolt of the Netherlands

After the 1520s, the surviving evidence of public discussion declines as the Lutherans turned into a Church and themselves limited or suppressed popular debate. The emphasis shifted from the priesthood of all believers to the importance of a learned ministry who would tell the people what to believe and what the Bible meant. We find similar developments in other parts of Europe later in the century.

From the point of view of the media, the battle between Catholics and Protestants is often presented as a war between a culture of the image and a culture of the book. This view is too simple. In the Catholic world, the standardization of religious practice associated with the Counter-Reformation fitted in as much with the needs of printers as of image-makers. There was an increasing demand for missals, breviaries and above all catechisms, and some printers, Christophe Plantin of Antwerp, for instance, enriched themselves by supplying these standardized products. Some of the laity read lives of the saints and other devotional works.

Nonetheless, there was a relative contrast between a Protestant book culture and a Catholic image culture. For example, long before the Counter-Reformation, at a time when it was dangerous to print Protestant literature in France, Italy or in the England of Henry VIII, the city of Antwerp was the home of a flourishing export business, printing bibles and pamphlets in French, Italian and English. On one occasion, on the instructions of the bishop of London (who seems not to have mastered the economics of printing), a Catholic English merchant in Antwerp, Augustine Packington, bought the whole edition of William Tyndale's *New Testament* (originally published in Worms in 1526), in order to burn it.

According to a contemporary source, Edward Hall's *Chronicle*, 'Augustine Packington came to William Tyndale and said, "William, I know thou art a poor man, and hast a heap of new Testaments and books by thee for the which thou hast both endangered thy friends and beggared thyself, and I have now gotten thee a merchant which with ready money shall dispatch thee of all that thou hast, if you think it so profitable for your self." "Who is the merchant?" said Tyndale. "The Bishop of London", said Packington. "Oh that is because he will burn them", said Tyndale. "Yea, Mary", quoth Packington. "I am the gladder", said Tyndale, "for these two benefits shall come thereof: I shall get money of him for these books to bring myself out of debt, and the whole world shall cry out upon the burning of God's word. And the overplus of the money that shall remain to me, shall make me more studious to correct the said New Testament, and so newly to imprint the same once again, and I trust the second will much better like you than ever did the first". And so forward went the bargain, the Bishop had the books, Packington the thanks, and Tyndale had the money.'

In the sixteenth century, Calvinists in particular encouraged a wave of iconoclasm that spread over much of Europe, directed primarily against statues (though stained glass also suffered). Sometimes the statues were smashed, sometimes merely removed. The movement was under way in the German-speaking world in the 1520s, supported by Andreas von Karlstadt in Wittenberg and Ulrich Zwingli in Zürich. It spread to Geneva and to parts of England and France in the 1530s. It reached its climax in France and the Netherlands in the summer of 1566, when image-smashing can be documented in twenty-five places between 10 August and 29 September. A map of iconoclasm (see Figure 11) suggests that in many places it was a reaction to news or rumours of image-breaking elsewhere. It is tempting to interpret this organized movement (the first on a large scale since the Byzantine Empire in the eighth century) as a reaction to the increase in the proliferation of images and especially in the communicative power of statues in the late Middle Ages and the Renaissance.

While Lutherans were not iconoclastic, so that Karlstadt was only able to remove the images from Wittenberg churches when Luther was away, communication through images was specifically prohibited in Calvinist areas. In a Calvinist 'temple', as in a mosque, the visual field of the worshipper was dominated by painted texts such as the Ten Commandments. It was the Calvinists who took the lead in two conflicts in the later sixteenth century: the religious wars in France from the early 1560s to the mid-1590s, and the Revolt of the Netherlands, from the 1560s to 1609. These conflicts are important in the context of this book because of the role played in them by the media and because the mixture of religious and political debates that they encouraged suggests that we may speak of the rise of a public sphere in these two neighbouring countries as early as the 1570s and 1580s.

The French Wars of Religion were media wars as well as conflicts with swords and guns, conflicts in which pamphleteering, image-making, image-breaking and oral communication were all important. Already in 1534 the French Protestants had turned to the press in order to publicize their ideas. Broadsheets or placards attacking the Catholic mass were printed in Switzerland, smuggled into France, and displayed in public places and even, briefly, on the door of the king's bedchamber. In the 1570s, the conflict turned into a triangular one when the powerful Guise family accused the government of being too tolerant of Protestants and organized a Catholic League with Spanish support. The League conducted what we would call a media campaign in which verses posted on walls, satirical images, fiery sermons and incendiary pamphlets all played a part.

That something can be said today about this campaign is largely due to the activities of the Paris lawyer Pierre L'Estoile (c.1546–1611), who made it his business to record rumours and sermons, and to paste otherwise ephemeral placards and engravings into his journal. It is thanks to L'Estoile that we know that the French civil wars were in part wars of images, many of them produced in one street in Paris: rue Montorgueil near Les Halles. On one side, a satirical 'Map of Popery' was in circulation, while the other side preferred the image of 'La Marmite Renversée', a large pot containing Protestants and atheists and cooking on the flames. When Henri III (ruled 1575–89) had his enemies Henri Duc de Guise and his brother Cardinal Guise assassinated, woodcuts immediately appeared commemorating their 'cruel deaths'.

Printed words played an even more important part in the struggle. Like Germany in the 1520s, France in the later sixteenth century was in an age of pamphlets, with more than thirty a year produced between 1559 and 1572. After the Massacre of St Bartholomew, in which many Protestants were murdered, the

The dates

8 Aug	Steenwoorde
3 Aug	La Chapelle d'Armentieres, Bailleul
4 Aug	Poperinge
5 Aug	Ypres, Estaires
6 Aug	Roubaix
8 Aug	Audenarde
20 Aug	Anvers
22 Aug	Gand, Veere, Breda, Boise le Duc, Amsterdam
22 Aug	Tournai, Malines
24 Aug	Valenciennes, Utrecht
25 Aug	La Haye, Delft
25 Aug	Leyde, Hulst, Cateau Cambresis
8 Sept	Leewarden
23 Sept	Maastricht

Key

——— Provisional boundaries

·············· Present frontiers of France, Belgium and Luxembourg

BRUSSELS Capitals

● Important town

GHENT Town where images were smashed

Scale
0   100 km

Fig. 11 The seventeen provinces and principal cities for iconoclasm in 1566.

pamphlets became more violent in their attacks on individuals such as the 'whore' or 'tiger' Queen Catherine de' Medici (1519–89). They also turned from religion to politics. Hence the conclusion of the historian Donald Kelley that in 1572 'modern political propaganda came of age'. Reaching a peak in the period 1588–94, and then declining in numbers when peace was re-established, pamphlets returned on a still grander scale during the political crisis of 1614–17, when a group of nobles rebelled against the king. More than 1,200 political pamphlets were produced in that short period. Cardinal Richelieu, who ruled France in partnership with King Louis XIII between 1630 and 1643, may well have learned about the political importance of the media from that crisis. At all events, he inspired the foundation of an official newspaper, the *Gazette*, in 1631, and on occasion sent items of news to the editor for inclusion in it. Jean-Baptiste Colbert, the most important of Louis XIV's ministers from 1661 to 1683, was even more media-conscious than Richelieu. The creation of a favourable image of the king, for a foreign public as well as a domestic one, via reports in the press, official histories, poems, plays, ballets, operas, paintings, statues, engravings and medals, was carried out by a team of artists and writers, supervised by Colbert.

The public role of the media was, if anything, still greater in the Netherlands than it was in France, beginning with the revolt against Philip II of Spain or, as the Dutch now call it, the Eighty Years' War, from 1568 to 1648. More than 7,000 pamphlets from this period still survive in Dutch libraries. The print runs of pamphlets were commonly from 1,000 to 1,250, but they were quickly reprinted in response to demand. It was the pamphlets, for example, which spread the so-called 'Black Legend' of Spanish despotism, obscurantism and fanaticism. The writers in the service of the rebel leader, William the Silent (1533–84), presented Philip II as a tyrant who had failed to respect the traditional liberties and privileges of the cities of the Netherlands.

Printed verses glorifying the rebels and denouncing Philip II as 'Herod' or 'Pharaoh' and the Spaniards as the descendants of 'unbelieving Jews' were also in circulation, probably more widely than the pamphlets since they were sung and heard even more often than they were read. Printed images also made a contribution to the rebels' campaign. For example, a woodcut of the execution of the counts of Egmont and Hoorne in 1568 by order of Philip II soon circulated in the Netherlands, the captions telling the viewers what to think of the events illustrated.

The Dutch pamphlets were not produced continuously but clustered in response to major historical events, notably in the periods 1578–85, 1598–1606, 1618, and 1647–8. A sudden increase in production around 1607 has also been noted, in other words, a few years before the outpouring of pamphlets in the French crisis of 1614–17 mentioned above. The political pamphlet was becoming a part of Dutch political life. There was even a debate about debate, one dialogue, for instance, discussing whether or not everyone 'may express his opinion on affairs of state'.

It was surely no accident that it was in the Dutch Republic, and especially in Amsterdam, that the newspaper (first recorded in Germany in 1609) became a popular institution. Unlike the pamphlet, the newspaper appeared at regular intervals, usually once or twice a week, and the issues were normally numbered so that readers would know whether or not they had missed one. In the unusually literate, urban society of the seventeenth-century Dutch Republic, the temporary public sphere was becoming a permanent one. In contrast to its Dutch equivalent, the English pamphlet before 1640 was moral rather than political, but the situation was to change very quickly on the outbreak of the Civil War.

From the Puritan Revolution to the Glorious Revolution

The European media had plenty of news to report in the 1640s, a decade of crisis. In Portugal, the scene of a struggle for independence from Spain, the Lisbon *Gazeta* gave news of the war from 1641 to 1647. In France, pamphlets once again had a major political role, widely employed in the attack on the government and on the first minister Jules Mazarin in the civil war (1648–52) known as the 'Fronde'. Some 5,000 'mazarinades' were produced at this time, selling at a half or a quarter of a sou each, the total surpassing the productions of 1614–17, as the pamphlets of that period had surpassed those of the Wars of Religion. Issues of the official *Gazette* were much longer than usual between 1648 and 1650 because there was so much more news to report, and unofficial newspapers such as the *Courrier bordelais* were in circulation. After 1650, however, and still more obviously after Louis XIV's personal rule began in 1661, the French public sphere contracted again.

Like the Fronde, the English Civil War, otherwise known as the English Revolution, was conducted in the media: in speeches and sermons, in texts and images, and in ritualized actions such as processions and image-breaking. Once again we find a situation in which the elites were divided and both sides appealed to the people for support, with consequences which they were unable either to foresee or to control.

In important respects the English Civil War was a religious war, waged between the supporters of a Church of England that was close in liturgy, if not in doctrine, to the Catholic Church and, on the other side, the so-called 'Puritans', who believed in simpler forms of worship (tables instead of altars, no religious images, ritual reduced to a minimum, and so on). However, in the course of the wars the conflicts within the party of Puritans or 'Roundheads' (so-called because they wore their hair short) became ever more acute. Presbyterians, Baptists, Ranters, Fifth Monarchists and others attempted to convert readers and listeners to their own form of Christianity. Returning to the media, the clergy lost control of the sermon at this time and had to compete with lay preachers, some of them artisans, like the ex-tinker John Bunyan (1628–88), and some of them women, including the Baptist preacher Mrs Attaway.

In London at least, this was an age of politics by placard, by petition, and by demonstration. For example, in 1640 the so-called 'Root and Branch' petition against the bishops was signed by some 15,000 people, while more than 1,000 took the petition to Parliament. In 1642, Parliament received the *Petition of the Gentlewomen, Tradesmens Wives and many others of the Female Sex*. Artisans and apprentices were involved in politics on an almost daily basis. No wonder then that some recent historians of the period speak of the rise of mass politics, despite the problematic nature of that concept.

The middle years of the seventeenth century were great years for pamphlets and newspapers in which royalists and parliamentarians pressed their respective views. Between 1640 and 1663 a bookseller, George Thomason, an English equivalent of L'Estoile in Paris, was able to collect nearly 15,000 pamphlets and more than 7,000 newspapers, a collection now kept in the British Library and known as the Thomason Tracts. The outbreak of the Civil War also coincided with what has been called 'the outbreak of the English newsbook' in 1641. *Mercurius Aulicus* was a leading newspaper on the first side, *Mercurius Britannicus* a leading newspaper on the second, each producing its own version of events, and followed by *Mercurius Melancholicus, Mercurius Anti-Melancholicus, Mercurius Morbicus, Mercurius Phreneticus, Mercurius Pragmaticus, Mercurius Anti-Pragmaticus* and many others.

This explosion of printed matter was the context for the famous debate about the freedom of the press in which the Puritan poet John Milton took part, publishing his *Areopagitica* (1644), an attack on the Long Parliament's Press Ordinance and a defence of 'the freedom of unlicensed printing', criticizing censorship of all kinds on a variety of general grounds, not least that independent men should be free to choose. He associated censorship with Catholicism, noting that the popes had 'extended their dominion over men's eyes' by inventing 'the new Purgatory of an Index'.

Topical messages were not confined to pamphlets and newspapers. Political graffiti on London walls and other public places provide vivid illustrations of the extension of the public sphere at this time. Pictorial propaganda was prominent too. About 150 political prints have survived from the year 1641 alone, some of them attacking Charles I's ministers, the Earl of Strafford and Archbishop Laud (see Figure 12). The scene of Laud in a cage offers a clue to the style of the street theatre which flourished in London at the time, as it had done in German cities during the Reformation (see p. 66), while the trial of Charles I, followed by his public execution on a scaffold outside the Banqueting House in Whitehall in 1649, was a high political drama which compensated in part for the closing of the theatres in 1642. The continuing importance of oral communication is revealed in the so-called Putney Debates in 1647, in which a draft constitution known as the 'Agreement of the People' was discussed in an Army Council in which all ranks were represented, the claims of property were challenged and the extension of the franchise demanded.

Print was also important in the appeal to the people and the consequent extension of the public sphere. In 1641, no fewer than 20,000 copies of the *Grand Remonstrance* of the Parliament against the regime of Charles I were in circulation. Reports of debates in the House of Commons, printed for the first time, enlarged the audience for the speeches of MPs. The rise of printed petitions made a contribution to democratic culture, since they were a means for ordinary people to participate more actively in politics than before by lobbying Members of Parliament.

The great question, here as elsewhere in this study, is the extent to which the media and their messages changed people's attitudes and mentalities. Some scholars have emphasized the trivialization of political issues in the news-sheets, but the other side of the coin was the entry of national politics into everyday life.

Fig. 12 Richard Overton, *Canterbury, his Change of Diet*, title page, 1644.

One pious London artisan, Nehemiah Wallington, referred in his journal to more than 300 pamphlets. Another contemporary declared that *Mercurius Aulicus* did Parliament 'more hurt than 2,000 of the king's soldiers', a remark not unlike the comment on Salutati's letters (see p. 62). Looking back from the standpoint of a later generation and extending the metaphor, a writer in 1682 declared that he knew 'not any one thing that more hurt the late King than the paper bullets of the Press'. One writer literally used his pamphlet as a missile, hurling it at the royal coach in 1641. When the German general Erich von Ludendorff (1865–1937) announced during the First World War that 'words have become battles', he was uttering a commonplace, even if developments in propaganda techniques gave his remark a new point.

The precise effect of this explosion of news and comment remains a matter of controversy. Historians still debate whether English political culture was essentially local or national at this time, while noting that newspapers kept the provinces informed about national events and encouraged discussion and the drafting of local petitions in order to influence politics in London. Illustrating the claim by Deutsch in *The Nerves of Government* (1963) that a community is 'a network of communication channels', the spread of news forged closer links between the political centre and the regions, and in this way helped construct a national political culture.

As in the Germany of the 1520s, a public political sphere and even a popular public sphere came into existence in Britain, and especially in London, in the eventful twenty years between the summoning of the Long Parliament in 1641 and the Restoration of Charles II in 1660. In the words of Nigel Smith, 'Never before in English history had written and printed literature played such a predominant role in public affairs, and never before had it been felt by contemporaries to be of such importance.'

The Restoration of Charles II in 1660 presented its makers with the problem, common to such situations, of returning from a relatively open system to a closed one. The proliferation of competing news-sheets was replaced by the monopoly exercised by the *London Gazette*, an official newspaper on the French model (a more recent example would be *Pravda* in the age of Stalin or Brezhnev), and the licensing of books was reintroduced. In 1663 Sir Roger L'Estrange, whose disapproval of print has already been quoted (p. 15), was appointed to enforce government regulations, his title of 'Surveyor' of the press being a euphemism for 'censor'.

L'Estrange was well aware of what has been described above (p. 68) as the conservative dilemma, the problem faced by the Catholic Church in the age of Luther, whether to ignore the public criticisms put forward by the radicals or to fight them with their own weapons. He once wrote that 'a public mercury [a newspaper] should never have my vote, because I think it makes the multitude too familiar with the actions and counsels of their superiors'. Nevertheless, he edited no fewer than three news-sheets: first *The Intelligencer*, printed, in its own words, 'for the satisfaction and information of the people'; then *The News*; and finally, from 1681 to 1687, *The Observator*. As he wrote in *The Observator* in April 1681, 'Tis the Press that has made 'um mad, and the Press must set 'um right again.' In this way governments were being forced to contribute through journalism to the spread of a popular political consciousness which the elites generally deplored, and to the rise of journalists ('newsmen', as they were known in seventeenth-century England) as a new force in political affairs, later described as a 'fourth estate' (see p. 154).

The workings of the media regime of the Restoration period are illuminated by a major communications event of 1678, the so-called 'Popish Plot' to assassinate Charles II so that his Catholic brother James, Duke of York, could rule in his place. On 6 September 1678, Titus Oates, an ex-convert to Catholicism and an ex-trainee Jesuit, went to a magistrate, Sir Edmund Berry Godfrey, to tell him about the plot, and repeated his story to the Council on 28 September. Godfrey was found dead, apparently murdered, soon afterwards. When his funeral procession took place on 31 October, the House of Commons resolved that there had been a 'damnable and hellish plot contrived and carried on by the popish recusants for the assassinating and murdering [of] the king'. At the trial of the plotters Oates gave evidence, but failed to carry conviction, and from this time onwards he began to lose credibility, just as Senator Joe McCarthy (1909–57), with his stories of Communist plots, suddenly lost credibility with American public opinion in the 1950s. Oates was eventually convicted for perjury.

The best-known study of the Popish Plot, written by the historian John Kenyon, is marked by a robust common sense and vividly illustrates both the strengths and weaknesses of such an approach. Concerned to elucidate what actually happened or failed to happen, Kenyon concentrates on showing that there never was any plot, dismissing contemporary beliefs as irrational, as 'panic', 'hysteria', 'paranoiac fear of Catholicism', or even 'mass hypnotism'. The Popish Plot surely requires, however, to be studied in the manner in which the French historian Georges Lefebvre studied the Great Fear of 1789 (see p. 24), in which the role of the media of communication is taken into account. As in so many political crises, stereotypes played an important role – the treacherous Catholic, the subtle Jesuit, and so on. Popular memories of the Gunpowder Plot of Guy Fawkes and also of the Great Fire of London in 1666 (for which the Catholics had been blamed) were reactivated.

The official *Gazette* did not mention the plot at all, and since there were no unofficial newspapers in existence at the time, the news of events circulated indirectly, either by private letters or by word of mouth, in other words, rumour. The crisis thus illustrates with particular clarity the argument of Tamotsu Shibutani in his *Improvised News* (1966) that rumour flourishes when the supply of information is inadequate to meet the demand for it. In this case there was a rumour of mysterious 'night riders' in Yorkshire, Wiltshire, Gloucestershire and elsewhere, followed by reports of a French invasion. Printed images also spread awareness of 'The Horrid Popish Plot', notably a series of engravings on playing-cards representing scenes such as 'The conspirators signing the resolve for killing the king'.

Moreover, after the plot had been finally shown to have been a mere invention, its themes continued to be exploited by the Whig party, who were hostile to Catholics and wanted to limit the powers of the monarch. There was a direct link, therefore, with the so-called 'Exclusion Crisis' (1679–81), the point being to exclude Charles's brother James from the succession to the throne (James was next in line, since Charles had no legitimate male heir). The Whigs drew up petitions, published ballads and prints, and organized a number of processions, notably in London in 1679, 1680 and 1681 in which an effigy of the Pope was consigned to the flames. The bill for these political demonstrations was paid by the Green Ribbon Club, a Whig organization. On these occasions a professional writer, Elkanah Settle, was hired to design pageants of pope, cardinals, friars, inquisitors and nuns, and a bellman was employed to cry out 'remember Justice Godfrey'. Labels were placed on the figures to make sure that everyone understood the message. Images of the processions were also engraved and printed. An important contribution to the Whig cause (for which he was executed in 1681) was made by the engraver Stephen Colledge, who represented the king as a two-faced puppet-master or 'raree-showman'.

On the other side, the Tories complained – in print – of the abuses of the press, comparing the 'seditious libels' of their opponents with those of 1641. It has been calculated that between five and ten million copies of pamphlets were in circulation between 1679 and 1681, arguing the case for and against exclusion. More traditional media were not forgotten either. For example, the poet John Dryden (1631–1700) wrote or collaborated on the play *The Duke of Guise* in order to show what he called the 'parallel' between 1583 in France and 1683 in England, with the Whig leader, the first earl of Shaftesbury (1621–83), in the place of the duke and the Dissenters in place of the Catholic League. In other words, the parallel was a copy in reverse, with ultra-Protestants in England playing the role of ultra-Catholics in France. The play won the approval of Charles II, who asked Dryden to translate a recent history of Guise's Catholic League. Dedicating his translation to the king, Dryden suggested that a comparison of the events of 1584 in France and 1684 in England showed that 'the features are alike in all'.

In spite of everything, James Duke of York succeeded his brother Charles in 1685 and was crowned James II. Yet he was driven out three years later when the Protestant William of Orange (1650–1702), married to James's sister Mary, invaded England from Holland. The place of the media in these revolutionary events was an important one. At the outset, William's *Declaration* of the reasons for the invasion was printed and began to be distributed in England before the invasion even took place. The fact that we still refer to the events of 1688 as the 'Glorious Revolution' testifies to the power of an image which was consciously fabricated at that time. For example, the Lord Mayor's Show of 1689, entitled 'London's Great Jubilee', presented William III as a conquering Protestant hero. The text was written by a professional poet, Matthew Taubman (who had previously written against the Whigs), and the message was supplemented by ballads, processions, prints, medals, playing-cards and sermons. Particularly influential was the sermon preached by Bishop Gilbert Burnet (1643–1715) at St James's in December 1688 which was circulated in print soon afterwards.

Long-distance communication continued to be difficult. In North America, news of the events of 1688 took time to arrive. The landing of William of Orange and the flight of James II occurred in November and December, 'at the wrong time of year for speedy reports to reach New England'. Thus, William's arrival in England was not known in Boston until early April 1689. In Carolina, William was proclaimed king even later than in New England because the news of his accession had taken longer to arrive.

While the importance of the English Revolution of the mid-seventeenth century in the history of the media is well known, less attention has been paid by historians to this sequence of events. They have noted, however, the lapse of the Licensing Act in 1695, which ended not only the censorship system but also the control of printing through the Stationer's Company, a control which had lasted since the Company had been granted a Royal Charter in 1557; and the Stamp Act of 1712 which, through levying stamp duty, attempted to curb the nascent power of the newspaper press.

There had been a spate of political memoirs and printed sermons in the years between, notably the sermon preached against the Whig government in 1710 by the High Tory divine Henry Sacheverell (*c*.1674–1724), which sold 40,000 copies in the space of a few days. Sacheverell's sermon illustrates the way in which a performance in one medium might be echoed or mirrored in another, while the fact that the text sold ten times as many copies as Luther's *Address to the German Nobility* (see p. 63) provides a measure of the increasing importance of printed matter in European culture.

Most significant of all was the rise of an unofficial periodical press, including newspapers such as the *Post Man*, the *Post Boy* – both founded in 1695 – *The Flying Post* and *The Protestant Mercury*. These papers were longer than the official *London Gazette* and appeared more frequently, three times a week instead of twice. They were also considerably more informative. Circulation figures appear to have been quite high: 6,000 copies of the *Gazette* at the beginning of the eighteenth century, 4,000 copies of the *Post Man*, 3,000 copies of the *Post Boy*.

It was such unofficial newspapers which turned the earlier temporary public sphere into a permanent institution, making politics part of the daily life of a considerable proportion of the population, especially in London. Newspapers subject to stamp tax and to paper duties, were often read aloud and discussed in coffee-houses, a political forum in which craftsmen as well as gentlemen, and women as well as men, had a voice. Other kinds of information were also becoming more public. The Stock Exchange and the newspapers spread economic information. Science, too, entered the public sphere, thanks to public lectures as well as to the *Transactions of the Royal Society* (see p. 58), which carried news of recent experiments and discoveries, even if the Society's meetings remained at most semi-public, open only to the members of the club.

It was this British culture that produced the radical politician John Wilkes, whose extraordinary career as a defender of liberty and a hammer of the political establishment depended on popular support which was mobilized through the media, not only in newspapers – notably the *North Briton* – but in political prints, handbills and processions, while Wilkes's distinctive features were reproduced on medals, buttons, jugs, snuff-boxes and teapots. For a long time, festivals have carried political messages, as we have seen (see p. 36). What was new in this period was the rise of what the nineteenth century would call a 'demonstration' – an event, not always festive, organized in support of a particular policy.

Another novelty was what we might call the institutionalization of the political print, which now appeared regularly, and not only in times of crisis. Prints encouraged critical thought about politics by satirizing both sides (the Whigs commissioned attacks on the Tories, and vice versa). Not even the royal family was spared. The Duke of Cumberland was represented as a butcher for his brutality in suppressing the Jacobite rebellion of 1745, while the Prince Regent, later George IV, was a regular target of visual criticism in the early nineteenth century.

Enlightenment and Revolution in France

On the Continent of Europe, with the exception of the Dutch Republic, the development of a permanent public sphere lagged behind Britain. In France, for example, the Fronde was followed by the long reign of Louis XIV (exercising power from 1660 to 1715), in which the media were controlled and public criticism of the regime was minimal. The situation changed, however, in the course of the eighteenth century and no history of the media can afford to omit the French Enlightenment, a leading part of a European movement of education, criticism and reform which had other centres in Scotland and Switzerland and affected North and South America as well.

The metaphor of 'light' was taken seriously in the definition of the movement by its participants. The light was that of 'Reason', a keyword of the time, set against faith and superstition, tradition and prejudice. Another keyword of the period was 'critical'. In his emphasis on rational and critical thought in the eighteenth century, as in his emphasis on the idea of 'the public', Habermas repeated or translated into twentieth-century terms what 'enlightened' people were already saying about themselves. Urging reform rather than revolution, they viewed their role as educational, in the widest sense of the word 'education'. The media were their requisite instruments.

In this movement, a central part was played by French thinkers, the so-called *philosophes*, among them Voltaire (1694–1778), Rousseau (1712–78), Diderot (1713–84) and D'Alembert (1717–83). Calling themselves 'men of letters', they have sometimes been described as the first intellectuals, independent of patrons, or even the first intelligentsia, in the sense of being systematically critical of the regime under which they were living. They tried to spread their message widely, inside and outside France, and to women as well as men – though they did not try to reach the 'people'. Voltaire, in particular, was contemptuous of what he called the 'mob' (*canaille*).

These men of letters thought and wrote within a system in which censorship was still in place, although administered more mildly than it had been in the age of Louis XIV. Journals, for example, were not allowed to deal with political subjects. These official restrictions made the oral culture of coffee-houses politically important, like the culture of the salons, in which aristocratic ladies organized intellectual conversations. Private correspondence, not least with sovereigns such as Frederick of Prussia (ruled 1740–86) and Catherine of Russia (ruled 1762–96), was another way in which the *philosophes* spread their ideas.

Artistic genres such as plays, paintings or historical studies were sometimes the vehicle of political messages. *The Marriage of Figaro*, for example, by the French playwright Pierre-Augustin Beaumarchais (1732–99), had its première in 1784 after difficulties with the censors, who suspected that the play was a satire on the regime. The political sentiments of Beaumarchais were toned down in the Italian libretto of Mozart's opera (1786), but something of the message remained.

Above all, the famous *Encyclopédie*, published between 1751 and 1765, was an important vehicle for politics. Originally planned as a four-volume translation from the English of Chambers' *Cyclopaedia*, the *Encyclopédie* turned into an independent work in thirty-five volumes. D'Alembert, Diderot, Voltaire and Rousseau were among the many contributors to volumes which were intended as a means to awaken political consciousness as well as to acquire information. The publication of the *Encyclopédie* was a major event in the history of communication. Only the wealthy could afford to buy it, but cheaper editions followed and many more people could consult the work in public libraries.

Another reaction to censorship was the organization of clandestine communication (see p. 43), whether in print or in manuscript, whether the books were smuggled from abroad or produced secretly in France. French booksellers referred to these clandestine publications as *livres philosophiques*, a general category which included pornographic as well as heretical and politically subversive works. The American historian Robert Darnton suggests that pornography was linked to Enlightenment and Reform via a process of desacralization. The attack on the sexual conduct of the wife of Louis XVI, Marie Antoinette, entitled *Les amours de Carlot et de Toinette*, may have encouraged not only reform but revolution as well. The ways in which royal families are presented in the media may have far-reaching political consequences.

As in the case of the movements described earlier in this chapter, the involvement of the 'people' in the French Revolution of 1789 was both cause and consequence of involvement of the media. A similar point might be made about the American Revolution of 1776. The cause of American independence, which drew on British precedent – the seventeenth-century English Grand Remonstrance was one source for the American Declaration of Independence – was advanced not only by pamphlets but also by newspapers. There were already forty-two different newspapers in the American colonies in 1775 and some of them, such as the *New York Journal*, the *Philadelphia Evening Post* and the *Massachusetts Spy*, advanced the revolutionary cause by describing atrocities committed by the British army. Over the long term they created a national political culture through the news they reported (as in England during the Civil War) and assisted the emergence of a new imagined community, defined against the British. A French visitor to America, after noting the frequent reprinting of Thomas Paine's pamphlet *Common Sense* in the periodical press, claimed that 'Without newspapers, the American Revolution would never have succeeded'. Other European travellers commented on the number of journals in existence in the United States. By 1800 there were 178 weeklies and 24 dailies.

As for the French Revolution, its relation to the Enlightenment which preceded it has often been debated. By the late eighteenth century, the French government recognized public opinion as an entity which needed to be addressed, and in so doing helped the opposition to overthrow the old regime; in this way, the Revolution might be described as a continuation of the Enlightenment by other means. The appeal to reason, personified as a goddess, and to the 'rights of man', treated as universal, followed Enlightenment traditions. The *philosophes* were venerated, and the body of Voltaire was taken in solemn procession to be interred in the Pantheon in 1791. Nevertheless, the revolutionary programme was more radical. It was to change the system, not to reform it. The reorganization of the calendar, making 1792 into 'Year 1', was an important symbolic act, a declaration of independence from the past.

Historians used to see the Revolution as primarily a response to the economic and social problems of the 1780s. More emphasis is now placed on the invention of a new political culture and the 'construction' of a new community of citizens, in which a place was created alongside the two privileged orders or 'estates' of the clergy and the nobility for the 'third estate' (lawyers, merchants, artisans and peasants). In this work of invention and construction a crucial role was once again played by the media.

Printed matter played an important part in the French Revolution, which began with calls for a free press. The Comte de Mirabeau (1749–81) adapted Milton's *Areopagitica* (1788), Marie-Joseph Chénier set out a forceful *Denunciation of the Inquisitors of Thought* (1789), and Jacques-Pierre Brissot produced a *Memoir on the need to free the press* (1789). Brissot was thinking especially of newspapers, for by the time that his memoir appeared events were moving too fast for books or even pamphlets. There was an explosion of new publications, with at least 250 newspapers founded in the last six months of 1789. Different papers aimed at different target audiences, including peasants (to whom *La feuille villageoise* was addressed). The size of such news-sheets was usually small, but the *Gazette nationale* imitated the large format of the English papers.

The Revolution was good for the press, since there was plenty of exciting news to report and no lack of readers either. The cook who confessed in 1791 to reading four newspapers (see p. 51) may not have been so unusual in her time. In its turn, the press was good for the Revolution. It has been suggested by Jeremy Popkin, for example, that the periodical press was 'indispensable to give legitimacy to the new law-making of the Revolution by making that process public'. All the same, the power of the press should not be exaggerated. In 1789, most French people could not read. Hence the contribution of all the parts of the system of communication needs to be considered, as it has been in the case of earlier movements such as the Reformation.

Oral communication was particularly important. The Revolution was a time of intense debate, of speeches in the National Assembly and in the political clubs newly formed in Paris and other cities. The debates were conducted in a new 'revolutionary rhetoric', appealing to the passions rather than to reason and relying on the 'magic' of words such as *liberté, fraternité, nation, patrie, peuple* and *citoyen*. Outside the assemblies and clubs, rumour was even more important than usual at this time when another rapid succession of dramatic events took place. The notorious 'Great Fear' of 1789, discussed above (p. 24), was simply the most important of the many rumours of the Revolution.

Visual communication, including iconoclasm, was also important. The destruction of religious images expressed a perception of the Church as part of the old regime. There was also secular iconoclasm or 'vandalism', as it was called at the time, as witnessed in the destruction of the statues of Louis XIV to be seen on two of the main squares of Paris until 1792. On the positive side, a new language of images was created in order to serve the new regime. The painter Jacques-Louis David (1748–1825), for example, was active on behalf of the Revolution, both in and out of his studio. His painting of the assassinated Marat was a contribution to the martyrology of the Revolution. More than 6,000 prints were produced in the revolutionary period to extend the political debate to the illiterate. A woodcut of the fall of the Bastille, for instance, symbolized the fall of the old regime. Even fans and plates carried political messages such as 'Long live the Third Estate' (*Vive le tiers état* or *Union and Liberty*; see Figure 13). So, once again, did playing-cards.

The Revolution may be described as a long-running political theatre, often 'black', with the public executions of Louis XVI, Marie Antoinette and later of leading revolutionaries such as Danton and Robespierre as the most dramatic scenes. There were also public festivals, whether in Paris (especially the large open space of the Champ-de-Mars) or in the provinces: the Festival of the Federation, for instance, or those of the sovereignty of the people, of the Supreme Being, and of Reason. The painter David was the designer and choreographer of some of these festivals. Their huge scale (to twentieth-century eyes, reminiscent of the Nuremberg Rally or the Mayday parades of the USSR) expressed the new democratic values of the time by allowing thousands of people to participate. They were also expressions of a process of secularization if only in the sense of

Fig. 13 Political plate, c.1790.

what the French historian Mona Ozouf calls a 'transfer of sacrality' from the Church to the State.

The conscious mobilization of the media in order to change attitudes may be described as propaganda. Originally a religious term, coined to describe the propagation of Christianity, the word 'propaganda' acquired a pejorative meaning in the late eighteenth century, when Protestants used it to describe the techniques of the Catholic Church. During the French Revolution, the term was adapted to politics. The revolutionary journalist Camille Desmoulins (1760–94), for instance, compared 'the propagation of patriotism' with that of Christianity, while the royalists in exile denounced the 'propaganda' of the Revolution. The new word referred to a new phenomenon. Although the uses of images and texts to shape attitudes goes back a long way in human history, the self-consciousness and the scale of the revolutionary media campaign was something new.

According to Habermas, 'The Revolution in France created overnight . . . what in Great Britain had taken more than a century of steady evolution; the institutions . . . for critical public debate of political matters.' The limitations of this French 'public sphere' have since been pointed out, notably its virtual exclusion of women. Nevertheless, the French media played a necessary role both in the destruction of traditions and the invention of new ones, the attempt to create a new political culture without either Church or king. It is no accident that the phrase *opinion publique*, like the term 'propaganda', came into regular use at this time. Conversely, the notorious guillotine entered the language of communications, whether to refer to a machine used by printers to trim the edges of sheets, or to an attempt to end parliamentary debates on a particular topic.

As in the case of England after the Restoration of Charles II, France under Napoleon (ruled 1799–1815) experienced a kind of return to a pre-revolutionary situation. Yet things could never be quite the same again as long as people remembered what had happened. The power of the media resided in its capacity to reactivate memories of the revolutionary past. The long-standing analogy between the press and the army (see above p. 75) was reactivated by Napoleon, who declared that 'four hostile newspapers are more to be feared than 100,000 bayonets'.

To return to a debate which has echoed throughout this study, and will continue to do so, it would be absurd to deny the creativity of individuals such as Diderot or Robespierre in the politics and in the communication system of the Enlightenment and the Revolution. As we have seen, this communication system included speeches, images and festivals as well as printed matter. Nonetheless, in thinking about the way in which printed matter encouraged political consciousness, while a more acute political consciousness led in turn to a rise in the consumption of printed matter, it is difficult to avoid a phrase like 'the logic of print', just as it is difficult, when speaking of a later period, to avoid a phrase like 'the logic of technology'.

Revolution (and empire later) gave a stimulus to science, including the science of communication, beginning with roads. Engineers were honoured – and their education promoted. So, too, was invention. Between 1792 and 1798 a new invention project was proposed each year. The pioneer of the telegraph was Claude Chappe (1763–1805), a young experimenter with electricity, who believed that revolutionaries should reward experiments which 'are useful to the public'. He presented a memorandum to the Legislative Assembly in 1792, urging it to support a semaphore system of conveying messages which would receive a quick response from tower to tower. It would unify the nation, an argument strengthened in the following year after France went to war with the Habsburg Empire: it now had military significance. The first semaphore line between Paris and Lille was built for communicating with the Army in the north, and one of Napoleon's first initiatives was the rapid building of a line between Lyons and Milan. At the same time universality was proclaimed, as it was in declarations of rights and in the metric system. By the time the electric telegraph was developed (see p. 109), French power could not influence the decisions of other countries, and France itself preserved its semaphore system or hybrid arrangements based on it after it had become obsolete.

The story in Britain was the opposite. The British government turned down offers from Francis Reynolds, 'the father of English telegraphy', in 1816 to provide 'an expeditious method of conveying intelligence', but with the rise of industry, described in the next chapter, private investors sponsored both railways and electric telegraphy. Reynolds himself received a knighthood in 1870 when the development of communications was entering a new phase.

Varieties of Public Sphere

This chapter has tried to work with, and also in some ways against, the idea of the rise of the public sphere associated with Jürgen Habermas, who, replying to his critics, has claimed that pushing the idea of the public sphere back into the sixteenth and seventeenth centuries involves 'changing the very concept of the public sphere to such a degree that it becomes something else'. For our part, we have emphasized the structural weaknesses of this sphere in old regimes and distinguished two kinds of public sphere, temporary and permanent, or structural and conjunctural.

We have moved from the German Reformation in the 1520s to the American and French Revolutions via civil wars in the Netherlands, France and England. We have noted a sequence of similar situations in which elites who were engaged in bitter conflict appealed to the people and in which the media, especially the printed media, helped raise political consciousness. In each situation, a crisis led to a lively but relatively short-lived debate which might be described as the establishment of a temporary or conjunctural public sphere.

Some at least of the characters in this long-running story were aware of their predecessors and attempted to build on their achievements. For example, the English Civil War was viewed at the time as a kind of replay of the late sixteenth-century French Wars of Religion. The Exclusion Crisis was also perceived in terms of the French religious wars, with Shaftesbury in the place of Guise (see p. 70). The seventeenth-century English Grand Remonstrance became a model for the American Declaration of Independence. Milton's *Areopagitica*, as adapted by Mirabeau, was used in the French campaign for freedom of the press, while the execution of king Charles I was cited as a precedent for the guillotining of Louis XVI.

Precedents were recorded in print, with pamphlets ensuring that rebellions were remembered and thereby assisting in the construction of what might be called a tradition of revolution, while the newspaper and periodical press turned the process of criticizing authority into a cumulative one. The press was already a force in society by 1789, alongside the clergy, the nobility and the rest. In Britain it was to sustain authority more than subvert it during the long wars against Napoleon. The wars were ultimately won through superior economic and naval strength, but many contemporaries attributed the victory to superior moral (and religious) qualities.

This history, however, as was suggested at the beginning of this chapter, was not one of linear but of zigzag progress. It moved from one region in Europe to another, often with one step backwards after two steps forward, and it has to be traced within a changing global geography. The word 'discoveries' came into use as the oceans of the world were opened up. Nonetheless, from the point of view of the media, we do not yet see 'one world'. Islam, as we have seen, displayed considerable resistance to print. It was only after 1800 that the press and revolutionary political movements appeared together in the Middle East.

In East Asia, where print culture came into existence long before it did in the West, the consequences differed from those in Europe. What Benedict Anderson calls 'print capitalism' certainly existed, especially at the popular level. For example, the eighteenth-century Japanese prints now sought by collectors originated as posters advertising actors, tea-houses, courtesans, and even brands of sake. However, in China and Japan alike, print was controlled more closely by the state than in Europe, delaying the development of a public sphere for centuries. Whether or to what extent China has a public sphere today remains a matter for debate.

In the case of Europe from the Reformation onwards the fragmentation of religious as well as political authority had made it impossible for governments fully to control printing, which had a strong economic thrust behind it. That thrust became more forceful, and even apparently irreversible and irresistible, in the nineteenth and twentieth centuries, as printing became one of a far wider range of media technologies, verbal and visual, driven by new forms of power, ultimately making for a new convergence within a global setting.

In retrospect, as at the time, printing with movable type by independent entrepreneurs stood out as an explosive combination, although a substantial proportion of the printing was concerned with economic activities unrelated to the emerging of the media. The failure of governments in Europe fully to control it left the way open for other developments in communication which began with transportation and were quickly seen, like the rise of steam-driven industrialization, as constituting a 'revolution'.

Commerce, Industry and Communication

Technology could never be separated from economics, and the concept of an industrial revolution preceded that of a communications revolution – long, continuing and unfinished. The second concept, clearly formulated only in the late twentieth century, had already begun to take shape in the nineteenth. Following what Charles Knight (1791–1873), pioneer of cheap books and a popular press, called a 'victory over time and space', time (and distance) were redefined under the influence first of the railway and the steamship and then of a cluster of new media – telegraph, radio, photography and moving pictures.

Even before the railway, contemporaries were already comparing the French revolutionaries Danton and Robespierre with James Watt (1736–1819), hailed as the inventor of the steam engine, and Richard Arkwright (1732–92), the first 'factory king', who began, like many cotton mill owners, by employing water power not steam. Napoleon soon came into the picture as well. His had been victories in war, Watt's and Arkwright's were victories of peace, and they were imagined, often in biblical language, as inventions with global consequences. Even the deserts of the world could be transformed:

> Steam! – if the nations grow not old
> Why does not thou thy banner shake
> O'er sea-less, steam-less lands, and make
> One nation of mankind?

Before an 'industrial sequence', later called 'industrialization', began, ending with technology based on science, the first technological inventions were proudly – but seldom without contention – acclaimed, particularly in Britain. Merchants preceded industrial entrepreneurs as they looked across the oceans for economic opportunities, materials and markets, dependent for success on communicating information. Daniel Defoe, author of the novel *Robinson Crusoe* (1719), had observed thirteen years earlier how 'the Merchant by his Correspondence reconciles that infinite variety which . . . by the Infinite Wisdom of Providence [has] been scattered over the Face of the World . . . Every country communicates to its other corresponding country what they want . . . and [there is] not a country so barren, so useless, but something is to be found there that can be had nowhere else.' There were new connections and new ways of living. The concept of an 'industrious revolution' preceding an 'industrial revolution' has been developed by Jan de Vries, historian of the Netherlands. It influenced both attitudes and habits.

Defoe was also interested in inventive projects which were to change the range and locations of commerce; and later in the eighteenth century the inventor James Watt's business partner, Matthew Boulton (1728–1809), who moved from the production of 'toys' to steam engines, could boast that he had established 'a correspondence in almost every mercantile town in Europe which regularly supplied me with orders'. 'Power', he believed, was 'what all the world wants.'

4 From Steam to Electricity

In boasting that he could offer all that the world wanted – 'power' – Boulton was dependent on Watt's steam engine patents, the first of which was taken out in 1769, five years before Watt joined him in the most famous of all partnerships between inventor and businessman. Before the 1760s the number of patents taken out in a year in Britain rarely exceeded a dozen: in 1769 the figure was thirty-six, and in 1783, when the American War of Independence came to an end, it reached sixty-four. Many were concerned with power-driven communications.

Steam power had a long history, stretching back to the ancient world, and it was used in mines for decades before it was used to move machines. By the time that Watt's patents expired in 1800, the steam engine had established itself as the most important of inventions, the invention on which many other inventions depended. It was described with exaggeration by Dionysius Lardner (1793–1859), a prolific writer on machines and steam power and editor of a *Cabinet Cyclopaedia*, as 'the exclusive offspring of British genius', 'fostered and supported by British capital'. It was in France, however, where because of ample water supplies and navigable rivers and canals the application of steam power to industry was relatively low – as it was in new American industrial communities, like Lowell in Massachusetts ('spindle city') – that in 1848 a well-known writer asked pertinently, as he looked back to 1789, 'what speculative discovery of the mind has exerted as much influence as the discovery of steam power?' That was in a year of further political revolutions in France and other European countries, and the writer was Ernest Renan (1823–92), author of a controversial life of Jesus. In the United States, a Lowell manufacturer, Erastus Brigham Biggelow (1814–79), had already described how, as steam power was increasingly applied, it was now possible 'to achieve what the ancients dreamed of in their fables'.

One new achievement was speed – surpassing greatly the speed of the horse. (Units of horse power were still used in relation to steam as they were to be later to the internal combustion engine.) There had already been an emphasis on speed before the advent of steam; now, however, it became an imperative. As the poet Samuel Taylor Coleridge (1772–1834) put it in 1826:

> Keep moving! Steam, or Gas, or Stage,
> Hold, cabin, steerage, hencoop's cage –
> Tour, Journey, Voyage, Lounge, Ride, Walk,
> Skim, Sketch, Excursion, Travel-talk –
> For move you must! 'Tis now the rage,
> The law and fashion of the age.

Cartoons as well as pamphlets and novels carried the message. As a character in George Eliot's novel *The Mill on the Floss* (1860) put it, 'the world goes on at a smarter pace than it did when I was a young fellow . . . It's this steam you see.'

Within these perspectives, 'industrial revolution' and 'communications revolution' can be seen as part of the same process – with a transportation revolution coming first in a technological sequence which seemed to have its own logic, particularly after electricity provided a new, if at first more mysterious, source of power than steam. (The word 'electronics' came much later.) In the twentieth century, television preceded computers just as the printing press preceded the steam engine, radio preceded television, and railways and steamships preceded automobiles and aeroplanes. There were delays in the sequence, each of which needs to be explained. 'The practical flying-machine', a focus of aspiration, had to wait for the invention of the internal combustion engine to become a technical possibility. Telegraphs preceded telephones, and radio began as wireless telegraphy. Later, after the invention of wireless telephony, it was employed to usher in an 'age of broadcasting', first in words then in pictures.

In dealing with the advent of steam power, which for long seemed to have started it all, David Landes, a distinguished American historian of the long process of industrialization, concentrated on the 'substitution of mechanical devices for human skills', the replacement of 'human and animal strength by inanimate power' and 'a marked improvement in the getting and working of raw materials'. There was nothing final, however, in the association of these developments with steam, as contemporaries recognized. Instead, a continuing process of industrialization had begun during which further human skills were acquired, new forms of inanimate power were developed – including, after electricity, nuclear and solar power – and substitute materials were devised through the advances of chemistry and, in the twentieth century, materials science.

The process of invention was at the centre of what most contemporaries saw as progress, frequently extolled in the media. One of the bodies fostering it in eighteenth-century Britain was the Society for the Encouragement of Arts, Manufactures and Commerce, founded in 1754, which set out to divide inventions into categories, of which those relating to transportation were particularly prominent. 'Inland navigation', 'longitude at sea', 'wheels, carriages and roads' figured as early as 1760 on its lists. In the nineteenth century, the Society for the Diffusion of Useful Knowledge, founded in 1827, was nicknamed 'The Steam Intellect Society'.

In all countries, both in the age of steam and in the subsequent age of electricity, it became a matter of pride to be the first to secure an invention, although it was seldom easy to establish the claim. Many inventions were arrived at independently in different places in processes which, it was recognized at the time, crossed state frontiers. Litigation concerning patent rights was a frequent occurrence. Legal disputes were struggles for power as well as for money, the question of how much depending both on how long a patent could be continued and how vulnerable it was to challenge. The law, frequently invoked, varied from country to country. Yet rhetoric was abundant with talk of 'conquering Nature'. As an agile versifier put it in 1776, the year of the American Declaration of Independence and Adam Smith's *Wealth of Nations*:

> The time may come when nothing will succeed
> But what a precious Patent hath decreed;
> And we must open on some future day
> The door of Nature with a patent key.

The 'future day' mattered as much to British inventors and businessmen – supported not only by versifiers but by great poets – as it did to French revolutionaries. It was in France, indeed, that the term 'industrial revolution' was first coined in 1827 by a political economist, Adolphe Blanqui.

For Erasmus Darwin (1731–1802), the grandfather of the great biologist Charles Darwin, living on the edge of Britain's Black Country and writing in the opening year of the first French Revolution of 1789, transportation was the main key to the world of the future:

> Soon shall they arm, UNCONQUER'D STEAM! afar
> Drag the slow barge, or drive the rapid car;
> Or on wide-waving wings expanded bear
> The flying chariot through the fields of air.

Darwin, a medical doctor, was a member of the Lunar Society, a West Midlands circle of friends formally constituted as a society in 1780, and Boulton and Watt also belonged to it. The members were conscious of their distance from London, although the time taken to reach it by so-called 'flying carriages' fell sharply (in good weather) after the building of turnpike roads. Their mileage increased five times between 1750 and 1790.

The practical form of transportation which most interested the members of the Society was not road traffic or steam locomotion but traffic by canal which in face of opposition was already transforming the economic life of the Midlands; and one of the members of the Society, the potter Josiah Wedgwood (1730–95), who had a business interest in the subject, contributed greatly to the canal phase of transportation history. The first phase reached its peak in Britain in 1790–3 when cheap capital encouraged a canal 'mania' in Britain and fifty-three canal and navigation bills were authorized by Parliament. This enthusiasm anticipated the railway mania of the 1840s. Speculation figures as prominently as investment in the later history of the media, including the history of the Internet. So, too, did the pressure to legislate. How or whether to use the law to regulate communications processes were fundamental questions then as now.

In continental Europe, with miles of navigable rivers, canals were a familiar feature of the landscape before they became so in Britain, and a canal era began there at the end of the seventeenth century. In 1810 in France, the completion of the St Quentin Canal linked the North Sea and the river systems of the Scheldt and Lys with the English Channel via the Somme, and with Paris and Le Havre via the Oise and the Seine. By then Napoleon was emperor, and Britain was engaged in protracted wars against him. The 'Louisiana Purchase' from Napoleon by the United States in 1803 had given it control of a main navigable waterway which, by the end of the nineteenth century, was to become part of a continental navigation network which included four thousand miles of canals. There had been only a hundred miles in 1800, but between 1817 and 1825 the Erie Canal, a vital link in the network, had been built by the state of New York, opening up the first American West.

Before Britain was drawn into armed conflict with pre-Napoleonic revolutionary France in 1793, Darwin was completing his verses *Botanic Garden* (1789–91), dealing with far more than transportation as he eagerly enlisted 'the imagination under the banner of science'. Meanwhile, the young William Wordsworth (1770–1850), who, like Coleridge, saluted the French Revolution as a new dawn, was extolling in his poem 'An Evening Walk' (1788–9):

> ... those to whom the harmonious doors
> Of Science have unbarred celestial shores,
> To whom a burning energy has given
> That other eye which darts thro' earth and heaven.

Within these perspectives science and technology were one.

In fact, their relationship was complicated. Neither the word 'scientist' nor the word 'technologist' had yet been invented. 'Scientist' was a new word in 1840, while the word 'technology', only coined in France in the *Encyclopédie*, was not yet used in Britain. Nonetheless, the word 'invention', preceded as it was by the word 'discovery', was part of the daily late eighteenth-century vocabulary, along with 'improvement'. Linked as it often was to play, not to purpose, the word 'toy', as the French appreciated before the British, was part of the same vocabulary. The desire for novelty might foster it as much as what came to be called in retrospect 'economic necessity'. One of the locomotives which took part in the steam locomotive trials of 1829 – won by George Stephenson's 'Rocket', a word with a late twentieth-century future – was named 'Novelty', still very much a favourite word of the nineteenth century.

One of the outstanding figures of that century, Karl Marx (1818–83), saw the invention of the steam engine as the great breakthrough in human history, separating past from present and opening up a revolutionary future. In the *Communist Manifesto* of 1848 he dwelt eloquently on 'the accomplished wonders of industrialization', but foretold that revolution would come not through technology itself but through class struggle between the capitalists who owned and controlled steam engines and machinery and the exploited industrial proletariat who worked them. In his *Grundrisse* notebooks, written in the mid-1840s, he listed the main industrial changes since the French Revolution and explained that 'Nature builds no machines, no locomotives, railways, electric telegraphs ... etc. These are products of human industry: natural material transformed into instruments of the human will.'

Marx's reference to 'electric telegraphs' brought in the first electrical invention that was to begin the process of reshaping what came to be called the 'media'. Yet it was on steam and on the relationship between steam and print that he still focused as he went on to ask 'What became of *Fama*, rumour, fame, when Printing House Square, the home of the London newspaper, *The Times*, spread news abroad as well as at home?' The newspaper, originally called in 1785 *The Daily Universal Register*, had been given its familiar name three years later by its proprietor John Walter I (1739–1812), who had served his apprenticeship with a bookseller who was also a publisher. In 1814 a huge steam printing press, made out of iron and patented in England by Frederick Koenig, had been installed by his son, John Walter II, in the headquarters of *The Times* in Printing House

Square: it not only saved labour, but made possible the production of 1,000 impressions an hour. The newspaper could now go to press later and contain the most recent news.

The idea of using a rolling cylinder in printing was not new, but Koenig's cylinder was; and, as *The Times* of 29 November 1814 put it, without referring to steam, the copy of that first day was 'the practical result of the greatest improvement connected with printing since the discovery of the art itself'. Koenig was referred to as 'an artist'. He was not the first such person to be employed by Walter, however, and after he left the service of *The Times*, having extolled British patent law, there were further substantial technical changes in Printing House Square in 1828 when a four-cylinder steam press was installed. By then it was common to describe newspapers as 'social engines', with the stress not on steam, but on their power over opinion.

Marx did not observe (or know?) that *The Times* as a working organization established its ascendancy by its refusal to employ trade-union labour in an industry where 'combinations' or 'unions' of compositors and printers – skilled trades – had been strong since 1785. Before turning to Koenig, who himself had earlier turned to a book publisher, Walter had subsidized a British inventor to develop a press 'by which manual labour should be rendered nearly unnecessary'. Both Marx and his friend and associate Friedrich Engels (1820–95), who lived for most of his life in industrial Manchester, appreciated the power of the print media, however, and wrote for newspapers, among them – ironically in retrospect – the New York *Tribune*. They were both zealous communicators. As well as letters to each other, which fill several volumes, they wrote pamphlets and books, ranging from the *Communist Manifesto* to *Capital*, a classic of political economy.

Marxists were to draw a distinction between the economic substructure and the cultural superstructure, with the Italian Marxist Antonio Gramsci (1891–1937), who was deeply interested in the media, making a special contribution to the debate in the twentieth century, introducing the word 'hegemony', which was to influence most writing on the media in the future. In dealing with the substructure they focused on the gap between employers and employed and did not forecast a general rise in material wealth or the rise of mass media, particularly television, which more than anything else were to shape the cultural superstructure of the future. The media were involved in processes of persuasion as well as in the provision of information. In their own time, Engels derived his income from the substructure, and Marx, working in the magnificent new Reading Room of the British Museum, from the superstructure (and from Engels).

Theirs was a world mediated mainly through books and other forms of print, including travel books, spanning space, as well as newspapers chronicling time. During their lifetimes, the number of books on political economy, most of them setting out a different version from theirs, greatly increased, but in all European countries they were still outnumbered by books on religion, dismissed by Marx and Engels as opium for the people. Yet even in an age of events, when news was in greater demand than ever before – particularly during the Crimean War (1853–6), when special correspondents were sent out to cover it and artists and photographers to illustrate Crimean scenes – there was still a substantial market for printed texts of pulpit sermons which proclaimed the eternal. In the twent-ieth century there was to be talk of television not only as photo-journalism or as mass entertainment but as a modern version of religion.

The most creative literary form in nineteenth-century prose was the novel, a word which did not establish itself until late in the eighteenth century, when many novels had already been published. Earlier in the century, a number of writers, among them Defoe, had focused on the new ('original') and 'strange and surprising' – adjectives that formed part of the title of *Robinson Crusoe* – and the urge for novelty was later given a different twist in England (just how differ-ent has been a matter of argument between literary scholars) by Henry Fielding (1707–54), whose first writing was for the theatre, and his rival Samuel Richardson (1689–1771), a printer whose *Pamela* (1741) was written in the form of letters. There were continuities here, as everywhere, but also, as Fielding put it in *Tom Jones* (1749), which he called 'a comic epic poem in prose', a consciousness that he was entering 'a new province of Writing'.

The annual production of works of fiction in Britain, which had averaged only about seven in the years between 1700 and 1740, rose at least threefold between 1740 and 1770 and more than doubled again between 1770 and 1800. By then, the novel form, highly adaptable, attracted women writers as well as large numbers of women readers. Its full potential was still to be realized and was to spill over into television and film. In 1750, one of the great contemporaries of Fielding and Richardson, Dr Johnson (see above p. 49), who had little to say about women writers and readers, had carefully distinguished new fiction from older 'heroic romances' dominated by 'giants, knights and imaginary castles'. 'The works of fiction with which the present generation seems more particularly delighted, are such as exhibit life in its true state, diversified only by accidents that daily happen in the world'. It was Johnson who suggested that 'no man reads a book of science for pure inclination. The books that we do read with pleasure are light compositions, which contain a quick succession of events.' Johnson's opinion, however, of journalists who dealt, often inadequately, with the flow of 'real events' was low: he called them 'blackguard newspaper scribblers'.

Between 1700 and 1750 there had been big changes in the world of publish-ing, with one important new periodical, the *Gentleman's Magazine* (1731), launched by a printer and bookseller, Edward Cave ('Sylvanus Urban'), and copied less successfully by others. Johnson wrote for it. It appealed to more varied tastes than *The Spectator* (see pp. 58–9) as it combined information, including details of inventions and entertainments. Already it aired many of the issues that were to be raised later in the history of the media, including the rela-tionships between author and audience and between content and form.

Booksellers were known as 'middle men' between writers and readers before the word 'media' was used. And there was already the sense of a 'market'. As Fielding's friend and collaborator James Ralph wrote in *The Case of Authors* (1758):

> Book-making is the manufacture the Bookseller most thrives by: the rules of Trade oblige him to buy as cheap and sell as dear as possible . . . Knowing best what Assortment of Wares will best suit the Market, he gives out his Orders

accordingly; and is as absolute in prescribing the Time of Publication as in pro-
portioning the Pay . . . The sagacious Bookseller feels the Pulse of the Times, and
according to the stroke, prescribes not to cure but to flatter the Disease: as long
as the Patient continues to swallow, he continues to administer; and on the first
Symptoms of a Nausea, he changes the Dose. Hence, the Introduction of Tales,
Novels, Romances, etc.

Later in the century a distinction was to be drawn between booksellers and publishers, a distinction beginning to be apparent in Samuel Johnson's great dictionary of 1755. In the past, the word 'publish' had had a religious connotation, that
of announcing 'glad tidings of great joy to all mankind'. Now with a growing dif-
ferentiation between printers and publishers, as great as that between poets and
Grub Street 'hacks', publishing came to be associated with 'putting a book into
the world'.

Putting out more 'things' into the world, which, backed by advertising,
was to become a major preoccupation in the centuries ahead, depended in
the long run on the advance of technology, but in its initial stages in Britain
this was a matter more of extending craft skills than of utilizing scientific
knowledge. This was also the case across the Atlantic, where Benjamin Franklin
(1706–90), who loved and printed books – and played with electricity – claimed
in 1783 at the end of the American War of Independence that 'there was no
important manufacture' in which 'workmen', learning at the job, 'have not
invented some useful process which saves time and materials or improves the
workmanship'.

In eighteenth-century France there was a closer relationship between scientific theory and new technical developments, and both were extolled by government during the Revolution and under Napoleon. One post-Napoleonic French
thinker, Saint-Simon (1760–1825), attracted a group of disciples, the Saint-
Simonians, who, in a tradition that looked back to Colbert, attributed a key role
to the state in technical and economic development. 'Wherever the public interest is at stake,' wrote one of them, Michel Chevalier (1806–79), 'the government
must intervene.' Saint-Simonian influences were actively at work in France
under the regime of Napoleon's nephew, Napoleon III (1848–70).

Technology was a word introduced into the United States in 1828 – around the
time that the term 'industrial revolution' was first being used in France; and in
1832 the British contemporary, mathematician and political economist Charles
Babbage (1792–1871), published his *On the Economy of Machinery and Manufactures*, welcoming the fact that the 'labour of a hundred artificers is now performed by the operations of a single machine'. Babbage, who was familiar with
what went on in Printing House Square, invented a mechanical computer, which
he described as an 'engine'. A sign of the times, it failed to secure government
financial backing, but it was on public display, at a gallery of scientific instruments at King's College in the Strand in 1843.

Meanwhile, there were intimations that the United States – which before 1848
was without an academy or a comparable institution to the Society of Arts –
would stand out in the future as a 'republic of technology', not merely satisfying
but inventing human needs. The process was to acquire irreversible momentum,
although after 1848, as before, there were to be economic booms and slumps,

international in their scope, identified as trade cycles, which were a concomitant of capitalism for Marxists and non-Marxists alike. Some economists, notably Nikolai Kondratieff (1892–1938), have traced 'long waves' too, one associated with electricity, one a century later with the Internet (see p. 231). The Austrian economist J. A. Schumpeter (1883–1950) produced the model of an economic system propelled by pushes in technology driven by innovative entrepreneurs.

Geopolitics, the geography of state power, as well as science and economics have always influenced the way in which media technology has developed: which country came first in invention was as much a matter of contention as which individual, and in the twentieth century it mattered that Soviet Sputnik (1957) ('co-traveller') came before the USA's Telstar (1962). Co-operation in space was achieved only after the collapse of the Soviet Union. Historical oblivion has been reserved for particular rejected inventions, whatever their origin – or their inventors – which did not lead to economic results, but with every invention that did produce such results there was a change in historical perspectives. It is only now, at our present stage in media history, in the early phases of the 'age of the Web', not a new metaphor, that we can see clearly how different sequences of communications development have related to each other in different cultures. In envisaging the future – and dreaming about it – myth as well as science has often been invoked: Icarus, who tried to fly, figures as well as Prometheus, who stole fire. Marx talked of Vulcan, the stoker of furnaces.

In the seventeenth century Francis Bacon had forecast 'the opening of the door of Nature'. His vision of a Solomon's House in his *New Atlantis*, written before 1620, incorporated a 'College of Inventors' which would include 'engine houses', where 'engines and instruments for all sort of motions were prepared', two galleries for 'Inventors Past', and 'spaces or bases for Inventors to come'. Within the House 'we imitate flights of birds . . . have ships and boats for going under water and brooking of seas . . . and curious clocks', even some 'perpetual motions'. Bacon, unlike Leonardo da Vinci, left no sketches of new machines: Erasmus Darwin did. In the mid-nineteenth century, when parts of the western world were becoming a Solomon's House, the great German organic chemist Justus von Liebig (1803–73) wrote that Bacon's 'name glows like a shining star', and Charles Darwin (1809–82), following his own logic of development (if sometimes reluctantly) after publishing *Origin of Species* in 1859, asserted that he worked on 'true Baconian principles'.

The British historian Thomas Babington Macaulay (1800–59) was as eloquent as Bacon himself when, in an essay about him, published in 1837, the year Queen Victoria came to the throne, he extolled the benefits for the human race that had been achieved under the influence of discovery. As Bacon had predicted, Nature had been harnessed, bridges had been built, spanning 'great rivers and estuaries', and distance had been conquered. 'Intercourse', 'correspondence', 'despatch of business', had all been facilitated. Considered over time, Baconian philosophy had been 'a philosophy which never rests'. Its law was 'progress'.

For Herbert Spencer (1820–1903), a later writer and a sociologist who depended confidently on his own unaided thinking, progress was 'not an accident but a necessity . . . It [was] part of Nature'. And he publicized this proposition in the year 1851 when progress was made visible at a Great Exhibition of All the Nations in London's Crystal Palace. There was to be a nineteenth- and twentieth-century sequence of exhibitions, always making the most of new communications devices, widely reported in the press. Many exhibitions were international in character, as were the ideas behind them. Spencer's influence in the United States, which staged a great Centennial Exhibition in 1876, was greater than in Britain.

Spencer, however, did not deal in detail either with the world of the media or with the world of work, which changed as much as the world of things in the nineteenth century through urbanization as well as through industrialization. When large numbers of workers were concentrated under one factory roof, new forms of collective communication developed, as they did also when large numbers of people who had not known each other before were concentrated in the large new industrial centres, among which Manchester, a shock city, provided the first example. Merely through the massing together of people, it could be claimed, intelligence and energy were being communicated to the socially deprived. For one knowledgeable English observer, writing in 1823, before the word 'socialism' was coined, 'the operative workmen being thrown together in great numbers had their faculties sharpened and improved by constant communication'. Within their ranks the leaders who emerged, talking of 'union' rather than of competition, thought of themselves as leading a 'movement', a metaphor derived from transport. Another metaphor, 'highway', was to be reborn in the 1990s and applied to the 'electronic revolution' (see pp. 217, 247).

The mere presence of urban crowds roused by militant leaders or, almost as dangerously, gathering together as 'masses without leaders', might stir as much apprehension among the propertied as the language that they used, just as fear of 'the mob' had done in pre-industrial times; and in the late nineteenth century, particularly in France, psychological and social scholarship began to focus on the crowd. In 1895, Gustave Le Bon published his influential book, translated a year later as *The Crowd*, and in 1901 G. Tarde published his *L'Opinion et la Foule*, not translated into (American) English (in edited form) until 1969, as part of a volume called, with a revealing change of words, *On Communication and Social Influence*.

Whatever the language, and however great the differences between Le Bon and Tarde, the latter aware of the importance of the media, the idea of a 'mass society' had made its way into general parlance, particularly in continental European countries, by 1914. It was complemented in a cultural context in the twentieth century by the words 'elites', 'mass society' and 'mass culture'. For James Bryce, writing about politics (and what came to be called 'the mass media') in 1900, 'the mutual action and reaction of the makers or leaders of opinion upon the mass, and of the mass upon them' was 'the most curious part of the whole process by which the formation of opinion is produced'.

Another element should figure in any such calculations, particularly in the two countries best known to Bryce, Britain and the United States. That was the burgeoning of voluntary associations, some calling themselves 'philosophical', others 'statistical', some with specific policy objectives concerned with housing, health or education. Most of them produced reports and surveys, often the most effective instruments of communication in socially segregated cities, like Liverpool and Boston, London and New York. At the end of the nineteenth century French observers reckoned that a large majority of British adults belonged to an average of five or six voluntary organizations, which included trade unions and friendly societies, while the American historian A. M. Schlesinger called his country 'a nation of joiners'. Almost a century later, an American political scientist and sociologist, Robert Putnam, fearing that for various reasons this was no longer true, gave warnings about the likely consequences not only for American society, but also for democracy.

Before Marx, the acute French observer and analyst Alexis de Tocqueville (1805–59) paid tribute to 'the power of association', which is now generally regarded as the driving force behind what is called in America the 'non-profit sector'. For Tocqueville it reached the apotheosis of its development there – even before the advent of the railroad which made the opening up of the West possible. The non-profit sector was to grow in importance in the twentieth century. So, too, was the principle of 'self-regulation' as an alternative to state regulation. In this there was a sharp contrast between the United States and France.

Before the phrase 'mass market' was coined there was much talk of 'the millions' by salesmen of all kinds on both sides of the Atlantic, in the first instance by publishers of cheap books and periodicals, the most eloquent and best informed of them Charles Knight (see p. 86), one of the founders of the Society for Diffusion of Useful Knowledge, who in 1834 started a review called *The Printing Machine, a Review for the Many*, and, eleven years before that, Archibald Constable in Glasgow had contemplated a series of books that 'must and shall sell not by the thousands or tens of thousands, but by hundreds of thousands – ay by millions'. In the twentieth century a new *-ism* was to be born, 'consumerism', which through the concept of a 'consumer society' was to reshape historical perspectives as much as new technology. Paris, nineteenth-century birthplace of the retail department store, had led the way, but Liverpool, London, New York, Helsinki and Tokyo followed.

The store was, indeed, a big city phenomenon everywhere, a place to spend time in as well as money. Patterns of spending mattered increasingly. It was an American writer, Thorstein Veblen (1857–1927), who introduced the idea of 'conspicuous consumption'. This was a process, like the introduction of 'scientific management' into work, which involved psychology as much as economics or technology. So did advertising.

By the time Veblen was writing, after two or three generations of industrialization, the pace of life had speeded up even faster than Knight anticipated, and a sense of routine or system had been imposed on much economic activity. Both the factory system and the railway system had attached new significance both to discipline and to time. The seasons counted for less in towns and cities as the working day was announced by mill hooters, not by church bells:

> And at the appointed hour a bell is heard
> Of harsher import than the curfew knell;
> A local summons to unceasing toil.

PUNCH, OR THE LONDON CHARIVARI.—June 25, 1881.

"WHAT WILL HE GROW TO?"

Fig. 14 King Steam and King Coal watch anxiously the Infant Electricity. A *Punch* cartoon of 1881 pitting two technologies, old and new, in symbolic opposition. They were to co-exist. Electronics was a twentieth-century development.

The railway system depended on schedules set out in timetables. (There had been postal timetables in Italy from the late sixteenth century, canal timetables in Holland from the seventeenth century, and coach timetables in Britain and France from the eighteenth century.)

Bradshaw's complete list of British railway times first appeared in 1839, to be followed by European and American supplements; and on both sides of the Channel and of the Atlantic 'missing the train' became a metaphor, like 'on track'. Habermas was to conclude later that the world had now become 'a systems world' with a new calendar.

In the United States it had become so only through struggle, the kind of Social Darwinist struggle approved of by Spencer in the name of 'natural selection' and condemned by Arnold Toynbee (1852–83) when he popularized the term 'industrial revolution' in lectures that he delivered on the subject, published posthumously in 1884. Industry now seemed to be one piece.

Nonetheless, there was scope for a new breakthrough as Schumpeter made clear when he associated electrification with enterprise and with the breaking of routines. This must also be associated with the rise of 'experts', including a growing corps of electrical engineers who had to struggle to establish their profession alongside that of civil and mechanical engineers. Some of their first labours were to apply electricity to trams and to railways, and in time they too settled into their own routines in the twentieth century.

For all the conflicts and the breakthrough, twentieth-century language in the age of electricity could still echo the language of steam. Thus, William Shockley (1910–89), one of the American inventors of the twentieth-century electronic transistor, was still in his senior year at Hollywood High School in 1927 when he wrote in a composition:

> Our age is eminently mechanical. We travel from one place to another at relatively monstrous speeds; we speak to each other over great distances, and we fight our enemies with amazing efficiency – all by the aid of mechanical contrivances.

Shockley did not then mention anything electrical or anything to do with the media, although in 1925 he had constructed a crystal set to listen to radio. In 1956, however, having moved on to the California Institute of Technology, where he studied quantum mechanics, he was to share a Nobel prize for Physics. When the miniaturization of electric circuits was beginning to transform all aspects of technology, he was not alone in forecasting a new radical breakthrough. Yet demand for transistors was slow to build up and it was only after the advent of the integrated circuit that it began to rise sharply (see p. 223). The first commercial customers were interested in small portable radios, and it was these, not the electronic devices that they incorporated, which were called transistors.

5 Processes and Patterns

This chapter examines one-by-one the story of the various new communications devices which prepared the way, long before the transistor, for what has been called with only a touch of exaggeration 'the media revolution of the twentieth century'. Railways come first because they set the pattern for much else to follow in technology, economics, politics and management, and, not least, in the world of the imagination. It was no accident that in 2000, in the corridors outside the office headquarters of Novel, a late twentieth-century hi-tech company in Silicon Valley, there were paintings of great American locomotives. A British traveller to the United States, writing in 1851, had commented on 'the natural affinity between Yankee keep-moving nature and a locomotive engine . . . Whatever the cause, it is certain that the "humans" seem to treat the "engine", as they call it, more like a familiar friend than as the dangerous and desperate thing it really is.'

Railways

Not surprisingly, the title of Albro Martin's study of American railroads (a word preferred there to 'railways') was *Railroads Triumphant* (1992). In it he described how the railroad idea took hold in America with remarkable speed; how poorly built, if cheaply, the first American railroads were until after the Civil War; and how the great age of railroad-building followed between 1868 and the end of the century. There were around 35,000 miles of track in 1865: by the mid-1870s there were nearly 200,000.

The last decades of the century witnessed impressive industrialization, while fortunes were being made by railroad tycoons and a popular railroad folklore was being created. Again there was always a view from above and a view from below, even in a country where everyone was a citizen and no one a subject. 'There are a briskness of step and a precision of speech about the people of a railway creation that you never find in a town that is only accessible to a stage driver', wrote Benjamin Taylor in his book *The World on Wheels* in 1874. 'The locomotive is an accomplished educator. It teaches everybody that virtue . . . we call punctuality. It waits for nobody. It demonstrates what a useful creature a minute is in the economy of things.' Building railroads demonstrated, too, both the problems in creating a system – junctions, signals, gauges, places for travellers to stay (not forgetting the danger of ambushes) – and the accompanying excitement in America of unifying a continent, a triumph recorded both in folklore and in the press.

The most dramatic moment in the story of American railroads was the hammering of a golden spike into the ground on the spot where two locomotives met, one arriving from the east, the other from the west, on 10 May 1869. This symbolic ceremony marking the completion of the first transcontinental railroad was commemorated in a photograph by A. J. Russell, which was widely circulated around the United States as a wood engraving a month after the event. The news had been circulated immediately by telegraph: a wire attached to the golden spike made it possible for distant crowds to hear every stroke of the hammer. There were spontaneous celebrations in San Francisco and Chicago. Church bells rang, and the mayors of San Francisco and New York exchanged telegrams.

Chicago, one of America's youngest cities, was to become the world's largest railroad centre. One great locomotive, the Exposition Flyer, was to carry thousands of people there in 1893 for the huge Columbian Exhibition, a celebration of Columbus's 'discovery of America' 401 years before. Many of them travelled from small towns, large numbers of which had come into existence (also with attendant ceremony) as a result of the arrival of the railroad. The American poet Walt Whitman (1819–92), excited by the basic technology, called the railroad the realization of Columbus's dreams, 'the marriage of continents, climates and oceans'.

A British writer had already written eight years earlier (in *Macmillan's Magazine*, May–October 1861) of the opening up of the world not only to migrants but to tourists – and it was they who realized most clearly that the world was small, not huge. 'We are now infinitely more familiar than our forefathers were' with the 'idea of the limited dimensions of the Earth, a tiny ball, axled eight thousand miles.' There were also psychological dimensions: 'a well-known use of travel consists in the self-reliance, and the general inventiveness which it develops'. Yet fascination with foreign places could be shared at a distance. Travel books and novels relating to foreign countries had a wide circulation – both before and after improvements in physical transportation.

Another writer on the European side of the Atlantic claimed in January 1878, in Britain's *Quarterly Review*, that 'our railways may be said to mark the furthest point which the advance of European civilization has reached':

> They have done more than anything achieved by former generations to modify the influence of time and space. Common and familiar instruments of our business and pleasure . . . they may be described, with literal truth, as the most striking manifestations of the power of man over the material order of the universe. The mightiest monuments of classical or pre-classical times are but feeble triumphs of human skill beside the work of the railway engineer, who has covered the face of the earth with iron roads, spanning valleys and piercing mountains, and traversed by fiery steeds fleeter than ever sped through poetic dream.

Such language, infused with metaphor, was not uncommon in the nineteenth century, early, middle or late: it flourished alongside the statistical tables and a huge pictorial collection of prints and paintings dealing with the medium of railway transport, to be followed by posters and films. There was music, too, throughout the process – and poetry. Whitman described the 'fierce-throated' locomotive as 'the type of modern, the pulse of the continent', and in every continent the ancient metaphor of the journey took new forms. One widely circulated European engraving showed a spiritual railway to heaven:

> From Earth to Heaven the line extends
> To life eternal where it ends.

You might take the wrong track at a junction and you could easily be shunted off the railway. This was a new version of John Bunyan's *Pilgrim's Progress*.

It was in Europe that there developed a 'railway literature' – Bunyan was one of the chosen authors. The publishers W. H. Routledge introduced a shilling series of reprinted fiction called 'The Railway Library' in 1849. Two years later, W. H. Smith secured a monopoly of bookstalls on the London and North-Western Railway, with other lines to follow. Cheap German Tauschnitz editions of 'the best in literature', well known to travellers, were not on sale there or anywhere else in Britain, but were easily obtainable at railway stations in Switzerland, Italy or Spain as well as Germany. Widely used guide books, particularly those of Karl Baedecker (1801–59), were carried around by the world's first 'tourists', many of whose other needs were met by Thomas Cook (1808–92), British travel entrepreneur.

For British contemporaries, who regarded railway communication as the triumph of the steam age, 'we who lived before railways and survive out of the ancient world', as the novelist W. M. Thackeray put it, 'are like Father Noah and his family out of the Ark'. Another novelist, Charles Dickens, was ambivalent in his reactions. He described railways as 'the power that forced itself upon its iron way', 'defiant of old paths and roads, piercing through the heart of every obstacle', and in one of his finest novels, *Dombey and Son* (1848), he chose to employ metaphors of death as well as of progress. This novel stands out in the literature of communications as J. M. W. Turner's painting *Rain, Steam and Speed* stands out in the realm of art, with French Impressionists adding memorably to the international collection of paintings of locomotives and stations later in the century.

Britain led the way in railway development, with only forty years separating Watt's 'conversion of the steam engine from a scientific toy to a veritable implement of human service'. The opening of the railway line between Liverpool and Manchester in 1830 (attended by disaster – the death by accident of an important minister, William Huskisson) was as much acclaimed as the golden spike ceremony in America by a later generation. The immediate comment of a Scottish newspaper on the event was that it 'established principles which will give a greater impulse to civilization than it has ever received from any single cause since the Press first opened the gates of knowledge to the human species at large'.

Railway development in an age of 'carboniferous capitalism' had not only introduced passengers to unprecedented speed, but had generated a huge demand for coal and iron, lowered business costs, opened up markets, stimulated employment in many industries, and created new and sometimes damaged old communities. The maps of Britain and the United States looked different (very different in the 1870s) from what they had been half a century before. In Britain, London was at the point of convergence – no railway 'main line' passed across it – and in the provinces, apart from new railway towns like Crewe and Swindon, it was for the most part existing communities that were linked together. In the

United States, entirely new communities, which grew quickly, were brought into existence. The scale of enterprise was continental rather than national.

The economics of development was never straightforward. Eager buyers of railway shares in the Britain of the 1840s learned bitter lessons about the difference between investment and speculation before such shares became part of settled mid-Victorian portfolios. There were years of mania and there were years of crisis. Risk was never easy to ascertain. The career of George Hudson (1800–71), the 'railway king', with his headquarters in York, collapsed in ruins in 1849: Dickens called him 'The Great Humbug'. There were certainly far more railway plans than railway lines or railway stations and, whatever the economics, not all engineering problems could be foreseen. There was an obvious need for regulation in the public interest as more and more lines were built, but this was not always forthcoming. There was a battle in Britain about the width of gauges: as late as 1865 there were no fewer than thirty places in Britain where passengers had to change trains for this reason. The Great Western Railway, with a broad gauge, favoured by Isambard Kingdom Brunel (1806–59), builder of much besides railways, did not convert fully to what became the standard gauge until 1892, more than thirty years after his death.

By then, many records had been broken on the Great Western, one of a small bevy of companies that survived into the twentieth century. From the start there had been an incentive for business amalgamation, as there was to be in twentieth-century communications media, but in 1844 there were no fewer than 104 separate companies. As total mileage tripled between 1850 and 1900, when there were almost 19,000 miles of track, four main groups emerged, each with its own territory, its own organization and its own statistical records relating to speed as much as to numbers of passengers carried. On the Great Western, Daniel Gooch's Actaeon did the journey from London's Paddington Station to Exeter non-stop in 1844, an achievement comparable to that of the most famous twentieth-century British locomotive, the Flying Scotsman, belonging to the London and North Eastern Railway – No. 447 – which in 1934 recorded 100 miles per hour on the line from London to Edinburgh.

Every country, like every railway company, has its own history with its own landmark dates. By 1845 there were already nine countries in Europe with railways (with Britain having exported a large proportion both of the iron and of the locomotives); in 1855 there were fourteen. Outside Europe, where Britain often secured railway business through Thomas Brassey (1805–70), the greatest nineteenth-century contractor, there were railways in five continents by 1855. Brassey and his partners often took their labour with them. Thus, when they were constructing railways in Australia in the early 1860s, they organized the transport of two thousand experienced 'navvies' from England and Scotland. The word 'navvies' was inherited from the canal age, and like the skilled engineers they faced many risks.

The story of Indian railways – the creation of British engineers – is unique. Work on the first two lines did not begin until 1850, and it was not until 1853 that the first locomotive in India, the Lord Falkland, pulled a train from Bombay to Thana, a distance of less than twenty-five miles. Yet as early as 1844, at the height of the British railway mania, one of the world's railway visionaries, Rowland

McDonald Stephenson, had prepared a scheme for linking by rail Bombay, Calcutta, Madras and Delhi; in his simple words, free from rhetoric:

> The first consideration is as a military measure for the better security with less outlay, of the entire territory [then controlled by the East India Company], the second is a commercial point of view, in which the chief object is to provide the means of conveyance from the interior to the nearest shipping ports of the rich and varied productions of the country, and to transmit back manufactured goods of Great Britain, salt, etc. in exchange.

This line of argument appealed to the Marquis of Dalhousie, the Governor-General of India, who wrote a landmark minute on railways to the Directors of the East India Company a few days after the line from Bombay to Thana was opened. 'The commercial and social advantages which India would derive from their establishment' were, he 'truly believed', 'beyond all present calculation'.

What neither Dalhousie nor the railway engineers ever fully anticipated was the popularity of railways to Indians. As early as 1855, an English-language newspaper, *Friend of India*, could observe in the socially stratified language of the period that 'the fondness for travelling by rail' had become 'almost a national passion among the lower orders' and that thereby it was 'producing a social change in the habits of general society far more deep and extensive than any that has been created by the political revolutions of the last twenty centuries'. By 1900, India had more than 25,000 miles of track, some of the most costly to build in the world, as against Britain's 18,000, France's 22,500, Germany's 30,000, Russia's 23,000, Canada's 17,500 and the United States's huge 260,000 miles.

In every country there were railway accidents, some horrifying, which became one of the staples of periodicals and of newspapers (and later of radio and television). Disasters were also depicted pictorially in engravings, some of them melodramatic. In Roman Catholic countries, like Spain and Mexico, popular *ex voto* art in the last decades of the nineteenth century portrayed people saved from railway disasters just in time by angelic or divine intervention.

Ships

The story of steamships fascinated contemporaries as much as the story of railways. It was appropriate, therefore, that a British historian of shipping, A. Fraser MacDonald, chose, as the title of his 1893 book on the subject, *Our Ocean Railways*. Between 1776 and 1940 no fewer than thirty million immigrants from Europe reached the favourite destination, the United States, some political refugees, some ambitious young seekers after fortune, some both. The Statue of Liberty (1886) was designed by a Frenchman, Frédéric Auguste Bartholdi, with a substantial contribution to the cost of its pedestal being collected from readers of a popular and aptly named American newspaper, *The World*.

The wearing journey across the Atlantic had been greatly speeded up by steam power. Americans had been prominent in developing steam for water transport, taking advantage of their many lakes and rivers as sources of water power; and already, before Independence, in 1763, William Henry of Pennsylvania had constructed a steam engine in advance of Watt, having visited England three years

Fig. 15 *The Laying of the Transatlantic Cable*, 1865. The *Great Eastern* (22,500 tons) was the only ship able to carry it. The task was not completed until July 1866.

before. In 1785, after Independence, John Fitch, a Connecticut mechanic, tried out a boat with paddle wheels, 'a boat that carried fire', which he patented within the following two years. In 1788, James Rumsey is said to have propelled a steam boat up the River Potomac, and he secured a patent in France three years later. Robert Fulton, who had stayed in Europe, both in Britain (including Scotland) and France, used a Watt engine when in 1807 he constructed the *Clermont*, which carried passengers on pleasure trips along the Hudson River. The first steamer to make an ocean voyage was Colonel John Stevens's *Phoenix*, which steamed thirteen miles from Hoboken to Philadelphia in 1809. The *Savannah* crossed the Atlantic ten years later.

It was not until 1839 that the British ship *Sirius* completed a transatlantic voyage entirely by steam – in eighteen days and ten hours. A few hours later, the *Great Western*, specially constructed for the journey, arrived in New York from Bristol in fifteen days and fifteen hours. Four years after that, Isambard Kingdom Brunel's *Great Britain*, the first large iron ship to have a screw propeller, was launched by Prince Albert in Bristol and did the journey in fourteen days and twenty-one hours. Brunel's *Great Eastern* received the most lavish press publicity of all when it crossed the Atlantic in 1865, having laid the first transatlantic cable. By then, Samuel Cunard, born in Canada in 1787, had established the British and North American Packet Company with a fleet of five sister ships, on the first of which, the *Britannic*, Charles Dickens travelled in 1843.

The peak year for the building of new sailing ships in Britain was 1864, and even after that steam did not completely supplant sail. Nor was the switch from sail to steam the only significant development. When the first steel ship, the *Serbia*, took to the seas in 1881, it was also the first ship to be fitted with electric light. The turbine, invented in Britain, was a major technological change. Meanwhile, canals which linked oceans, the Suez and the Panama, shortened travel times. The former, opened with pomp (and the music of Verdi's opera, *Aida*) in 1869, was the dream of a Frenchman, de Lesseps, who believed, like St Simon, one of the people who inspired him, that between them industry and communications could transform history. For practical reasons, many British businessmen shared this belief, and Thomas Cook was present at the opening of the canal. A less well-known date in its history was 1887, when ships passing through the canal were for the first time furnished with electric headlights to allow travel by night. This cut a long journey by sixteen hours.

During the 1880s there was ample evidence of a dramatic new burst of invention – with steam power giving way to electricity, and with 'the media' at the centre of the activity. American streets began to be lit by electricity before American homes were, and in New York harbour 'the illumined face of the Statue of Liberty now shone out upon the dark waste of waters'. Electricity as spectacle preceded the introduction of electric plugs. Nonetheless, it was during this decade and the next that there was the first talk of a future 'push-button' society. The concept of time was now being transformed even more drastically than it had been in the late eighteenth and earlier nineteenth centuries when it was standardized in time zones. Local time differences disappeared, although not all at once or everywhere.

In 1884, representatives of twenty-five countries met in Washington and, after considerable debate, a system was adopted based on Greenwich as the prime meridian. Already Britain, Sweden, Canada and the United States had adopted it. France, objecting to the choice of a British meridian, did not adopt it until 1919, although its government fully accepted the idea of standard time. At an International Conference on Time held in Paris in 1912 the French pressed for accurate time signals to be transmitted around the world. This time, France, where Marcel Proust was exploring in words the mysteries of time, was chosen as the site, and the first signals were transmitted from the Eiffel Tower on 1 July 1913.

The Mail

Railways and ships carried not only people and goods across time zones, but also letters – an indispensable mode of communication, both national and international. By the end of the century they also carried postcards. The first Post Office postcards, 'open post sheets', had been introduced in Austria in 1869, and in Germany and Britain in 1870. They raised interesting issues, such as privacy, that were relevant to other media of communication: 'Why write private information on an open piece of cardboard that might be read by half a dozen persons before it reached its destination?' It did not much matter whether they read it or not, particularly after picture postcards were introduced during the following decade, with France, Germany and Switzerland leading the way. What was written on them became increasingly standardized.

In 1900 the English journalist G. R. Sims described in *The Referee* how at the top of a mountain in Switzerland, a favourite tourist country, 'directly we arrived at the summit, everybody made a rush for the hotel and fought for the postcards. Five minutes afterwards, everybody was writing for dear life. I believe that the entire party had come up, not for the sake of the experience or the scenery, but to write postcards and to write them on the summit.'

The speeding up of the mail had preceded the introduction in Britain in 1840 of the world's first adhesive, perforated postage stamp, an attractive art object bearing the young Queen Victoria's head, and remarkably soon to become a 'collectible'. The adhesive postage stamp itself was an important nineteenth-century invention, but the word 'stamp' was not new, nor, of course, particularly in the United States, was the idea of a stamp tax. Nonetheless, the stamp as an object was pre-paid, as was the cheap penny postal rate, and uniform over the whole country, wherever the destination. A by-product was the ready gummed envelope.

The poet Coleridge's son Hartley hailed the penny post as an invention beneficial to all:

> . . . the best of Ministerial measures
> That wings the feathers of young Cupid's wings
> Father and mother, sister, brother, son
> Husband and wife, pronounce one benison.

This, however, was an idealized version of what had happened. Illiteracy rates, though falling between 1840 and 1870, were still high, and intermediaries had to be employed by many of the poor both to write outgoing letters and to read incoming ones. The political leader Richard Cobden welcomed the penny post not only on political grounds – it made it possible to mobilize opinion in favour of free trade – but on moral grounds too. There was now a new spur to become literate.

The British postal system developed before the national educational system was devised. Rowland Hill (1795–1879), creator of the system and a passionate advocate of popular education, called the Post Office a 'powerful engine of civilization', and for his brother Matthew, writing in 1862, 'the amount of [Post Office] correspondence will measure with some approach towards accuracy the height which a public has reached in true civilization. As when, for instance, we find that the town of Manchester equals in its number of letters the empire of all the Russians, both in Europe and in Asia we obtain a means of estimating the relative degrees of British and Russian civilization.' Other commentators drew the same conclusion when making comparisons with the past rather than looking sideways and making comparisons with other continents.

Both kinds of comparison were made by backbench Conservative MP Henniker Heaton thirty-five years later at the time of Queen Victoria's diamond jubilee, when all the technical and social achievements of the nineteenth century were under review, particularly in the press. An enthusiastic spokesman for an imperial penny post, Heaton claimed, mainly with private letters in mind, that when the Queen had come to the throne in 1837, 'the masses were almost as restricted to oral communication and local commerce as their ancestors were under the Stuarts, or as the Turks are under Abdul Hamid'. Different parts of the country were each absorbed in their own interests, knowing no more of other communities than 'one Russian village knows of another a hundred miles away. The gentry and professional men in the rural districts, and the citizens of the great towns, maintained sufficient intercommunication; but while the more elevated points were then ringed with light, darkness reigned below.'

The contrasting images of darkness and light belonged to the new age of electricity, yet the two had been contrasted sharply in the eighteenth century by Enlightenment writers, and it was then that the post first began to be significantly speeded up. The language of the masses which Heaton used belonged firmly to the nineteenth century, however, to some extent replacing the language of 'class', a word associated with industrialization. Yet expectations, often expressed in sentimental language, that a penny post would greatly increase the volume of private working-class correspondence were not realized in the first decade of its implementation. It was the middle classes who benefited most from the new flat rate of postage, and the continued speeding up of the post was achieved in response to business demands, not to the demands of the 'masses'. Mid-Victorian articles or paintings and engravings of the peak hour at London's much publicized General Post Office in St Martin's Le Grand identified plainly just what 'business' meant at that time: they could usefully be compared with paintings and engravings of the great railway stations. Nearly half of London's 161 million letters in 1863 came from within the city and were delivered within its inner area twelve times a day.

When Heaton urged the introduction of an imperial penny post in 1890, he found other arguments besides business benefit. It would not only stimulate trade, he maintained, but would symbolize both 'imperial unity' and 'Anglo-Saxon brotherhood'. There were Americans, notably Elihu Burritt (1810–79), 'the learned blacksmith' who, like Heaton, wanted a cheap universal post in the interest of universal brotherhood. It was New Zealand, however, not the United States that was the first country to take action – in 1901, the year Queen Victoria died.

The United States did not issue its first postal stamps until 1853, the year when the rail link between New York and Chicago was being completed, but from the start it was a cheap post, and the number of items it carried doubled to 7.4 billion between 1886 and 1901. One of the direct consequences was a growth in mail-order retail business, although some of the products purchased were carried by private firms, the best-known of which was Wells Fargo. The American Post Office, staffed through patronage, did not carry the authority of Europe's Post Offices, which were required by government, or took it upon themselves, to determine national policies relating to railways, telegraphs, telephones and later what came to be called 'telecommunications' as well as postal services.

A general postal union, the Union Postale Universelle, was founded in 1874 with Britain as a founder member: one British company, De La Rue, was then producing stamps for many different countries in the world, and one of the rules of the Union was standardization of the colours of stamps. Nine years earlier, an International Telegraphic Convention had been signed in Paris by twenty countries, which then formed the International Telegraph Union: Britain was not invited at this time because its telegraph service was then in the hands of private companies. One of the delegations represented in Paris – that from Turkey – had to travel part of the way to Paris on horseback.

A hundred years later, when the Union celebrated its centenary – its head-quarters had been set up in Berne in Switzerland in 1868 – the issues that it was dealing with as an intergovernmental organization were of a radically different kind: two years before, it had organized the world's first Conference on Space Communications. The first International Radiotelegraph Convention had been held in Berlin in 1906, and in 1932 at a conference in Madrid, dealing with radio wavebands, a new name was adopted, the International Telecommunications Union. In 1947, following two further conferences in Atlantic City, it became a specialized agency of the United Nations.

Telegraphs

Telegraphy was the first great electrical breakthrough, described in 1889 by Britain's Prime Minister, the Marquess of Salisbury, as 'a strange and fascinating discovery' which had had a direct influence on the 'moral and intellectual nature and action of mankind'. It had 'assembled all mankind upon one great plane, whence they can see [*sic*] everything that is done and hear everything that is said and judge of every policy that is pursued at the very moment when these events take place'.

Whether 'all mankind' was placed in that position was not obvious, but it was certainly obvious that politicians now had at their disposal a powerful new instrument. They praised it, however, in general terms. Thus Dalhousie, on leaving India in 1856, had composed a final minute for the Governors of the East India Company, referring to 'Uniform Post' and 'Electric Telegraph' along with railways as 'three great engines of social improvement, which the sagacity and science of recent times had previously given [he might have said 'restricted'] to the Western Nations'. Dalhousie was speaking for many people in power. Rail-ways – carrying people, goods, newspapers and books – and telegraphs – the first nineteenth-century electrical invention to carry 'messages', public and private – were directly related to each other in his and their minds.

If, with hindsight, railways, followed by bicycles, automobiles and aeroplanes, seem to belong to the history of transportation, and telegraphy, followed by tele-phony, radio and television, seem to belong to the history of the media, any such separation is artificial. The development of the telegraph was closely associated with the development of railways – instantaneous signalling methods were nec-essary for safety reasons on single tracks – although there were some telegraph wires that followed not railways but canals. Babbage looked for older associa-tions when he suggested that every church steeple should be used as a telegraph pole. There were classical allusions too. The fall of Troy, it was stated, had been signalled to Argos.

In one country – Australia – the telegraph was more important than the railway. In 1830, the total population, held back by 'the tyranny of distance' (see p. 23), numbered no more than 70,000, and was dependent on the postal service, 'a people's service', costly but never questioned. Official communication over short distances was by semaphore, an optical mechanical system, until the gold rush of the 1850s, when the opening of the first telegraph line between Melbourne and Port Melbourne on 8 March 1854 preceded by six months the opening of the first railway line between the two places: for several years this was the only profitable railway line in Australia. The subsequent story of the telegraph has been told in gripping fashion by Ann Moyal in her *Clear Across Australia, a History of Telecommunications* (1984). By contrast, the story of railways built by government was patchy – and bedevilled by differences of gauge – although mileage increased from 1,600 to 10,000 between 1875 and 1890. Peak mileage was to reach 26,000 in the twentieth century.

The coming of long-distance links by cable was obviously of enormous importance to Australia and New Zealand. They were forged slowly, as cable links by land and sea crossed Europe and Asia, arriving in the Australian port of Darwin via the Indonesian archipelago in 1872. Even then, they had to make their way across central Australia, where lonely telegraph operators might live more than a hundred miles from their nearest neighbours. At first the service was costly, but by the 1880s costs had fallen significantly. It was only with telephony that private benefits began fully to accrue.

The laying of submarine ocean cables of telegraph wire, a huge, but difficult, achievement, would have been impossible without the improvement and expansion of ocean steam transport, with global commerce acting as the main spur. The technical achievement itself rightly impressed contemporaries, and when Charles Bright, who laid the first transatlantic cable in 1858 (although it did not work), was given a knighthood at the age of twenty-six, *The Times* described the cable as 'the greatest discovery since that of Columbus, a vast enlargement . . . given to the sphere of human activity'. For Dickens, 'in an age of express trains, painless operations, crystal palaces . . . and a hundred curiosities such as our grandfathers and grandmothers never dreamt about', the telegraph was 'of all our modern wonders the most wonderful'.

From the start, the social and economic effects of the telegraph were regarded in Britain as being as impressive as the technical achievement itself. It was due to the enterprise of the first private company, the Electric Telegraph Company, a writer in the *Edinburgh Review* suggested in January 1869, that the telegraph, 'to the ordinary world little more than a philosophical curiosity', was converted into 'an empire of general intercommunication'. The writer was analysing and assessing the various economic and social results of telegraphic development, not all of them foreseen, in the year after Parliament, under Disraeli's Conservative government, had passed the Telegraph Act of 1868, which transferred the management of the telegraph system from private companies to the Post Office.

Like canals, railways and ocean highways, the telegraph linked national and international markets, including stock exchanges and commodity markets (cotton, corn and fish, for example). It also speeded up the transmission of information, public and private, local, regional, national and imperial, and this in the long run stood out as its most significant outcome. Distance was conquered as information relating to government, business, family affairs, the weather, and natural and manmade disasters was transmitted, much of it in the form of news. Agencies were brought into existence to carry news across the frontiers, the first of them the Agence Havas, founded in Paris in 1835. The Reuter Telegram

Company, founded in London in 1851 by Baron Julius Reuter, who had arrived there from Germany, was always known simply as Reuters. It was Julius who in 1859 supplied news of Napoleon III's battles in Italy and the text of the Emperor's twenty short despatches that he sent each day to the front. There was no American news agency until 1892 when Associated Press (AP), known at first as the Associated Press of Illinois, was launched.

The main inventions in telegraphy, as in many other fields, were arrived at independently and in different countries in a cumulative process which did not have one single inventor. Nor was one single scientist associated with the theory of electromagnetism, although in France, André Marie Ampère (1775–1836), who extended the work of the Dane Hans Christian Oersted (1775–1851) gave his name to the unit in the current-carrying element in the electro-circuit. In Britain, James Clerk Maxwell (1831–74) formulated in 1864 the basic mathematical equations relating to what came to be called the electro-magnetic field.

In Britain the first successful, if unlikely, partners in telegraphy were William Fothergill Cooke and Charles Wheatstone, and it was with them that the invention of the telegraph was to be particularly associated. Their joint patent of 1837 bore the magnificent description 'Improvements in Giving Signals and Sounding Alarms in Distant Places by means of Electric Currents transmitted through Metallic Circuits'. Cooke himself used less formidable language when he claimed that the telegraph would enable the railway line to become a 'highway', the image to be brought back to life in the United States in the early 1990s. The image, then fresh, appealed immediately in 1842 to the *Railway Times*.

In the United States it was Samuel Morse (1791–1872), artist by training, son of a Yale-educated minister, who devised a dots and dashes code, which could be read at forty words a minute and came to be used universally in telegraphic transmission. The basic instruments Morse operators used were a key, a relay and sounder, a register, a battery and a circuit change. Meanwhile, far away in a different continent, William B. O'Shaughnessy, an assistant surgeon in the Indian Army and a telegraph enthusiast, was carrying out telegraphic experiments in Calcutta, hanging iron wire on trees in the early 1840s, although the first telegraph line between Calcutta and Bombay was not to be completed until 1854.

There were international contacts from the start. Cooke had listened to Professor Muncke lecturing on telegraphy at Heidelberg University and had seen a demonstration of a needle telegraph devised by a Russian diplomat, Baron Pawel Schilling. Morse had addressed the Académie des Sciences in Paris in 1838 and, having been forestalled by Cooke and Wheatstone's telegraph patents in London, had patented his own device in Paris in 1838 two years before patenting it in the United States, where a new Patent Law had been passed in 1836 and a new Patent Office established. A young Canadian of Irish extraction, Samuel Walker McGovan, who introduced telegraphy to Australia, had worked with Morse and his colleague Ezra Cornell, inventor of the first telegraph insulators. The first long-distance message sent in 1872, after Australia had been connected to Europe and Asia via Darwin, was 'Advance Australia', although it ended with the hope that the 'submarine cable connection would long speak words of peace'.

The very first telegraphic message had been British. It passed between Cooke and Wheatstone – a physicist who was also interested in music and invented a concertina – who had originally worked independently, viewing each other with some suspicion. Using a needle system, Cooke telegraphed Wheatstone from Camden Town station one week after the formal opening of the London and Birmingham Railway in 1837, and Wheatstone replied at once from a dingy room, lit only by a candle, at Euston station, having experienced what he called in his own words 'a tumultuous sensation' such as he had never felt before: 'all alone in the still room, I felt all the magnitude of the invention 'pronounced to be practicable beyond cavil or dispute.' Such recollections of first sensations and of first conversations were to become part of the folklore of the media. The telephone, radio, television and the Internet were to provide others. Morse's first message was 'What hath God wrought?'

In a military context – always critical in the history of telecommunications – telegraphy affected both planning and operations on land as well as at sea, just as semaphore telegraphy had done during the revolutionary and Napoleonic Wars. It was organized through 'chains of command' and 'general' and 'special' orders. The first time it was used significantly on an operational scale was during the Crimean War when a 340-mile cable was laid across the Black Sea. Its value was demonstrated even more strikingly during the American Civil War when more than 15,000 miles of telegraph line were in use and more than a thousand operators worked the system. By then, Reuters were telegraphing across the Atlantic details of battles and of much else. In 1889 they were to start a 'Special India and China Service', and thereafter for almost a century India, in the words of Reuters' historian, Donald Read, was 'destined to play a central part in the Reuter Empire within the British Empire', an empire which came to depend on an 'All-Red Line' of telegraphy. There were also to be close links with Japan.

The first phase of telegraph development in Britain had come to an end in 1846 with the creation of the Electric Telegraph Company, five years before the announcement that a cable from London to Paris had been completed. It was made just after Queen Victoria, enthusiastic about the new system as she was about most inventions, but not yet Empress of India, had declared the Great Exhibition closed. Two years after that, the Electric Telegraph Company merged with its rival, the English and Irish Magnetic Telegraphic Company, to form the new Magnetic, with imposing offices not far from the Bank of England (see p. 114).

As telegraphic business expanded, key questions were continually raised about the respective roles of private and public enterprise, of state and market. 'Is not telegraphic communication as much a function of Government as the conveyance of letters?' the *Quarterly Review* asked in 1854, when no fewer than 120 provincial newspapers, then at the height of their influence, were receiving columns of parliamentary news by telegraph. Comparisons were drawn with other countries where the system was state-controlled, like Switzerland, where for every 100,000 people there were 6.6 telegraph offices as against 5.6 in Britain.

In the United States, the state had been involved at first, when Morse secured public funds to build an experimental Washington to Baltimore overhead line: its role thereafter was very different from its role in Europe. The Post Office department might state firmly that 'an instrument so powerful for good and evil' could not 'with safety be left in the hands of private individuals uncontrolled by law', but it was never likely to provide continuing adequate investment. At first private investment was inadequate too, and the subsequent decision to hand the telegraph to business was crucial in the history of United States communication. As a result of it, a massive corporate enterprise, Western Union, which acquired that name in 1854, was to take shape. (See p. 115.)

In France, state control of communications had been deemed essential from the start for different reasons, but because semaphore devised by the Chappe brothers had been introduced successfully during the Revolution (see p. 184) – and there were more than three thousand miles of semaphore lines in operation during the 1840s, all operated by the Ministry of War – progress in electrical telegraphy was slow. A law of 1837 laid down that there should be a continuing government monopoly in distance communications, and ten years later the French Minister of the Interior reiterated firmly that telegraphy should be an instrument of policy, not of commerce. Whatever the subsequent constitutional regime in France, his successors agreed. Very similar attitudes towards *l'espace nationale* were to characterize twentieth-century French policy in relation to radio and telecommunications.

In the pre-1848 European regimes, telegraphy arrived before revolution, and it was inevitable that in the Habsburg Empire Metternich, given his anti-liberal policies, would urge that the telegraph should be a government monopoly, closed to the public, as was the case in Prussia. It remained so, too, after the 1848 revolutions which overthrew him, although when telephony was introduced later in the nineteenth century there were to be surprising developments in Hungary (see p. 147). In Russia, Nicholas I connected St Petersburg to Warsaw and on to the German border by semaphore, and a branch line from St Petersburg to Moscow was opened, with towers, each manned by six men, five to six miles apart. Nicholas banned the circulation of any information concerning electrical telegraphy on the grounds that it would be subversive, even though a Russian nobleman, Baron Schilling, had devised a system using a battery-powered galvanometer and a binary code.

Before and after 1848, one country – Belgium – where the telegraphy lines, like the railways, were state built, seemed to be setting an example. Its lines were said in 1869 to have been 'excellently planned and cheaply constructed', so that as a consequence the tariffs charged, always a matter of concern in Britain, were comparatively low. At that date the stock market accounted for half the traffic and 'family affairs' for 13 per cent. By contrast, the press accounted for only 4 per cent and government for 2 per cent.

Inside the British Post Office, one ambitious official, Frank Scudamore, who had already created a Post Office Savings Bank, was strongly of the opinion that the Post Office should take over the telegraph companies, and by the Telegraph Act of 1868 it duly purchased them, along with the telegraphic business of the railway companies. The measure, supported by the Liberal politician W. E. Gladstone (1809–98), then in opposition, who was soon to become Prime Minister, and by Chambers of Commerce and the press, was fiercely, but unsuccessfully, opposed by the railway and telegraph companies, closely linked through interlocking directorships, an interesting early example of concentration of media control.

The railway companies were a major interest in Parliament also, straddling both sides of the House and showing their power as early as the 1840s, when a young Gladstone, then President of the Board of Trade, was forced to withdraw a clause in his 1844 Railway Regulation Bill, giving government authority to buy up (i.e. nationalize) railways that had started operating after the Bill became law. The Railway Regulation Act, as finally passed, prescribed that all future railway companies should provide third-class accommodation on at least one train a day travelling in each direction. These so-called 'parliamentary trains' (a hybrid too) were to survive deep into the twentieth century.

In 1868, a financial deal was reached with the telegraph companies before the Post Office took them over. Critics had warned in vain of the likely 'stagnation and dreary routine inseparable from official regulations' that would follow nationalization, but the government pledged that telegraphs were now to be treated like postal services and that a uniform rate would be introduced for a twenty-word telegraphic message irrespective of distance. In 1844 there had been no such railway regulation after the nationalization clause had been withdrawn.

The Post Office monopoly was to run into financial problems in the nineteenth century, although the number of messages transmitted rose from 6.5 million just after the Act had been passed to 26.5 million ten years later, a huge increase in comparison with other European countries and, indeed, with the United States. Yet more than comparative statistics were involved, for as Post Office losses on unremunerative traffic, described by critics as a 'subsidy', increased with the number of messages transmitted, there was bound to be parliamentary and public criticism which raised other media issues also. The press, which enjoyed the benefit of what to the Post Office were unremunerative rates, could defend them on the grounds that they stimulated interest in the news (see p. 157). It, too, constituted an interest.

After the move to public ownership, many of the directors of the old private telegraph companies, with compensation money in their pockets, acquired holdings in telegraph companies dealing in overseas business, and a large new merger, the Eastern Telegraph Company, was founded in 1872, which for almost a quarter of a century paid dividends of between 6.5 and 10 per cent. It was one of several concerns which at the end of the century buttressed British dominance in the international cable business.

There was an acknowledged imperial interest in this, for, as an official committee put it in 1902, it was 'desirable that every important colony or naval base should possess one cable to this country which touches on British territory or on the territory of some friendly neutral'. Commercial incentives were said to come second. 'After this there should be as many alternative cables as possible', and these 'should be allowed to follow the normal routes suggested by commercial considerations'. Not surprisingly, suspicion of British financial interests, there from the start, grew in continental Europe towards the end of the nineteenth century, and Paris journalists pondered in 1894 as to whether 'the security of other nations' could be upheld if Britain controlled 'all sources of information'. Americans went on to ask the same question.

In parts of the British Empire the telegraph was a major unifying influence across distant lands, carrying more messages per mile than were carried in Europe. Four years after it was opened, the line from Toronto to Quebec, for example, handled twice as many messages per mile as British lines were carrying. In Australia, the *Melbourne Argus* could declare in 1854 that 'To us, old colonists who have left Britain long ago, there is something very delightful in the actual contemplation of this, the most perfect of modern inventions . . . Anything more perfect than this is scarcely conceivable, and we really begin to wonder what will be left for the next generation upon which to expend the restless enterprise of the human mind . . . Let us set about electric telegraphy at once.'

By the 1850s, even before the great move westwards, the United States was proud of its achievement in telegraphy. As a popular song of 1860 put it (and there were parallel songs in Britain):

> Our Fathers gave us liberty, but little did they dream
> The great results that flow along this mighty age of steam:
> For our mountains, lakes and rivers, are all a blaze of fire,
> And we send our news by lightning, on the telegraphic wire.

By 1846 there were more than 1,000 miles of American line, including a stretch of 450 lines between New York and Buffalo. A telegraphic link between New York and San Francisco was completed in 1859. By the end of the Civil War, which greatly stimulated telegraphic business – and the business of Western Union, in particular – there were 37,000 miles of line.

Apart from assisting in the construction of the first telegraph line, government in Washington played little part in this story, which was left to unregulated private enterprise – with market forces clashing, often dramatically, in the early years of what has been called 'reckless expansion'. According to A. D. Chandler, American business historian and author of an indispensable book, *The Visible Hand* (1977), the competitive telegraphic companies then formed were the first modern business enterprises to appear in the United States. Yet out of competition between many firms came oligopoly, with few firms competing imperfectly, and out of oligopoly attempts at monopoly.

The giant Western Union, which was favoured by advantageous leasing and franchising arrangements and benefited from its alliances with railroad interests, claimed that monopoly was natural. Between 1870 and 1890 its corporate profits in real terms rose even in years when major sectors of the American economy were depressed, and the number of its offices increased from 3,972 to 19,382. The largest of these were in New York, where no fewer than 444 telegraphers were employed in a huge operations room. Thomas Edison (1847–1931), most famous of all American inventors, began his long career as an operator in Western Union's Boston office in 1868.

By 1890, 80 per cent of the country's message traffic was in Western Union hands, and critics of monopoly, although always in evidence, could be dismissed airily with the maxim that it was 'the result of an inevitable law that the business shall be mainly conducted under one great organization'. Morse himself had wished from the start that a telegraphic network would make 'one great whole

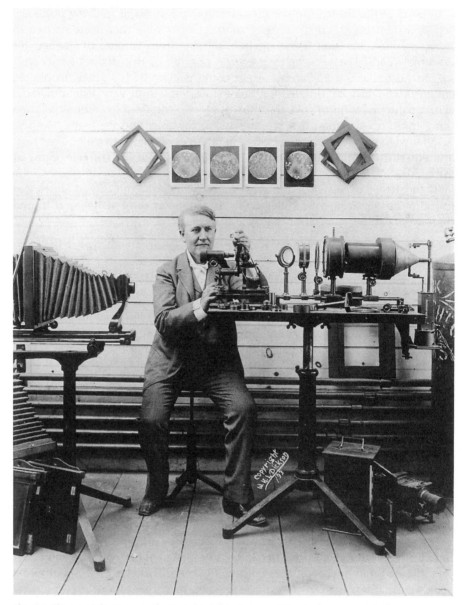

Fig. 16 Thomas Edison at work. Both his laboratory and his study were workplaces. 'Inventor of inventors', he had more inventive ideas than anyone before or since. He secured his patent for the phonograph in 1878 two months after applying: the Patent Office had known nothing like it before.

like the Post Office'. During the last decades of the century there was a further argument for monopoly: it alone would make possible the pursuit of necessary innovative research.

There was no shortage of this. With the development of Duplex, a single telegraph line could be used for the transmission of two messages, in opposite directions; and when in 1874 Quadruplex was devised by Edison, this doubled the capacity yet again. Five years later, a great national telegraphic strike by the Brotherhood of Telegraphers of the United States and Canada was totally broken by Western Union, and the ultimate challenge to the telegraphic business was to come not from workers within but from the advance of telephony outside.

Telephones

The story of the telephone, which became an instrument both of private and public communications, began some years earlier, in March 1876, when Alexander Graham Bell (1847–1922), an American inventor born in Scotland, patented his 'telephone', a word first used in 1796 for a purely acoustic method of communication. In 1837 the American C. G. Page had discovered that rapid changes in the magnetization of iron produced a musical note, 'galvanic music', and some of the experimenters who followed in his wake used a diaphragm to increase the output of sound. Notable amongst them was Philip Reiss, a teacher in Frankfurt who claimed that he had transmitted 'intelligible speech'.

Such a claim was too ambitious: if speech had been received, it must have been accidentally for short periods. Only Bell could claim correctly that he had made the telephone work. He demonstrated it at the great Centennial Exhibition in Philadelphia in 1876, and his first telephone call to his partner Thomas Watson is another message that has passed into folklore: 'Mr Watson come here, I want you.' There was an element of royal telephone folklore in Britain too. Queen Victoria, who had Bell presented to her in 1876, listened attentively to Kate Field singing 'Comin' Through the Rye' on what she described as 'the most extraordinary' model telephone, which Bell had brought with him.

In 1876, it has been suggested, 'there was no need for the telephone. Society did very well without it.' But this comment, which could never have been made about the telegraph, is misleading. Received at first with incredulity, in the twentieth century the telephone was to become a 'necessity' for many people, both in the office and the home – later, indeed, with the mobile phone, in the street. The *Scientific American* had already suggested comprehensively in 1880 that it would usher in 'a new organization of society – a state of things in which any individual, however secluded, will have at his call every other individual in the community, to the saving of no end of social and business complications, of needless goings to and fro.'

It was an Australian Professor of Engineering at Melbourne University who stated in an address of 1897 that 'if a prediction of coming achievement had been made to any intelligent person in 1837 . . . of all modern inventions, the telephone would have aroused the greatest scepticism'; and it was Sir William Thompson, the Scots scientist, later Lord Kelvin (1824–1907), who, after trying out Bell's telephone in Philadelphia, where he was a judge at the Centennial Exhibition, described it as 'the most wonderful thing he had seen in America'.

Thompson, one of the first people in Britain to install electric light bulbs in his home, brought back to Britain two Bell telephones which he and Sir William Preece (1834–1913), a key figure in Post Office history, who became its Chief Engineer, displayed in 1877 to members of the British Association for the

Advancement of Science. In the same year, an American woman journalist, hired by Bell, presented a *Matinée Teléphonique* to coincide with the opening of Parliament. In Australia, news of the invention reached Sydney and Melbourne in the same year via the printed word – articles in the *English Mechanic and World of Science* and in the *Scientific American*. Immediately, Australians set about trying to produce home-made telephones.

Bell, who had worked earlier on the problems involved in teaching the deaf to speak, had conceived of the idea of transmitting speech by electric waves in 1865, and in 1874 fashioned a phonautograph, a word coined by another experimenter, which was modelled on the structure of the human ear. His 1876 device was patented on his birthday in March 1876. It had been applied for on 14 February, the same day as another American inventor, Elisha Gray, had also applied for a telephone patent. Litigation, won by Bell, was to follow, with the victory being controversial at the time and remaining so since. The liquid transmitter that Bell used in his message to Watson was similar to that devised by Gray.

Nor were Bell and Gray the only two inventors who figured in the early story which involved what would now be called a convergence of two long histories, that of acoustics and that of electricity. At first, however, communication was only one way, and the first Bell patent application was described as 'an improvement in telegraphy': remarkably, it did not refer specifically to speech. This technical limitation was quickly lifted in 1876, and the second patent application brought speech in also. The first prospectus of the Bell Telephone Company, issued in July 1877, stated unequivocally that 'the telephone actually speaks and for this reason it can be utilized for nearly every purpose for which speech is employed'.

Business came into the story as well, converging with technology. Having failed to interest William Orton, Chairman of Western Union, Bell set up a private company in 1877, which three years later was converted into a public company, National Bell. Realizing that he had made a serious mistake, Orton turned hopefully to Edison, 'inventor of inventors', for technical guidance. Edison then produced a successful carbon transmitter, which led Bell, a David facing a Goliath, to consider litigation, but an out-of-court deal was reached in November 1879, from which Gray benefited modestly too. The terms were that Western Union would become the sole equipment manufacturer for Bell devices and that the operation of the telephone system would be left to a new National Bell Company, which could make use of all the relevant Western Union patents.

The deal worked for several reasons. One was that National Bell attracted as its General Manager an outstanding individual – Theodore Vail (1845–1920), a cousin of one of Morse's assistants, who had managed the American railroad postal network before joining National Bell. Under his effective leadership, the company was to grow in strength, successfully defending all Bell's patent rights which were subjected to no fewer than six hundred challenges before they expired in 1893. While they lasted, National Bell enjoyed the same kind of business advantage that Boulton and Watt had enjoyed a century before. Bell, now a rich man, lived until 1922, keenly interested in every aspect of telephone development – and in much else in the field of telecommunications.

Fig. 17 'Weavers of Speech'. A telephone advertisement for the Bell Telephone Company, drawing on metaphors with a 'mythical past and a technological and commercial future'. There is a Wagnerian twist to the weaving and a pictorial hint of the World Wide Web.

From the start Bell had proved himself to be more than an inventor, offering the world a 'vision', as Vail was to do. After visiting Britain in 1877, he set out what he called 'a grand system', 'something which might sound utopian', a 'universal network reaching into homes, offices and workplaces'. This required the invention of switchboards and exchanges, however, as well as necessary improvements in the transmission of speech; and although the beginnings of these came quickly too – the first switchboard was installed in New Haven in 1878 and the first exchange in London was opened in Coleman Street in 1879 – it took time for the telephone to 'come within the means of the ordinary householder'. It was a doctor in Lowell, a city once more figuring in communication history, who suggested a numbering system in 1880, but dialling did not arrive until 1896 (in Milwaukee).

Mechanized switching, with which the name of A. B. Strowger, a Kansas City undertaker, is usually linked, was introduced in La Porte, Indiana, in 1892: for the first time subscribers could make a call without the aid of an operator. Yet the introduction of mechanized exchanges was slow, even in the United States; and in Britain, outside the City of London, where a Strowger exchange was installed in 1897, only Epsom, Surrey, near the Derby racecourse, had a similar system installed in May 1914. Darlington – of railway fame – got one later in the year. It was not until 1927 that an automatic system was opened in London.

During its very early years, many people associated the telephone as much with entertainment for a scattered audience as with point-to-point, one-to-one communication between individuals, and for this reason alone the telephone must figure larger than the telegraph in the pre-history of broadcasting. Nonetheless, the same association had been made earlier between entertainment and the telegraph: in 1848, *Punch* had reported as a pseudo-news item songs being sent by telegram from Boston to New York. In 1876, *Nature* forecast that 'by paying a subscription to an enterprising individual who will no doubt come forward to work this vein we can have from him a waltz, a quadrille or a galop just as we desire'.

One of the predictions of the *Springfield Republican* in 1877 was that by means of the telephone 'all the music of a prima donna could be distributed over the country while she was singing, thus popularizing good music to an extent as yet unknown'; and far away from Springfield, in Switzerland, an engineer relayed a Donizetti opera in 1879. It was further away still, in Hungary, that the most enterprising and most sustained project for using telephones for entertainment was devised by a Hungarian inventor, Theodore Puskas. He had worked for the Edison company, had exhibited at the Paris Electricity Exhibition of 1881, and had secured exclusive rights to develop the telephone in Hungary in the same year.

Puskas was assisted by his brilliant friend Nikola Tesla (1856–1943), a pioneer of electricity and of the use, in particular, of alternating current, the form of power favoured by Westinghouse. Born in Croatia, Tesla was frequently drawn into argument about the merits of electrical systems, whereas another pioneer of electricity, the American writer Park Benjamin, without going into differences, relied on rhetoric in his book *The Age of Electricity* (1887) when he described the multiple uses of electricity as 'simply legion'. One of them was directly bound up with what became broadcasting. 'It will talk in our voices hundreds of miles away [it was far from doing that then]. It will record the votes which changed the destiny of a great nation or set down the music of the last popular melody.'

This was what Puskas was seeking to do when he inaugurated (and his brother continued) a Telefon Hirmondo service in Budapest in 1893 which offered subscribers what in effect was the world's first broadcasting system. Providing his subscribers with long flexible wires and two smooth round earpieces in their home, he offered a daily schedule of items to which they could listen, including news bulletins and summaries of the newspapers, stock exchange reports, 'lectures', sports news and 'visits to the opera'. There was also a weekly children's programme, along with 'linguistic lectures' in English, Italian and French.

The word 'Hirmondo' had its roots in the past: it was translated as 'news announcer' and recalled the older term 'town crier'. The daily schedule, announced to subscribers, pointed to the future. One of the first English writers on the work of the 'station', Arthur Mee, who became editor of *The Children's Newspaper* in 1908, called it, railway-fashion, a 'timetable': the magazine *Invention* called it a 'programme'. Mee's own vision was global: 'If as it is said to be not unlikely in the near future that the principle of sight is applied to the telephone as well as that of sound, earth will be in truth a paradise, and distance will lose its enchantment by being abolished altogether.' Telefon Hirmondo had no more subscribers in 1910 than it had in 1897 (6,000), but it survived the outbreak of the First World War.

This Hungarian service was far more ambitious and successful than a parallel Electrophone Company in Britain, which in 1884 offered, for an annual subscription, connections to theatres, concerts and, not least, church services – the sermons were to be delivered by 'the most eminent divines' – and a United States venture, which had begun seven years after the London company, folded in 1904, the Telephone Herald in Newark, New Jersey. Various 'theatrephone' schemes in Paris also collapsed, despite the interest of Marcel Proust, who foresaw many of the other uses of the telephone. While the 'pleasure' telephone was developed as an instrument of entertainment – it was thought of by some commentators largely as a 'toy' – Bell was right in forecasting that the 'serious uses' of the telephone would prevail. His foresight was always ahead of the current technology.

Different though the telephone system, with its subscriber base, was from the telegraph system, the British government, backed by the courts, decided in 1880 that, within the terms of the Telegraph Act of 1868 (see p. 110), the telephone was a telegraph. The decision followed a merger between the British Bell and British Edison companies which encouraged the Post Office, supported by strong telegraph interests, to acquire control of all telephone activity in Britain. It was to be operated largely through a licensing system, with licensee companies being required to pay a royalty on their business, but the Post Office maintained some exchanges of its own, for example, at Newcastle-upon-Tyne, and there were also a number of municipal telephone companies, for example, Hull, the longest surviving of them all. The National Telephone Company, the biggest of the licensees, acquired a near monopoly, however, before being taken over completely by the Post Office in 1912.

By then, a national trunk system had been developed – again slowly – and international traffic had increased. A submarine cable link between England and France was opened in 1891, but there was no full national link-up until four years later. Across the Atlantic, the first long-distance line, completed in 1880, was between Boston and Lowell, and by 1892 there were open lines between New York and Chicago and by 1915 between New York and San Francisco. Two American inventions, the wave filter and the loading coil, made such communication increasingly economical: the substitution of amplifiers or repeaters of an electronic type for electro-mechanical repeaters is said to have heralded a new era.

By comparison with the United States (and Canada), progress in extending telephone use in Britain, which led the world in the manufacture of cables, and in other European countries had been slow. Indeed, in Britain there was no sense, as *The Times* put it in 1902, that the telephone was 'an affair of the million'. It was rather a 'convenience for the well-to-do and a trade appliance for persons who can well afford to pay for it'. 'An overwhelming majority of the population do not use it, and are not likely to use it at all except perhaps to the extent of an occasional message from a public station.' A year earlier, the Chancellor of the Exchequer had claimed that 'telephonic communication is not desired by the rural mind', while in Canada, the United States and Australia it was in the rural areas where the telephone was most in demand. The expiry of Bell's patents in 1894 favoured commercial exploitation, and after 1893 'independents' came into the picture as telephone use expanded. Evidence was now accumulating that the telephone was facilitating decentralization, allowing scattered families to communicate more easily, making farm life less isolated, and changing marketing methods, medical practice, politics and journalism. It was changing social habits too, not least those of women, soon happy 'to chat on the phone'. There was, indeed, an emerging 'telephone language and culture'.

As was to be the case years later, in the history of the Internet, fears were expressed on both sides of the Atlantic that 'truth' might be in jeopardy. Indeed, before the adjective 'phoney' was coined, *Punch* had complained not of telephonic but of telegraphic 'fibs':

> What horrid fibs by that electric wire
> Are flashed about! What falsehoods are its shocks!
> Oh! Rather let us have the fact that creeps
> Comparatively by the Post so slow
> Than the quiet fudge which like the lightning leaps
> And makes us credit that which is not so.

In 1902 H. G. Wells was more concise: 'The businessman may sit at home . . . and tell such lies as he dare not write.'

This was not the only line of criticism. The intrusion of the telephone into the home was often under attack, as television intrusion was to be decades later. Swearing on the phone raised ethical issues. Should it be treated as an offence? 'Telephone crime' was isolated from its context. In 1907, an article in *Cosmopolitan Magazine*, again anticipating articles almost a century later dealing with the Internet, was entitled 'The Telegraph and Telephone Companies [and here they were treated as associated, not as competing, agencies] as Allies of the Criminal Pool Rooms'. Not surprisingly, other critics thought of them as 'Allies of the Police'. There was agreement, however, that telephones were the 'Allies of the Press' and of the banking and stock exchange systems, the latter called upon to provide necessary capital for the development of telephone systems.

As early as April 1877, when New York stockbrokers were already using the new medium, a telephone news message concerning one of Bell's own lectures was broadcast as a news item from Salem to the *Boston Globe*. In London as early as 1880, *The Times* set up a telephone link with the House of Commons in order to include the reporting of late-night debates in the next day's editions. By 1900, the daily mass journalism of the United States had come to depend more on telephonic than on telegraphic communication. In France there was a different emphasis. The French word for 'exchange' was '*central*', and this suggested a very non-American (and non-British) way of looking at what came to be thought of as a network. As late as 1922, Paris was said to be spurning the telephone: 'almost a half century after its invention the telephone remained a tool reserved essentially for professional men'.

The United States was far ahead of all European countries in telephone distribution by 1900, with one telephone for every sixty people. Sweden came first among European countries with one for every 215. France had one for every 1,216 and Russia one for every 6,958. In 1904 there were 6.5 telephones per hundred persons in Manhattan and the Bronx and only 1.4 in London. The dynamic American drive, well expressed in the title of a 1914 article in *McClure's Magazine*, 'Telephones for the Millions', came from the American Telephone and Telegraph Company (AT&T), which had been brought into existence in New York in 1885 as a long-distance network subsidiary of National Bell, located from the start in Boston; and in an imaginative move (in two senses) in 1899, AT&T became the parent company, and New York the corporate headquarters. Another electrical equipment manufacturing company, Western Electric, had already been assimilated in a cumulative process starting in 1881.

Vail's ambition from the start had been to control what he thought of as 'the nervous system' of the American business and social community, through what he recognized would have to be a regulated rather than an unregulated monopoly. Local operations could and should be decentralized, carried out by licensees, but integration was essential. Returning to AT&T in 1900, having made a fortune outside it, Vail took over its presidency in 1907 and two years later engineered the buy-out of Western Union, the major telegraphic company (see p. 115). He also tightened control over the finance of the licensing companies.

Whatever Vail might write about the importance of control and regulation, there were strong American objections, local and national – and inside and outside government – to the monopoly of AT&T as an alternative to competition. 'We do not ask the government to fight our battles,' the National Association of Independent Telephone Exchanges, founded in 1897, declared in 1910, 'but we do ask for protection against outrageous methods of warfare, which are illegal and detrimental to the public welfare.' In what became a struggle of Social Darwinian proportions Vail had one particular advantage, however. He believed in research, while most of the independent companies did not, and a generation after the expiry of the original Bell patents, the Bell Telephone Laboratories, to be known worldwide, were to be formally set up in 1925.

In relation to the question of monopoly, a compromise between what appeared to be radically different approaches to thorny issues, practical as much as theoretical, had been reached in 1913 and was reaffirmed after the First World War in the Graham Act of 1921. In 1913 AT&T disgorged Western Union, made its distance toll lines available to independents, and agreed to work with the Interstate Commerce Commission and to obtain prior approval for the opening up of new telephone systems. The Graham Act, acknowledging this, exempted AT&T from the provisions of anti-trust legislation; and although AT&T continued to face hostility from opponents of monopoly and from 1934 onwards was subjected to regular questioning in the Federal Communications Commission (see p. 187), on the eve of the Second World War it controlled 83 per cent of all United States telephones and 98 per cent of long-distance toll wires. It also had a total monopoly of overseas radio telephony. It was the largest company in history.

There were parallels overseas, with different countries reaching out slowly towards an ideal of 'universal service', as they had done in the evolution of their postal systems, but relying mainly on their Post Offices to dictate telecommunications policy. While after 1918 the number of telephones per thousand persons continued to increase, with an interruption during the Great Depression and the

Second World War, it was not until the 1950s that the rise began to be identified as a major social trend on both sides of the Atlantic.

Wireless

The early history of wireless has more to do with telegraphy than with telephony, although after the development of broadcasting the Puskas pedigree acquired a new significance in retrospect. In 1925 Sir Frank Gill, who took the chair in British Post Office talks leading up to the creation of the BBC, emphasized how 'telephony had some of the properties both of the letter and the newspaper. It can be clothed with privacy . . . or it can be broadcast to millions simultaneously.'

The science behind wireless had a long history, even predating the work of German scientist Heinrich Hertz (1857–94). It was he who corroborated experimentally the brilliant theoretical work a generation earlier of the British scientist James Clerk Maxwell (1831–74), who without apparatus had formulated in 1864 the basic mathematical equations relating to the electromagnetic field. Both Hertz and Maxwell died young. Oliver Lodge, born in 1851, was to die an old man in 1940, and it was he who demonstrated Hertzian waves, as they were immediately called, at the Royal Institution in 1895. He also invented a 'coherer', as he called it, a Hertzian wave receiver with an iron filing tube, without ever quite realizing the economic importance of his own work. For him the coherer was a pedagogical device.

There were radio pioneers in other countries too, such as A. S. Popoff (1859–1906) in Russia, Edouard Branly (1844–1940) in France, and Augusto Righi (1850–1920) in Italy, so that when Guglielmo Marconi (1871–1937) arrived in Britain in June 1896 to demonstrate what he called 'improvements in transmitting electrical impulses and signals', a writer in the *Quarterly Review* could judge that 'Mr Marconi' had 'only introduced another mode of doing what had been done before'. It was 'his nationality, his youth, and the unworthy attempts to belittle his success' that had 'attracted the attention of the Press'. 'It is well', the anonymous author concluded, 'that the Press should occasionally wake to the rapid forward strides of practical science. Civilization has advanced more by the aid of the working engineer than of the talking politician.'

Marconi had, in fact, been talking, if not to politicians, then to civil servants, naval officers and soldiers as well as to scientists, including A. A. Campbell Swinton, a prophet of television (see p. 129), to whom he had an introduction and who extended him an invitation to meet Preece, who had informal talks with him at the Post Office (see p. 118). One of the naval officers had already begun experimenting with radio himself a year earlier, quite independently from anyone else, and he and Marconi now carried out field trials with the British fleet on similar lines to trials being carried out with the Russian fleet by Popoff. Necessity, not the advancement of science, drove them. Iron-clad ships demanded new modes of signalling, just as the 'iron horses' of the railway had needed them two generations before.

Within this context, wireless, the culmination of nineteenth-century communications history, was thought of simply as a substitute for wired telegraphy, just as automobiles, the high point of nineteenth-century transportation history,

Fig. 18 The young Guglielmo Marconi. He arrived in London from Italy in February 1896 with a bundle of wireless devices. He set up his Wireless Telegraph and Signal Company in 1897.

were thought of as horseless carriages. It followed that radio would be of most practical use on the oceans or in large, sparsely populated continents, and the fact that its signalled messages, all in Morse, could be picked up by people for whom they were not intended – its broadcasting dimension – was deemed to be not an asset but a serious disadvantage. Likewise, the automobile was a luxury product, and no one envisaged a car in a suburban house with a garage any more than a similar house would later be associated with a 'wireless set'.

In visiting England Marconi wanted quick results, and when he founded his Wireless Telegraph and Signal Company in 1897 he concentrated primarily on devising and selling wireless apparatus to large-scale commercial and governmental customers. He had royalty in mind too: in 1897, more than a hundred messages passed between Queen Victoria at Osborne House in the Isle of Wight and the Prince of Wales's royal yacht outside Cowes, where the Prince lay ill in bed. Marconi had no vision of radio as a widespread medium. Nor, indeed, did he use the word 'radio'. And in this he was not alone. In 1899, for example, *The Electrician* contended that 'messages scattered broadcast only waste energy by travelling with futile persistence toward celestial space'.

Preece, a founder member of the Society of Telegraph Engineers, which was created in 1871 and changed its name in 1889 to the Institution of Electrical Engineers, was cautious about the prospects of Marconi's patents even within the context in which Marconi himself placed them; and even after Marconi had transmitted messages across the Channel to France in 1899 Preece warned that 'wireless telegraphy in its present form and limited speed' (a genuine limitation) could not be placed in the same category as 'the old system'. Bureaucratic rather than entrepreneurial in his approach to communications development, he believed as a fact that 'it is about the worst thing possible for an invention [like Marconi's] to get into the hands of a company. We have only to look at the telephone to be convinced of this.' Nonetheless, Preece's stance did not go unchallenged. *Chambers's Journal*, reporting one of his speeches, placed it alongside an item called 'Her Majesty's Pigeon Messengers'.

There was immediate popular excitement, as the writer in the *Quarterly Review* noted in 1898, about the medium of transmission of Marconi's messages – 'the illimitable, incomprehensible, exquisite medium, the ether'; and he suggested, in dated fashion, that a better term for the system would be 'etheric telegraphy', for 'it was not really wireless'. Wires were used 'at each end as a part and parcel of the apparatus'. Another writer claimed that the 'miracle' of wireless consisted in the fact that it was, above all, 'mysterious', like X-rays, newly discovered in 1895. It was the nearest the world had got to telepathy.

Its potential only became apparent to most people, as it did to experts who claimed to speak with authority, when radio entered the home, first in the United States, and then in Britain and Holland. Yet before new institutions had been created to offer 'programmes', an amateur network of radio enthusiasts, known as 'hams', had forged national and international links, most of them using Morse, others telephony. They were described with foresight in 1912 in an American book by H. Collins, *The Wireless Man*, as, potentially at least, 'the largest audience in the world'. There were then estimated to be 122 wireless clubs in existence in America.

It had become possible to write in terms of size of audience only because of a series of inventions in the period between the 1890s and 1920s, some of them the product of careful scientific research, others encouraged by the special circumstances of the First World War, when radio was employed for military purposes. Nonetheless, the future applications of technology could have been predicted if social factors had been taken into account, rather than underplayed when wireless was in the pipeline. For example, when Sir William Crookes, in a much-quoted British article of 1892, offered 'the bewildering possibilities of telegraphy without wires, posts, cables or any of our present costly appliances granted a few reasonable postulates', he did not suggest what would happen next.

Marconi followed his own line of development, stirring the American imagination when in 1899 he accepted a paid commission from James Gordon Bennett Jr., owner of the *New York Herald*, to cover the America's Cup yacht races, and capturing both American and European imaginations in 1901 when he sent a wireless message two thousand miles across the Atlantic to Cornwall from Newfoundland. There was a business twist to this story. The Anglo-American Telegraph Company held the telegraphic monopoly in Newfoundland and had the Marconi team expelled from the island, which was then independent of Canada.

Subsequent publicity did not need to be contrived. In 1904, wireless hit the headlines when it was used to report the arrest of Dr Crippen, a murderer fleeing from England to Canada by sea with his mistress. Eight years later, it was the Marconi station in Long Island which picked up the SOS messages from the sinking *Titanic* and sent the news on to the White House: a man later to be famous (see p. 131), David Sarnoff (1891–1971), was the operator. In 1906, the second World Congress on Wireless Telegraphy, held in Berlin – the first had been held in 1903 – had agreed that SOS should be the standard distress call signal. Berlin was in fact outside the Marconi empire: the Germans now had their own Telefunken wireless system managed through a subsidiary of Siemens and Allgemeine Elektricitäts Gesellschaft, established in 1907, with indispensable government backing. It had a research and development budget and established radio stations in many parts of the world. It challenged Marconi's existing patents and attempted to prevent him from acquiring new ones.

Marconi had formed an American subsidiary company in 1899 and still faced no corporate competition from America in 1901 except from cable companies. One early historical study – *Radio: Beam and Broadcast* by A. B. Morse in 1925 after the beginning of broadcasting – told the story of radio development mainly through the patent office records of 'inventions in use today or their lineal forebears'. This was a story which took a new turn in the United States after the formation in October 1919 of a new body, the Radio Corporation of America (RCA), a civilian version of the naval and military monopoly that had controlled radio during the war. It forcibly took over all Marconi's patents. If Marconi had been an American citizen, his highly successful American company might well have survived.

RCA was a government-sanctioned company, which established close connections with AT&T, General Electric and Westinghouse, now building civilian wireless sets, but it and they had to concern themselves not only with patents and competitors but with the competing claims for access to the radio spectrum of government – and of the armed forces in particular – and of the now greatly enlarged peaceful army of radio 'hams', an army with battalions also on the other side of the Atlantic.

By the terms of the Radio Act of 1912, the first such act to be passed in the United States, 'ham' radio messages were restricted by law to wavelengths of 200 metres or less, a limit raised in certain states to 425 metres in 1915. Despite military and naval pressure, there had been resistance inside and outside Congress to any regulation. 'We have been brought up with the idea that the air was absolutely free to everyone.' Why should it not be? The same question was to be raised in Britain as well as in the United States after the First World War, when amateur broadcasting had not been permitted for naval and military reasons. In 1921, for a spokesman of the Wireless Society of London, now largely committed to radio telephony, 'every Englishman is entitled to hear what is going on in his ether providing his listening apparatus does not annoy his neighbours'.

In all countries most 'hams' used cheap crystal sets made by themselves. It was fortunate for them that it had been discovered in the late-nineteenth century that several types of crystal would serve as detectors of wireless waves which could be listed and classified, as they were between 1908 and 1911. There was one well-known crystal rectifier on the market before 1914 – the Perikon – a brass point resting on the surface, polished or unpolished, of a piece of silicon, a substance with a more romantic future even than the hams themselves. The first detailed history of the transistor and 'the birth of the information age' was to be called *Crystal Fire*.

In Britain, by the terms of the Wireless Telegraphy Act of 1904, all transmitters or receivers of wireless signals had to have a Post Office licence, and the Marconi Company held a 'General Licence' in 1920 to 'conduct experimental telephony'. It met with tough opposition, however, from the Wireless Telegraphy Board, where there was strong military representation, after it started to broadcast Marconi concerts from Chelmsford. Such broadcasts, the Board argued, were not only interfering with defence messages but were turning wireless, which was 'a servant of mankind', into 'a toy to amuse children'; and in the light of their advice permission for Chelmsford to broadcast was rescinded in the autumn of the same year.

This in turn led the 'hams' to protest. Now seeking both to communicate with each other and to listen to radio programmes put out for them, they drafted a petition signed by sixty-three wireless societies which forced the Postmaster-General, who himself had called the concerts 'frivolous', to think again. When he yielded in December 1921, he took care to state that the resumption of the concerts would be 'for the benefit of the Wireless Societies'. There was still no sense of a 'great unseen audience'.

The first Marconi Company station to provide half-hour concerts after the resumption was Writtle, near Chelmsford. The first concert, described modestly by its makers as 'an engineers' do', was broadcast on 14 February 1922 and the last on 17 January 1923. The engineers proved themselves to be bright and highly informal broadcasters: gramophone records were a staple, but they broadcast the first radio play, *Cyrano de Bergerac*. Peter Eckersley, natural leader of the group, was to become first Chief Engineer of the BBC, which was set up in the autumn of 1922 before Writtle closed.

Before 1914 there were three outstanding inventors, one British, one American and one Canadian, who led the way towards sound broadcasting. In 1904, Ambrose Fleming (1849–1945), a Professor at University College London – he had attended Maxwell's lectures – devised the thermionic valve which was described long before the microchip as 'the tiniest little giant in history'. A yet bigger step forward was taken two years later by Lee de Forest (1873–1961) in Palo Alto: he added a third electrode in the form of a grid between the cathode and anode of Fleming's diode valve, described in the United States as a vacuum tube. The latter was a British Marconi Company patent, as was an important valve patent by H. J. Round, and there were patent conflicts which lasted even beyond the expiry of the Forest patent in 1922. Indeed, it was not until 1943 that the United States Supreme Court decided that Forest had sole claim for his triode or 'audion' as he called it. This was more than an improvement: it enabled weak radio signals – not only in Morse but in words and music – to be amplified and longer distances to be covered. It was with pride that Forest called himself 'the father of radio'.

The third man in the trio, Reginald Fessenden (1866–1932), a Canadian, used a high frequency alternator to put on the 'first event' in the pre-1914 decade, a wireless concert broadcast by him from Brant Rock, Massachusetts, on Christ-mas Eve 1906, and picked up in places as far away as the Caribbean. Fessenden himself played the fiddle, sang Christmas carols and presented Handel's *Largo* on his phonograph. 'If anybody hears me', he told his unknown audience, 'please write to Mr Fessenden at Brant Rock.' Some years later, Forest, who had broad-cast from American naval vessels, reached a different and unknown audience when he sent out messages from the Eiffel Tower in Paris which was already broadcasting time signals (see p. 106).

Forest, who is said to have lacked business sense but to have been 'a born ham', had seen the need for such a service before 1914. He had insisted, therefore, that he should go on presenting broadcast concerts after he had negotiated a deal with AT&T in 1914, whereby he sold the Company his audion patents while at the same time agreeing to stay out of point-to-point voice transmission by radio from specific senders to specific receivers. Forest wanted to concentrate on transmitting music – and opera, in particular – into people's homes, and in 1910 he broadcast direct from New York's Metropolitan Opera, with Enrico Caruso as one of the soloists. He already thought of broadcasting as a medium, and believed, before the technology was ready – particularly that relating to the pro-duction of receivers – that it could become big business. While Europe, but not the United States, was at war, he broadcast the Yale/Harvard football game in 1916, and on election night in the same year a six-hour coverage of the results of the presidential race which took Woodrow Wilson (1856–1924) to the White House. (He erroneously reported that Wilson had lost, as did some sections of the press.)

Even as late as 1916, most British wireless experts, including leading figures in the Wireless Society of London, which had Crookes and Lodge as honorary members, were unconvinced that wireless telephony had a future of the kind that Forest envisaged; it was not 'quite clear', one of them wrote in 1913, 'from what quarter the first definite demand' for wireless telephony would come. Yet in the same year the *Illustrated London News* had shown pictures of British lis-teners in evening dress, absorbed in listening through earphones not to words or music but to time signals.

The President of the Society in 1914 was Campbell Swinton, both far-seeing and cautious. He told its members that with a little imagination one could picture in the not too distant future wireless receiving stations that would be spe-cially set up in halls resembling picture palaces and that people would be able to go there and 'hear *viva voce* all the prominent speakers of the day, although they might be speaking hundreds of miles away'. But that was not to be the shape of the future. Wireless telephony, like telephony, was to invade the home. A London magistrate, writing in 1924, was to call it 'a new bond of interest to the family' in an article entitled 'The Revival of Home Life'.

This aspect of its future had been realized after Forest by Arthur Burrows (1882–1947), who worked for the Marconi Company during the war, collecting, editing and distributing intercepted wireless messages, and across the Atlantic by David Sarnoff (see p. 127), who was to become the first commercial manager of RCA. During the war, Sarnoff had conceived of 'a simple Radio Music Box . . . arranged for several different wavelengths which should be changeable with the

throwing of a single switch or pressing of a single button'. 'The problem of transmitting music had already been solved', he claimed, and no imagination was
needed 'to forecast it'. And music could be supplemented by 'news items, lectures and scores'.

Sarnoff was thinking of broadcasting, although he did not then use the word,
which was derived, like the words 'culture' and 'cultivation', not from technology
or industry but from agriculture: broadcast seed was seed scattered freely, not in
drills or in rows. The scattering, as we have seen (see p. 125), had been thought
of at first as a commercial disadvantage. Yet once broadcasting began to be conceived of as a 'medium', the disadvantage was transformed into a rationale.
Sarnoff wished to make 'radio a household utility in the same sense as the piano
or phonograph'. He also suggested that every new subscriber to the service
should be sent copies of the Marconi Company's house journal, *Wireless Age*,
which had changed its name from *Marconigraph* in 1913.

Ironically, it was the British forecaster, not the American, who incorporated
advertising into his broadcasting vision. 'There would be no technical difficulty',
Burrows explained, 'in the way of an enterprising advertisement agency arrang-
ing for intervals in the musical programme to be filled with audible advertisements, pathetic or forcible appeals – in appropriate tones – on behalf of
somebody's soap or tomato ketchup.' There were other ironies. For the financing of broadcasting programmes Sarnoff put his trust in a superpower consortium of radio manufacturers and dealers, covering the whole country, not
dissimilar to that which the British Post Office eventually summoned in London
in 1922 and out of which the BBC emerged as a monopoly. For Sarnoff 'the industry itself' had 'the responsibility of maintaining and supporting suitable broadcast stations so that the sets which are sold to the public and bought by them
may not represent a refrigerator without ice'.

The BBC, which was set up as a monopoly largely for technical reasons,
derived its initial income not from advertising but from royalties from the sale
of wireless sets and licence fees. It was made a monopoly because of the government's decision that since there were competing claims for access to the
scarce spectrum, there should be only one broadcasting organization. In the
United States, with no Post Office in the background – and with limited will to
regulate the spectrum – such a solution was not considered. RCA could not act
as a monopoly. Nor did AT&T, as a 'common carrier', succeed in an effort in the
early 1920s, to promote programming by selling network time on a toll basis to
would-be customers in the same way as it sold telephone time to subscribers.

American broadcasting was to be developed quite differently. A remarkable
radio boom in 1922, described as canal and railroad booms had been, as a
'mania', took the United States by surprise; and in response a large number of
stations of all kinds emerged, some associated with newspapers, others with
retail organizations, some with cities, some with schools and universities. As one
observer put it, 'anything that could speak was called a broadcasting station'. As
early as May 1922 the Department of Commerce had granted more than three
hundred licences for broadcasting. The first stations were known, as Chelmsford
and Writtle were to be in England, by their call signs, and what was said to be
the first of them, KDKA, had been started in 1920 in Pittsburgh. The man who

initiated it was a radio amateur, Frank Conrad, a Westinghouse engineer, who used a department store to advertise his 'wireless concerts'. Westinghouse was particularly interested when it found out that gramophone records which Conrad played sold better in the store as a result of his broadcasts.

Station turnover was high, and at first they all used the same wavelength, 360 metres, creating 'chaos in the ether', the 'ruin' which had been forecast before the war. By the end of 1922 the number of licences had reached 572. Newspapers and periodicals produced radio supplements, encouraging the public to buy sets. A hundred thousand were sold in 1922, and more than half a million in 1923. By 1925 there were five and a half million radio sets in use in the United States, nearly half the world's total. The number of individual broadcasting ventures was to fall – and powerful networks were eventually to emerge, the first of them NBC, the National Broadcasting Company, launched in 1926 as a 'public service'; the second CBS, the Columbia Broadcasting System, created in 1927 by the man who became Sarnoff's chief rival, William Paley (1901–90). He had started in radio by advertising his father's cigar business and had worked through the agency of United Independent Broadcasting.

The share of the networks increased from 6.4 per cent of broadcast stations in 1926 to 30 per cent in 1931. For the hams, pushed into the background, there was continuing excitement in trying to pick up the most distant messages, but for those local owners of radio stations who tried, as in Chicago, to concentrate not on the far but on the near, there was disappointment as increasing network power expressed itself in increased programming by formula. For those 'ham' enthusiasts who were totally uninterested in the content of the messages picked up, radio was a sport. For the networks radio was big business, with broadcasting of live sport one of its attractions.

Advertising became the financial dynamic. Criticized in many sections of the press, it had been attacked, too, in 1922 and 1923 by Herbert Hoover (1874–1966), future President of the United States, then an active reforming Secretary for Commerce: in a remarkable phrase he declared it 'inconceivable that we should allow so great a possibility for service and for news and for entertainment and education, for vital commercial purposes to be drowned in advertising chatter'. He was wrong, yet in 1927, when the first government legislation setting up the Federal Radio Commission was passed (a limited exercise in regulation), it carried the language of 'public interest, convenience, necessity'.

Edgar Felix, an early radio merchandizing consultant, looked back enthusiastically at the process of expansion before there had been any regulation:

> What a glorious opportunity for the advertising man to spread his sales propaganda. Here was a countless audience, sympathetic, pleasure seeking, enthusiastic, curious, interested, approachable in the privacy of their own homes.

Westinghouse concurred. 'Broadcasting advertising', the company asserted, was 'modernity's medium of business expression. Operating through increasingly sophisticated campaigns, it made industry articulate. American businessmen, because of radio, are provided with a latch key to nearly every home in the United States.' Frank Arnold, NBC's Director of Development, went so far as to call broadcasting 'the Fourth Dimension of Advertising'.

It was not seen as such in Britain nor in most European countries. The Netherlands led the way in regular broadcasting, putting out programmes from The Hague in November 1919 by PCGE, a station set up by Nederlandse Radio-Industrie. Until 1927 there was only one Dutch transmitter, which was shared, unusually, although in line with Dutch history, by five 'pillar' organizations, with their roots below, each with a religious affiliation. British broadcasting took a different course. While the British Broadcasting Company did not receive its licence from the Post Office until January 1923, it broadcast its first programmes on 14 November 1922. Burrows read a six o'clock news bulletin at two speeds (slow and fast) into an ordinary telephone receiver connected to the Marconi Company's 2LO transmitter. Far away in the Antipodes, New Zealand broadcast its first radio messages on the same day.

How to allocate scarce wavelengths was a matter of hard national bargaining, which became international in 1926. A Geneva Plan for European wavelengths, hammered out by engineers, was adopted in July of that year; and a year later a World Wireless Conference at Washington, the first such conference since 1912, examined what Hoover called 'the congestion of the lanes on which communications are conducted'. A further conference in Prague in 1929, one organized by governments and broadcasting authorities, left national administrations, including that of the Soviet Union, not represented at Geneva or Washington, to make detailed allocations within a total allotted to them. Each year the Soviet Union celebrated 7 May, the anniversary of a Popoff radio demonstration in 1895, and the first public broadcast was made in 1919, but there was little radio listening on a mass scale until the late 1920s.

In all countries concerned with the development of broadcasting, the activity was being left to newly organized broadcasting institutions, local, regional and national, which grew rapidly during the 1920s. They employed the same radio technology, but had different structures. Some were commercial; some were government controlled; some, like the BBC, being shaped by John Reith (1889–1971), who gave his name to an adjective 'Reithian', were neither commercial nor government controlled. Nonetheless, whatever their structure, they had to share what has been called the 'role of cultural brokerage' with the gramophone record industry, the cinema, the performing arts, sporting bodies and 'to some extent the newspaper'. Each of these had its own history and its own organization. So did what later came to be called telecommunications. There were clashes there, national and international, before the merger in 1929 of the 'Eastern Group', a powerful combination, and the Marconi Company, no longer chaired by Marconi, to form Cable and Wireless, a company with a lively future.

There was a symbolic point in time, after broadcasting had established itself, when the story of early wireless came to an end, a point of silence. Marconi died on 20 July 1937, and the next day almost all the wireless stations of the world, including broadcasting stations, which had never greatly interested him, were silent for one or two minutes. It was a unique moment in their history.

Cinema and Television

In 'normal times' radio brought more noise into the world, including background music, much disliked by people who felt that music deserved careful listening.

Meanwhile, the history of the cinema, at first silent cinema, which stretched back before Marconi, did not serve as a model for Reith; and in the United States, as in Britain, the origins of radio and cinema were quite different. There was to be interaction, however, between radio and television, the broadcasting of pictures as well as words. In its original form, television did not permit viewers to turn an international knob, as manufactured radio receivers did, although there was growing international traffic in pictures, with the production and control of the pictures on the television screen controlled by broadcasting bodies which had dealt in sound before pictures at a time when cinema was showing pictures without sound.

The development of both cinema and television depended on the camera, and that had a long history behind it: the *camera obscura* (dark chamber) had been an artist's tool for centuries. The new nineteenth-century camera was developed first in France and in Britain and then in revolutionary fashion in the United States. As early as 1802, a member of the Wedgwood family had written a 'Description of a Procedure for Copying Paintings onto Glass and for making Silhouettes by the Effect of Light on Silver Nitrate', but it was a French experimenter, Joseph Nicéphore ('bringer of victory') Niepce, who produced by what he called 'heliography' the first 'photograph from life' soon after the end of the Napoleonic Wars. (The word 'photograph' was coined by Wheatstone.)

Niepce informed the Royal Society in London of his success in 1827, but it was his younger partner, Louis Daguerre, taken on in 1829, who developed the first precise photographic images, which he called daguerreotypes, releasing details of his photographic process in Paris 'in the interests of the sciences and the arts' in 1839. The state, proud of French scientific prowess, acquired monopoly rights in his work, but immediately renounced them and declared photography 'open for the whole world'. The announcement was less dramatic than it seemed, however, for the invention had shrewdly been patented earlier in London, where it remained protected. Nevertheless, there was competition.

Also in 1839, in London, William Henry Fox Talbot (1800–77), who had worked concurrently with Daguerre, employing a quite different process, using silver nitrate and producing 'negatives' on paper, demonstrated his 'calotypes', what he called 'photogenic drawings', to 'lovers of science and nature' at the Royal Society. Calotype images were softer than daguerreotypes, and as early as 1840 a Swiss, Johann Baptiste Isenring, is said to have discussed a method of colouring them. It was not until 1861, however, that the first true three-colour photograph was taken by a great scientist famous in other fields, James Clerk Maxwell (see p. 111): it could only be viewed through a projector. The subsequent development of colour photography was a twentieth-century venture.

The first daguerreotypes, highly successful, were unique objects, thought of as expressions of art which did not allow for multiple reproduction, and their success can be measured statistically. The number of daguerreotypists in different countries grew rapidly, beginning in France, where there was talk of *daguerréomanie*. There were ten thousand of them in America by 1853, among them Samuel Morse (see p. 111), and in Britain some two thousand photographers were registered in the Census of 1861, a year when the *Photographic News* described photographic portraiture as 'the best feature of the fine arts of the millions that the ingenuity of man has yet devised. It has swept away many of the illiberal distinctions of rank and wealth.' Nevertheless, photography won special royal and political favour. Victoria and Albert bought their first daguerreotypes in 1840; Daguerre dedicated one to Metternich.

There was a legal struggle in London about Daguerre's patents, and it was only after overtures from the Royal Society in 1852 that Fox Talbot's patents were relaxed in 1854. Already a new wet glass-plate era had begun in 1851, the year of Daguerre's death, when Frederick Scott Archer, one of the first twelve members of Fox Talbot's Calotype Club, invented a collodion process which sharpened calotype images. (Collodion was guncotton dissolved in ether.) The process of technological advance continued, with even 'slight improvements in processes' and 'slight variations in results' being discussed in animated detail – in the words of Lady Eastlake, the wife of the President of London's Photographic Society – 'as if they involved the future of mankind'.

Not everything was 'slight', however, and there were interesting new experiments in stereophotography: the slogan of the London Stereoscopic Company was 'no home without a stereoscope' and, for good measure, 'no school' either. Yet the stereoscope turned out to be a 'fad', a word increasingly used in the history of the media, and photographic improvement took a different course when, during the 1870s, plates of dry gelatine, which could be produced industrially, came into use in Britain, France and the United States. Meanwhile, the size and price of cameras fell, as an enterprising American, George Eastman (born in 1854, a bank clerk turned photographic manufacturer), developed a wide market. Keenly impressed by everything new that was on display at the Centennial Exhibition in Philadelphia in 1876, Eastman contributed twelve years later to the list of items one of the most famous things of the century, the Kodak camera, usable by everyone everywhere. He thought correctly that Kodak was a name which would be memorable in every language. He had a slogan for it too, 'You press the button, we do the rest.'

No fewer than 90,000 cheap Kodaks were sold within five years. As compared with later cameras, they had no focusing apparatus and only one speed on the shutter – the art went out of photography – but they had an exposure time of only one-twentieth of a second, and were sold ready-loaded with a roll of negative stripping paper sufficient to produce one hundred pictures. When these had been taken, the camera was packed up and shipped to the Eastman plant where it was unloaded, charged with fresh film and returned to the customer in ten days. In this, as in other ways, the United States was setting the pace in the evolution of a consumer society lavishly, if briefly, recorded in snapshots. Like the telephone and the wireless set, the box camera was produced for domestic use. And it was produced for the millions. So also, in time, were the electrical domestic appliances – in a wider range than prophets of electricity had anticipated. The technology, which had to become 'user friendly', but did not always do so, was to develop throughout the twentieth century, but design was to be influenced also by fashion.

It was not only in the United States that the new social trends – which also reflected demographic change – were evident. Industrialization had greatly increased material wealth and hours of leisure in all industrialized countries, and there were many examples of luxuries that had become necessities. Food and other products, including imported tropical items, were branded, and advertising, some of it electrical – the neon sign, for example – was being used both to launch products and to increase their sales. Cities everywhere had grown in size, spreading out into new suburbs, with trams ('gondolas of the people', as Richard Hoggart was to describe their British versions) and underground railways making possible day-to-day personal movement in and out of the city. The commuter preceded the computer as the world prepared for the flourishing of what came to be called the 'mass media' – with an old medium, the press, leading the way.

The introduction of the 'moving picture' was the biggest technological change, although before it became practical a debate had already taken place concerning the claims of photography to be an art form, anticipating similar debates in relation to the cinema. Fox Talbot had had no doubt, and one photographer, Julia Margaret Cameron, who illustrated Tennyson's *Idylls of the King*, has been called 'the Rembrandt of English photographic art'. In the same group were the Swede Oscar Gustav Rejlander and the Englishman Henry Peach Robinson, who set out to explain how and why there were as many 'individualizing' features in a good photograph as there were in a drawing or painting.

Moving pictures were to revivify the argument, but their origins were mechanical and belonged to the world of toys. They had names less memorable than Kodak – Praxinoscope, Phenakisti[s]cope and, after photographs began to be used instead of paintings, Kaamatographs. The first man successfully to employ a camera sequence to convey the sense of movement – there had been many earlier unsuccessful attempts – was 'Eadweard Muybridge' (1830–1904). His chrono-photographic series of horse movements, taken for the horse-loving Governor of California in 1872, proved that there were times when a horse was trotting when all its feet were off the ground.

'Muybridge', Edward Muggeridge, was an Englishman born at Kingston upon Thames, whose personal experiences included being charged with murder and acquitted. He publicized his work in *Animal Locomotion* (1888) and *Animals in Motion* (1899). In parallel, a French physician and university professor, Etienne Marey (1830–1906), publicized his own work in *Le Mouvement* (1894): he recorded multiple images of birds in flight on a single film. Muybridge opened a 'Zoopraxographical Hall' at the Chicago Columbian Exhibition of 1893, where a photographic display of leaping horses and gymnasts was a great popular attraction.

One year later, Edison, who had set up a laboratory at Menlo Park in 1876, an earlier Exhibition year, put on sale his patented kinetoscope, a device which made it possible to watch a moving film individually with an eye piece. Inspired by Muybridge and possibly by Marey, he set out to do for the eye what the phonograph (see p. 145) did for the ear. His practical ambition, however, was limited: he first conceived of the kinetoscope in the context of a peepshow, with one person at a time, having paid a coin, looking through it in a penny arcade. Edison did not believe that using it to project images onto a screen would be as financially profitable, but between 1893 and 1895 two of his technicians, W. K. L. Dickson and William Heise, shot a number of interesting twenty-minute films in the world's first film studio, the Black Maria. They included 'Bar Room Brawl' and 'Edison in Laboratory'.

In November 1895 Max and Emil Skladanowsky screened nine films in Berlin, using their Bioskop system – they included gloved kangaroos engaged in a boxing match – and a month later Louis Lumière (1864–1948), seventeen years younger than Edison, introduced his 'cinematograph', a *nouveauté du jour*, to an audience of thirty-five at the Grand Café in Paris, going on in 1896 to present films to a bigger audience at the Empire Music Hall in London's Leicester Square. The London programme was very mixed, beginning with an overture and including a group of Russian dancers and juggling acrobatic acts. One of the films shown was *The Arrival of the Paris Express*, another *Boating in the Mediterranean*.

Lumière was one of two brothers who made films which would later be called documentaries. Maxim Gorki (1868–1938), the Russian writer, who saw and admired some of them, said that the film was 'born from life'. There were other film-makers, however, like Georges Méliès (1861–1938), who had a background in magic and who believed that illusion was the strength of what came to be called 'the cinema'. Other film-makers looked to the stage. Indeed, in 1906, one observer maintained that 'instead of taking the place of the illustrated paper, as the cinematograph did, at first almost exclusively, it was taking the place of the theatre'. In fact, the film form was to prove as adaptable as the novel on which it drew; and while for some film-makers (to be treated by sophisticated critics as *auteurs*) their aim was art, a new mass audience was brought into existence through film, far bigger than that ever created by the theatre, in what was to be called the 'golden age of the cinema'. This was to be a term applied to other media, including broadcasting, which again created a wide variety of programmes.

That took time, however, as long a time as it took the cinema to develop its own forms and its institutions, although Edison was a quick convert to the new medium, benefiting from his patents and working closely with Eastman. France dominated early production, but there were active film-makers elsewhere, including Britain, where Brighton was an early centre. Their work has been reappraised in recent years. 'The Cinema of Attractions', as it has been called, drew on a rich variety of traditions of performance. For example, one English film-maker, R. W. Paul, who started his film life by duplicating Edison's kinetoscope, which was not then patented in England, produced in 1896 a 26-second film of Derby Day. In America in 1898 a young cartoonist, J. S. Blackton, was shown sketching Edison and In France Pathé Frères produced the first *Life of Christ* two years later.

The passion play inspired many film-makers, including Americans. By 1914, the United States was second in the film export market and Hollywood in California, at the centre of the golden age to come, had already made its first film. Hollywood was still 'a pepper tree-lined village' with orange groves only recently (1903) integrated into the growing metropolitan complex of Los Angeles. Nevertheless, even before 1914 there were 'film stars' there, among them Charles Chaplin (1889–1977), born in London and with a background in British vaudeville.

In the cinema business, which was strongly influenced by market considerations, there was a bigger division in Europe between production and distribution than there was between performance and production. Music hall proprietors and showmen were the first people in Britain and France to put on films, and it was not until 1904 that films could be rented rather than bought, and not until later in the decade that special halls for showing them were opened, the first of them in Britain at Colne in Lancashire. The first American film theatre was opened in Pittsburgh in 1905. In France Charles Pathé created his own projection halls. So too did Gaumont, who gave his name to a chain of them. Another word used in the naming of the theatres or halls was 'bioscope', the word that had been used by a German inventor.

During the 'golden age' the largest cinemas – a word adopted later on to describe buildings – were to be turned into glamorous 'dream palaces', offering other entertainment besides films, including music played on mammoth Wurlitzer organs and coffee and cakes in cinema cafés. There were still cinemas that were flea pits, however, although in silent days they too had live pianists accompanying the film on the screen. Between 1913 and 1932 the number of cinemas in the city of Liverpool, to take one example, rose from thirty-two to sixty-nine (while the number of theatres fell from eleven to six). It was estimated that in 1932 no fewer than four out of ten people in Liverpool were going to the cinema once a week and one in four twice a week.

Meanwhile, slowly but inexorably, film business passed out of the hands of what Gilbert Seldes, American author of a pioneering analysis *The Great Audience* (1951), called 'aggressive and ignorant men without taste or tradition, but with a highly developed sense of business' into the hands of bigger corporations. In 1909 Provincial Cinematograph Theatres Ltd was set up in Britain with an initial capital of £100,000. Twenty years later, there were two huge concerns formed through mergers: the Gaumont-British Picture Corporation (1927), which had connections with Fox Films in the United States and owned three hundred cinemas, and Associated British Cinemas (1928), connected to First National (American) and Pathé, and which, starting with twenty-eight cinemas, within a year had eighty-eight. A third company emerged in 1933, the Odeon Circuit, although it did not make films.

The pattern of film-making had been affected by the existence of Edison patents, national not international, and in 1908 an attempt was made by the ten leading American production and supply companies, all using Edison patents on the basis of an agreement with Edison, to establish a monopoly merger, the Motion Picture Patents Company. By the time that it was, so-called 'Independents', a term used previously in relation both to art and to business, had arrived in Hollywood. So, too, had Chaplin, who had worked first in New York in the Keystone Studios of Mack Sennett (1888–1960), starring in slapstick comedies. Chaplin's first Hollywood film, *Making a Living* (1914), won him world-wide praise and the most lavish of contracts. There could have been no stars without fans, and both were in evidence before the rise of Hollywood. So also, through the theatre, were so-called matinée idols.

Chaplin's reasons for moving to Hollywood were bound up with his work, not with the desire to make still more money. Tiring of Sennett's 'custard pie wars', which followed a formula, he founded his own studio and company, United Artists, in 1919, with Douglas Fairbanks (1883–1939), Mary Pickford (1893–1979) – who had also acquired star status, the first woman to do so – and D. W. Griffiths (1875–1949). Fourteen years older than Chaplin, Griffiths had, in 1915, produced one of Hollywood's early 'classics' (a term to become common in the future), *The Birth of a Nation* (1915). This was a long film, played entirely with white actors and with huge crowd effects, and it has been as frequently reinterpreted since 1915 as any Verdi opera. At the time, President Woodrow Wilson described watching it as being like reading history 'by flashes of lightning'. He did not comment on its length.

Already by 1920 there was talk of 'Chaplinitis', with an accompaniment of products to go along with the films – songs, dances, dolls and even cocktails, a combination to become familiar in film and, later, in sport; and Chaplin's films of the 1920s, particularly *The Gold Rush* (1928), were to acquire a mythical character. Characterized as 'the Tramp' or as 'the Little Fellow', Chaplin was praised for his grace as well as for his humour, for his timing as well as for his pathos: Sennett considered him 'the greatest artist who ever lived'. His fame was to continue to grow while a host of other stars – quite different from himself – had emerged, for example, Rudolf Valentino (1895–1926), 'the great lover'. After America's unprecedented boom of the 1920s had been succeeded by the equally unprecedented depression, which began in 1929, Chaplin's *Modern Times* (1936), presenting assembly lines in the kind of factory plant associated with automobile manufacturer Henry Ford (1863–1947), was to fascinate social historians as much as *The Birth of a Nation* had fascinated Wilson in 1915.

There were other films produced during the 1920s and 1930s which achieved the same reputation. For example, Fritz Lang's *Metropolis*, made in Germany in 1927, is a haunting portrayal of city life. Lang (1890–1976), born a year after Chaplin, had dealt directly in myth too (*Die Niebelungen*, 1924), and had initiated atmospheric crime films with his *Dr Mabuse der Spieler* (1922). His first 'talkie', the thriller *M*, made in 1931, was his own favourite.

Like the novel, the film was an international form, and among the acknowledged great directors were the Russian Sergei Eisenstein (1898–1948), the Japanese Akira Kurosawa (1910–98) and the Swede Ingmar Bergman (1918–), whose father was a Lutheran pastor and chaplain to the Swedish royal family. In the history of the novel, however, there had been no single city centre, nor was there to be, as Hollywood, with its powerful studio system, was for the 'movies'. From abroad, for various reasons, including politics, both performers and directors were drawn towards it. Chaplin, who never became an American citizen, was to emigrate eventually in 1952, when an anti-Communist witch-hunt led by the FBI was taking place. There had long been a censorship system in Hollywood, too, taking the form of a code. The man who devised it in 1930, W. H. Hays (1879–1954), had served as American Postmaster General under President Harding, and had been recruited to serve Hollywood in 1923.

The business context of film and novel was completely different. Among the Independents who moved to Hollywood, Adolph Zukor (1873–1976), having helped to destroy the Motion Picture Patents Company, turned to 'integration' himself, passing from production to distribution. It was he too who led the way

Fig. 19 *The Jazz Singer*. Crowds gather to see Al Jolson in the world's first 'talkie', a Warner Brothers film, in 1927.

from Hollywood to Wall Street, when in 1919 he raised funds through an issue of $10 million of preferred stock, the first major attempt to finance cinema from the capital market. Two years later he controlled more than three hundred cinemas. Complaints were now being made, as he had heard them made before, that he had made it difficult for small and independent producers or distributors of films to enter into or remain in the moving picture industry or market, or to lease individual pictures of merit. It was to remain difficult, for, as in radio corporate structures had hardened. The moguls ruling over the system were there to stay.

One new concern emerged, however: that owned by Warner Brothers, who had grown from nickelodeon operators to become giants in the film industry. They were to employ and to create many stars in a wide range of films, and it was through their enterprise, recorded in film, that *The Jazz Singer*, the first famous film in sound, was made in 1927, ushering in cinema's golden age. (While it was being made, Walt Disney's Mickey Mouse was on the drawing boards.) *The Jazz Singer* cost $500,000 to make and netted five times as much in box office receipts, the ultimate test of any commercial film. In 1928, the capital assets of Warner Brothers were valued at $16 million: in 1930, with the financial crash of 1929 intervening, they stood at $230 million.

It was difficult for film interests in other countries to face up to Hollywood, although with the end of silent films and introduction of sound the existence of the world's many languages, described in broadcasting circles as a Babel, gave non-American film producers an opportunity which, whatever the differences between the American and English languages might be, was absent in Britain. Different national cultures were expressed in film, often unconsciously, sometimes deliberately, with France throughout and Germany until the advent of Hitler in 1933 emphasizing the role of film as an art. The sense of there being creative *avant gardes* involved in film was strong. There were film-makers who drew sharp distinctions between their products and commercial films shown in cinemas. In the nineteenth century George Gissing had anticipated what they would say in what he wrote about literature in his novel *New Grub Street* (1891).

There was a new twist in the 1930s. The Depression stimulated the making of films that expressed the social conscience of their makers. In Europe, some of them were influenced by makers of documentaries, socially motivated and aiming at 'authenticity'. In Britain John Grierson (1895–1972) was their pioneer during the late 1920s. (A decade later, in 1939 he was given charge of the National Film Board of Canada.) Radio was influential too. For André Malraux in France, the talkies only became an art form when directors realized that their model should not be the gramophone record but the radio feature.

There was little in common between radio features and film documentaries and the lavish musicals in colour which were made towards the end of the 1930s, like *The Wizard of Oz* (1939) or the epic *Gone With the Wind*, released in the same year. During the Second World War they were to be watched by huge audiences, and after the war they were to take on a new life. Newsreels were another separate category, and there were even separate newsreel cinemas, the most successful of them outside railway stations. Most of the pioneer companies were French, with Pathé's *Animated Gazette* putting out a daily edition before 1914. Like its rival Gaumont, it presented a special women's edition during the 1920s. Fox-Movietone arrived from across the Atlantic in 1929 to produce a British product during the 1930s, complete with sound – and the soon familiar voice of Leslie Mitchell – after Lord Rothermere, owner of the *Daily Mail*, joined up with Fox to create British Movietone News, one of five newsreels. By 1933 the Big Five were producing an average of 520 newsreels per annum.

In Britain, a protectionist attitude towards the cinema had been evident in government circles from 1927 onwards. Hitherto, the government's only measure of control over the industry was an Act of 1909 which gave local authorities the power to license buildings used as cinemas and to censor films. (The industry itself set up a British Board of Film Censors in 1912.) The government acknowledged in 1927 that, while it saw no reason to offer financial assistance to the British film industry, there were grounds for intervening, because of the magnitude of what were described in Parliament as 'the industrial, commercial, education[al] and imperial interests involved'. In 1926, only 5 per cent of the films shown in Britain were actually made in the country. The British Cinematographic Films Act of 1927, described by Jeffrey Richards as 'a marked breach with the prevailing doctrine of free trade', controlled advance and block booking of films, introduced a quota system (maintained in a further Act of 1937) and created a Cinematographic Films Advisory Committee to advise the Board of Trade on the administration of the Act.

Neither the film industry nor the newsreel companies faced any serious challenge from television in 1927 or in 1933. Indeed, there was virtually no regular television in any country, although the word had been invented – in French – in 1900, and before that there had been a long pre-history of nineteenth-century experiment, going back, it has usually been claimed, to 1839 (see p. 133), the landmark year in the history of photography. Following Edouard Becquerel's experiments, Willoughby Smith, one of the telegraph engineers who supervised the laying of the transatlantic cable (see p. 105), noted in 1873 the correlation between the odd behaviour of selenium resistors and sunlight, and in the same decade a French lawyer suggested how selenium might be used in a scanning system. What he had in mind, however, was the transfer of single images, instantaneous but 'fugitive', rather than of continuous images on a screen; and when three years later, an Englishman, Shelford Bidwell, demonstrated 'picture telegraphy' – necessarily of poor definition – to the Physical Society in London, it was the precursor of fax rather than of television.

The technical basis of all television is different from that of the transmission of still pictures which Bidwell demonstrated. It involves the scanning of an image by a beam of light in a series of sequential lines moving from top to bottom and from left to right. Each section of the image, as the light passes over it, produces signals which are converted into electrical impulses, strong or weak. The impulses are then amplified and transmitted along wires or through the air by radio waves which are reconverted into light signals in the same order and the same strength as they were at their original source. Their capacity to appear to the human eye as a complete and moving picture on a screen depends on the retention of vision. No progress could be made until the valve amplifier, the key to radio telephony, had been invented.

There are two possible techniques of scanning – mechanical, by a disc, and electronic, by an electronic beam – and before 1914 there had been experiments with both. Paul Nipkow, a Berlin science student, had conceived of the first mechanical scanner in Germany in 1884 – although he never made one. It was a mechanical instrument (*Elektrisches Teleskop*), a rotating disc, spirally perforated with small holes through which a strong light shone. Electronic scanning, which was to prove to be the key to mass television, was identified as such by Campbell Swinton in 1908. He suggested 'the employment of two beams of kathode rays [note his use of the 'k' as in 'kinema'], one at the transmitting and one at the receiving station, synchronously deflected by the varying fields of two electromagnets':

> So far as the receiving apparatus is concerned [and he did not call it a television set] the moving kathode beam has only to be arranged to impinge on a sufficiently sensitive fluorescent screen, and given suitable variations in intensity, to obtain the desired result.

When Swinton wrote those words, he did not know of experiments being carried out in St Petersburg by Boris Rosing, a professor at the Technical Institute, who applied for a patent in 1907 proposing a television system using a cathode tube as a receiver. The work on such tubes had started in Germany, but Rosing carried it much further, developing prototypes, only to see his work lapse in Russia during the First World War.

After the Revolution, Vladimir Zworykin, one of Rosing's pupils, who emigrated twice to the United States (on the first occasion he could not find work), successfully patented a complete electrical television system in 1923. Later he joined RCA, taken on by Sarnoff (in secret) to run a laboratory, and he developed a new camera tube, the 240-line iconoscope, which he described, without demonstrating it, to a conference in Chicago in 1933: it was, he said, 'a new Version of the Electric Eye'.

There is an immense difference between forecasting on the basis of scientific knowledge, as Zworykin did, and popular speculation about future pictures on a screen. Yet the former kind of projection of the future does not always take account, as Marconi well knew, of the need for enterprise and publicity as well as knowledge. Popular forecasting could be closer to reality in certain respects, if wildly remote from it in others. A writer in *Lightning*, one of the many popular science magazines of the 1890s, was more right than wrong when he explained in 1893 that

> Before the next century shall expire the grandsons of the present generation will see one another across the Atlantic, and the great ceremonial events of the world, as they pass before the camera, will be executed at the same instant before mankind.

Yet another writer seemed to have the cinema more than the home in mind when he forecast that

> the showman of the future will be able to travel with a Derby or a Leger, a Cesarewitch or a Jubilee Stakes; with the Gentlemen versus Players [cricket] match [that was not to survive for reasons which he did not forecast], the Amateur [Boxing] Championship, the Varsity Boat Race, or a big turn with gloves at the National Sporting Club; to show you the spectators, principals, umpires, referees, judges, horses, jockeys, boats, water, playing fields, and all, and treat you to a day's sport whenever you want it and whenever you plan to have it.

Like many other forecasters, the writer was comparing eye and ear. Neither writer focused on the devices, including screens, which would enable 'viewers', a word of the future, to follow distant events.

When, a generation later, the first publicity gathered around practical television the situation had changed. Television sets ('televisors') were being put on sale in the late 1920s: they had not been discussed much before. And the focus in Britain was now on a particular inventor, a Scot born in Helensburgh, John Logie Baird (1888–1946), a son of the Manse. A lonely man, ingenious, diligent and shabby – his first mechanical scanner was made out of a hat-box – Baird, nonetheless, appreciated the need for publicity, dependent as he was on raising funds from others, and consequently did more to publicize television on both sides of the Atlantic than any other single person. Baird, too, had his 'first', indeed two of them. Working with a young assistant, V. R. Mills, he was thrilled to see his fingers appear on the screen. Even more thrilling for him, he saw the head and shoulders of his office boy, William Taynton, who had been scared by the intense white light of the arc lamp used in his studio by Baird. Baird was so pleased that he gave Taynton half-a-crown.

It seemed even more of a landmark date when, on 30 September 1929, after protracted negotiations with a reluctant BBC, Baird was given permission to launch an experimental television service. The President of the British Board of Trade, granting it his blessing, told viewers (still not described as such) that he looked forward 'to this new applied science to encourage and provide a new industry, not only for Britain and for the British Empire but for the whole world'.

A year earlier, the eminent philosopher and mathematician Bertrand Russell had warned his readers that while 'apparatus' had been constructed 'capable of transmitting more or less recognizable pictures of still life objects, such as a drawing, a page of writing or a stationary illuminated face', there 'did not exist nor, as far as one can see, is there likely to exist in the near future, any apparatus capable of transmitting a real life moving picture such as the Boat Race or the Derby'. Russell was as wrong as H. G. Wells had been at the beginning of the twentieth century when he discussed the future of aviation. Television had already become a reality 'in fact' when a Pirandello play was televised in July 1930.

Baird's relations with the BBC – and the Post Office, which had to approve of experimental television broadcasting – were complex not so much because the corporation was suspicious of television – some of the BBC's leading executives were – but because it was suspicious of Baird himself and, above all, of his business associates, one of whom, Isidore Ostrer (for a time) ran Gaumont British, the film company, and acquired a newspaper, the *Sunday Referee*. Baird was interested in every aspect of television, including long-distance, colour and big-screen television, but he found it just as difficult to work in the United States, where he was thwarted by entrenched American radio interests, as he had done in Britain.

All these factors, as well as technology, determined the future of television, including its timing, and from the start all the business advantages were on the side of large organizations rather than individual inventors. One of these companies was the newly merged Electrical and Musical Industries Ltd (EMI). There was no exchange of information during the 1930s between EMI, the Marconi Wireless Company, RCA and Baird, who was left on the sidelines, as was an American inventor, C. P. Jenkins, who had contributed earlier to the development of the cinema projector. Like Baird, he experimented with mechanical scanners.

A second American inventor, Philo Farnsworth, born on an Idaho farm, who worked on developing an all-electric television system, using quite different apparatus from Zworykin, was luckier. He joined the Board of Philadelphia Battery Company, Philco, a rival of RCA, which produced radio sets, including sets for automobiles. Farnsworth left Philco amicably and financially secure, but before doing so he assigned his own patents to Baird who had by then turned to electronic scanning. Meanwhile EMI, with access to RCA patents, built up a remarkable team, directed by another Rosing pupil, Isaac Shoenberg, who had worked earlier with the Marconi Company, and including Alan Blumlein, 'a genius who showered idea upon idea'. Using an Emitron camera, they set out to develop a 405-line system for Britain. At the same time, Telefunken in Germany, with gramophone as well as radio and television interests, was experimenting with a Zworykin design.

Both in Germany and in England, two television systems were pitted against each other during the mid-1930s in a conflict that reached its climax in Britain when the two were brought head to head in trials – as had been the case in railway history – in the autumn of 1936. In January 1935, an official government inquiry had recommended the inauguration of a limited but ultimately 'general' service (without making clear-cut suggestions about finance) and the setting up of a Television Advisory Committee; and in response the BBC organized the first television transmissions from Radiolympia, the main radio trade fair, in August 1936. The first programme was called *Here's Looking at You*. The trial started in earnest on 2 November, when on the toss of a coin the Baird system was given the first run: it described its installation as having been built 'with typical British thoroughness as solidly as that on a battleship', while Marconi-EMI confidently chose as its slogan 'The System of Today and Tomorrow'.

The first studios used by the BBC were at Alexandra Palace, a great North London centre of nineteenth-century entertainment, complete with organ and racecourse. Baird himself was working then in the Crystal Palace. The advanced new technology of television was thus developing in London within Victorian shells. Yet it was the EMI technology which was really advanced; as Cecil Madden, who dealt with the programmes, put it, working in the Baird studio was 'a bit like using Morse code when you knew that next door you could telephone'. This judgement was not untypical. When the BBC engineer D. C. Birkinshaw had seen for the first time in 1934 the Marconi-EMI system, equipped with new Emitron cameras, he had had no doubt that it would triumph: 'A picture not produced by mechanical means. No whizzing discs, no mirror drums, silence, lightness, portability. It showed the way things were going.' He was right. Baird, who had done more than any other person in the world to publicize practical television, duly lost the contest – and with it far more. He went on working in television until his death, but his company was placed in the hands of the receiver in 1939.

One of the engineers who had worked with Baird and who became a consultant on radar, part of a system that met war needs, put Baird's work into long-term perspective. 'He was', Jim Percy wrote, 'right at the end of the mechanical age. He thought in terms of wheels and sprockets and devices that spun around. He really wasn't with the electronics age at all. He hardly knew how a cathode tube worked. But he created a demand . . . If it hadn't been for Baird shouting and yelling and putting his crude 30-line pictures over London, we wouldn't have had television in this country before the War. He demonstrated that television *could* be done if not the way it should be done.'

In other European countries, without a Baird, electronic television won more easily, and in Germany, Fernseh, a subsidiary of the camera company Zeiss Ikon, like Baird, lost out to its rival. Meanwhile, the production of cameras and television sets made progress both in the Netherlands and in Sweden. The Philips Company built a Dutch iconoscope in 1935, and in the same year began 180-line experimental transmissions, later changing the definition to 450-lines, then 405, as in Britain; and when war broke out in 1939, Philips television sets were on sale, capable of being used either in Holland or in Britain. In Sweden, experimental broadcasts, licensed by the Swedish Board of Telegraphy and Radio AB, a subsidiary of the W. M. Ericsson Telephone Manufacturing Company, began in 1939.

In France, there were experiments by Baird subsidiaries before an iconoscope was installed at the Paris Exhibition of 1937, and a new station was opened in the Eiffel Tower by the Administration des Postes, Télégraphes et Téléphones. Using 455 lines, the station was said in 1939 to have a top capacity of 45,000 watts, making it the most powerful television station in the world.

Meanwhile, television in Britain was suspended at the beginning of the Second World War, and although television in Germany and France continued, if not on a regular basis, it was not revived in London until 1946, still for a strictly limited audience. 'The Age of Television', described in the next chapter, was not to begin until the 1950s (see p. 188). In the United States and Japan, 525 lines were used: in Europe mainly 625. There were to be different concerns and different chronologies, but the same problems of control were raised as had been raised in radio broadcasting.

Gramophones

One of the first inventors to interest himself in the transmission of pictures was Edison, but he had been more concerned during the 1870s with the transmission of words and music. It is interesting, therefore, to compare the early history of the cinema with the early history of the gramophone industry. One took people out of the home, and the other, as television was to do, kept people in it. Before Edison became involved, however, it was a French photographer, Nadar, who conceived in high-sounding language of an 'acoustic daguerreotype which faithfully and tirelessly reproduces all the sounds subjected to its objectivity'. Like Sarnoff long after him, Nadar suggested 'a box in which melodies could be caught and fixed, as the *camera obscura* captures and fixes images'. He called his machine a phonograph.

Edison, who at the age of thirty was described in some American newspapers as Professor Edison, turned conception into fact, interested in more than the mere recording of sound for contemporaries. After meticulous and well-recorded team research, he patented a mechanical 'telegraphic reporter' in 1877, the year after Bell's telephone patent, in which a disc, covered with paper, turned on a turntable and an engraving stylus suspended on an arm marked a series of dots and dashes in a spiral. Edison had no doubt that he was capable of recording and reproducing the human voice, and in the *Scientific American* he described his discovery as a 'wonderful invention capable of repeating speech countless times by means of automatic recordings'.

A telephone subscriber, Edison maintained, could connect his telephone to a phonograph – the same word – which 'with each call' would 'inform the exchange that he [was] out and that he [would] be back at a certain time. Similarly, one subscriber who calls another and finds him out will be able to say what he wants to and have this recorded on a phonograph.' In this instance, Edison was ahead of his time, as were prophets of the mobile phone. He also noted, as did Bell, who built a 'graphophone', the possible use of the phonograph as an office dictating machine, which would complement another major nineteenth-century invention, the typewriter, of which there were many versions.

As always, journalists went further (at first) than he did in contemplating multiple uses. For *Leslie's Weekly*, the phonograph would 'turn all the old grooves of the world topsy-turvy and establish an order of things never dreamed of even in the vivid imaginings of the Queen Scheherazade in the 1001 Nights Entertainments'. Edison would not have liked this language, but by 1878 he too was suggesting ten possible uses for his phonograph. It might be 'liberally devoted to music', but the fourth of its uses would be to serve as 'a family record', 'a registry of sayings, reminiscences, etc., of family members and their dying words'. The *Electric World* of 1890 tantalized its readers with a further attraction: 'Fancy an interview with Gladstone or Bismarck reproduced not only in their words but with the very intonations of the great statesmen.' The writer was thinking not of classrooms but of phonographed newspapers entering the home. Edison's talking machine actually recorded Gladstone, the poet Robert Browning and Cardinal Manning.

During the early years of the phonograph industry, when market progress was slow, there were fierce struggles between Edison and Bell interests before an outsider, Jesse H. Lippincott, a businessman from Pittsburgh, managed to secure control of both in 1888, only to go bankrupt rapidly two years later. The following year there was a new company to take into account, the Columbia Phonograph Company; and even before that Emile Berliner (1851–1921), an inventor of German origin, who had worked at first with Bell but had severed his connection in 1883, had entered the scenario. Berliner drew on the work of other inventors as he developed a new grooved disc-playing machine, which he called a gramophone, in 1888. Further developed technically by Eldridge Johnson, who introduced clockwork drive and controlled speeds, it was the gramophone which was to become the successful product of the immediate future.

The technology behind the two products was different, but so too were the intentions of the inventors. Deeply interested in the quality recording of classical music – Berliner was a music lover – he opted for the use of a mould to duplicate sound recordings. For him, repeatability mattered more than it did initially to Edison or Bell. Very quickly Edison recognized that Berliner's flat gramophone discs, 'plates' as he called them, which came to be known as 'records', were more popular than his own cylinders, but in the first decade of the twentieth century, after a patent sharing deal in 1901 and the expiry of other Edison patents in 1903, the price of cylinders fell. New technical processes were largely responsible.

Company structures were complex and differed on the two sides of the Atlantic. In the United States, the Victor Talking Machine Company was set up in 1901 which acquired a hold over the American gramophone industry for more than half a century. Its approach followed what Michael Chanon has called 'a consumption model': the record was being dealt with like a book and not like a photograph. Successful performers were to make larger amounts of money out of their recordings, however, than most authors made out of their books. Thus, the Italian tenor Enrico Caruso, who made his first quality recording in 1901 and his first million-selling record in 1904, went on to earn two million dollars from his records by the time of his death in 1921.

The organization of music, classical and pop, and the fortunes of musicians, based on performing rights, were to be transformed through the introduction of what was called at first 'mechanical music'. So too, however, were the lives of the listeners. Not all at once, the gramophone took the place of the piano in the home, a very different looking object, with a familiar image to go with the music, that of a listening dog. (The His Majesty's Voice label, known throughout Europe, had been devised by a painter who had first depicted an Edison machine in one of his paintings.) More than image was involved, however, for in the long run, through recording and broadcasting, there was a remarkable improvement in the quality both of performance and of recordings. Meanwhile, the Victor Talking Machine Company's revenues increased sevenfold between 1902 and 1917, when the United States entered the First World War. In 1914, it was one of nearly two hundred American gramophone companies, compared with eighty companies in Britain, and by the end of the First World War it had capital assets of just below £38 million.

In continental Europe, where other gramophone companies had emerged, the story began with Pathé Frères in France, formed in 1898, which produced cylinder gramophones before switching to discs in 1906. The switch was more general, although in Britain cylinders were far more popular than discs until a financial crisis in 1908, when many businesses dropped out in what a trade journal called 'a good winnowing . . . separating the wheat from the chaff'. 'In an industry like this, still in the throes of development', it generalized, 'this is always so.' Business revived, however, between then and 1914, with Germany playing an increasing part in international trade.

After the First World War, the Victor Talking Machine Company was selling four times as many records in 1921 as it had done in 1914, and rival companies, too, seemed strong in Britain and continental Europe. Unlike the cinema industry, however, the gramophone industry was to face a major crisis between 1929 and 1932. It survived the Great Depression, but only six million records were sold in 1932, 6 per cent of the total sales in 1927. The golden age of the record, if not of the gramophone, was still to come.

Conclusions

This chapter and the previous one have charted within a chronological frame the development of communications from the advent of steam power through into the 1920s and early 1930s, when there were many media instruments and when new media organizations were created, some of which very quickly became institutions. There were different pedigrees in each branch of what ultimately came to be called a single media industry, but there were economic, social and technological connections and overlaps, recognized by contemporaries. *Science Siftings* chose to start with railways, when, as early as 1892, it observed how 'we are all learning to move together, act together, achieve in vast companies'; and in the same year, *The Electrical Engineer*, charting what had already been done in relation to the spread of message services, could conclude that 'still the cry is for quicker communication'.

Fig. 20 Alfred Harmsworth, first Viscount Northcliffe, greatest of British press tycoons, seen here in 1911 with members of the Astor family. His passion was automobiles.

It was not only individuals, like Wheatstone or Vail or, above all, Edison, who provided the connections. There were geographical connections too. London and Paris were always on the communications map. So, too, after its emergence from the Midwest plains of the United States, was Chicago. Detroit figured too. Yet far smaller places, like Lowell, moved on and off the map at several points in time; and Hollywood in the west was to transform the setting in which it found itself, as Silicon Valley was to do half a century later.

Two late nineteenth-century and early twentieth-century innovations in transportation, one mentioned at more than one point in this survey, affected the overall picture – automobiles and aeroplanes – with the advent of bicycles serving as a prelude to the automobile, which still, at the end of the nineteenth century, was a luxury product. The making of bicycles offered an apprenticeship, too, to some of the inventors involved. Thus, in Britain, Edward Butler, who produced the first petrol-driven engine capable of being attached to an automobile, had begun by designing a petrol-driven bicycle, and William Morris (1877–1963), later Lord Nuffield, repaired bicycles in Oxford before and after he repaired motor cars. It was a mechanic from Coventry, which became a centre of the British automobile Industry, John K. Stanley, who built the first Rover safety cycle in 1885.

Alfred Harmsworth, later Lord Northcliffe (1865–1922), founder of *Answers* and the *Daily Mail*, worked for the cycling magazines *Wheel Life* and *Bicycling Times* before he moved onwards into motoring, his greatest love, and at the same time became a 'media mogul'. In 1902, he published a still readable book, *Motors and Motor Driving*. In the United States, Hiram Maxim (1869–1936), son of the inventor of the Maxim gun and himself the inventor of an automobile, wrote with hindsight in his autobiography that 'the bicycle could not satisfy the demand which it had created. A mechanically-propelled vehicle was wanted instead of a foot-propelled one, and we now know the automobile was the answer.'

It was not the answer for those people who in the twentieth century could not afford to buy automobiles, even after they had ceased to be a luxury, for bicycles not only continued to coexist with automobiles (as old and new media coexisted), but were to remain the dominant form of transportation in late twentieth-century China. Meanwhile, Japan became a major producer both of bicycles, some from the 1960s onwards luxury products in themselves, and of auto-mobiles. There was a psychological angle, too, as well as an economic one, to the development of transportation as a medium, as there was to advertising and collecting. The bicycle could be considered, as Marshall McLuhan was to consider media like radio and television in the 1960s, as an 'extension' of man. The man on the bicycle was not just a man and a machine. He was a 'faster man'.

The different parts of the bicycle, like the different parts of the railway (tracks, locomotive, stations, signals), had their own prehistory – steering (1817), pedals (1839), front-wheel cranks (1861), pneumatic tyres (1890) and geared front-drive (1889–96) – and there were many intermediate products, including French *velocipedes* (in English 'bone-shakers') and tricycles. They were all associated, not only with individuals (women as well as men) or with families, but collectively with clubs. They were a 'democratic' mode of transport. Automobiles were to acquire the same stamp only after Ford, as influential a figure in his lifetime as Watt or Boulton, set the pace. His famous Model T, which took to the roads in 1908, was based on the principle, unattractive to fashion designers, that one automobile should be like another automobile, a standardized product sold at the lowest possible price.

Automobiles, thought of at first as luxury products, must be considered among the cluster of inventions which ushered in a new age which has been called both 'the Age of the Automobile' and 'the Age of Broadcasting'. They were pioneered in France and Germany, with Gottfried Daimler and Karl Benz producing a four-stroke gasoline-burning engine in 1885. Rudolf Diesel used heavier liquid fuels. They might have been electrical products, but for various reasons such an option was rejected and they came to depend on an oil industry, international in scale, but with a distinctive geopolitics of its own, which gained in importance with the advent of aircraft and air traffic. The geopolitics of the Middle East, in particular, were to be transformed. And in the long run coal seemed doomed.

The social consequences of the inventions were from the start ambivalent. Some inventions encouraged privacy, others threatened it. Some generated new problems (accidents, pollution). Some promised and provided new freedoms, among them the 'freedom of the road'. Yet while red flags to limit speed had been waved away long before the first 'freeway' was built, the freedom of the road pointed to the necessity for control of traffic and speed. Newspapers, proud of their freedom in Britain and the United States, in particular, emphasized the need for it in editorial leaders which often contrasted with the advertisements they displayed.

As in Chapter 1, therefore, which dealt with the period before the advent of steam, it is difficult in retrospect to treat the history of the nineteenth-century communications complex in purely linear terms, although in that century a self-conscious sense of progress, while challenged, usually unified the story as contemporaries saw it. At the Paris Exhibition of 1900, the climax of the century, in front of the Palace of Electricity building an electrically powered cascade of water fell on a basin containing an illuminated and sculpted group 'representing Humanity conducted by Progress' overturning figures of Furies representing 'the Routine of Present and Past'. Visiting the same exhibition, the percipient American writer Henry Adams meditated on the cult of the electrical dynamo, which he compared with the cult of the Virgin Mary.

There had been more than symbolic significance in the switch from steam to electricity during the last decades of the nineteenth century, for it was the electrical inventions, which demanded a new infrastructure, that seemed to point most clearly to the future. A *Punch* cartoon of February 1899 showed 'Electricity giving Steam Warning' within the context of submarine cable and land telegraphy. The caption read: 'I don't want to get rid of old and valuable servants but I am afraid that I shall not be able to keep either of you much longer.' A far wider context might have been chosen. Steam had had its gospel, intelligible to large numbers of people. Electricity, a natural force, fascinated new generations without being as intelligible. At best it had a mission.

Nevertheless, electricity also had what Carolyn Marvin has called a 'priesthood' – men who possessed special knowledge and carried distinctive authority. Women did not figure in it, however, except when they were called upon to depict 'the goddess of electricity' or more prosaically 'the Electric Light'; indeed, one of Marconi's daughters was called Electra.

In fact, a large variety of different occupational groups was covered by the new word 'electrician'. Profit preoccupied only a number of them, among them the creators of the modern media of communications, 'media for the millions'. Only in retrospect, however, could they be called cultural entrepreneurs. Others concerned with electricity were providing what was thought of as a utility, and the development of utilities, among them the supply of water, depended upon the introduction of infrastructure systems, whether publicly or privately owned.

In the next chapter which, like Chapter 2, focuses on particular periods and particular clusters of events, personalities and tendencies, four overlapping periods are identified, as they were at the time, to each of which a label was attached: 'the age of the Press', 'the age of broadcasting', 'the age of the cinema' and 'the age of television'. Such labels tend to be attached to particular periods according to what seems for a variety of reasons to be the dominant technology. The press did not always give its name to the age when it became the dominant medium, but it publicized all labels, even devised them. The chapter deals briefly with the three generally acknowledged functions of the various media – information, education and entertainment – and describes the different ways of dealing with them.

6 Information, Education, Entertainment

As the previous chapters have shown, the importance of information in what in the twentieth century became an almost sacred trinity – information, education and entertainment – was fully recognized long before the popularization of the terms 'information society' and 'information technology' during the 1970s and 1980s. The elements of the trinity itself had, however, not always been identified in the same language. 'Information' had usually been described in the seventeenth and eighteenth centuries as 'intelligence', 'education' as 'instruction', and 'entertainment' as 'recreation', 'pastime' or 'amusement'. Similar terms existed in other European languages. In the nineteenth century the words 'elevation' and 'uplift' were key words in the vocabulary, and 'trivial' information was separated from 'useful' information, while 'entertainment' was deemed 'rational' or 'debasing'.

Both education and entertainment had long histories stretching back to the ancient world, in the settings of academies, libraries, games, theatres. So too had 'intelligence'. The verb 'inform', derived from Latin, originally meant, both in English and French, not only giving facts, which might be incriminating, but 'forming the mind'. The importance of information was already clearly appreciated but was stressed still further in the commercial and industrial society of the nineteenth century, when notions of speed and distance were transformed. As Sydney Chapman put it in a book on the Lancashire cotton industry, published in 1904: 'during the last century the amount and the accuracy of information at the disposal of dealers increased enormously; moreover, the time elapsing between an event and the general knowledge of an event has dwindled to a small fraction of what it used to be.' The same point had been made in Walter Bagehot's *Lombard Street* (1873), centre of the City of London. It is notable that it was in nearby Threadneedle Street that one of the first merged telegraph companies, the Magnetic, had built imposing new offices in 1859. In 1884, the compiler of what he called 'the first statistical dictionary in any language', M. G. Mulhall, claimed that between 1840 and 1880 world banking had increased elevenfold, three times as fast as commerce and twenty times faster than population – the latter, in Britain, in particular, largely concentrated in cities and towns.

There were more changes than continuities in education and entertainment during the nineteenth and twentieth centuries, most of them explicable in economic and social terms, provided that technology, treated as a social activity, involving people and products as well as patents, is always incorporated in the analysis. Technology both requires and produces social and organizational change. Institutional change is often more difficult to achieve, and there was much talk in the nineteenth century of an 'age of transition'. There were

institutional differences, too, within what came to be considered in the twentieth century as a media complex; and even then schools and universities were
markedly different, at least in principle, from newspaper offices, radio and television studios, theatres, cinemas and sports stadiums, although they could – and
often did – incorporate each or all of these. It is as true of education as it is of
technology that it both requires and produces social and organizational change.

In the flow of history, or to use an alternative metaphor, 'the march of time',
industrialization, which, as we have seen, increased both wealth and leisure,
gave new meaning to each element in the trinity. While it demanded a more substantial and reliable circulation of information, both for financial reasons and
for the control of industrial processes, it also required in the long run a broader
public access to education, beginning at school, at which attendance became
compulsory in Britain in 1880 and in France, fully secularized, in 1882. (Prussia
had led the way in the eighteenth century.) Mass literacy was now deemed essential, just as continuing education and computer literacy came to be in the last
decades of the twentieth century.

In the long run, too, industrial advance called for greater opportunities for relax-
ation, active or passive, in the form of recreation. The first national Education Act
in Britain was passed (belatedly) in 1870, to be preceded in 1850 by the first Public
Libraries Act and to be followed in 1871 by the first Bank Holiday Act, laying down
that certain days should be national holidays. Previously, holidays had been
linked directly both in Roman Catholic and in Protestant countries to the seasonal
and the religious calendar, and some of them were local. Increasingly, through the
media, they were linked in the twentieth century to new rhythms of work and play
and in the process were commercialized. Yet Thanksgiving remained the great
home festival in the United States and pre-Lent carnival in places as different as
New Orleans, Trinidad, Rio and Cologne. In Britain, no newspapers were published on Christmas Day or Good Friday. In the Muslim world, which gained in
importance in the late twentieth century, the great fasting season of Ramadan survived: it commemorated the first revelation of the Koran. In countries where there
had been revolutions, their anniversaries now entered the calendar.

Work rather than play was at the heart of a Victorian gospel, as preached by
Samuel Smiles (who was translated into both Arabic and Japanese), and
remained a necessary aspect of human existence, underwritten in most scriptures. In increasingly secularized and urbanized societies it was treated explicitly as a social necessity, both in years of high unemployment, cyclical or
structural, and in years of technological labour-saving advance. The automation
of industrial processes, including the manufacture of armaments, was extended
through electronics and affected and continues to affect employment just as
directly as it affected and affects the media – with immediate human consequences. *Cybernetics*, the science of automatic control and communications
processes in animals and machinery, was the title of a pioneering American
study by Norbert Wiener (1894–1964), published in 1948.

Long before automation became a subject of discussion during the next
decade, work patterns, workplaces and the context and meanings of work had
changed substantially. The first change had come in the late eighteenth and early
nineteenth centuries when 'industry', thought of earlier in the eighteenth

century as a human quality, came to be treated separately from agriculture and eventually identified as the non-agricultural sector of the productive economy. In the late twentieth century it was to be a word that was also applied to agriculture, the share of which in the labour force – and gross national product – had declined dramatically. A second change came with 'scientific management', based on time and motion studies, developed first in the United States and adapted in various forms in quite different countries. The automobile manufacturer Henry Ford, with his standardization of product and assembly lines, was a hero in the Soviet Union.

In the late twentieth century the word 'work' began to be applied also to leisure, travel and sport. Sports became sport (though the plural was retained in the United States); entertainments became entertainment (on both sides of the Atlantic). Leisure, tourism, sport and, not least, 'heritage' were all now treated as industries or, eventually, as sectors in one industry. Sport, in particular, illustrates trends. Locally organized at first, it was to become 'global', and 'amateur', at first, it was to become largely professional, with 'rules' being drafted in the nineteenth century and modified later. In the twentieth and twenty-first centuries professional footballers were – and are – told to work by managers who might hire or fire them for their 'work effort' (the managers themselves, including national managers, are themselves hired and fired), while journalists often judged – and judge – players' and managers' performances on the field in these terms. Some of the players were – and are – exceptionally highly paid celebrities, relying on agents of the kind that most actors, musicians and authors had come to depend upon since the 1890s. Their private lives off the field are published in the media. They also have their own 'halls of fame'. A minority of them have gone on to become highly paid journalists.

The twenty-ninth General Assembly of the European Broadcasting Union, held in Athens in 1978, was the first European occasion when all aspects of the organization of sport were covered, but by the 1990s the organization had been completely transformed. The words 'spectator sports' lost much of their meaning. Spotlit by the media, sections of which, often through patronage, sometimes through communications mergers, acquired an economic interest in sport, they became as commercialized as 'the food chain' had become under the influence of supermarket retailing. The detail is as interesting as comparisons across time. The adjective 'historic' is often attached to the detail of the scenes of Derby Day or of Superbowl, national events which are now part of a media calendar. A number of international events, particularly the Olympic Games, which were 'revived' in Athens in 1896 – their location in 2004 – are a staple of all the media, which directly influence their location and their image. The German Olympics of 1936, stage managed (and filmed) by the Nazis, received massive attention. So, too, did the first Games to be held in an Asian country, in Tokyo, Japan, in 1964: they might have been held there earlier had it not been for the Second World War.

There was a technological dimension too. The 1912 Stockholm Olympics, for instance, saw the first use of electrical timing equipment for running events. New and smaller cameras, carefully grouped and placed, made it possible for viewers to see more of the action. This was merely a beginning. Slow motion replays fascinated viewers and were studied by the athletes themselves. So, also, week by week, were televised incidents on the football, cricket or baseball field, involving referees and umpires as well as players, now under perpetual media scrutiny. The camera could become a referee. In the late twentieth century, television too had an influence on the timing of sports, even on their rules. It came to control their finance, and through the finance much else.

The dividing lines between information and entertainment became increasingly blurred during the 1950s and 1960s, both in newspapers and in the electronic media, and were later to become even more hazy. Producers showed established sports to the sound of music. Hitherto, spectators had sung songs and chanted before and during games: now players chanted as well and (for money) sang songs off the field. Producers of sports programmes introduced them with entertainment items. There were some 'crazy gang' sports, like wrestling, which television companies bought in as a World Wrestling Federation 'product' solely for the purpose of entertainment.

This was not an entirely new phenomenon, however, as is revealed in the history of the press – long before Harmsworth launched his halfpenny *Daily Mail* in London in 1896, with the explicit object of entertaining as well as informing. His was the first daily newspaper to include a women's page, and 'stunts' were as much part of his strategy as features. Nor was education left out of his range. As a distinguished Liberal journalist, J. A. Spender, observed, 'he and his imitators influenced the common man more than all the education ministers put together'. Technology was made to count – and extolled. 'It is no secret', readers of the first copies of the *Daily Mail* were told, 'that remarkable new inventions have just come to the help of the Press. Our type is set by machinery. We can produce 200,000 papers per hour, cut, folded.'

The Press – The 'Fourth Estate'

There had been references to the importance of technology in the history of the press two generations earlier than Harmsworth and after Koenig (see p. 91), when America took over the lead from Britain in printing technology (the type-revolving press). Popular journalism, nevertheless, did not rest on technology. Nor did the arguments for defending 'old' journalism. On this side of the Atlantic *The Times*, the dominant organ of the press in London, was treated itself during the 1830s, '40s and '50s as a 'fourth estate'. The person who is said to have coined the phrase was the historian Macaulay, although he was referring to the Press Gallery in Parliament rather than to *The Times* or the press as a whole. The medieval concept of an 'estate' – Lords Spiritual, Lords Temporal and Commons – had been broken in revolutionary France, but it survived residually in Britain in the two Houses of Parliament, and the new term 'fourth estate' was used as the title of a book on the press by F. Knight Hunt, a journalist, in 1850. The term became accepted not only in Britain but in several other European countries and even in the United States. Indeed, in the twentieth century, the American periodical *Broadcasting* was to print proudly on its cover the words 'The Fifth Estate'.

The Times, described in 1871 as 'the greatest journal the world has ever witnessed', was an expensive paper, not a 'mass journal', and it lost some of its own dominance in Britain after stamp duties, reduced in 1836, were abolished in 1855 and the paper duties were repealed in 1861. Long before that, however, the 'penny press' had appeared in New York before it appeared in London, the first successful newspaper being the New York *Sun* (1833), which was started by a struggling job-printer, Benjamin Day. When he disposed of it in 1838, it was selling 34,000 copies, many of them at street corners. Much of the information it contained related to ordinary people – and the police. A totally fictional account of life on the moon, 'The Moon Hoax', was part of the entertainment which it provided.

More innovatory and more comprehensive in vision was James Gordon Bennett's New York *Herald* (1835). 'My ambition', wrote Bennett (1795–1872), born in Scotland, 'is to make the newspaper press the great organ and pivot of government, society, commerce, finance, religion, and all human civilization.' Religion mattered seriously in this list: 'a newspaper can send more souls to heaven and save more from hell than all the clubs and chapels in New York.' J. G. Bennett Jr (1841–1918) followed the same confident approach: Stanley's mission to Africa to discover Livingstone was financed by him. Technology was part of the Bennetts' vision also. In 1854, Bennett Sr experimented with a method of printing using a metal plate impression of type rather than the type itself. This was genuine innovation, and by the 1870s printing by stereotypes had spread widely. In Paris, *La Presse* was using the stereotyping process as early as 1852.

Eleven years before that Horace Greeley (1811–72), coiner of the phrase 'Go west, young man, go west', who had been involved in journalism before Bennett, launched his New York *Tribune*, the 'Great Moral Organ', which he hoped would be self-sufficient in its supply of news. There were then twelve daily newspapers in the city. While the *Tribune* included articles sent from Europe by Marx (many of them written by Engels, see p. 92), it deliberately excluded some domestic news, refusing to print details of crimes, reports of trials, and theatre plays. The *New York Times* (1851), 'a sane and sensible newspaper', founded by a young reporter from Greeley's staff, Henry Raymond (1820–69), followed a professedly balanced line, in the twentieth century explicitly separating 'news' and 'views'. 'We do not believe that *everything* in society is either exactly right or exactly wrong; what is good we desire to preserve and improve; what is evil to exterminate and reform.'

In this case – and others – the American press freed itself from party political ties which had figured prominently in its early development. How free it was in practice was a matter of law as well as of politics. The First Amendment, incorporated in a Bill of Rights passed by Congress in 1791, stated that 'Congress shall make no law respecting an establishment of religion, or prohibiting the free exercise thereof; or abridging the freedom of speech or of the press.' The language seemed plain, and it influenced all subsequent American history, but just what the amendment would mean in changing circumstances was left to the courts – and to public discussion. It was never certain. Justice Learned Hand maintained that 'right conclusions are more likely to be gathered out of a multitude of tongues than through any kind of authoritative selection', while Justice Oliver Wendell Holmes (1841–1935) introduced the metaphor 'free market place of ideas'. Broadcasting (see p. 173) was to be treated differently from the press; it was to be subject to regulation, one of the grounds being that because of the scarcity of space on the radio spectrum, if it had not been regulated the 'multitude of tongues' would have sounded like gibberish.

Legal judgments and public data became entangled with arguments about monopoly. Anti-trust legislation and implementation, themselves the cause of clashes of opinion as well as of interests, centred on the term 'public interest' which was also proclaimed in the 'fairness' doctrine' developed by the Federal Communications Commission, set up in Washington in 1934 by the Federal Communication Act. The doctrine imposed a two-part duty on broadcasters – to devote a reasonable time to controversial issues of public importance and to provide reasonable opportunity for contrasting viewpoints on such issues to be heard. It was a doctrine that did not survive deregulation of the American electronic media in the 1980s and 1990s but, of course, the First Amendment did. For this reason alone, the media history of the United States has been different from that of all other countries, one of which, Sweden, had an old press law of 1766, protecting freedom of expression.

From the start, the press in New York was only one element in an American press which was never centralized and continued to rest on a local base. So, too, did the press in France and Italy, although Paris was the centre of French mass circulation papers, beginning with *Le Petit Journal* in 1863, selling a quarter of a million copies a day, then said to be the largest circulation in the world. (There were as many disputes about which was the largest as there were about which was the first invention, but with no patent law at stake.) *Le Petit Parisien* followed in 1876, *Le Matin* in 1882 and *Le Journal* in 1889. In Britain, while *The Times* was losing ground to competition in London after the repeal of the Stamp Act and the end of the paper duties, the provincial press thrived during the middle years of the nineteenth century. In 1864, there were ninety-six provincial dailies as compared with eighteen in London, and Edward Baines, owner of the liberal *Leeds Mercury*, could proudly proclaim that out of a total annual newspaper circulation of 546 million copies 340 million were provincial publications.

The English provincial press was to lose much of its influence in the late nineteenth and twentieth centuries, when, for a variety of reasons, information – and entertainment, too – came to centre on London. Yet one nineteenth-century newspaper, the *Manchester Guardian*, which had become a penny paper in 1855, acquired a national audience under the talented and highly responsible leadership of C. P. Scott (1846–1932). It was not until 1952, however, that it put news on its front page, eight years before moving its printing office to London, having already dropped Manchester from its name. It was Scott who said of television that nothing good could come of it: the word was half Latin and half Greek.

Scott and his family thought of the *Manchester Guardian* as a 'quality newspaper', a British term, and *The Times* was so regarded in the 1950s long after the term 'fourth estate' had passed out of fashion. The *Daily Telegraph* fell into the same 'quality' category, although it had not appeared to be likely to do so when it started as a daily paper on the eve of the repeal of the stamp duty. With a reduction of its price from threepence to a penny – and a doubling of its size – it immediately gained a circulation more than twice that of *The Times*. It also had on its staff the country's best-known mid-Victorian journalist, G. A. Sala, who was one of the contributors to Dickens's *Household Words* (1850). Dickens himself was the first editor of the *Daily News* (1842).

How different British newspapers and various sections of the population viewed the abolition of the stamp and paper duties – and the advertising duties – is of strategic importance in the history of the British media. Excise duties on paper, imposed in the reign of Queen Anne – and later raised – had been considered by radicals as 'taxes on knowledge', and their abolition was hailed by the *Morning Star* as 'a red letter day in all English calendars'. For the *Daily Telegraph* it was of fundamental importance that the production of paper would henceforth be 'governed exclusively by commercial rules'. It would not only be newspapers that would benefit from repeal. 'Every class of literature would benefit too – Shakespeare, Milton and Shelley' as much as the 'railway literature available on W. H. Smith's bookstalls'. Repeal, it went on, opened up for writers a 'proportionately extensive field for the activity of genius and of talent which they never before enjoyed'.

Echoing Richard Cobden, who made moral claims for the freedom of the press as lofty as those for the penny post (see p. 107), the *Daily Telegraph* added that in future a newspaper would be considered as 'a far more formidable and trustworthy authority than any Attorney-General or official censor of the Press'. The use of the word 'authority', as much of a key word in the Victorian vocabulary as the word 'progress' (see p. 96), is interesting, not least because it was to be much used in the twentieth century in relation to broadcasting. For Cobden, who had written in 1834 that 'the influence of public opinion, as exercised through the Press', was the 'distinguishing feature in modern civilization', opinion mattered even more than information. And he wrote this at a time when the most lively editors and distributors of a radical press, dealing in unstamped newspapers, dismissed in Whig and Tory circles as a 'pauper press', were braving and often experiencing imprisonment.

Their protest was to be swallowed up in Chartism, an avowedly working-class movement, which fought for democratic freedoms in parallel with, sometimes in opposition to, occasionally in cooperation with, Cobden's Anti-Corn Law League, but always in hostility to 'Whiggery'. Most working-class leaders, pre- and post-Chartist, believed that 'knowledge is power', a motto emblazoned on every issue of the unstamped *Poor Man's Guardian*, first published in 1831. They also believed that knowledge, by which they meant more than information, could be derived from pamphlets and books as well as from newspapers, including, while it lasted, the influential Chartist newspaper, the stamped *Northern Star*, founded by the Chartist leader Feargus O'Connor (1794–1855) in 1838, and published at first in Leeds. The *Star* included much information that would never have entered the pages of *The Times*, drawing on the willing services of local correspondents, but keeping a place for poetry too. There was also Chartist fiction. It made money by being representative as much as by mobilizing opinion.

In the history of the press each country had its own landmark date. In France it was 1881, when after protracted and comprehensive Third Republic debates a new Press Law began with the stirring words '*La presse est libre*'. Old restraints were removed, including the requirement for newspapers to deposit caution money against the possibility of fines for libel and other offences. *The Times* in

London saluted the new law with the words 'a better press makes exceptional laws needless'. In 1848 all German restraints on the press had been removed, but they were back again within three years.

In some countries, including imperial India, new repressive laws were still being passed late in the century. Bismarck cracked down on the socialist press in 1878, and far away in the same year an Indian Vernacular Press Act placed new controls on vernacular newspapers. Three years earlier, the Japanese Press Law of 1875 laid down that 'the Home Minister [might] prohibit the sale or distribution of newspapers or if necessary seize them when it is deemed that articles disturbing to the peace and order or injurious to morale' were contained in them. In most countries press laws were difficult to enforce. Tsarist Russia had a clandestine press which was directly involved in politics.

In all countries, whatever the state of the law, the press had established itself by 1900 as a force in society that would have to be reckoned with as much in a democratizing future as it had been in an authoritarian past. Print was to remain a basic medium long after electronic media had appeared, with journals, books and encyclopedias flourishing alongside newspapers. Technology was not the determining factor. The first Australian news-sheets were handwritten, but the *Sydney Morning Herald* was founded in 1831 and published daily from 1840. There were newspapers in every Canadian city ten years later. Far from the cities and their expanding suburbs, forests were being cleared to produce wood pulp.

The processes of change were complex, and as the cost of printing fell and mass readerships were built up, the content of those newspapers which did not claim to be 'quality newspapers' included more entertainment and less information. Their style, too, was less formal. Yet even so-called 'tabloids' were not a standard product, as some histories of newspapers have tended to suggest. They were competing not only with each other but with other media of communication and with other products not associated with communications, some of them a source of their own advertising revenue.

While the role of journalists, the men who gathered news – there were few women before the 1890s – and of the editors who selected, arranged, presented and interpreted news had always been controversial, it became even more so as sales rose. Most important of all, new generations of entrepreneurial owners emerged. In the United States, William Randolph Hearst (1863–1951) and E. W. Scripps (1854–1926) were building up huge chains. Hearst, who had cinema interests too, ended his days in a fairy-tale palace in California, not far from Hollywood, living with a Hollywood star, Marion Davies. His story was to move Orson Welles to produce one of the most powerful of all films, *Citizen Kane* (1941). The products of the Hearst press were attacked as 'yellow journalism'; the products of the Scripps press could be attacked too as 'liberal and pro-labor'.

In Britain, Harmsworth, who abandoned magazines (but not encyclopedias) for newspapers after 1900 – and acquired *The Times* in 1908 – was not the first of the magnates to turn to 'chat'. The poet and essayist Leigh Hunt (1784–1859) had started a paper called *The Week's Chat* in the 1820s, and in 1881 George Newnes (1851–1910) had launched *Tit-Bits*, described as 'the first snippets paper', which was selling 350,000 copies a week seven years later. Harmsworth saluted it as 'the beginning of a development which is going to change the whole face of journalism'. It would appeal to 'the hundreds and thousands of boys and girls' leaving the new Board Schools set up by the Education Act of 1870.

It was claimed in 1881 as 'a remarkable phenomenon of modern times' that between five and six million penny publications, weeklies and monthlies, circulated in London alone, but this was less 'modern' than it seemed. Nor was it as directly related to the Education Act as has been suggested, even at the time. As early as 1858 the novelist Wilkie Collins (1824–89) had written (anonymously) an article in *Household Words* entitled 'The Unknown Public'. Literacy was already increasing before the 1870 Act and there was a buoyant demand for reading matter very different from that on offer to the educated public. What happened in the 1880s and 1890s was that the ideal of an informed 'public' was giving way to the realities of 'the market' in the media as in the economy. The force of radicalism diminished, and it was not only Conservatives who talked of 'giving the public what it wanted'. Publishing was a business, for some, like any other.

The novel, shrinking in size from the standard three-volume work which had been the staple earlier in the century and was to disappear in the 1890s, was still the major literary form, but for Gissing and for Henry James (1843–1916), the great American novelist who lived in England, journalists now seemed to be taking over, with seedy publishers in the background. So it also seemed to the historian W. E. A. Lecky (1838–1903), writing in 1888 on the occasion of the co-incidental deaths of the constitutional lawyer Sir Henry Maine (1822–88) and of the poet and critic Matthew Arnold (1822–88). 'Literary talent', he declared, was being 'pulverized and absorbed in the daily or weekly Press.' 'I suppose', Lecky concluded, 'that there has never been a country or an age in which so large an amount of excellent literary talent has been so devoted to writings which are at once anonymous and ephemeral.'

Thirteen years later, in the year of Queen Victoria's death, another, now better known, historian, G. M. Trevelyan (1876–1962), who was to leave his mark on the twentieth century's interpretation of its past, could complain in the periodical *The Nineteenth Century* that the Philistines had now captured the Ark of the Covenant, by which he meant the printing press. He was borrowing the term 'Philistine' from Arnold for whom the formative decade of the nineteenth century had been the 1860s. As for the 'Ark of the Covenant', it had, of course, a far longer pedigree than 'the Fourth Estate'.

It is important not to oversimplify processes affecting both journalism and fiction or their chronological sequence. As in film sequences, it is necessary to skip across time. The right language is not that of cause and effect. Arnold had not been sure himself that the Ark of the Covenant, a description which he himself would not have used, was safe even in the middle years of the century in what Trevelyan thought of as a golden age of the press. Advocate of 'sweetness and light', Arnold, quintessentially highbrow, was unhappy, indeed, about the role of communications in general:

> Your middle-class man thinks it the highest pitch of development and civilization when his letters are carried twelve times a day from Islington to Camberwell . . . and if railway trains run to and from them every quarter of an hour. He thinks it is nothing that the trains only carry him from an illiberal, dismal life at Islington to an illiberal, dismal life at Camberwell.

Such an attitude towards communications was accompanied in Arnold's case by a fear of the unenfranchised and, after some of them had been enfranchised in 1867 and 1884, he was equally uneasy about the first new voters, 'the democracy as people are fond of calling them'. 'They have many merits, but among them is not that of being, in general, reasonable persons who think fairly and seriously.'

The 'new journalism' – and Arnold may have been the first person to use this term – was, Arnold believed, 'feather brained' as it tried to attract the readership of the recently enfranchised. Arnold's influence on twentieth-century cultural studies was to be profound (see p. 199), but in his own time he largely left out 'entertainment' when he considered the role of the press. Nor did he examine carefully the opinions of people who had been disenfranchised before the Reform Acts of 1867 and 1884. As an inspector of schools he was pessimistic about the chances of the press serving as an educational force. Writers who thought of themselves as 'Christian Socialists' were optimistic, however, with J. M. Ludlow claiming in 1867 that while 'the cheap newspaper and periodical' could not perhaps be 'defined strictly as educators':

> For good or evil, and probably on the whole for good, they are very powerful ones. . . . Notwithstanding the many sins and shortcomings of the newspaper press, the working man of today, with his broadsheet for a penny is by its aid a man of fuller information, better judgement and wider sympathies than the workman of thirty years back who had to content himself with gossip and rumour.

Certainly the most articulate working men, including ex-Chartists, had hailed as a great victory the abolition of the stamp duty in 1855 on the anniversary day of Magna Carta.

With the great victory won, there was more than a touch of irony, even for optimists, in what was to follow. There was more gossip and rumour in 1900 than in 1800. Most of the newly enfranchised turned to the press for diversion – even escape – in larger doses than for information and knowledge – or poetry. Thomas Wright, a 'workingman' friend of Arnold, who loved irony, put no trust even in the Education Act of 1870. 'The extension of elementary education . . . if left to its simple self, will give us a large number of people able to read the police intelligence of the lower types of weekly newspapers, and willing to read little else.' The founder of the popular Sunday newspaper *Reynolds News*, which built up a large circulation by dealing in items other than political information, including 'police intelligence', was himself a former Chartist.

Yet G. W. M. Reynolds (1814–79) was no more the founder of the kind of journalism that was to be called 'new' than Harmsworth twenty years later. It was the wrong adjective. Before the beginning of the nineteenth century, entertainment (or diversion) figured as prominently as information in many newspapers, particularly those published on a Sunday and distributed by 'horn boys' calling out their names in the streets. In 1812 there were eighteen, few of them designed for 'working-class' readers. The *Sunday Times*, which appeared in 1821, originally called itself the *New Observer* – the *Observer* dates back to 1791 – and *Bell's Life in London and Sporting Chronicle*, which appeared in 1822, advertised itself as 'combining with the NEWS of the WEEK a rich REPOSITORY of FASHION, WIT and HUMOUR, and interesting INCIDENTS of HIGH and LOW LIFE'. In 1886, appropriately, it was to be incorporated into *Sporting Life*.

Another Bell production, *Bell's Weekly Messenger* (1796–1896), focused also on crime, scandal, sex, disasters, epidemics and the turf. So did the still surviving *News of the World*, launched in 1843, and Edward Lloyd's many publications that have not survived. Lloyd (1815–90) had begun his working life, like a number of Chartists, as a newspaper vendor and bookseller in London's East End. His first venture into journalism was his *Penny Sunday Times and People's Police Gazette*, and two years later he launched his *Lloyd's Illustrated Sunday Newspaper*, the first newspaper to sell a million copies, after it had changed its title to *Lloyd's Weekly News*. Lloyd raised his capital from the sale of Old Parr's Laxative Pills.

Even before the beginning of the nineteenth century, therefore, before the spread of literacy and the coming of the railways had offered the press unprecedented opportunities to increase circulations, 'The Ark of the Covenant' had not always been treated as reverentially in Britain as Trevelyan, drawing on Whig traditions, implied. Nonetheless, Whig traditions had been strong at the beginning of the century. Indeed, the new Whig periodical, the *Edinburgh Review*, founded in 1802, had described the press as being 'wrought with a power which in reverence may be assimilated, if aught human may be so assimilated, to the working of Almighty wisdom'.

Outside the Whig tradition to which Trevelyan – and his forebear, the historian Macaulay – belonged, another periodical, the *Westminster Review*, founded in 1824 by admirers of the philosophic radical Jeremy Bentham (1748–1832), had left out all religious metaphor when it described newspapers in the language which Cobden was to use, as 'the best and surest civilizers of the country. They contain within themselves not only the elements of knowledge, but the inducements to learn. . . . It is necessary to have seen a people among whom newspapers have not penetrated to know the mass of miscellaneous prejudice which these productions instantly and necessarily dissipate.' For the *Westminster Review*, as for Charles Knight (see p. 86), a more telling term than the Ark of the Covenant was 'March of Intellect', a more purposive march than the 'March of Time'. One of the writers in its first number stressed that at last 'the public' was everywhere coming into its own, not least in literature where 'flattering dedications' to patrons were 'defunct'. 'All our great poets write for the people.'

In the early nineteenth century, therefore, more was involved in the argument about the press than access to information or improved education. The newspaper was a symbol as well as a medium. Walter Bagehot (1826–77), editor of *The Economist*, outside the Whig tradition, quoted the memorable words of Dickens that London was 'like a newspaper. Everything is there and everything is disconnected. There is every kind of person in some houses; but there is no more connection between the houses than between the neighbours on the lists of births, marriages and deaths.'

Bagehot thought of his age as an 'age of discussion' and believed that newspapers and periodicals were necessary opinion-forming agencies for making discussion possible. Yet he did not stop there. He was fascinated by the context within which communication – or the lack of it – took place. For him, while there was an educational dimension to the dissemination of ideas, there was always a social and political dimension too. It was axiomatic to him that in politics 'the form of government becomes liberal in the exact proportions as the power of public opinion increases'. But would it remain liberal?

Before Bagehot, before Arnold, even before Dickens, another novelist, Edward Bulwer Lytton (1803–73), in his *England and the English* (1833), an early anatomy of Britain, had included a section on the press which looked forwards as well as backwards:

> If the sevenpenny paper were . . . to sell for twopence what would be the result? Why, the sale being extended from those who paid sevenpence to those who can afford twopence, a new majority must be consulted, the sentiments and desires of poorer men than at present must be addressed; and thus a new influence of opinion would be brought to bear on our social relations and our legislative enactments.

Lytton raised other issues too, some already old, including the question of the relationship between 'partisanship' and 'objectivity' in a 'free press'.

This same question had been raised in late eighteenth-century America in the very year of the First Amendment which was to make subsequent or later American media history distinctive. The purpose of the newspaper, John Fenno, first publisher of the *Gazette of the United States* (1789), maintained, was 'to hold up the people's own government in a favourable point of light and to impress just ideas of its administration by exhibiting FACTS'. What were 'just ideas'? What were 'Facts'? The *Gazette*, which printed on its front page 'an epitome of the present State of the Union', was subsidized by Alexander Hamilton and the Federalist party, and Thomas Jefferson was not alone in believing that all Federalist newspapers dealt in 'lying and scribbling'. Fenno put his trust in unknown American readers of the kind that Wilkie Collins identified. 'Our citizens may be deceived for a while, and have been deceived, but as long as the presses can be protected we can trust to them for light.'

William Cobbett (1763–1835), most partisan of writers, whose writing career spanned both sides of the Atlantic – America first – defended political partisanship as vigorously as he defended any of his causes. In his *Political Register*, first published in Britain in a twopenny version in 1810, dubbed 'Twopenny Trash', he was as aggressive as he had been when he was writing under the pseudonym 'Peter Porcupine' in the United States. In 1816 the *Register* was said to be selling 40,000 to 50,000 copies a week. It could never be claimed, however, that Cobbett dealt simply in facts. His robust journalism led directly to political action. The sub-title of his pamphlet *The Poor Man's Friend* (1826) was 'a defence of the Rights of those who do the Work and fight the Battles'.

There was a conservative element in Cobbett's outlook, but most English Conservatives of his time were bound to object to his Tory radicalism, a supremely English product. Many of them were hostile also towards the 'March of Intellect', for them a subject of satire, although the press had one Conservative defender, George Canning (1770–1827), a future Prime Minister, who had edited a periodical, *The Anti-Jacobin*, in his youth, and who in an address to his Liverpool constituents in 1822 had referred to 'the mighty power of public opinion embodied in a free Press'. He even compared it with the power of steam.

Not all liberals were so impressed. The historian and sociologist Sismondi (1773–1843), married to a Wedgwood but writing from a background in Switzerland and in Italy, observed bluntly in 1823 that, while 'the daily Press is a power', its object was 'not public good, but to get the largest number of subscribers'; and John Stuart Mill (1806–73), son of Bentham's close friend James Mill (1773–1836), a militant Utilitarian, who believed strongly in the need to mobilize public opinion, suggested bluntly that 'more affectation and hypocrisy are necessary for the trade of literature, and especially the newspapers, than for a brothel keeper', an image that was to recur. Meanwhile, Sir Robert Peel (1788–1852), a Conservative who had emerged from a different background from that of Canning, described public opinion as comprising 'a great compound of folly, weakness, prejudice, wrong feeling, right feeling, obstinacy and newspaper paragraphs'.

The Times, even as it was coming to be thought of as a fourth estate in itself, was never without a variety of critics, among them the radical William Hazlitt (1778–1830), who wrote brilliant essays on 'The Spirit of the Age' in 1823. While admitting that *The Times* was entitled to the character it gave itself of being the 'leading journal of Europe', Hazlitt did not find it to his taste. 'It might be imagined to be composed as well as printed with a steam engine.' By contrast, Peel, alarmed by the support for parliamentary reform of its powerful editor, Thomas Barnes (1785–1841), during the stormy years from 1830 to 1832, called it the 'great, principal and powerful advocate of reform', and the Tory counterpart of the *Edinburgh Review*, the *Quarterly Review*, founded in 1809, described it as 'the most profligate of the London newspapers, and the most impudently inconsistent in everything except malice and mischief'.

Barnes certainly listened to his readers but, knowing the political aspirations of many of them, he felt that at historic moments, like the Reform Bill crisis of 1831, he had to stir them as well as listen to them. *The Times* was 'The Thunderer'. It was in literature what brandy was in beverages. 'John Bull, whose understanding is rather sluggish . . . requires a strong stimulus. He consumes his beef and cannot digest it without a dram, he dozes composedly over his prejudices which his conceit calls opinions; and you must fire ten-pounders at his densely compacted intellect before you can make it comprehend your meaning.' Barnes was focusing on his middle-class readers, many of whom secured the vote in 1832, but what he was saying was to be echoed in alternative language by different editors in a wide range of political and social circumstances.

Twelve years later, Benjamin Disraeli (1804–81), one of Peel's fiercest critics, put into the mouths of his characters in his novel *Coningsby* phrases like 'God made man in his own image, but the Public is made by Newspapers', 'Opinion is now supreme and opinion speaks in print', and the representation of the press 'is far more complete than the representation of Parliament'. But among other novelists Anthony Trollope (1815–82), who hated Disraeli and at one time hoped to be a politician himself, did not believe that 'this was a good thing'. *The Times* for him was Jupiter, god of gods, but journalists working for it deserved neither respect nor esteem. They had long been regarded as hacks, but they were now becoming something worse: 'intruding busybodies'.

Their ranks were to be augmented from the 1860s onwards by university-educated 'intellectuals', a term little used in Britain at this time, and they also became organized collectively. A National Association of Journalists was created (in Birmingham) in 1886, later to be given a Charter and renamed the Institute of Journalists – it included editors as well as reporters – and a National Union of Journalists, a genuine trade union, was founded in 1907. These journalists were not trained, however, as they were beginning to be in the United States. For them, journalism was a craft to be learned through experience. So it was also for most Americans, although other forces were at work there. As early as 1869, 'Press scholarships' for journalists were offered at Washington College in Virginia: the defeated commander of the Southern army, Robert E. Lee (1807–70), thought that journalism could strengthen post-Civil War society in the south. As late as 1908, Missouri started America's first school of journalism, headed by a Dean.

In the north, in New York, the media capital, Columbia University was to become the main provider after 1912, although it was a graduate school. The man who conceived of its role, Joseph Pulitzer (1847–1911), after whom coveted prizes were to be named (eight in specific fields of journalism, six in 'letters'), was born in Hungary and had taken over *The World* in New York in 1883. He envisaged that the training of journalists would be based on the contribution which the press had made to 'the idea of progress, especially the progress of justice, of civilization, of humanity, of public opinion, and of the democratic idea and ideal'. This was not a Whig but an American Progressivist perspective. It implied, however, that while schools of journalism would not all be of the same type or quality, the history of journalism in most of them would be approached in a particular way.

Among journalism's classic texts were essays by Robert Ezra Park (1864–1944), who had been a newspaper reporter and who now stands out as one of the founders of the Chicago School of Sociology. The newspaper, Park suggested in 1916, was 'the great medium of communication', and it was 'on the basis of the information which it supplies that a public opinion rests'. Another great journalistic name in the American pantheon was that of Walter Lippmann (1889–1974), much-quoted newspaper columnist: his 'Today and Tomorrow' column, begun in 1931, was syndicated in 250 newspapers, one in ten of them outside the United States.

'Many people buy a paper', Lippmann recognized, 'because their own lives are so dull that they want the vicarious thrill of reading about a set of imaginary people with whose gorgeous vices they can, in their fancy, identify themselves.' Yet he probed more deeply than this, and deservedly won two Pulitzer prizes. His influential and often reissued book *Public Opinion*, published in 1922, remains the best known of all books on the subject. Lippmann suggested that the power of the press was expressed less in the personality of the editor of a newspaper than in the flow of the news itself. In a complex modern world news was inevitably selective, and readers, dependent on what was on offer – 'condensed stories' – found it increasingly difficult to make informed judgements of their own. They were offered 'stereotypes', 'pseudo-reality' on public issues. Lippmann's idea of the 'public sphere', like that of Habermas (see p. 60), was hard to sustain when it seemed that media distorted and advertisers manipulated.

The idea remained an ideal, however, and most American schools of journalism – there were 84 of them by 1917 and 812 by 1987 – believed in maintaining ideals in a complex society and culture. An Association of Trades of Journalism was founded in 1912 and an Association for Education in Journalism in 1949, and in 1924 a *Journalism Bulletin* was produced, to be converted into a quarterly in 1930 and to be followed in 1974 by a periodical, *Journalism History*. How to relate journalistic training to the changing world of communications remained – and remains – a matter of debate even in Britain, where between 1919 and 1939 the only University Diploma for Journalism in Britain was offered at London University. In the United States, James W. Carey, Dean of the College of Communications at Illinois, within which a department of journalism was located, was a leader in his field and believed that school programmes should contribute to historical scholarship. Other schools of communication and of journalism, however, were turning to 'media studies' within a changing cultural context.

Neither the idea nor the ideal of a 'fourth estate', nor the hope of creating a progressivist political force, ever seemed relevant to many journalists or proprietors, some of them as interested in pictures as in words. The *Illustrated London News*, founded in London in 1842, offered instead a 'panorama of the world', an offer to be taken up by television *Panorama* programmes more than a century later. The first pictorial daily newspaper, the *Evening Illustrated Paper*, was one of a growing range of British evening dailies founded in 1881: another was Harmsworth's *Evening News* (1894). (The *Daily Mirror* was to be launched in 1903.) The evening papers went through many editions, the first of them appearing in London as early as 11 o'clock in the morning: 'Read All About It' was daily advice. Meanwhile *Punch*, a weekly, renowned for its cartoons and its puns and founded a year earlier than the *Illustrated London News*, had made its way from London, where it was firmly based, into many Victorian provincial homes, along with *The Times*. Radical in its origins, it described itself variously – through pictures as well as through words – as 'watcher', 'curator', 'protector', 'chastiser', 'lancet'.

In 1860, under the editorship of John Thaddeus Delane (1817–79), the mid-Victorian *Times*, in an age when periodicals influenced opinion more than newspapers, exercised some of these functions itself. Its leaders were read avidly at breakfast time both in homes and in clubs, and its supply of foreign intelligence was superior to that which could be found in any other newspaper. It was in that year, before the repeal of the paper duties, that it was said by an outside observer that 'it leans upon no single class, represents no exclusive party, advocates no separate interest. It claims to embody and to express, and to a great extent it does embody and express, the current opinion of all the intelligent and informed sections of the British community.' This was certainly Delane's goal. 'The first duty of the Press is to obtain the earliest and most correct intelligence of the events of the time, and instantly by disclosing them, to make them the common property of the nation.'

By the end of the nineteenth century the climate had changed, and press headlines, replicated in street placards and shouted out in the streets by news boys – as familiar a sight on the streets of London and Birmingham (and other towns and cities) as on the streets of Chicago or New York – were more important than long leaders or even longer reports of parliamentary proceedings. The emphasis was on 'stories', accompanied or supplemented by what came to be called 'features', some deliberately appealing to women, and from the 1880s onwards by gossip columns and interviews. 'Stories' had been sought in 1800, but as the century went by they came in faster, and editors expected them to do so, while journalists told the stories in fewer words and in shorter paragraphs.

Some stories were now making their way into advertising. Already in the eighteenth century, national and local newspapers had appeared with *Advertiser* in their titles. Advertising has a long, only partially told, history. As has been noted (see p. 46), ink, very appropriately, was advertised in the seventeenth century, and in the eighteenth century patent medicines – note the word 'patent' – with tea, cocoa, soap and tobacco to follow. In 1900, when many consumer products were standardized, the advertisements might be long and increasingly pictorial in character, directing attention to nationally 'branded products', not only in the press but in brightly coloured posters, triumphs of chromolithography. As we have described, it was in the United States, where the first advertising agencies were established between 1880 and 1914, that advertising expenditure broke all records. The total, which rose from $40 million in 1881 to over $140 million by 1904, reached the billion dollar mark in 1916. There was to be further breaking of records on both sides of the Atlantic – and with more than one medium involved – during the late 1950s and 1960s.

It is interesting that Harmsworth, who advertised the *Daily Mail* on poster hoardings and in the sky, thought that to 'display type' for advertising in the pages of his newspapers was 'vulgar'. Words made images. Harmsworth paid the editor of the *Daily Mail* more than any other journalist in the country and did much to establish the image of Fleet Street, a different image from that of Madison Avenue in New York, the centre of its advertising agencies, or of brightly lit Times Square, the centre of entertainment as well as of the offices of the *New York Times*. Behind all three places and their images, however, there were powerful economic bases. It was one of Northcliffe's go-getting henchmen, Kennedy Jones, who told John Morley (1838–1923), a writer of essays and books, including the biography of Gladstone, and an editor of periodicals, that 'you left journalism a profession, we have made it a branch of commerce'.

The most controversial figure in the history of late Victorian and early twentieth-century journalism was W. T. Stead (1849–1912), who succeeded Morley, a very different kind of political journalist, as editor of London's influential *Pall Mall Gazette*, widely read in the London clubs in 1885. Morley himself had succeeded a very different kind of editor, Frederick Greenwood (1830–1901), known to his contemporaries as 'the Prince of Journalists'. Before Stead, who was the son of a Congregationalist minister, the *Gazette* was said to have had 'nothing vulgar or flashy or sensational about it'. Now it blended stirring leaders with muck-raking news items, many of them related to campaigns, the most notorious being that against juvenile prostitution, which he labelled 'white slavery'. In an article in 1886, published in the *Contemporary Review*, entitled 'Government by Journalism', Stead argued that the press was far more than a check on Parliament. It was a 'Chamber of Initiative'.

Stead remained editor of the *Gazette* for only five years, founding soon afterwards, with financial support from George Newnes, the immediately profitable *Review of Reviews*, indispensable for historians of the world's press. He also wrote a sensational book, *If Christ Came to Chicago*, but failed in an attempt in 1904 to establish a newspaper of his own – what he called a 'paper of the home'. He was one of the passengers to go down in the *Titanic* in 1912, the subject of press comment that Stead would have savoured and of several late twentieth-century films.

Stead had begun his journalistic career in 1870, the year of the first national Education Act, as a highly successful editor of the provincial halfpenny morning paper in Darlington, the *Northern Echo*, a paper with an adventurous twentieth-century future. Harold (later Sir Harold) Evans, a later editor of the *Sunday Times*, who was dismissed in 1982 by his proprietor Rupert Murdoch, also began his journalistic career on the same paper. There have been few more eloquent advocates of the public's 'right to know' than Evans, who in a 1974 address published by Britain's Granada Television, wrote:

> Governments as well as citizens need a free and inquiring press. With a volatile, pluralistic electorate, and a complex bureaucracy, a free press provides an indispensable feedback system from governed to the governing, from consumers to producers, from the regions to the centre, and not least from one section of the bureaucracy to another.

The political and social context of this address was quite different from that in which Delane or Stead had moved. And so, too, was the media constellation. Evans's wife, Tina Brown, had become for a time editor of the *New Yorker*.

The *Sunday Times* under Evans introduced a glossy colour magazine in 1961, packed with advertisements – and it was not alone in this – and a large section of the provincial press consisted of free newspapers, paid for largely through local advertising. 'Investigative' journalism was now as familiar a key word as 'muck-raking' (a word derived from Bunyan) had been in early twentieth-century America. The printed media were involved in far more than 'front-page history', and complaints about their journalistic operations were now coming not only from political leaders or sophisticated novelists, but also from ordinary people, disturbed by threats to their privacy.

This was a story, little told in the media, that skips across time – and place. It was in the United States that muck-raking journalism flourished decades before Evans, laying the foundation for what the American historian Richard Hofstadter has called 'The Age of Reform'. Proud of their contribution to the making of it, great journalists like Lincoln Steffens (1866–1936) established their reputations through both newspapers and periodicals, notably a new magazine, *McClure's*, very different in content and style from old magazines like the *Atlantic, Harpers* and the *Century*. The 'muck-rakers' were suspicious of tycoons of all kinds, including press tycoons, whose British counterparts could generate extra suspicion when, in addition to wielding power, they received public honours. Harmsworth, who was to become a Viscount in 1917, was not the first newspaper proprietor to enter the British honours list. Algernon Borthwick, proprietor of the *Morning Post*, a confidant of Lord Palmerston, was knighted in 1880, and made a baronet by Salisbury and a peer in 1895. In the same year as

Harmsworth became a Viscount, he met Ford and Edison on a visit to the United States, finding, to his satisfaction, that the former was no more interested in money 'than I was', and that the latter 'hated the Germans like poison. They stole all his patents.'

The role of proprietors in British journalism, 'muck-racking' or 'stridently patriotic', was under attack during the first decade of the century precisely in those circles, Whiggish and Liberal, within which Trevelyan had moved. For L. T. Hobhouse (1864–1929), a so-called 'new liberal', the press of 1909 was 'more and more the monopoly of a few rich men' and far from being 'the organ of democracy' – what radicals had hoped for – it had become 'rather the sounding board for whatever ideas commend themselves to the great material interests'. Yet this was too simple a contrast to draw then and later. Some rich proprietors thought that they were representing the public more than Parliament did, while others, like the Quaker George Cadbury (1839–1922), who in 1899 acquired the *Daily News*, determined that it should propound his own principles. He immediately expelled betting information and tips from the newspaper, and Hobhouse was his first candidate for its editor.

Cadbury went on to acquire provincial newspapers in the belief that it was better to spend money 'trying to arouse my fellow countrymen to take political action than it was to spend it on charities'. Another great Quaker family, the Rowntrees, believed in doing both. The *Northern Echo* was under Rowntree Trust control before the war, as was the influential weekly *The Nation*, which in 1931 was to merge with the *New Statesman*, one of the most influential weeklies of the inter-war years.

One of the more successful sponsors of the 'new journalism' before 1914 was C. A. Pearson (1866–1921), who founded the *Daily Express* in 1900. He had earlier established *Pearson's Weekly* in 1890, which had as its motto 'To interest, to elevate and to amuse': on one occasion he daubed its copies with eucalyptus oil to try to make his readers immune from influenza. Joseph Chamberlain (1836–1914), to whose controversial tariff reform campaign Pearson gave valuable, sometimes strident, support, called him 'the greatest hustler' he had ever known. In 1903, Pearson purchased the *St James's Gazette*, and a year later acquired the *Standard* and the *Evening Standard*, to be followed by a cluster of provincial papers, including the *Birmingham Daily Gazette* and *Evening Dispatch*.

There was no shortage of politics in Pearson's papers, the most important of which were in 1919 to pass into other hands – those of the Canadian Max Aitken (1879–1964), who in 1917 became Lord Beaverbrook. Surviving Northcliffe, who was fourteen years older than himself, Beaverbrook was to serve during the Second World War in Winston Churchill's cabinet. He had already written a classic study of the role of politicians, including Northcliffe, during the political crisis of the First World War, when Herbert Asquith was replaced as Prime Minister by David Lloyd George. 'Bravo, Lloyd George' had been the happy *Daily Mail* headline.

Northcliffe was keenly interested in exploiting the power of the press, not only in politics but in the advancement of new technology. In aviation he sponsored Blériot's flight across the Channel in 1909, and the new medium of radio in 1920, when he arranged for the Australian singer Dame Nellie Melba, the 'Australian nightingale', to broadcast from Chelmsford. Whatever the headlines might read – and in the text of the *Daily Mail* it was asserted that 'Art and Science had now joined hands' – there were not enough headphones in the *Daily Mail* office to go around on that occasion. In Paris, a phonograph record of Melba's performance was made in a radio operations room below the Eiffel Tower.

If Northcliffe had not become mentally disturbed and died in 1922, the year of the foundation of the BBC (see p. 130), he might have played as important a part in the history of broadcasting as he had done in the history of the press. Beaverbrook, who survived him, had a more ambivalent attitude towards the new medium. He was opposed to 'radio manufacturers taking control of it', but he was totally distrusted by the BBC's first Managing Director, John Reith. After Reith stated in 1923 that 'freedom of the air would result in chaos', the *Daily Express* headline ran: 'Fighting Freedom'.

A more open critic of Beaverbrook than Reith was the Conservative leader Stanley Baldwin (1867–1947), who made the headlines early in 1931, a year of financial crisis and political drama, when he accused Fleet Street newspapers of 'aiming at power without responsibility', adding that such power had been 'the prerogative of the harlot through the ages'. Supported by *The Times*, whose editor Geoffrey Dawson was close to official Conservative party sources, Baldwin had himself been a target. Northcliffe's heir, Viscount Rothermere, along with Beaver-brook, threatened to oppose those Conservative candidates at the next general election who would not promise to campaign for 'Empire Free Trade'.

During the following decade, leading up to the Second World War, Rothermere was to support the Fascist leader Sir Oswald Mosley (1896–1980): 'Hurray for the Blackshirts', one *Daily Mail* headline ran. Beaverbrook's *Daily Express*, very much the organ of his own opinions, was to promise its readers on the eve of Hitler's invasion of Poland that there would be no war. In Britain this was the age of the press barons, which was well described in the second volume of a magisterial study, *The Rise and Fall of the Political Press in Britain*, published in 1985 by an American historian, Stephen Koss, who placed the adjective 'apparent' before 'baronial power'. The popular press in his judgement could stimulate or provoke opinion, but it could not determine how its readers would react.

There was much else to appeal to readers, nevertheless, in their newspapers, including crosswords and, above all, sport. Politics often came last, and as far as that was concerned, there was much misinformation: it was always necessary, as the poet W. H. Auden put it, for readers to read between the lines. But the Second World War, which changed so much, altered the mood, and the political power of the press was shown to be limited in 1945 when, in face of all the guidance offered by the *Daily Mail* and the *Daily Express*, the first daily newspaper to reach the two million circulation mark, Winston Churchill was heavily defeated and the Labour Party won the general election.

At this point, in particular, in media history, it is necessary to probe deeper and to compare press and radio as media influences on information and opinion. It is necessary, too, to look at social and political history as well as at the history of the media themselves. There were many reasons for the victory of the Labour Party in 1945, and Churchill, renowned for his war-time BBC addresses to the nation, did not strike the right note in his partisan election broadcasts. Nor did it help him that he seemed to be getting advice on strategy from Beaverbrook. Meanwhile, Clement Attlee (1883–1967), who had started his ministerial career as Postmaster-General, and his Labour Party colleagues enjoyed the powerful assistance of the *Daily Mirror* in 1945, which had become a genuine tabloid in 1934 – with advice from the American advertising agency J. Walter Thompson. Its favourite strip character, 'Jane', was better known in 1945 than Attlee.

Whatever the sources of press appeal in 1945 – and the limitations on its influence – the circulation of national newspapers had risen during the war, having climbed only slowly during the 1930s, when the circulation of provincial newspapers declined. Koss ended his book with the appointment of the first Royal Commission on the Press in 1947, which devoted 150 pages to the education and training of journalists. He included a postscript, however, noting the later demise in 1960 of established newspapers. In 1960, the *News Chronicle*, heir to the nineteenth-century liberal *Daily News*, disappeared. In 1964, the *Daily Herald*, founded as a Labour newspaper in 1912, with trade-union backing, was transformed into the *Sun*, when it was given a misleading new slogan, 'a newspaper born of the age we live in'; and the funeral took place in 1967 of *Reynolds News*, a paper which had unequivocally belonged to an earlier age.

The *Daily Herald* had got into financial difficulties as early as 1930, during the Depression, when 51 per cent of its shares were acquired by Odhams Press; 49 per cent stayed with the trade unions. The new *Sun* lost even more money, and after five years of uncertainty and strain was sold in 1969 to a young Australian newspaper owner, Rupert Murdoch, still in the process of making himself a media tycoon. In the same year he had acquired the *News of the World*, and in 1981, following in the wake of Northcliffe, he bought *The Times* from its Canadian owner Roy Thomson (1894–1976), who had himself bought the paper ten years earlier. Having started his career in the Canadian newspaper and radio business, Thomson had secured a foothold in Britain through his acquisition of a major share in one of Britain's first independent television companies, Scottish Television, which presented him, in his own unforgettable words, with 'a licence to print money'.

The twentieth-century concentration of media power became a matter of increasing public concern between 1961 and 1981. It blurred not only most of the possible lines between information and entertainment (with a little education thrown in), but most of the political party dividing lines between left and right, and, not least, all the dividing lines between media. Murdoch's empire stretched into film and television; Thomson's had included the travel business too, the business on which he eventually concentrated. Cecil King (1901–87), Northcliffe's nephew, had acquired control of the large *Daily Mirror* Group in 1933, to be renamed the International Publishing Group (IPC) in 1963. It had a stake also in Associated Television; and after taking over Odhams it was responsible for around two hundred periodicals – weeklies, monthlies and quarterlies. King was involved in conspiratorial rather than party politics against Harold Wilson (1916–95), Prime Minister of the Labour government in 1968, and this forced him out of the chairmanship of the Group.

The best known of the IPC periodicals, *Woman*, had been launched by Odhams in 1937, price twopence, and had half a million readers by the end of the year. In 1945 it had three-quarters of a million readers, and at its peak in the late 1950s, three and a half million. Outside the Northcliffe circle, the most distinctive weekly publication had been the *Picture Post*, founded in 1938, with highly topical political articles and highly memorable photographs; it not only reflected war-time attitudes on the left, but had a strong influence on them. Through it, Stefan Lorant, a refugee from Nazi Germany, using a small Leica camera, raised British pictorial journalism to a new height. The owner of the paper, Edward Hulton (1906–88), who had started his proprietorial career in 1937 with *Farmers' Weekly*, was knighted in 1957, the year that he closed *Picture Post*. Two years later, the whole Hulton group of periodicals was taken over by Odhams before Odhams in turn was incorporated in IPC.

It is interesting to compare *Picture Post* and *Life* magazine, founded by Henry Luce (1898–1967) in 1936, thirteen years after *Time*, and almost simultaneously with the monthly film newsreel, *March of Time*. Its prospectus was eloquent – 'to see life; to see the world; to eye witness great events; to watch the faces of the poor and gestures of the proud . . . to see things thousands of miles away, things hidden behind walls and within rooms, things dangerous to come by . . . to see and be amazed; to see and be instructed.' With none of the campaigning drive of Lorant, Hulton and Tom Hopkinson (1905–90), the last editor of *Picture Post*, who was deeply interested in the education of journalists, *Life* lived up to the prospectus, which was distributed to advertisers before it reached the public. In a telegram sent earlier in 1936, Archibald MacLeish (1892–1982), poet and essayist, had told Luce that 'the great revolutions of journalism are not revolutions in public opinion but revolutions in the way in which public opinion is formed'.

Public opinion was to be formed in different ways, just as the pursuits of entertainment and education were also to be moulded in separate ways, and the route through topical photojournalism had changed significantly before Luce's death in 1967. *Life* itself, offering in colour a record for all time of history in the making, was to die in 1972 after seeking to compete frontally with television, most of which was in black and white. Luce had had to cope with news magazines, his own *Time*, and *Time's* competitors, *Newsweek* and *US News and World Report*, the combined circulation of which rose between 1961 and 1970 from 5.38 million to 8.47 million. After his death the first of these, *Time*, was at the centre of what became a huge economic conglomeration, consisting in the first instance of *Time* and Warner Brothers and later, in 1995, including Ted Turner, who, from an unlikely base in Atlanta, had created against the odds (and the old networks) a global news network, CNN (Cable News Network), built from nothing.

In these circumstances the American newspapers had to adapt, as they had to do when computerization arrived. The old newspaper office set-up, with its composing room, where reporters used typewriters and where copy was cut and edited, was to change as radically as the printing processes. Yet 'hot lead' had still not given way everywhere to 'offset' printing before the first electronic editor's terminal was marketed in 1973. There were still old smells and old noises in newspaper buildings, and these, later to seem quaint, provided the background in the brilliant political film *All the President's Men* (1976). As in the nineteenth century, copy was being laid out time and time again at different stages of the production process. And sales were falling. The number of newspaper copies sold per household (smaller in size than in the nineteenth century) fell from 1.12 in 1960 to 0.88 in 1974. In social terms, the inner city on which the old local newspapers had focused had lost much of its grip on a wider area, which now included not only suburbs but 'exurbia' – stretching out beyond them.

When the owner of the New York *Sun* had acquired three other metropolitan newspapers during the 1920s to launch the *Herald Tribune*, he had been able to choose from fourteen, and in 1963 twelve of these were still operating. But the *Herald Tribune* itself disappeared in 1958, and twenty years later there were only three. In 1977, Anthony Smith, experienced in Britain in radio, television and film, was invited by the George Marshall Fund of the United States under the auspices of the International Institute of Communications – an interesting example of international cooperation – to study the changes taking place in newspaper publishing in a number of countries.

What was happening in other countries was not dissimilar to what was happening in the United States and in Britain, although national policies varied even between neighbours. In Sweden, which lost fifty conservative, thirty liberal and several of its social democratic newspapers between the 1920s and the 1960s, a loan fund and joint-distribution rebates were introduced by the state in 1970 and further state subsidies followed, particularly to low-coverage newspapers. There were also establishment grants for new papers. Norway pursued a parallel policy. Denmark did not. In Sweden and Norway, the extinction of party newspapers represented for most party members a total disaster.

International comparisons made during the late 1970s showed that after a decade of economic adversity the Swedes 'consumed' more newspapers per thousand of the population than any other people except the Japanese, that they came next to the United States in the per capita number of telephones and that 95 per cent of them had television sets. In such comparisons the media were now usually treated as one, with the United States as the main reference point. The rise of broadcasting – first radio and then television – had led to a decline in newspaper advertising from 45 per cent of all advertising in 1935 to 23 per cent in 1995, but the combined share of newspaper and television advertising in the total was more or less constant – 46 per cent as compared with 45 per cent.

It was not only television which had posed a challenge to the press. Once the press had been forced to concern itself with other media, both in business and in cultural terms, it had to examine possible future changes in its own role. They were not new questions. In Britain, one of the first people to speculate on media relationships and their implications was Lord Riddell (1865–1934), then proprietor of the *News of the World*, which in 1909 already had a circulation of more than four million, the year when Riddell became a peer. Faced with sound radio, not with television, Riddell was friendly to the new medium, but he raised many interesting issues, some of which were being raised on the other side of the Atlantic.

> What effect is radio going to have on life? (By the way I do not like the description 'wireless': why describe a thing as a negation?) Are people likely to read less?

> Are they going to talk less? Are they going to be better or worse informed? Are they going to go to the theatre and music less? Are those who reside in rural districts going to be more or less satisfied? Who can tell?

Riddell went on to place his questions in what was an extended time frame. 'So far as the present generation is concerned, I believe that those accustomed to read and who like reading will continue to read whether they use the radio or not. But what about the next generation brought up on radio? Are they going to prefer information through the medium of the eye or that through the medium of the ear?'

The next generation (and there was already much talk about it) was to be able to acquire information (and, even more, entertainment) on the screen through the medium of the eye, the 'universal eye' of television. Indeed, already in the same issue of the *Radio Times* that Riddell posed his questions, a 'listener', a new and then controversial word, suggested in a letter to the editor that it was 'not too much to prophesy that within ten years television will be as advanced as radio telephony is today'. The word 'viewer' was not yet thought of, but when the BBC started a second periodical in 1929, more highbrow than the *Radio Times*, it called it the *Listener*.

When television did arrive, it raised more questions than those which Riddell had asked about radio. As Kenneth Baily, then television critic of the *Evening Standard* and associate editor of *Television*, put it in 1949:

> Thousands of people, and then people in millions, are going to become subject, to some degree, to their household screen. What will it mean to them? Good or ill? With this new power there are likely to be no half-measures; it will choose its way, and then do what it cannot stop itself from doing.

Technological determinism was not the answer, as the third section of this chapter, on 'The Age of Television', will show, but more attempts were to be made to provide answers about the social consequences of television than had ever been asked about radio.

The Age of Broadcasting

It is necessary, nonetheless, to begin with what the BBC always called 'sound broadcasting' rather than with television, both because of its intrinsic interest and because, at least in the beginning, the same institutions that had ushered in the age of broadcasting were responsible for ushering in the age of television too. And each institution had its own history. They were usually institutions more than organizations: in the United States, NBC and CBS thought of themselves in this way, and in Britain the BBC was universally thought of as such. As early as 1926, the Archbishop of Canterbury said so, and afterwards the BBC was to be compared with the Church of England over which he presided. In 1940, R. S. Lambert, a former editor of the BBC journal the *Listener*, turned to a different institution, claiming in his book *Ariel and All His Quality* that 'in the field of art, intellect and politics' the BBC exercised through patronage 'all the power once exercised by the Court'.

One of the great radio reporters of the war, and equally well known on both sides of the Atlantic, Ed Murrow (1908–65) was almost an institution in himself, recognized as such for his broadcasts from London during the Battle of Britain. For MacLeish, by then Librarian of Congress, his were broadcasts that 'destroyed the superstition of distance'. Now invaluable as historical records, at the time they made everything alive. MacLeish himself had opened a new chapter in American radio with a verse play *The Fall of the City*, broadcast in 1937, with Orson Welles cast as a radio announcer. Another CBS broadcast in 1938, in which Welles again figured as an announcer, was a much transformed version of H. G. Wells's *The War of the Worlds*. His announcement of Martian landings generated panic, but it could also be described by Dorothy Thompson as 'the news story of the century' that made 'a greater contribution to an understanding of Hitlerism, Mussolinism, Stalinism and all the other terrorisms of our time than all the words about them that have been written by reasonable men'.

Within two years, most European broadcasting stations were in the hands of the Nazis, and the demand for 'real' news was greater than ever. In providing it, radio, for the first time, had a marked advantage over newspapers, an advantage which was somewhat resented in the United States but greatly appreciated in Britain. Before the war, the BBC had been restricted in its news operations, particularly their timing and content, by the press and by news agencies. Now, with the support of the Ministry of Information, a new and unpopular ministry, it was liberated. It was host, too, to many European broadcasters, seeking for political liberation, standing out as the 'Voice of Freedom' and going on to broadcast at its war-time peak in as many as forty-five languages, including Tamil, Thai and Japanese. At home, it had the responsibility for maintaining morale, and among the range of entertainment programmes that it broadcast, Tommy Handley's *ITMA* passed into legend. How the BBC interpreted 'views' in war-time through a range of broadcasters, most of them not professionals, was of special importance. American radio, too, turned increasingly to volunteers from outside the profession, a critical cohort in the propaganda of democracy, a propaganda in which Hollywood excelled.

War provides a necessary but unusual vantage point from which to survey these aspects of broadcasting, just as it does for a survey of technological change, for example, radar and rocketry. A war of words was being fought between 1939 and 1945, and in democratic as much as in totalitarian countries the microphone became a potent weapon. It had already been employed during the 1930s by Adolf Hitler (1889–1945) and Josef Goebbels (1897–1945), the manager of the Nazi propaganda machine, as it had been before that in the Soviet Union. At the very first Nazi radio exhibition in 1933, Goebbels, who was then engaged in destroying the independence of the press, stated forcefully that radio would be to the twentieth century what the press had been to the nineteenth. At the huge, cleverly staged Nuremberg party rallies the microphone was handled like a megaphone – just as it was in the Soviet Union in public squares and buildings.

Wired radio was favoured, too, because it could be controlled, and the people's radio sets, which were being produced during the late 1930s, kept other countries' radio out. Neither Lenin (1870–1924) nor Josef Stalin (1879–1953), both associated with pamphlets appearing in their names, set out to be active broadcasters, however, and Soviet programmes were dull, replete with dubious statistics and appealing only to party activists. The press was rigorously controlled. In

Fig. 21 In the stadium. Adolf Hitler, assisted by his Minister of Propaganda, Josef Goebbels, used the microphone as a megaphone. Here, alone, separated from his huge audience, he addresses a rally.

Fig. 22 At the fireside. Franklin D. Roosevelt uses radio to chat to his fellow citizens. He put his trust in what he considered democratic communication. Note *his* audience.

the United States, where the press was largely hostile to Franklin D. Roosevelt (1882–1945), who came to power in the same year as Hitler, the President used the microphone quite differently in his 'fireside chats', seeking to make his listeners feel that he was present with them in their homes. Nor was this his only use of radio. His eight chats represented only 8 per cent of his radio addresses between 1933 and 1936: one of them on a public holiday was heard on 64 per cent of American radios.

None of these uses of the radio had been part of the British experience, however, so that in dealing with the move from peace to war the BBC, which during the first years of its history had been required by government to keep out of all controversial broadcasting, had to adapt its structures and its policies more than any other great broadcasting organization. Nevertheless, the range of its pre-war programming was far wider than that in any other country, particularly the United States, and it maintained this advantage during and after the war. In its overseas transmission it continued to take pride in broadcasting 'the truth'. In its domestic programming it now abandoned much that had been considered fundamental in its early years, a special pattern of broadcasting on Sundays, for example, and unwillingness to broadcast too much 'pop music'.

At the start of the war, obeying government instructions, the BBC broadcast only a single programme, but as early as January 1940 it launched a new Forces Programme as an alternative to the Home Service. Broadcast throughout the world, this completely changed the BBC's pre-war programme balance, which separated out Sunday from every other day of the week, and after the war was over in July 1945 it became the so-called 'Light Programme'. This was one of three programmes for the home audience, of which the Third was a minority cultural programme, more prestigious abroad, perhaps, than it was in Britain. Through these moves, the 'great audience', the praises of which had been sung by Reith as much as by Seldes, was now being split up, although Sir William Haley (1901–87), then Director-General, would never have used the word 'fragmentation': he expressed the hope that listeners would graduate from one programme to another, Light to Home, Home to Third.

There were no signs of such policies in American radio: the networks remained firmly in control, although the US War Department had its own network with 1,800 outlets in 1944. In the war-time Soviet Union also, no efforts were made to introduce relaxing programmes. Soviet printing presses were 'vying with machine guns and artillery as weapons of war', and poets, novelists and song writers were mobilized in the cause. Stalin used the words 'brothers and sisters' in his first radio address on 3 July 1941, and a few weeks later a main radio feature was the reading of letters from men and women at the front. After the war, there was to be a greater emphasis on 'culture', defined and monitored from above by Andrei Zhdanov and his associates.

In examining American and Russian as well as British experience, it is necessary to go back to the beginnings; and in Britain, Reith, briefly the wartime Minister of Information, could combine personal history with institutional history as he looked back. A Scot and an engineer by profession, son of a minister and born in a manse, Reith was only thirty-three years old in 1922 when he was appointed General Manager of the British Broadcasting Company, a commercial company with restricted dividends – inconceivable in the United States – and had served for five years in that capacity before becoming Director-General of the new British Broadcasting Corporation. He had largely engineered the change of structure set out in 1926 in a Royal Charter, which stated that the BBC was required to provide information, entertainment and education, and that it should be governed by a Board of five governors, appointed by the Crown for five-year terms on the recommendation of the Prime Minister. They were to be trustees and not managers, for it was Reith's conviction, more than an opinion, that the management of broadcasting had to be in the hands of broadcasters, independent both of government and of business.

What governing the BBC meant was to be interpreted in different ways in the future, in peace time as well as in war, by different Boards of governors and by different individual governors, but Reith's philosophy of social responsibility survived in Broadcasting House long after his departure from the BBC in 1938. His ideas had been set out in one of the most revealing books about the formative years of broadcasting, *Broadcast Over Britain* (1924), written at great speed while Reith was under the kind of great pressure that he liked. Lord Riddell posed questions (see p. 172); Reith both asked questions *and* answered them.

When he entered broadcasting, Reith wrote, there had been no 'sealed orders to open': 'very few knew what [it] meant: none knew what it might become'. Even by 1924, however, he had anticipated its challenges in long-term historical perspective in a way that Riddell had not:

> Till the advent of this universal and extraordinary cheap medium of communi-
> cation a very large proportion of the people were shut off from first-hand knowl-
> edge of the events which make history. They did not share in the interests and
> diversions of those with fortune's twin gifts – leisure and money. They could not
> gain access to the great men of the day, and these men could deliver their mes-
> sages to a limited number only. Today all this has changed.

Reith had a strong sense of mission. To have used broadcasting simply as a
medium of entertainment, he believed, would have been to 'prostitute' it. He did
not wish to offer people merely 'what they wanted'. The BBC had to set standards.
'It should bring into the greatest possible number of homes . . . all that is best in
every department of human knowledge, endeavour and achievement.' There was
more than a touch of Matthew Arnold here, although Reith probably did not
realize it. For him, in his own words, 'the preservation of a high moral tone'
was 'obviously [note the adverb] of paramount importance'. He attached great
importance to religion. He never ever used the words 'mass media' or 'mass
communications'.

A monopoly was the natural instrument to achieve Reith's mission, even a
'brute' monopoly – he chose the adjective himself years later – for only a monopoly could defy a cultural Gresham's law stating that the bad drives out the good.
What the bad and the good were, of course, was a matter of argument. Even
at the time, Reith's stand, refusing to seek 'the lowest common denominator',
seemed authoritarian to his critics, and with the passage of time it appeared rigid
and ultimately obsolete. Yet it won unofficial and official support, as Vail's
defence of the AT&T's position did in the United States (see p. 123). In August
1922, a *Manchester Guardian* leader affirmed confidently, before Reith had been
appointed, that 'broadcasting is of all industries the one most clearly marked out
for monopoly', and twelve years later, in the light of experience, *The Times*
observed that it had been wisely decided 'to entrust broadcasting in this country
to a single organization with an independent monopoly and with public service
as its primary motive'.

More to the point, the official Crawford Committee, appointed in 1926 to
inquire into the future of British broadcasting, agreed with Reith's line of thinking that monopoly was a matter of mission more than of technology – to cope
with scarce frequencies. While conceding that 'special wavelengths or alternative services' might provide an escape from what it called 'the programme
dilemma' – there was then only one programme – the Committee trusted that
they would 'never be used to cater for groups of listeners, however large, who
press for trite and commonplace performances'. Its decision to set up a public
corporation by Royal Charter was hailed by the Fabian socialist W. A. Robson as
'an invention in the sphere of social science no less remarkable than the invention of radio transmission in the sphere of natural science'.

By the year 1927, when the Federal Radio Commission was set up in the United
States to deal with broadcasting issues, at first it was designed to be temporary.
Already American radio had diverged quite significantly from Britain's. It was
mainly a means of entertainment, although the word 'service' was widely used.
It had a very different attitude to political (including election) broadcasting. By

Fig. 23 John Reith, architect of British broadcasting, appeared in many cartoons, including *Punch*, where he could figure as Prospero. (The BBC's house magazine is called *Ariel*.) 'The isle is full of music, sounds and sweet airs that give delight.' This cartoon shows him outside the new Broadcasting House.

1930 there were approximately 14 million radio sets in use, and that was the beginning, against a background of depression, of its 'golden era', when it was, above all else, a mass medium. Local stations might provide future folklore, as they were to do a generation later when Garrison Keillor's *Prairie Home Com-*

panion, originally a programme on Minnesota Public Radio, was broadcast nationally, but during the 1930s national networks were in control.

The main difference in international approaches to radio, however, was in relation to advertising. In no country was broadcasting 'manna from heaven', 'as free as air', but Britain's financing of it from licence fees (not from general taxation) was diametrically opposed to America's financing of it from advertising, which involved rating of sponsored programmes and the taking off the air of such programmes if they did not attract sufficient listeners. During the 1950s segmented advertising (with targets) was establishing itself, helped by psychological research. The argument about the merits of the two systems had never ended. 'The Cash is still the Key', ran a headline in the BBC's house magazine *Ariel* in 1979.

Nonetheless, the British and American systems were only two of the many broadcasting systems which evolved in the 1920s, although each of them served as models. There were many hybrids, as there always were in telecommunications. Canada was particularly interesting since, given its powerful neighbour, it was never likely to follow it as a model. Broadcasting was used quite deliberately there, like transportation policy earlier, to reinforce national identity. Spill-over broadcasting from the United States greatly disturbed the Canadian Radio League and influenced directly the Canadian Radio Broadcasting Act of 1932, the setting up of the Canadian Broadcasting Commission, CBC, and the subsequent creation of the Canadian Broadcasting Corporation in 1936. This was modelled on the BBC, but from the start it incorporated a commercial element: a segment of specifically Canadian advertising was introduced.

Before 1945, the Soviet system, built on Marxist–Leninist foundations, did not serve as a model. Nor did Nazi radio. Italian radio, propagandist though it was, offered no model either, although because it broadcast propaganda in Arabic, it drew the BBC into its first foreign language broadcasting before the war in 1938. French radio, never a model, had been run since 1928 by a public broadcast service organized by the Post Office in competition with thirteen private commercial stations. The audience was relatively small, and in 1939 the public service was placed under the control of a newly established Office for Public Information. Following the German invasion of France in 1940, which was backed by clever German radio propaganda, the service lost all credibility.

Each radio system, even the French, had its advocates. Some countries developed their own institutional identities: more rested on an uneasy coexistence of public service and commercial broadcasting. NHK (Nippon Hoso Kyokai) in Japan, before and after the war, with its Board of Governors, seemed the closest to the BBC. It was founded in 1926, dependent on licence fees, but, unlike the BBC, it was subject to government control which was tightened even before the Japanese invasion of Manchuria in 1931, when the number of licence holders had reached a million. There was pressure before and after Japan's war with China in 1937 to concentrate on broadcasts that would extol 'the national spirit', including 'theme of the day' broadcasts which incorporated the national anthem, patriotic songs, and calls on the Emperor's subjects to bow in the direction of his palace. Ironically, the Second World War was to end with an unparalleled broadcast by Emperor Hirohito (1901–89), which few listeners understood because of the highly formal court language that he spoke.

After Japan was occupied, the status of NHK as a 'juridical person' was confirmed in the Radio and Broadcasting Law of 1950, which was designed to guarantee freedom of expression in broadcasting; and only after that date did NHK face competition from commercial broadcasters, most of them associated with newspapers. Likewise, it was while Germany was occupied – and in its case divided – that the framework of its post-war broadcasting systems was set for it by two very different occupying powers. In Eastern Europe, the main function of radio (and later of television) was now defined as 'the formation of socialist state consciousness': the Soviet system had become a model, as it was in central Europe. In federal West Germany, a highly decentralized radio system was devised after 1945, largely under British influence, with nine regional public law broadcasting stations, each offering three different radio programmes.

There could be no 'great audience' in such circumstances, but there were other distinctive elements from the start in Germany. Suspicion of broadcasting on the part of the press, which was dominated by powerful financial interests, represented in particular by the Springer group, based in Hamburg and Berlin, limited innovation in broadcasting; and the existence of spill-over listeners in the East – and later of viewers – was a fact of political importance before German reunification in 1989. The mass market was left to the press. The fifth article in the Basic Law of the new German state in 1949 specifically made a free press an integral element in the constitution, but it did not foresee the triumphs of the Springer group: Springer's *Bild-Zeitung* (*Picture Post*) sold four million copies a day. In Italy, fewer newspapers were sold to a smaller proportion of the population than in any other European country (in 1975, 99 per thousand compared with 441 in Britain), but newspapers were important institutions, recognized as such. There was also a mass weekly, *Oggi*, to be set alongside *Paris Match*. The Italian broadcasting agency, RAI, Radiotelevisione Italiano, promoted the policy of targeting a unified Italian public, but it was often compromised by overt political interference.

Whatever the country, whatever the regime, whatever the agency, whatever the period, the *raison d'être* of all broadcasting was the offer of programmes to a large unseen audience. For a variety of reasons, largely historical, different countries, using basically the same technology, did not present the same range of programmes or in the same manner, but in all of them there was an operational division of labour, however simple, as there was in the film industry. All kinds of 'studio' programming, beyond the totally informal, involved, with the development of magnetic tape recording, pioneered in Germany, scriptwriters (until scripts as such were largely abolished); producers, usually working behind glass screens; presenters, working in front of them; and performers, not all of them necessarily full-time professionals. Engineers were always behind the scenes too, and the extension of 'outside broadcasting', called for by listeners in all countries, would not have been possible without them.

In the United States, where from the start broadcasting was integrated into the business system, there was a division, as there was in the press, between on the one side programme-makers and programme presenters of all kinds (often the highest paid of all – the 'celebrities') and on the other side, the salesmen who collected advertising revenues. It was inevitable that in the process a programme ratings system would be developed which would become more sophisticated than the programming. Sponsors would measure statistically the impact of radio programme scheduling as they would later measure the audiences for television programmes (peak and non-peak), and this would largely determine the bill of fare that they would offer.

The Reithian BBC avoided ratings as guides to policy, and carried out no listener research of its own until 1937. By 1945, however, it had developed a sophisticated internal system which considered the quality of particular programmes as well as the numbers listening to them. The A. C. Nielsen Company in the United States, founded in 1923, which devised the first direct measurement machine, the Audimeter, in 1941, had established what were generally accepted ratings figures. By the time that it turned to television in 1950, it had become as established an institution as the advertising agencies which preceded the rise of broadcasting and which organized often highly expensive radio and later television campaigns. The agencies, which developed a distinctive marketing language, were subject to the same process of concentration as radio (and later television) companies.

In Britain, where there was nothing monolithic about the broadcasting process, there was a marked division between those people, 'creative' or not, who were directly involved in programme-making and those who administered it and sorted out its finance. Lines could, however, be crossed. For one of the most eloquent among creative administrators, Huw Wheldon, who joined the BBC in 1952, the BBC was 'the sum of its programmes, no more no less'. The patterning of programmes, which for him necessarily incorporated arts programmes, was never fixed, although there were programmes scheduled at the same times each week, some with a very long life: many listeners did not want to see them die, and when they were dropped it was often amidst controversy.

Weather forecasts were included on the programme list everywhere, in Britain relatively early, on 26 March 1923. In mountainous Switzerland and rural America they were a major selling ploy for radio sets. From the start, sporting events were also popular in most countries, despite the frequent lack of co-operation on the part of sporting vested interests. Religious programmes were broadcast in many countries, and in Britain the week ended with a religious Epilogue and a long Amen. In Roman Catholic countries there were differences of opinion about whether or not the Mass should be broadcast. Meanwhile, Radio Vatican, following in the wake of the newspaper *Osservatore Romano*, developed its own restrained style.

The main form of pre-war broadcast entertainment in Britain was 'Variety', an odd name, described by *The Times* in 1934 as 'the bread and butter of broadcasting'. In the United States it was the name of a professional periodical. It had its origins in the theatre, and the first programme broadcast (30 January 1923) was called appropriately *Veterans of Variety*. (However, not all veterans adapted themselves to the broadcasting experience.) Cabaret had a different class appeal. In the United States, the *Amos 'n' Andy Show*, with its origins in nineteenth-century black-and-white stage minstrel shows, survived depression and war, heading pre-war ratings, and after twenty-one years it remained in Nielsen's top ten in 1950 before transferring to television. Its programme form was open-ended, leading the way to the serial.

The word 'programme' has two usages in Britain, as will have become clear: first, for an overall more or less continual broadcast transmission, in the days of television to be described as a 'channel'; and second, for the individual components in the broadcasting so transmitted. Many individual programmes have had their histories recorded, but there have been few comparative studies across national frontiers of the balance of constituents (programmes in the first sense). Television has fared better. Several of its genres have had specialized monographs written about them.

The balance changed over time, notably in Britain – more during the 1960s, a decade of social and cultural conflict, than between 1945 and 1960 – when television was beginning to offer an alternative service. Portable transistor radios had presented a social and cultural breakthrough in Britain, Europe and the outside world, including the Arab world, where, as Daniel Lerner pointed out in his influential book *The Passing of Traditional Society* (1958), they became symbols of modernization (see p. 53). The desert as well as the beach was the place to observe how they were used.

In Europe, one of the drives to make established broadcasting institutions change their programming a little later was dealing with 'pirates'. Radio Caroline, broadcasting from the North Sea, was the first (1964) of a cluster of pirate stations to defy authority and broadcast mainly pop music to Britain and other European countries. After attempts to handle the situation by law – and such attempts were rarer in Britain than in the United States – the BBC itself created a new Radio 1 in 1967, which provided much the same fare as the pirates (largely rock music) and employed some of the pirates themselves. By then, there were four radio channels (1, 2, 3 and 4) instead of three (Home, Light, Third).

Radio 4 took over the mainstream element in the Home Service, the programme to which listeners turned for 'comprehensive coverage of news and comment on the news', and Radio 3 took whatever remained of the old Third Programme, which had itself become a generic music programme in 1964 and 1965. Local radio was introduced also, for the first time since the earliest days of the old British Broadcasting Company, when a high-power long-wave transmitter at Daventry was opened in 1926 and a regional scheme introduced in the following year. The changes made in the 1960s were highly controversial inside and outside the BBC, but the new pattern quickly established itself. For Frank Gillard, who had made his name as a war-time broadcaster, reporting from the Front in a brilliantly organized programme, *War Report*, radio had the great advantage of being 'relatively cheap and simple', an advantage which was of special importance in education, while television was 'costly and cumbrous'. While radio may have been shaken up by television, until then it could compete successfully with newsreels and after then it was never superseded by it.

There was just as big a shake-up in the Netherlands, where there had been a unique broadcasting structure before 1939, largely shaped by religious bodies. A new Broadcasting Act of 1967 introduced two new stations, TROS and VOD, directly designed, with the experience of the pirates in mind, to entertain.

Fig. 24 Transistor radios transformed life on the beach and in the desert where there was none. Radios were mobile, a key asset in media history (note the mobile phone), portable and cheap. Transistors had a bigger history, a key invention in the development of the laptop computer and, most generally, of miniaturization.

Indeed, although one of the later drives in radio came from radio journalists anxious to launch a continuous news programme, it was not until 1974 that the Minister of Culture insisted that TROS should include any news bulletins at all. 'Trossification' left its impact on traditional broadcasters, although the Act defined the purpose of broadcasting as that of offering a 'comprehensive pro-gramme' in 'reasonable proportions' of 'different programme categories'. They were 'to satisfy the population's cultural, religious or spiritual needs'.

In the United States, the purposes of radio broadcasting could never have been so defined. Nor did American radio, by then largely local, live up to the chal-lenges of the time as much-criticized BBC and Dutch radio did. Before the war, 'soap opera' received its name from fifteen-minute daytime dramas sponsored by Colgate-Palmolive and Procter and Gamble. There was a Palmolive Hour, too, and a Maxwell-House (coffee) Hour. News was slow to enter the charts after Lowell Thomas, despite press complaints, began reading news regularly on NBC in 1930, and it was not until 1934 that it took its place in the schedules, often in headlines and snippets. Some celebrities were to pass directly from radio into television. *The Fleischmann Hour* introduced Milton Berle, who began as a nightclub and theatre comic. One event that stands out in broadcasting history was transmitted on radio only: on 30 October 1938, six million people were lis-tening to CBS's *Mercury Theatre on the Air* when ballroom music was interrupted by an authoritative account of an invasion from Mars. *The War of the Worlds* had begun.

After the post-1945 advent of coast-to-coast television, a new stimulus was given to local radio, but as the prime night-time listening audience for radio fell from 17 million homes to 3 million, little was done to improve the range of pro-gramming until the number of available channels increased. The coming of the transistor radio, first offered as a de luxe item in the United States in the early 1950s, and the rapid development of automobile radio guaranteed that pop music, including 'country and western', punctuated by brief news bulletins, would remain staple fare. Only over time – and with the sense that the narrow scope of the radio spectrum no longer mattered – did generic classical music provide an alternative, as later still did 'community radio'.

The sub-title of a 1964 article by Desmond Smith on 'American Radio Today' in *Harper's* magazine was 'the listener be damned'. It was a very different message from that of the editor of London's *Daily Mirror* in face of criticism from government, 'Publish and be Damned'.

> The aims of radio [Smith stated] are identical in kind, but different in magnitude from television's. American radio, as any listener can tell, is an even more docile slave of the commercial dollar. Radio's standards are worse than television's, if that is possible, because radio can only survive, in an atmosphere of shrill sales-manship, as a bargain advertising medium for the local merchant, department store [back to the beginnings of radio] or used car lot.

In 1946, the share of local advertising in radio revenue had been 34 per cent: in 1963 it was 70 per cent. Yet profits from local station operations were high, and it was ironic that with radio in the doldrums as an imaginative medium the FCC had partially to freeze the granting of new licences in 1962.

Perspectives were to change somewhat in the 1970s, a decade which began with the creation of a National Public Radio and ended with the number of FM (frequency modulation) listeners, less vulnerable to interference with their reception, exceeding the number of AM (amplitude modulation) listeners for the first time. The story of FM involved business more than technology. An engineer, Major Edwin H. Armstrong, originally a friend of Sarnoff, became an enemy as Sarnoff came to see FM, which was demonstrated to him in 1933, as a danger to the network system; and although Armstrong was allowed to build an experimental station in New Jersey in 1939 and FM became popular, war held back progress. Moreover, it stagnated until 1957. Appalled by the attitudes of the FCC and driven relentlessly into the law courts, Armstrong committed suicide in 1953 by jumping off a skyscraper. In the history of FM there were parallels with the slow development of UHF in television, although FM made listening, particularly to classical music, far more satisfying, while UHF in many places made viewing less so.

It is possible to make a number of generalizations about the age of radio broadcasting, before television became the dominant medium. Nonetheless, it is almost impossible, as it is in the case of television, a medium far more frequently studied, or, indeed, in the case of the automobile, to separate out its influence on attitudes and habits from other influences on culture and society. Like the postal system, it set out to reach the whole population even in the most remote places, in a quite different way from other media like the press and the cinema. Everywhere it was 'a good companion', consoling as well as entertaining, informing and educating, and everywhere it carried with it unique blessings for the blind, the sick, the lonely and the housebound. In retrospect, at least, the pictures it evoked linger as much as the words offered on it.

The extent to which radio broadcasting established a common culture in countries where this was held up as an ideal is debatable. It was limited, largely by class, however defined, but jokes were shared, as were stories, before the process of fragmentation set in. Its economic consequences were substantial, apart from the creation of huge new industries. Even where, as in Britain, there was little or no integration with the business system through advertising, newspapers and periodicals – and, not least, exhibitions – could use the existence of broadcasting to sell products, including wireless sets. There was also a special appeal to women. As early as 1928, the *BBC Handbook* included an advertisement 'to the women of Britain', who, having installed 'wireless' and thereby 'kept your husband away from the club', were urged to go one step further and 'make your home comfy and cheerful by having Hailgloss Shades and globes in your lights'. The advertisement bore the caption 'The Pleasures of the Hearth'. Sitting around the hearth has come to seem nostalgic: the hearth itself as well as the wireless set have now largely disappeared.

For its fiftieth anniversary in 1972, the BBC invited Alasdair Clayre, writer, singer and broadcaster, to produce a number of radio programmes examining the impact of broadcasting on people who had grown up with it. He began with *Children's Hour* (1922), presented by 'uncles' and 'aunts' – would-be family figures, reinforcements for parents, not substitutes for them. Politics came next in Clayre's survey, with McLuhan, one of the people being interviewed, stressing not entirely convincingly, how radio broadcasting had pushed into the forefront 'tribal chiefs', but drawing no distinctions between broadcasting politics in Britain and Germany, between Britain and the United States or, indeed, between Britain and Canada. Music came third. There had been an unprecedented access to classical music, and the audience for it had greatly increased: gramophone and radio had become interdependent. A commercial British radio station, Classic FM (1992), was to prove it after the BBC lost its monopoly. Meanwhile, background music, including muzak – 'wallpaper for the ears' – was a largely new phenomenon in all countries.

Looking at the trinity of entertainment, education and information, entertainment certainly changed in character after the arrival of sound broadcasting in the home, although not as dramatically as it was to do during the 1980s and 1990s. The cinema was usually an alternative popular attraction with the 'Big Five' dominating both production and distribution – Metro-Goldwyn Mayer, Paramount, Warner Brothers, RKO and Twentieth Century Fox – and with syndicated columnists in the newspapers publicizing (and sometimes damning) the stars of the screen. Oscars, first awarded in 1927 by the American Academy of Motion Picture, Arts and Sciences, were always an occasion for a media event. Radio publicity never had the same popular appeal. As for education, the educative role of radio broadcasting, like television broadcasting, was greater than its formal educational role, although in Britain the BBC concerned itself both with school and adult education almost from the start, and the conception of the 'Talk' as an art form, limited in length and carefully scripted, as strange to French listeners as it was to American, had its origins in adult education.

The first national broadcast to schools in Britain was in April 1924, and by 1939 there was an elaborate apparatus of schools broadcasting, organized by a largely independent Central Council for Schools Broadcasting, which did much to keep schools alive and alert during the Second World War. There was also towards the end of the war a system of Forces Educational Broadcasting, keenly supported by the Adjutant General of the Army. The scheme was not phased out until 1952 when a 'Further Education Experiment' was begun. Both the Forces scheme and the Experiment focused attention through research on intelligibility: how many broadcasts could people actually understand? The answer was fewer than the people producing them realized.

Broadcasting was never simply a mode of transmission, however, for, as its historians have pointed out, broadcasting served at least some of the functions set out by Habermas when he wrote of a 'public sphere'. Most of the broadcasters were middle class, accents had to be 'standard', and there was no talk of interactivity, but it 'widened horizons' (this became a cliché) and stimulated not only hobbies but reading. Librarians usually deemed it an ally, not a foe. A radio programme could lead to a run on bookshops as well as on libraries.

In the United States, early radio had been developed by educational institutions as in no other country in the world, but by the late 1920s they were losing influence as well as numbers; and in 1934 when a new Federal Communications Act replaced the FRC with a Federal Communications Commission concerned with telecommunications as well as radio, there was organized pressure to stake out and support educational programming. Yet the new FCC favoured stations catering for 'the entire listening public within the listening area of the station' and showed no interest in supporting educational stations. Nor did Congress show interest either. Despite philanthropic as well as academic support, by 1935, in the words of Robert W. McChesney, they had 'washed their hands of broad-cast policy' in this and other fields.

This had further implications also in relation to the provision of information through broadcasting. In European countries, broadcasting had done much by 1935 to raise the general level of information, and it continued this task during the war and beyond the introduction of television, when news broadcasting took a new direction. In the United States, hopes had been expressed in 1922 that radio would galvanize 'democracy', a term then used more often in the United States than in Britain, through enhancing a citizen's sense of participation. It was Herbert Hoover, not Roosevelt, who put the point most clearly. Radio for him was 'revolutionizing the political debates that underlie political action under our principles of Government. . . . It physically makes us literally one people on all occasions of general public interest.' That was so in Britain also, notably at the time of the abdication of Edward VIII: his 1936 radio broadcast was introduced by Reith himself.

But how much had that to do with democracy? Ten years earlier, Reith's task as company manager of the BBC (and that was before he became Director-General of a public corporation) had been to maintain the independence of the BBC – or as much of it as he could – when the nation was divided by a general strike in 1926 and when there were people in power, as there were to be in later crises, who wished to take over the BBC. Only an official newspaper and clandestine Labour sheets were available during the strike, and the role of the BBC as a monopoly was bound to be controversial. Reith had many worries but no doubts. There were to be far more doubts in the future.

The Age of Television

Sound broadcasting on both sides of the Atlantic and in many other parts of the world, whatever its pattern, was so well established by the mid-1930s that it was never easy for those engaged in it – whether as proprietors, managers, presenters or performers – to decide how television with its long pre-history would or could fit in (see p. 141). Moreover, although there was a minority of dedicated enthusiasts, the economic situation everywhere was unfavourable to rapid development. In the United States, which might have taken the lead, the early years of the decade before America's New Deal were years of depression when the growth in sales even of automobiles was under threat.

Despite Sarnoff's employment of Zworykin (see p. 142), it was always the word 'experiment' which stood out when television was mentioned in the 1930s, as it still was in Britain. When the decade which ended in war was almost over, television was on public display at the New York World Fair in 1939 at which Roosevelt spoke: there was even a 'Television Hall of Fame'. But it was not until 1941, the year when the United States entered the war, that NBC and CBS, keen rivals, began limited but scheduled television broadcasting in New York. It was not one of the networks but an ambitious newcomer without a radio base, DuMont Laboratories, in which Paramount Pictures was an investor, that continued regular television programmes throughout the war. Sarnoff and William Paley, founder of CBS, were away on non-combatant media-related service, and the third network, ABC, turning to television in 1943, had too many financial problems to be an effective initiator.

When the Second World War ended there was still little sense of excitement about television in radio and film circles, and below the surface there may have been apprehension. Nor was there any group available to put on pressure, like the 'hams' who had played such a critical part in the early years of wireless. Decisions had to be taken from above, and, given strong radio interests, the FCC did not help either. It was involved in protracted arguments about technology, including colour television and the choice of VHF rather than of UHF, and when it froze the setting up of all new stations between 1945 and 1949 this did particular harm to DuMont.

In so-called informed circles there was a misconception about the prospects for television. Only the higher income groups would be attracted to it, it was believed. Yet this was shown to be a serious misconception even before the freeze ended. With few programmes on offer, the production of television sets rose remarkably from 178,000 to around 15 million between 1947 and 1952, and in the latter year there were more than 20 million sets in use. More than one third of the population now possessed one: the figure for 1948 had been 0.4 per cent, with a significant proportion of the sets not in homes but in bars. Even in 1948, however, *Business Week*, enraptured by a post-war boom, could call television 'the poor man's latest and most prized luxury' and proclaim the year 'Television Year'. RCA was in step: the price of its stock in that year rose 134 per cent on the basis of sales of sets.

A real mass audience was beginning to grow explosively each week, while cinema attendances were going down, despite the popularity of the description 'Age of the Cinema' and Hollywood's sloganized claim that 'Movies are Better than Ever'. In 1953, President Eisenhower wrote in his diary: 'If a citizen has to be bored to death, it is cheaper and more comfortable to sit at home and look at television than it is to go outside and pay a dollar for a ticket.' Average weekly cinema attendance fell from 90 million in 1948 to 47 million in 1956. The number of cinemas had peaked to 20,000 in 1945, then fallen to 17,575 in 1948, and had slumped to 14,509 in 1956. From within Hollywood, some attempts to push for pay television failed in face of radio network power, although that took time to assert itself. And some film companies set out to secure television licences. Thus in 1948, Twentieth Century Fox tried to buy ABC. One way out, that of selling films to television companies, was not taken until the mid-1950s.

By then no one was talking of 'the Age of the Cinema' and Hollywood, far from a Dream Factory, had been torn apart by Senator Joseph McCarthy, who had a 'television black list' of so-called pro-Communist performers drawn up for him. McCarthy used television, but was subsequently destroyed by it (and for other reasons). His own television appearances eventually proved counter-productive, and journalists Ed Murrow and Fred Friendly used the medium (without the backing of their company, CBS) to expose him. Some companies had not shown the hearings, and Murrow's own role in McCarthy's fall, through his programme *See It Now*, has been exaggerated.

There were many kinds of television programme, among which the McCarthy hearings were unique, although not as many kinds as there were in radio, and there were different line systems. The United States employed 525 lines – as did Japan – and many European countries employed 625. By the 1960s there was to be more programme traffic across frontiers than there was in radio and even in film, with Hollywood quickly coming into its own again on new terms, and with Broadway, which influenced much early American live television, quickly losing ground. There was no television equivalent, however, to turning the knob, a distinctively radio experience, as Citizens' Band radio was to be in the United States of the 1970s.

Drama was popular at first, and if the *New York Times* could complain that watching stage scenes being enacted on Broadway was not unlike looking at a series of picture postcards, there were optimists who thought of the new medium as 'cultural theatre'. There was also room at that earliest stage in American television history for local differences in the content and style of programming, quickly lost as the networks took over. The latter were helped in this by a technological advance, the development of magnetic videotape. Television programmes could now be broadcast at any time and in any place.

Already before then, some of the creativity had disappeared. This was a complaint in 1950 of Gilbert Seldes, who had served as a CBS director during the war, and who observed with interest, later in the 1950s, how Hollywood was quickly coming back into its own on new terms. The United States was by then televising far more film material (including old movies) than live features, including Westerns like *Gunsmoke*, which ran for twenty years, and *Disneyland*. Warner Brothers was the main provider: ABC, with a new president who had Hollywood connections, was the main purchaser. And a new generation of 'independents' was producing low-cost films which, if successful, earned substantial profits when shown in the cinemas. *On the Waterfront* (1948), with Marlon Brando, from the start a celebrity, was one. Some of the producers, like Otto Preminger, were prepared to defy Hollywood taboos.

Staple American television programmes were far more stereotyped. They included game shows, like *Beat the Clock*, quizzes – these were soon to raise ethical issues – and soap operas. One of the best-known programmes, not only in the United States, was *I Love Lucy* (1957). The long-running *Ed Sullivan Show* on CBS was 'rushed on to the air' in 1948 in an attempt to counter NBC's Milton Berle. 'Television is going the same way as radio as fast as it can: that is towards entertainment,' the editor of the Louisville *Courier-Journal* remarked in February 1956.

Not all non-American broadcasting companies wanted to move in the same direction, certainly not 'as fast' as they could. Nor did Italian film-makers, who were at the height of their creativity in difficult post-war years. In Britain, the BBC, operating in a land not of boom but of austerity, followed a completely different strategy when it put its trust in George Barnes (1904–60), a cultivated broadcaster, who was more at home directing its radio Third Programme than he was inside a television studio and who moved on from being head of television to become head of a new university. William Haley, the BBC's post-war Director-General, was uneasy about the medium itself, even though it was the BBC that had pioneered a pre-war regular but small-scale television service in 1936 (see p. 144). When, after a seven-year, war-time break, 405-line television was restored in June 1946 – the interrupted Disney cartoon of 1939 was the first item – it was called a 'resurrection'.

The number of television licences in Britain had reached only 14,560 at the end of March 1947, but the million mark was attained at the end of 1951, with a preponderance of low-income-group viewers: a BBC survey showed that 70 per cent of them had not been educated beyond the age of fifteen. It was claimed at first that television aerials were status symbols, put up for show, but there was very soon no doubt about the extent of genuine viewing. This became possible in large parts of Scotland, Wales and the north of England in 1952. There was now the potential for a mass audience.

A great impetus to viewing was Queen Elizabeth's Coronation, literally 'in sight of the people', in 1953. Around twenty million people were said to have watched it. (There was a large American audience, too, supplied with film transported by air.) Given that only just over two million British television licences had been issued at this time, large numbers of people must have been watching outside their own homes, some of them in cinemas, public halls and public houses. The commentator, Richard Dimbleby (1913–65), had become well known to radio audiences during the war and had moved naturally into television, becoming even better known as a presenter of *Panorama*, one of the BBC's leading information programmes, first broadcast in the same year as the Coronation. His two sons were to become equally well-known.

The number of radio-only licences reached its peak in 1950 (11,819,190), and fell to under 9.5 million in 1955 when the number of combined radio and television licences was more than 4.5 million. That was the year when Parliament, after protracted and often bitter debates, took away the BBC's monopoly. In a Conservative White Paper of 1952, one of a whole series of White Papers on broadcasting, what was later to be described as a 'Trojan Horse' clause, had pointed to the 1955 outcome: 'in the expanding field of television, provision should be made to permit some element of competition when the calls on capital resources at present needed for purposes of greater national importance make this possible'.

It was from inside the BBC that the man had emerged who was to play a major part in breaking its monopoly. Norman Collins (1907–82), for a time Head of the Light Programme and of BBC Television, created a Popular Television Association in July 1953, which won the support of *The Economist*, the editor of which asked the deceptively simple question, often asked in the United States and in continental Europe, 'Why should broadcasting be treated in a different way from other media, including the Press?' The Association operated in a different way from a pressure group, fighting its campaign against the BBC's monopoly in populist terms. One member of it attacked the BBC because 'it set out unashamedly to make people think, and from that it was only a short step to telling them what to think'.

The Americans, the campaigner failed to add, would never have permitted that, but the new competitive British television channel was not devised on American lines. Indeed, to many people – including French observers, hostile to all Anglo-Saxon pressures both on language and on culture – America served as a warning rather than an example, as it had done in the early years of radio (see

p. 131). British critics shared the sense of threat, and when regionally based commercial companies, described as 'independent' companies (some with press interests), were enfranchised, they were placed within the orbit of an Independent Television Authority (ITA), set up by Act of Parliament in 1954. The word 'authority' stands out in its name. It was the ITA that would control advertising on which the revenue of the companies would depend, limiting it to short advertisements placed between programmes. These would not be sponsored by business firms. 'Commercial breaks', however, now became a feature of the British viewing experience. Their length and character were regulated, but by the 1990s the process of regulation had been softened – with exceptions, like the end of tobacco advertising in stages, the first of them in 1965. Children's advertising was subject to far more critical scrutiny than it was in the United States. Meanwhile, the BBC was never reluctant to advertise itself – and its programmes – in what became increasingly lavish 'trailers' that intervened between the scheduled programmes of the day.

Competition in British television worked to the financial advantage of television producers and performers and a range of outside organizations, particularly in sport, while sharpening competition inside the BBC itself between professionals employed in television, many of them young, and those working in radio. For Antony Jay, a member of the pioneering BBC television team which produced the unscripted, popular programme *Tonight*, introduced in 1957, 'the BBC had been improved more by competition from within itself . . . than by competition directly with ITA'.

The advent of independent television had certainly given a new vitality to the British way of presenting news. Hitherto, news presentation had been superior in the United States, where Walter Cronkite had long ago embarked on a successful career of influence and, indeed, authority. He was a genuine professional, and in Britain, as in the United States, a sense of professionalism in both branches of broadcasting was becoming increasingly strong during the 1960s and 1970s.

It had been possible, through professional skill as much as through institutional policy, for the BBC to retain a competitive advantage in sport (*Grandstand*, 1958) and in comedy. British 'sitcoms' were more popular than drama series, although some of the latter gripped viewers abroad as well as at home: John Galsworthy's *Forsyte Saga*, seen in New York and Washington, was also watched in Moscow. *Hancock's Half Hour*, which moved from radio to live television in July 1956 and ran until 1961, focused on a comedian of genius, Tony Hancock (1924–68), a born entertainer: one of his most memorable programmes was about 'ham radio'. Another successful BBC television series, *Z Cars* (1962), focused on new-style mobile police, offering a complete contrast to *Dixon of Dock Green*, which dealt with old-style policemen on the beat.

In programmes like these – 'mirroring change' – the BBC, with an alert, if controversial, new Director-General, Sir Hugh Greene (1910–87), who took over in 1960, was responding to the new social circumstances and institutional changes of the 1960s more imaginatively than the commercial companies. Yet not everything that succeeded was planned to achieve this result. The programme *Dr Who* (1963), which went through as many changes as the 'time lords' who featured in it, started as a children's programme, but eventually became a cult, as did *Star Trek* in the United States, which successfully passed from television to the cinema and survived the disappearance of its original cast.

The BBC went further than the United States when it introduced satire. *That Was The Week That Was* (*TW3*; 1962), was a programme which treated all institutions and all people in authority irreverently, including the Prime Minister Harold Macmillan. Like the new weekly *Private Eye* (1961), it was an instant success. In drama, where there was more of a sociological than a satirical emphasis, Independent Television (ITV) had secured the services of a creative Canadian producer, Sydney Newman (1917–97), to run its highly successful *Armchair Theatre*, but he was 'poached' by the BBC in 1961 and went on to broadcast a similar, and equally contentious, series, *The Wednesday Play*. Drama flourished, but there were persistent critics on moral grounds (the most pertinacious of them Mary Whitehouse, who founded a National Viewers' and Listeners' Association, vigilantes of the screen).

Despite ample evidence of creativity coupled with controversy, the Pilkington Committee, skilfully lobbied by Greene, expressed alarm in its Report, published in 1962, that a decline in the BBC's ratings share would lead inexorably to a continuing lowering of standards; and, turning back to an old argument, familiar during the parliamentary debates on the end of monopoly, claimed that the companies were making excessive profits from 'the use of a facility which is part of the public and not the private domain'.

It was clear in the early 1960s that the BBC itself had not yet accepted the verdict of Parliament in 1954; and in its voluminous evidence to the Pilkington Committee, seven times the length of Tolstoy's *War and Peace*, and including a film, *This is the BBC*, it stuck to what Greene considered to be the high moral ground, quite different from the moral ground which Mrs Whitehouse, 'defender of the decent', trod. Independence was all. It knew, of course, that whatever the Pilkington Committee might say, the BBC itself would have to develop an adaptable strategy to defend public service broadcasting and the licence system on which its enterprise rested, whatever government was in power. Harold Wilson, Macmillan's Labour successor, accepted ITV enthusiastically: Tony Benn, to the left of his party but an enthusiast for new technology, did not believe – in a memorable phrase – that broadcasting could be left to the broadcasters.

By the early 1970s, when local BBC radio, part of the structural reorganization prepared during the 1960s, was being opened up to competition, as it was in other European countries, it was the unified nature of the British broadcasting system, including television and radio, rather than the differences between the BBC and the ITA (now renamed, after the development of local commercial radio, the IBA) that began to stand out – at least for some knowledgeable commentators and for IBA's Director-General, Sir Brian Young, a former headmaster of a public school, appointed in 1973. Governors, even chairmen of governors, were now being switched from one institution to the other, and professional personnel could move freely between them. Programmes, too, could start on one channel and move to the other. The only major difference seemed to be the continuing difference in finance. The BBC did not take advertising: the companies did. The BBC depended on a licence fee: the companies were driven by profit.

Both sides adapted themselves to changing circumstances, including the arrival of regular colour television in 1967, far later than in the United States, and the introduction of a separate and more expensive colour licence in 1968. For some time that sustained the BBC's finances. Other public broadcasting systems in countries as different as Canada and Portugal were to face serious cuts. Increasingly, broadcasting systems became 'mixed', with public service and commercial companies existing side by side, never within the same institutional framework as that of Britain. There were attempts in the United States also to rewrite the 1934 Communications Act, all of which failed.

The differences between Britain and the United States, where the networks remained immensely strong, was enormous. So also was their outreach. After their domestic television market seemed to have reached saturation point in the mid-1950s, powerful American television interests had begun to look abroad. In February 1955, there were 36 million sets in use in the United States and only 4.8 million in the whole of Europe, with 4.5 million of these in Britain. The explosion was about to happen; and by the mid-1960s there were television stations in more than ninety countries. The great global audience now reached over 750 million.

In the mid-1950s CBS already had affiliates in Havana, Mexico City, Puerto Rico and twenty Canadian cities, and it was outside Europe that the American style of commercial television, intent on offering the entertainment it believed viewers wanted and on avoiding all causes of political offence, spread most easily. In 1966, the well-informed Wilson P. Dizard, in a jargon-free and hype-free book, *Television, a World View*, dedicated to Murrow and written after the first phase of the 'television explosion' was over, estimated that by the early 1970s the 'great audience' would have doubled and that 'TV's influence would stretch from Minsk to Manila, from London to Lima, and on to the Nigerian up-country city of Kaduna where even now bearded camel drivers and local tribesmen sit in fascinated harmony before a teahouse television set watching *Bonanza*'.

Dizard noted that there were differences in programme styles as well as institutional structures in a world industry where the United States had a substantial lead in the export of its own programmes. In Latin America, for example, the *telenovela*, an indigenous form of domestic drama and cheap to make, became immediately popular. Individual episodes, lasting between half-an-hour and an hour, were shown each day except Sundays and public holidays: they were made only the day before. They sometimes offered alternative endings, asking viewers to express their opinions. In Japan, Samurai made their way across the centuries on to the 'small screen' and to other countries too. So did 'monsters from the deep'.

In Japan NHK had introduced television in 1953, to be followed later in the same year by the first commercial station, and there had been excitement on the Tokyo streets when thousands of people gathered to watch a live television broadcast of a wrestling match. Five years later, a Japanese royal wedding gave as great an impetus to viewing as the British royal wedding had done earlier: a million TV sets were sold. In that year, 1958, it was reported that Japan was becoming 'as TV obsessed as the US'. The 1964 Olympics held in Tokyo were a great national as well as international television attraction also, for colour television as well as for black-and-white. NHK, which spent more money on research than any other broadcasting organization, showed that in 1960 a Japanese adult spent three hours and eleven minutes a day on average watching television, and children even more.

In France and Germany, television development followed lines that might have been anticipated given the post-war history of radio broadcasting in both countries, and in France, in particular, a far longer period stretching back at least to the revolutionary and Napoleonic Wars, and even before that to Colbert, had to be kept in view. In 1946, all French political parties had supported legislation nationalizing all French radio and television, but seven years later, with television policy following radio policy, there were only 60,000 television sets in French homes. It required a five-year national television plan in 1954 to project forty-five transmitters, but it was not until it was abundantly plain that audiences were being lost to neighbouring broadcasting organizations, like Luxembourg and Monaco, that the tide began to turn.

After de Gaulle, who appreciated the political potential of television, had become head of state in 1958, the first efforts were made to modify the system, and in 1964 an autonomous new organization, L'Office de Radiofusion Télévision Française (ORTF), was set up. By then there were five million viewers as compared with nearly ten million in West Germany and nearly six million in Italy. In West Germany, television, like radio, had been left on Allied orders to the *Land* governments, with the first television station, Nordwest Deutscher Rundfunk, beginning its operations in December 1952.

The autonomy of ORTF was more dubious than that of the German and Italian services, but there could be no further change in France until after the resignation of de Gaulle in 1969, following the disturbances (*les événements*) in Paris in 1968. The big change still did not come, however, until after the death of de Gaulle's successor, Georges Pompidou. President Giscard d'Estaing then abolished ORTF in 1974, and in a far-reaching 'new deal' set up seven autonomous organizations, one to run radio, two to run television channels, one to run regional television, one to work an independent production company, supplying the rest, one to deal with the technological side of the operation, and one to handle research and archives. To preside over the whole elaborate, still monopolistic, structure, a High Audiovisual Council was created.

This was only one of a number of reorganizations in television structures. The most dramatic was in Italy. In 1974, decisions of Italy's Constitutional Court confirming the need for public service broadcasting based on objectivity and impartiality nonetheless opened the way for private broadcasting and, following a 1975 Broadcasting Act, for an extraordinary eruption of private companies, most of which did not survive. In 1978 there were no fewer than 506 local television stations and 2,275 radio stations. There were now more stations per person than in the United States. Ten years later, the Italian Court's Spanish counterpart made a similar decision, noting that since the constitution was silent on the question of broadcasting, no structure was explicitly forbidden. The constitutional principle of free speech might be deemed, it stated, to include the principle of the freedom to broadcast, a judgement unrecognized in the United States where telegraphy, telephony, radio and television operated under different legal principles from publishing.

The Italian scenario, which continued to evolve, was not copied, however, in Spain. In 1980 Silvio Berlusconi, future Prime Minister, started a quasi-national channel, Canale 5, going on to buy other Italian channels in 1983 and 1984. His business concern, Fininvest, now controlled three channels to RAI's three, a duopoly situation, which was sanctioned in law in 1990. RAI survived, however, as it survived the downfall of the two main Italian political parties, the Christian Democrats and the Socialists, and the long spell in office of Berlusconi from 2001.

In Britain, a Labour government had commissioned in 1974 a report on the Future of Broadcasting by a committee headed by Noel Annan (1916–2000). Reporting in 1977, it rejected schemes put forward within the Labour party, including the formation of a National Broadcasting Council and Commission and the splitting up of the BBC; and in 1980 the new Conservative government, headed by Margaret Thatcher, taking account of its recommendations but modifying them, decided to introduce a new Channel 4, outside the control of the IBA, but dependent for part of its revenue on advertisement. It would commission programmes from independent producers, growing in numbers and soon to grow still more, rather than make them itself. Channel 4 soon proved itself a highly innovative institution, drawing on programmes from abroad as well as from Britain, and some of the new British independents, with areas of speciality, were highly creative, in time constituting a new sector with overseas as well as with British interests.

Annan had made much of the diversity of voices and the lack of moral consensus in the Britain of the early 1970s. In France, however, where there was a strong left and right, President Georges Pompidou had claimed in 1970 that being a journalist in ORTF was 'not like being a journalist anywhere else': ORTF was the 'voice of France'. Giscard d'Estaing's new ORTF did not live up to the hopes placed in it. Broadcasting remained firmly in the hands of government, so that after the election of a socialist president, François Mitterrand, in 1981, all the senior directors in French television were dismissed and replaced by socialists.

A new study commission, appointed to set out a reform programme in France, recommended a new High Authority for the Audiovisual Media, old and new, and changes in the disposition of funds between the various programme sectors. In the subsequent legislation based upon it the language of monopoly was abandoned, but there was an increased stress on public service. Only a public authority had the right, it was reiterated, to take decisions about radio and television programmes 'for the French people'. Such sentences stand out, as they did in broadcasting reform legislation in other countries. There were no clauses dealing with finance, however, and many ambiguities in the sections on structures.

As television spread, leaving only a few countries like Tanzania and Guyana beyond its reach – both by governmental choice – there were some countries where only one voice was allowed to be heard and only a few privileged faces to be seen on the screen. Thus in Thailand, official regulations stated in 1965 that the first objectives of broadcasting were '(a) to promote national policy and common interests in the area of politics, military affairs, economics and social welfare, (b) to promote the loyalty of the citizens to the country, the religion and the king, (c) to promote the unity and mutual co-operation of the army and its citizens and (d) to invite citizens to retort to and oppose the enemy, including those doctrines which are dangerous to the security of the nation.'

Comment and Research

Contemporary comment on television, in countries where its pattern depended on debate, was stressing its global rather than its national implications, as Marshall McLuhan did when he introduced the concept of a 'global village' in 1960. (He had published *The Mechanical Bride, The Future of Industrial Man* in 1951.) His most-publicized books, which followed in sequence, beginning with *The Gutenberg Galaxy* (1962), directed attention to the intrinsic characteristics of particular media, including print, radio and television. In all of them he dwelt on the range of media ('hot' and 'cool', a distinction of his own) rather than on messages and their content, 'programmes'. He paid no attention to national differences or to social differences within countries which directly influenced, along with educational structures, patterns of control and the range of content, and styles of presentation. Nonetheless, when he generalized about village or globe, he was influenced by the unique national traditions and experiences of Canada.

McLuhan, whose words and images linger, was a commentator more than an analyst, and television has provoked more comment and stimulated more argument (and more cartoons) than any other medium in history, beginning perhaps in Britain with the comment of the *Daily Mirror* in 1950: 'If you let a television set through your door, life can never be the same again.' The American Ernie Kovacs's judgement that television is a medium 'because it is neither rare nor well done' is memorable. So, too, are the cartoons in the *New Yorker* which, like cartoons in *Punch*, began with the medium as gadget rather than as message and ended with the television experience.

There was little consensus about what television meant: it was the 'universal eye', but the architect Frank Lloyd Wright called it 'chewing gum' for both eyes. The criticism was strongest in the United States where the emphasis in network television, as in network radio, was on stereotyped entertainment, leading Newton Minow, the Chairman of the FCC in 1961 – an exceptional chairman – to speak of network television as a 'vast wasteland'. In London, Milton Shulman, a lively newspaper critic of particular programmes, called British television 'the least worst television in the world', but he noted also, like Lloyd Wright, how 'for most people the act of watching the box' had now become 'a habit rather than a conscious discriminatory act'. For Shulman, television was 'the ravenous eye'. For others it was 'the evil eye', *mal occhio*, destructive not only of individuals who gazed into it but of the whole social fabric.

Much of this criticism is now dated. Some of it, however, sounds curiously topical. For many critics, television was a reductive agency, trivializing the news as well as the other constituents of programming; for other critics, however, it was a negative force, distorting not only the news but the issues that lay behind it. McLuhan was quoted less often in the 1980s than he had been twenty years before. For Neil Postman, writing in 1986, we were now 'amusing ourselves to death'.

Yet if that had been all that there was to television, there would never have been as many debates as there were in most countries about decency, language, sex, violence and taste, or the standards or codes dealing with them. Nor would the law have been so prominently evoked, in particular in the United States. There, as we have seen, broadcasting was from the start treated quite differently from print; and cable television, when it arrived (see p. 236), was treated differently from network television, not only in the courts but by the FCC. Most legal action originated there. Both inside and outside the courts much of the debate centred on the role of the family, an institution in flux, about which it was even more difficult to reach consensus or even to generalize than it was about television itself. It was easy to say that children needed to be protected when television intruded into the home, but ideas on how to protect them might divide families.

The legal issues were complex, and the complexity increased with the advent of cable and ultimately the Internet. The debate on the influence of television on children was opened by Hilde Himmelweit in her *Television and the Child*, published with Nuffield Foundation support in 1958, which also considered the influence of television on adolescent and adult social and political behaviour, including violent protest. The United States contributed much to both debates. There has been no agreement on either, despite public demand to 'do something' and a vast amount of empirical research. In general, protecting children has been given more attention than educating them, content labelling and rating systems have been proposed and implemented, time zones have been introduced, within which certain types of programme would not be broadcast and, most recently, technical filtering devices have been devised.

Similar issues have arisen in film. As early as 1919, a now defunct periodical, called significantly *Education*, complained of 'the tendency of children to imitate the daring deeds seen upon the screen', with the imitation 'not confined to young boys and girls, but [extending] even through adolescents and to adults'. The Hays Production Code went into effect in 1931, and a new MPAA (Motion Picture Association of America) code in 1968. Within the home, different responses were necessary. The last response was technological, the invention of the Violence-Chip (V-Chip), an electronic device designed in Canada, which could be installed in television sets to identify television programmes which parents deemed objectionable. Politicians seized upon this device for their own purposes and in 1996, in a Communications Decency Act, Congress mandated that such a chip should be installed in every new television set sold in the United States. The Supreme Court ruled the Act to be unconstitutional in 1997 on the grounds that its provisions would abridge freedom of speech.

The best-known example of American action to use television positively in the interests of children leads back a generation before the Children's Television Act of 1990 to the Children's Television Workshop, created with Nuffield Foundation support, which devised the series *Sesame Street*, starting in 1969. A commercial product, deliberately designed to be entertaining as well as educational, teaching pre-school children how to read, the programme depended on team co-operation and collaboration similar to that of academics in the Open University (see p. 250). In the course of its long life, it was shown in 140 countries around the world and became a model for programmes like the Mexican *Plaza Sesamo*, the Brazilian *Vila Sesamo*, *Sesamstraat* in the Netherlands and *Iftah Ya Simsin* in Kuwait.

Nevertheless, it inspired almost as much controversy as enthusiasm, particularly in countries which had different attitudes towards children from those in the United States and did not wish to treat them as commercial consumers. It is refreshing to turn to the simplicities of Dr Maire Messenger Davies's British paperback of 1989 *Television is Good for Your Kids*, which itself used evidence derived from research like that carried out in Australia by Bob Hodge and David Tripp. Their in-depth study of 600 five-to-twelve year olds concluded that 'the *bête noire* of lobby groups, the cartoon, turns out . . . to be a healthy form, ideally adapted to children's growing powers'.

Empirical research on radio and television use or on particular programmes has sometimes, but not always, avoided theory, but with the expansion of twentieth-century universities and other institutions of higher education, many of them developing departments of media studies, it is not surprising that theory was given a prominent place and that the wide range of theories on offer frequently did not seem to relate pertinently to the experience of people working in the media. They were, indeed, far removed from them. Many theories concerned education, many semiology, fewer entertainment, and some of the most interesting 'news'. Columbia in New York, where Robert K. Merton and Paul Lazersfeld met in 1941, co-authored a remarkably wide-ranging article, 'Mass Communications, Popular Taste and Organized Social Action' in 1948. In Britain, a Glasgow University Media Studies Group opened up a sometimes bitter debate about 'news bias' in 1976 in a book called *Bad News* (there were to be sequels), prefaced with a quote from the French semiologist Roland Barthes that 'reluctance to display its codes is a mark of bourgeois society and the mass culture which has developed from it'.

In Britain, Richard Hoggart, the founder in 1964 of the Birmingham Centre for Cultural Studies, the first academic institution in Britain to deal with 'cultural studies', then a debatable and debated designation, had started his career in adult education and from 1960 to 1962 had served as a member of the Pilkington Committee on Broadcasting, whose views he succeeded in shaping (see p. 193). Before that he had published *The Uses of Literacy* in 1957, which drew on women's magazines for much of the material that it put under review. Universal literacy had come to be taken for granted (prematurely): Hoggart showed its current limitations years before the BBC introduced its first literacy initiative, the kind of campaign which was still regarded as necessary, perhaps more necessary, in 2001.

Along with another British academic, Raymond Williams, who had also started his career in adult education, Hoggart reshaped academic approaches in Britain to the media (taken as a cluster) and to their role in contemporary society. Williams's prolific writings, representing 'New Left' Marxism at its most analytical, include *Communications* (1962), significantly revised in its second edition

(1966), and *The Long Revolution* (1961). The second of these books, a sequel to his *Culture and Society* (1958), encouraged the study of changing media over a long period of time, beginning formally with the Industrial Revolution. The approach – which left out religion – was histrical, more through social, cultural and political history than through statistical analysis, although Williams as a Marxist never ignored underlying economics. Books figured more prominently in his account than newspapers, but radio and television were always given their place.

Daniel Boorstin's book on the media, *The Image*, was often quoted alongside Williams, although it was written within a very different American frame. It directed attention not only to 'pseudo events' manufactured by the media but to 'celebrities', known, unlike 'heroes', by their images rather than by their achievements. 'Formerly a public man needed a private secretary for a barrier between himself and the public. Nowadays he has a press secretary to keep him properly in the public eye.' Techniques of communication, including 'spin', have become far more sophisticated, if not always more effective, since then. As for the 'events', they were to be described by the Israeli scholars Elihu Katz and Daniel Dayan as 'media events' and treated as reinforcements of 'social integration'.

Neither Katz nor Boorstin drew on statistics. Others did, often heavily, including UNESCO which produced a series of reports on Mass Communication, the first of them in 1954, *Newspaper Trends 1928–1951*. These reports demonstrated that Canada was by far the main supplier of newsprint both before and after the war and that among the 120 countries which were consuming more than fifty tons of newsprint in 1951, the United Kingdom was consuming less in 1951 (599,000 tons) than in 1938 (1,250,000 tons). In the same year, 1938, Political and Economic Planning, a non-partisan organization, produced the first empirical report on the British press. Three post-war British Royal Commissions, reporting in 1949, 1962 and 1977, drew useful comparisons of readership across the century. In 1920, one in two adults read a daily newspaper of any kind – it could still be considered a luxury; in 1947, every ten adults read twelve daily newspapers and twenty-three Sunday newspapers. The total sales of national and provincial dailies were 50 per cent higher than they had been before the war, despite their smaller size, due to the shortage of newsprint. Thirty years later, total readership had fallen slightly, but the provincial press was in a stronger position than before.

The second issue of *Cultural Studies*, the provincial product of the Birmingham Centre, published in 1971, included a fascinating article by Stuart Hall, who was to move to a professorship at the Open University, on 'The Social Eye of *Picture Post*', and the third issue saw another long article by him on 'The Determinations of News Photographs'. Both threw light on the evolution of newspapers and of 'photojournalism', more highly developed in Germany before the Nazis took power than in any other country. Meanwhile, the Centre subjected entertainment to closer analysis than at any earlier time in Britain. There was also a fascination with 'sub-cultures'.

In Germany, writers of the so-called Frankfurt School, founded by Theodor Adorno (1903–69) and Max Horkheimer (1895–1973), had developed a 'critical theory' of the media before they were driven out of the country in 1934 and regrouped themselves in the United States. Marxist in its origins, like much

European analysis of the media, the School was once described by Ralf Dahrendorf as 'the unholy family of critical theory'. Yet when members of the School returned to Frankfurt after the Second World War, they stored their old papers in the basement and abandoned critical theory. Nonetheless, they invited the young Jûrgen Habermas to join them, and he spent an unhappy time with them before moving to Marburg and Hamburg. His first major work, published in 1962, *The Structural Transformation of the Public Sphere*, set out his ideal of a rational informed discussion of public policy described in the early chapters of this book.

This was the moment when cultural studies were emerging in universities, French and Dutch as well as British and German, when interest in the image (through the newspaper, television and film) and in 'history from below' was generating new kinds of scholarship and when university teachers and, above all, students were being recruited in increasing numbers from hitherto socially underprivileged sections of society. There was a social convergence that preceded technological convergence (see below, p. 216).

In the United States, where most pre-war research on radio had been 'body count' market research, leading into public opinion poll and ratings studies, one of the best-known and most influential researchers, Bernard Berelson, who had made his reputation with his studies of media content, announced in the *Public Opinion Quarterly* in 1959 that communication research was 'withering away'. It was a provocative judgement which led directly, if years later, to the publication in the summer of 1983 of a special number of the *Journal of Communication* entitled 'Ferment in the Field', which surveyed the whole American and world scene in communications research. A 'new type of (American) scholar' had by then appeared.

One of the most interesting – and brief – contributions was by James W. Carey (see p. 165), who, in referring to a new fashion for cultural studies, asked whether their spokesmen would be able to retain 'the cheery optimism of pragmatism and the insights of some of [their] forebears in facing the central issues of power and dominance in communications and society'. Cultural studies were for Carey 'an attempt to think through a theory or a vocabulary of communications that is simultaneously a theory or vocabulary of culture'. Would they cover all the relevant questions?

French scholars had moved into the field by different routes, and three of them, conscious that they were writing from within an electronic society, stand out, largely because of the influence they exerted on others. They were Guy Debord, Jean Baudrillard and Pierre Bourdieu. Debord's *Society of the Spectacle* (1970), a translation of a manifesto in French, published in 1967, with little empirical evidence to back it, argued that in societies where 'modern conditions of production prevail, all life presents itself as an immense accumulation of spectacles. Everything that was directly lived has moved away into a representation.' Thus, the spectacle became the world. The observation should be contrasted with the modest remark by an American writer on television, Richard Adler, that 'the small screen severely limits the effectiveness of spectacle'.

Baudrillard, who judged McLuhan's 'the medium is the message' to be 'the key formula of the age of simulation', turned to television as *the* medium of 'electronic simulation', pointing to 'the dissolution of television into life [and] the dissolution of life into television'. From a different tradition, Bourdieu, in a short, highly compressed, bestselling book, *On Television*, published in France in 1996 and in the United States in 1998, mentioned Debord only once and Baudrillard not at all. This was not unusual among theorists of the media who preferred parallel play to engaging with each other. Meanwhile, the editors of the British journal *Media, Culture and Society*, launched in 1977, made a valiant effort to keep British media scholarship in contact with continental theory.

While French university professors were beginning to discuss the media during the late 1960s with sharp differences of outlook, university students who were involved in *les événements* of 1968 in Paris were learning, like civil rights marchers in America, through experience, not through research, how to use television to ensure that they were seen and heard. Inevitably they were attacked mainly in newspaper correspondence columns, which have received less attention from media scholars than talk shows and access radio and television, growing in importance. Was it television, their critics asked, which was stirring them up and making them behave in a way that they would not have done had there been no 'Small Screen, Big World'? Protesters against the Vietnam War were soon to appear frequently on the American screen. Who were *they* stirring up?

There was ample debate on this question on the screen and more than ample blaming of television and, indeed, of all the media, which reached a climax when President Nixon's first Vice-President, Spiro Agnew, launched a premeditated but not unpopular attack on them in 1969. Richard Nixon (1913–1994) himself often used the phrase 'the press is the enemy'. Why, they asked, should the press and television set the agenda? Why should they determine the tone of argument? Politicians were elected, citizens paid taxes. What was the claim of journalists to exert power? These were questions that persisted long after 'revolting students' had passed from the centre of the stage. Indeed, they were topical at the end of the century and the beginning of the next.

How religion was affected by television had provoked a more uneasy long-term American debate than the effects of television on politics, particularly Republican politics. Jerry Falwell, star of *The Oldtime Gospel Hour*, which claimed 50 million viewers, had for a time mobilized 'moral majority' power. And in the 1990s, televised religion, 'the electronic church', became visible in Garden Grove, California, where the Revd Robert Schuller – a less stirring and less provocative gowned figure on the screen than the eloquent but personally vulnerable Jimmy Swaggert, or the presidential hopeful Pat Robertson – built a huge cathedral with 10,000 windows. By then, praised by Rupert Murdoch, he was giving weekly broadcasts to an audience of millions which stretched far beyond the United States. Religious television is still changing. No cathedral can contain it. The most global of televangelists, the American Billy Graham, never needed one. A football stadium would do just as well, and a raincoat just as well as an academic gown.

Whatever the style, there were persisting questions about journalists, whatever their medium, and their relationships with government and religious groups. The Vietnam War, followed by Watergate, raised basic questions both about the dependence of the media on official sources and the extent of press and

television influence on American politics (see p. 204). So, too, did the later reporting of President Clinton's personal life. Robert Manoff and Michael Schudson
began the book that they edited, *Reading the News* (1986), published before the
Internet raised other issues, with three old questions raised in different form by
Harold Lasswell (see p. 4). 'Every newspaper reporter should answer the questions, What? Who? Where? When? and Why?, adding How? and should do it in the
first paragraph as early as possible', adding that the questions, part of schools of
journalism catechisms, hid 'within their simplicity and their apparent com-
monsense a whole framework of interpretation'. In fact, the wide range of interpretation, which has little to do with technology, is explicable only in terms of
values, their glossing over as well as their expression.

The Dynamics of Change

The range of questions relating to television, some of them the same as the issues
raised in relation to the press, often had little to do with technology. It is interesting to compare the structure and dynamics of television as described in 1966
in Wilson P. Dizard's *Television, a World View* with Francis Wheen's *Television: a
History*, which appeared in 1985 in conjunction with an ambitious fourteen-hour
British Granada television series, which broke a taboo that television should
never investigate itself. The series was three years in the making and involved
hundreds of interviews in Europe, America, Asia and Africa. It demonstrated that
as television had made its way around the world both to democratic and authoritarian countries, leaving only a few countries untouched, it had won new friends
and made new enemies. The comment was now multicultural. Thus, the magazine *India Today* described the Indian television service in 1982 as being like 'a
slack, inexorably slow and malfunctioning government department, no different
from the local passport office': 'the tedium is the message'. And in the
Philippines, a Jesuit priest claimed that President Ferdinand Marcos worshipped
the media 'idolatrously', 'the way other people believe in God'.

A Japanese who was quoted as saying that television addiction had turned millions of his fellow countrymen into imbeciles might have taken as part of his evidence an opinion poll of 1982. When Americans and Japanese were asked what
single item they would take to a desert island (of the kind mapped by Sue Lawley
in Britain's radio programme *Desert Island Discs*), over 36 per cent of the
Japanese chose television, only 4 per cent of the Americans. At that time, two-
year-old children in Japan were on average watching three hours, thirty-one
minutes of television a day, either alone or with their mothers.

Much of Wheen's book was devoted to particular programmes, like long-
running soap operas, such as Granada's *Coronation Street* (1960), and to the
handling of particular events by television, in fact, fiction or 'faction' broadcasts,
prominent among them documentaries on the events of war. From the early
years of post-war television, the Cold War was in the background, and its influence could inspire propaganda and generate entertainment. So could the
Second World War. In Britain, *Dad's Army* (1968) returned to it, as did many
British programmes, a preoccupation disturbing to German critics. Thames
Television's *World At War* (1982) was produced by Jeremy Isaacs, who was first

Director of Channel 4 and a strong critic of the Glasgow Media Group's *Bad News*. The First World War had been the subject of a twenty-six-part series, organized jointly by the BBC, the Canadian Broadcasting Corporation and the Australian Broadcasting Commission. It drew on the reminiscences of more than 50,000 survivors, in a way impossible in previous centuries.

Vietnam, a long war with different phases, has been, as already suggested, a major influence on media history. It was the first war to be seen, if in selective form, on the screens, although the selective pictures of blood-shed that were shown did not so much horrify viewers as sag the credibility of President Lyndon Johnson. Newspapers had more influence on public opinion at that stage and later. In 1972 a highly successful and often repeated American sitcom *M*A*S*H* (1972), which ran to 251 episodes and did not close until 1983, was set during the Korean War. By then President Nixon had been forced to leave office in 1974 not because of war, but because of the domestic scandal of Watergate, pushed out not by television's Cronkite but by two junior reporters from the *Washington Post*.

During the previous decade civil rights battles in the United States had been transformed through television exposure. The assassination of Martin Luther King in 1968 was caught on the screen, but Kennedy's assassination had to be first announced in sound only – by Cronkite – before endless television pictures were released. (A British television series, bought by the United States, followed.) Terrorism provided a major theme on many occasions, for the cinema as well as for television. So too did space. NASA's officials were uneasy at first about using television, but for political as well as televisual reasons they soon changed their mind. When John Glenn went into orbit in 1962, the world as well as the United States saw his blast-off; and seven years later the first pictures from the moon provided a prelude for what was hailed as 'the greatest show in the history of television': the Apollo XI landing. It was seen by 125 million Americans and 723 million other people around the world. This was a scientific and technological as well as a media event (see p. 205).

Entertainment, eventually bound up inextricably with news and sport, has its own landmark events, frequently recalled on television and on film. One American programme in particular, *Dallas* (1979), 'the ultimate soap opera', has also been a subject of sociological research in many universities. Dealing dramatically with sex, wealth, power and family, irresistible in combination and suggesting that 'sun-belt' Texas was as 'communicable' to the world as the Wild West had been, it was shown, often in dubbed form, in more than ninety countries with governments of all political persuasions. Meanwhile, a very different kind of British comedy programme, *Monty Python's Flying Circus* (1969), with an appeal greater even than that of the equally innovatory *Goon Show* on radio, also captured an international audience. It used linking animation and revelled in absurdity, just as apparent when the television series was extended into film. *Till Death Do Us Part* (1966), yet a third kind of comedy programme, British as it was in essence, inspired American and German programmes *All in the Family* and *One Heart and One Soul*.

Educating, not entertaining, remained the priority for some of the first defenders of television against charges that it had an inevitable corrupting influence on

Fig. 25 The moon landing, 1969. The Americans tell the world they are in space. The successful Apollo project enabled Neil Armstrong to be the first human to walk on the surface of the moon. The Russian Yuri Gagarin had been the first human to orbit the earth.

society and culture and took up far more of viewers' time than they spent on any other activity. Two hundred and fifty million American man-hours a day were being devoted to watching television in the mid-1960s when Harry J. Skornia produced a well-received book, which won the praise of McLuhan, on *Television and Society: An Inquest and Agenda for Improvement.*

Should educating be treated as a separate task, segregated in separate channels or in separate broadcasting organizations? There were different answers. Japan introduced an entire NHK channel devoted to educational television in 1957. Britain took a different route and incorporated education into general programming. The idea of launching a separate educational channel had been supported by independent television companies but was opposed by the Pilkington Committee. It was 'independent television', not the BBC, which initiated a television service for schools in its regular programming, but in 1964 the new Chairman of the Schools Broadcasting Council, Charles Carter, the Vice-Chancellor of Lancaster, a new university, urged in face of much school teachers' opinion to the contrary that television 'opened up opportunities' which were 'as exciting as anything since the arrival of the cheap printed book'.

In the United States, the FCC reserved more than two hundred television stations for educational broadcasting in 1952, but most of them lacked adequate finance and would not have been able to operate without help also from the Ford Foundation which supported a National Education Television (NET) to produce programmes. Other foundations gave support also. The Ford Foundation also initiated pioneering formal and informal educational schemes in Latin America, India and Africa. So, too, did CETO, a British organization, the Council for Educational Television, financed by the Nuffield Foundation.

The American situation changed when in 1967 a commission set up by the Carnegie Corporation proposed the creation of a Corporation for Public Broadcasting and the Ford Foundation earmarked funds for a Public Broadcast Laboratory. Nonetheless, once established in 1967, the American public broadcasting system (PBS), with strictly limited funds, concerned itself as much with informing as with educating, and not entirely leaving out entertainment either, some of the entertainment consisting of drama imports from Britain. Entertaining, like educating, was a task which crossed frontiers. In Britain, the oldest public broadcasting institution in the world, the BBC, did not hesitate to import entertainment programmes from the United States. And under a communist regime, Serbs, Croats, Bosnians and Slovenes watched the *Forsyte Saga*.

Little information came out of Yugoslavia during the 1960s, but informing became a major concern everywhere, including Yugoslavia, during the late 1960s and 1970s when there was simultaneous talk both of 'lack of information' and of 'information saturation'. In the United States, in particular, there was a growing tendency to treat information as a commodity, created and distributed in an 'information economy', a term explored in the next section of this chapter. In January 1966, for example, Senator George McGovern, opponent of the Vietnam War, who six years later was to be Democratic presidential candidate, was reported as observing that 'just as we were beginning to feel comfortable about living in the space age, bold headlines in an IBM advertisement told us "there's growing agreement that we are now in an information age"'. It was time, therefore, to look both at its domestic and at its 'ripening international applications'.

They were interrelated and became more so after the oil crisis of 1973 which followed the victory of Israel in the Yom Kippur War. Arab pressure in OPEC, the Organization of Oil Producing and Exporting Countries, led to a quadrupling of world oil prices and to 'Third World' demands for a 'new economic order'. In that year, Britain and Europe as well as the United States were faced with economic and social crisis, and in Britain there were two general elections in one year, 1974. In the United States in the same year Richard Nixon, who had won a landslide victory against McGovern in 1972 and had subsequently extricated his country from the Vietnam War, was forced to resign – the first American President to do so – in the wake of the Watergate scandal (see p. 204). In these circumstances the mood of the 1960s gave way to unprecedented fears of social, political and constitutional breakdown.

It was not events in Britain and the United States, however, but Third World reactions to American dominance in information generation and distribution ('hegemony') that pushed information into the centre of international debate from the mid-1970s onwards. UNESCO, where much of the debate was concentrated, now became the forum for a North–South dialogue (a new term) in which the developed countries had the power and the developing countries a majority. This was the beginning of UNESCO's 'Second Development Decade', covered chronologically and analytically in Thomas McPhail's *Electronic Colonialism* (1987).

Even as early as 1959, before the beginning of the first such Development Decade, UNESCO had been asked by the Economic and Social Council of the United Nations Organization to prepare for the UN's General Assembly 'a concrete programme of action' to promote 'the development of mass media of information all over the world', but little was done until in the changed economic circumstances of the 1970s most of the countries, which had long described themselves as 'non-aligned', placed on a broad international agenda disparities not only of wealth and of income but also of information, pre-electronic as well as electronic. This was at a time when new attitudes towards the development process were taking shape in the United States and in Britain. The word 'modernization' had fallen out of favour, the word 'under-developed' had given way to the adjective 'developing', and alternative ways to 'development' were being considered.

The need for new approaches to communications issues and policies was emphasized in pioneering fashion in *Intermedia*, the journal of the International Broadcast Institute, which significantly changed its name to the International Institute of Communications in 1978. It explained in its leaders, with evidence culled not from the United States but from the Third World, that 'without information – without the opportunity to select, distribute and discuss information – one has no power. Those who lack information are often the most conscious of this relationship.' Most of its leaders were written by its committed Swedish director Edi Ploman, who had previously worked in Swedish radio and television, and who subsequently moved on to become a Vice-Rector of the United Nations University, with its headquarters in Tokyo. In the words of one leader, it had long

> been a frustration of the developing countries that their 'window on the world' is filtered through lenses chosen and fitted by the developed, industrial countries. Their own information infrastructure – their newspapers, television and radio stations; national and international microwave links and satellites; news agencies; training institutes; film production units – are few and scattered. Few countries have UNESCO's minimum requirements of ten copies of daily newspapers, five radio sets, two television sets and two cinema seats per thousand people. A journalist in Bombay can telephone London or New York more quickly and more easily than Kabul or Dar es Salaam.

In this statement, which did not yet include the phrase 'media environment', all the media were related to each other, and UNESCO was given a special role – that of setting standards.

Ironically, one country, Iran, which after the fall of the Shah in 1979 was to proclaim Islamic values in face of modernization, was for a time the centre of studies of development and the role that the media might play in the development process. The first editorial in the journal *Communications and Development Review*, which appeared in 1977 under the editorship of Majid Tehranian, was entitled 'Communications and Development: The Changing Paradigms', and this was followed by the report of a probing interview with Daniel Lerner. A later article was headed 'Modernity and Modernization as Analytical Concepts: An Obituary'.

Turning from Tehran to Paris, where, also ironically, the man who took over after the overthrow of the Shah, the Ayatollah Khomeini, was living in exile, the 17th General Session of UNESCO in 1972, one year before the international oil crisis effectively brought the 1960s to a close, had passed a 'Declaration of Guiding Principles on the Use of Space Broadcasting for the Free Flow of Information, the Spread of Education and Greater Cultural Exchange'. The Declaration asserted that cultural sovereignty and international control of the accuracy of news broadcasts were necessary. No fewer than fifty-five states accepted the Declaration, and only seven, with the United States most prominent among them, were opposed. There were twenty-two abstentions, among them the Soviet Union.

The demand for 'cultural sovereignty' was a protest against 'cultural imperialism', a concept developed in the United States by academics like Herbert Schiller, who also (1976) used the phrase 'cultural domination'. In Latin America, where cultural imperialism was at the centre of media and communications studies, commercial television was the most prominent target of attack. In the strong words of the Chilean delegate to a subsequent United Nations Working Group, competitive, commercial television, 'dragging down standards and offering the dregs of mass culture', constituted a 'source of concern for our educators, sociologists and statisticians and for all of us who participate in a cultural policy that seeks to ennoble rather than to degrade our people'.

Imbalanced information was a parallel complaint, gaining in weight as statisticians, among them Scandinavian communications scholars like Karle Nordenstreng, collected details of 'flows'. Geographers were to play an increasing part in communications research, not only studying flow routes and comparing them with the trade routes of the past, but also exploring through what came to be called 'phenomenological' geography the relationship between people and the world they lived in. A landmark work was J. Meyrowitz's *No Sense of Place* (1985) which argued that electronic media affected people not primarily through their content but by dissociating physical place and social place. 'When we communicate through telephone, radio, television, or computer, what we are physically no longer determines *where* and *who* we are socially.'

Critics of 'imbalance' continued to point out, along the lines of *Bad News*, that most of the news relating to the Third World was negative. It dealt only with such subjects as disasters, political and military intrigues, scandals, shortages and famines. Complaint shifted later to an attack on direct broadcast satellites (see p. 232), seen as a threat to cultural identity, and to the distribution of frequencies on the radio spectrum, still conceived of as a scarce communications resource.

The spectrum was a matter not for UNESCO but for the World Administrative Radio Conference (WARC), organized by the ITU, which had previously been concerned largely with technical questions. Now communications policies came to dominate its conference agenda. This was a shift of importance in the history of the International Telecommunications Union which, at a plenipotentiary meeting in Nairobi in 1982, set up an Independent Commission for Worldwide Telecommunications Development under the chairmanship of a British former diplomat, Sir Donald Maitland. Its sixteen members included, as his Vice-Chairman, the Costa Rican Minister of Information and Telecommunications, the Chairman of the Advisory Council to the Indian Prime Minister for the Planning Commission, and a former Chairman of AT&T.

While there were 600 million telephones in the world in 1982, half the world's population lived in countries which together had fewer than ten million telephones; and at its five meetings the Commission ranged not only over all the implications of this situation but on what it called 'dramatic advances in the technology of telecommunications [which were then] taking place'. The Commission's Report, *The Missing Link*, which appeared in 1984, made points often made in the 1980s, but unconfirmed since, that 'the appropriate technology from a Third World nation [might] be more advanced than the prevailing norm' and that a 'leap frog planning strategy' would work.

Before the publication of *The Missing Link*, UNESCO had appointed a different kind of commission, also at a meeting in Nairobi, that of its 19th General Session in 1976, when a highly contentious resolution was carried. This included what to many 'developed' countries was a notorious Article XII, attacked not least for its language which laid down that 'States are responsible for the activities in the international sphere of all mass media under their jurisdiction'. The new Commission, headed by an Irish politician Sean McBride, was given what he rightly described as 'the formidable task' of examining 'the totality of communications problems in modern society'.

Its members included McLuhan, the Colombian novelist García Márquez, a well-known Japanese journalist Michio Nagai, and the Director General of the Soviet news agency TASS. They were agreed on the need 'to approach communications globally', but even before they were appointed it was clear that in Cold War conditions they had no hope of winning universal support for any recommendations that they might make. In 1977 sharp divisions in approach between the United States and the Soviet Union had been all too apparent at the Helsinki Conference on Human Rights, and when the Commission's report, *Many Voices, One World*, appeared in 1980, their recommendations quickly passed into history. Indeed, the non-aligned countries were themselves divided after Indira Gandhi's repression of press freedom in the last phase of her long prime ministership of India between 1966 and 1977.

When in 1978 the 20th General Session of UNESCO carried a grandiosely entitled 'Declaration of Fundamental Principles concerning the Contributions of the Mass Media to Strengthening Peace and International Understanding, the Promotion of Human Rights and to Countering Racialism, Apartheid and

Incitement to War', Article XII was missing. Yet this 'masterly exercise in squaring the circle' – as a well-informed journalist called it at the time – was to look masterly only in the short run. When the United States, followed by Britain, disturbed by this and by other UNESCO policies, left the organization, it never again set out to deal with the 'totality of communications problems in modern society'.

The initiative in international intellectual debate now passed to academic spokesmen of 'free trade in ideas' – what the most able of them, Ithiel de Sola Pool, a Professor at the Massachusetts Institute of Technology, who favoured deregulation of all media, called in 1983 'technologies of freedom'. For Pool, who mentioned UNESCO only once *en passant* in his book with that title, published in that year, what the news media did, whoever owned them, was to create counterweights to established authorities. It was authoritarian governments, not traditional cultures, which were in danger. The cultures would flourish not on protection but on a fostering of their production capabilities and on reciprocal exchange. No culture could remain isolated. This continued to be the line taken by the United States in the late 1990s in a periodical, *Correspondence*, edited by the American sociologist Daniel Bell. In the spring of 2000 it drew on survey evidence to claim that of 186 countries in the world only 69 had a 'free press'.

Pool did not consider it necessary to scrutinize systematically media operations in democratic countries, nor did he dwell on global issues. He placed stress on 'electronic media as they are coming to be . . . dispersed in use and abundant in supply', allowing for 'more knowledge, easier access and freer speech than were ever enjoyed before'. Although he was in no sense a technological determinist, he hailed the demise of the typewriter and the prospect that 'not too far in the future nothing will be published in print that is not typed on a word processor or typed by a computer'.

Looking ahead towards a new millennium, he estimated that by the early 1990s there would be more than 600 million telephones and 680 million television sets along with millions of computer work stations. Pool had little to say about entertainment or the threat to local cultures from homogenized culture, although he welcomed the 'end of spectrum scarcity' and the advent of 'electronic abundance'. There would be more media choice.

It was the surprises and problems of an 'information society', resting on new communication supports, not quite the same as an 'information economy', that turned the term into one of the most familiar, if always controversial, of all twentieth-century labels. It could even be claimed that a McLuhanesque blessing had been conferred upon it. In *Understanding Media* (1964), McLuhan had already written that 'in the electronic age we see ourselves being translated more and more into the form of information, moving towards the technological extension of consciousness'.

The Information Society

One of the people who most fully articulated the idea of an 'information economy' and an 'information society', already in the air, was a young American, Marc Porat, then associated with the Aspen Institute, who published a paper, 'Global Implications of the Information Society', in its first form in 1977: it was commissioned by the United States Information Agency. The phrases had already passed into the language during the 1960s. 'Flow' was then the favourite noun – and verb. By then, too, the word 'information' had already been incorporated into the terms 'information technology' (IT), first used in management circles, and the mathematics of 'information theory'.

As has been noted, the medieval verb 'enforme, informe', borrowed from the French, had meant 'to give form or shape to', and the new term 'information society' gave form or shape to a cluster of hitherto more loosely related aspects of communication – knowledge, news, literature, entertainment – all exchanged through different media and through different media materials – paper, ink, canvas, paint, celluloid, cinema, radio, television and computers. From the 1960s onwards, all messages, public and private, verbal and visual, began to be considered as 'data', information that could be transmitted, collected and recorded, whatever their point of origin, most effectively through electronic technology.

Once more, in the late twentieth century as in the sixteenth, it was the French language which became a carrier of extended and changing concepts through the words '*informatique*' and '*informatisation*' which influenced not only ways of thinking and feeling about communication but the procedures and decisions of businessmen and the policies of governments. There was a clear link in French between these terms and computerization. Indeed, an essential French text by Simon Nora, Inspector-General of Finance, and Alain Minc, extolling an information society as the ultimate civilization, had immediate policy implications for the French government, and was called in English translation (1980) *The Computerization of Society*. It had been written by Nora as a report for the President of France, Giscard d'Estaing, with the title *L'Informatisation de la Société*.

There were other forces, however, behind changes in language. In the biological sciences, the discovery of DNA (deoxyribonucleic acid) – the major discovery of the 1960s – as the carrier of genetic information gave a new impulse to what was called an 'information paradigm'. Information was considered the organizing principle of life itself. The genetic code was *the* code, and transmission now became the favoured way of considering all kinds of information.

The word 'paradigm' itself was an unfamiliar word that had rapidly passed into general language. This followed the immense success of the American book by Thomas S. Kuhn, *The Structure of Scientific Revolutions*, which sold nearly 600,000 copies between its first publication in 1962 and 1984, the novelist George Orwell's year of communications doom. In fact, 1984 was a formative year, when the communications pattern, responding in particular to new technology, proved to be very different from that which Orwell had sketched fifty years before.

A different strand, more central to the emergence of the concept of an information society, was bound up with the development not of biology or of information technology but of economics and sociology (with politics seldom absent). Daniel Bell, author of *The End of Ideology* (1960), was aware of the work of his fellow American, the economist Fritz Machlup, when he published a second book, *The Coming of Post-Industrial Society, a Venture in Social Forecasting* (1974) in which he focused on the way in which the services sector of the economy was becoming more important than manufacturing. Bell's horizons were new, as was his terminology. He employed the prefix 'post', which was to become increasingly fashionable, in his title, and soon the adjective 'post-modern' was to establish itself. There was nothing new, however, in Bell's identification of a shift from manufacturing to services, a shift which had already been plain to the Australian agricultural economist Colin Clark, when he published his now neglected book *Conditions of Economic Progress* (1940).

Bell's analysis of the social implications of structural change, which paid little attention to the continuities within capitalism, whatever the dominant technology might be, were new and challenging, as was his account of the social framework of what he too called the 'information society'. Not surprisingly, his analysis led to criticisms from Marxists like Schiller, who published in 1981 *Who Knows: Information in the Age of the Fortune 500*, focusing on the financial promoters of the new society. Meanwhile, Machlup, who had first introduced the theory of a 'knowledge economy' in his book *The Production and Distribution of Knowledge* (1962), continued to update his data, demonstrating that in the course of a century the number of workers engaged in agriculture in the United States (the main reference group, as they were for Clark) had fallen from 40 per cent to about 4 per cent and that the proportion of information workers was rising, as it was in Britain.

The description 'information workers', the broadest of categories, far too loosely defined and analysed, sounded far more appealing than 'service workers'. The former seemed to constitute an attractive and dynamic knowledge-based group, free of ideology, who would transform not only their own country but, as the St Simonians had set out to do, the world. Peter Drucker, most successful and prolific of all analysts of change – he made no claims to predict the future – had drawn attention to their presence in 1969 in his book *The Age of Discontinuity*, the first part of which was devoted to 'the knowledge technology'. 'Learning and teaching were going to be more deeply affected by the new availability of information than other areas of human life.'

Yet for Drucker there was a considerable way to go. One large international company was already shipping computers at the rate of a thousand a month, but there was still no equivalent in the computer field of Edison's light bulb. Such an equivalent would be an 'electronic appliance' selling for less than a television set, 'capable of being plugged in wherever there is electricity and giving immediate access to all the information needed for school work from first grade through college'. Drucker clearly saw, too, that it would give access to much else in society besides information for school use, but he had no sense of what 'a future television set' might look like or be able to do. It was still thought of in most places as a successor to radio sets and gramophones, not as a herald of computers.

The development and impact of computers is dealt with in the next chapter. Here it is necessary to turn back to a range of other writings on 'information' which eventually overlapped with writings (and speeches) on 'globalization'. One of the most interesting in retrospect was a small, schematic and highly purposive book, *The Information Society as Post-Industrial Society* (1980) by Yoneji Masuda, a Japanese scholar, working in a country which by then was producing millions of microchips: it was published by the Tokyo Institute for the Information Society, which forecast that work would be dispersed in 'electronic cottages', that the media would be 'demassified' and human awareness heightened as a global flow of messages accelerated. It is not surprising, given this vision, that the other new label – 'post-industrial society' – would take over and would stick until new metaphors were coined. Masuda himself pointed to the one already mentioned when in a brief section called 'Globalisation: the Spirit of a New Renaissance' he put the spotlight on globalism: 'Information has no natural boundaries. When global information space is formed, world-wide communications activities among citizens will cross all national boundaries.' 'As distinct from conventional geographical space, "global information space" would be space connected by information networks.'

Conclusions

Following on chronologically after Chapter 5 – and in places overlapping with it – this chapter has shown that while technical innovation comes in 'waves' ('clusters') associated with economic trends, historical labels tend to be attached to societies according to what seems, for a variety of reasons, to be their dominant communications technology. The 'age of railways', described in Chapter 4, was one. The 'age of broadcasting' or 'the age of television', and the 'age of the cinema', described in this chapter, have overlapped. The press, which as a 'fourth estate' did not give its name to an age, gave publicity to the other labels, even devised them. In the case of the Internet, described in the last section of the next chapter, the word 'era', sometimes applied to broadcasting, was to be used more often than the word 'age', and old metaphors of navigation were to be employed.

Fig. 26 The press retains its power: police and photographers at May Day protests, London, 2001. Press photographers shaped press content.

In none of the ages, some of which were thought of – at least in retrospect – as golden, did one medium eliminate another. Old and new coexisted. The press remained a powerful force during the 1960s, and in some ways increased in importance after that date. Television, sometimes called 'the fifth estate', did not supplant radio, often dismissed when television was young as 'steam radio': cheaper to operate than television, it remained the dominant medium in Third World countries. The railway remained an important agency of transportation in 'First World' countries even while or even because the number of automobiles increased more rapidly than ever before. Letters still went by post. Yet as technological advance speeded up (with occasional lags), old technologies were being challenged and, above all, their institutional framework was having to be thought out afresh.

There was a backward-looking as well as a forward-looking aspect to the historical process. Interest began to grow during the 1960s and 1970s not only in steam locomotives, refurbished trams and vintage cars but also in the range of fears and expectations of earlier generations when what had become old technologies were new. 'Retro' was to become a favourite prefix a decade later in the United States. From the start, the word 'generation' was applied to computers as well as to people. Meanwhile, it was seldom appreciated that whatever the 'age', similar issues were raised concerning the relationship of 'ownership' of the media to 'content', of 'content' to 'structure', and of 'structure' to technology. All were bound up with 'control'. The need for information in every age has been associated with the effort to control the present and future for personal, political and economic reasons.

The next chapter in this book is concerned with what even at the time was thought of and has been thought of since as a major breakthrough in human history. Its title 'Convergence' is directly related to technology, to the history, briefly though it must be told, of the computer, the transistor, the integrated circuit and digitalization. It involves far more, however, than technology, dazzling – or intimidating – though some of the technology was. With a continuing process of innovation, inventing the future seemed to be the challenge as it had been when Erasmus Darwin (see p. 90) wrote his verses before the end of the eighteenth century.

The two words 'information' and 'convergence', which had already been brought together in the 1960s, were to be linked increasingly often during the 1970s and 1980s. Meanwhile, just as the advent of television had stimulated historians of the media to re-examine the implications of the invention of printing, so the development of new electronic technologies, culminating in the Internet and the World Wide Web, stimulated their successors to re-examine the implications of the sequence of nineteenth-century inventions covered in previous chapters. Thus, in 1986, James Beninger traced back meticulously to the nineteenth century and even earlier the origins of both technical and societal control, some of it built-in, with feedback through new mechanical and electronic devices. The 'governor', a mechanical device in Watt's steam engine, was an early example of control before the advent of electricity multiplied both the number of devices and the opportunities they offered. And in 1998, Tom Standage, with the Internet then at the centre of the picture, wrote a book on the telegraph and its 'online pioneers' with the title *The Victorian Internet*.

> Modern Internet users [he maintained] are in many ways the heirs of the tele-
> graphic tradition, which means that today we are in a unique position to under-
> stand the telegraph. And the telegraph in turn can give us a fascinating
> perspective on the challenges, opportunities and perils of the Internet.

He might have noted how images of the network and the web had been used outside technological circles during the nineteenth century.

Even earlier, an interesting 1974 study of the novelist Thomas Hardy by Ian Gregor had been called *The Great Web*; and in his novel *The Woodlanders* (to be turned into a twentieth-century film), Hardy himself observed that 'the lonely courses' of his characters 'formed no detached design at all, but were part of the great web of human doings then weaving in both hemispheres from the White Sea to Cape Horn'.

7 Convergence

Convergence was a useful, if overworked, word, freely employed by Pool and others before it became fashionable. From the 1980s onwards it was applied most commonly to the development of digital technology, the integration of text, numbers, images and sound, different elements in the media which have largely been considered separately in the previous periods of history covered in this book. During the 1970s, however, the word was already being used with reference to much else, in particular to what Americans called 'a marriage made in heaven' between computers, partners in other marriages also, and telecommunications. The less felicitous hybrid word 'compunications' was an earlier description. The dictionary definitions of the word 'communication' itself had changed during the previous twenty-five years. In 1955 the *Oxford English Dictionary* defined 'communication' as (1) 'the action of communicating, now rarely of material things and (2) the imparting, conveying or exchange of ideas, knowledge etc. whether by speech or writing or signs'. By the time that a 1972 Supplement to the *Dictionary* appeared, however, communication was described as 'the science or process of conveying information, especially by means of electronic or mechanical techniques'. The difference was enormous.

The word 'convergence' was subsequently applied to organizations as well as to processes, particularly the coming together of the media and telecommunications industries. It also had different and broader uses in relation to whole societies and cultures, including British society and culture: D. L. LeMahieu, examining the concept of a common culture and the limits to it in his illuminating book *A Culture for Democracy* (1988), included a chapter called 'Sight and Sound: Studies in Convergence'. Jeremy Black chose 'Convergence' as part of the title of his book on Britain and Europe, *Convergence or Divergence, Britain and the Continent* (1994), while Boorstin, in his fascinating, but now dated, book, *The Republic of Technology* (1978), used it in its most general sense – 'the tendency for everything to become more like everything else' – adding, first, that 'technology dilutes and dissolves ideology' and, second, more illuminatingly, that 'while communication was once an inferior substitute for transportation it is now often the preferred alternative'.

Boorstin might have had railroad transportation mainly in mind. Instead, as society became more 'mobile', the favourite term of transportation that was to make its way into the convergence rhetoric of the 1990s was 'highway'. Different societies and cultures which started their historical journeys separately were now said to be travelling together on the same 'information super-highway'. As early as 1972, a freelance journalist Ralph Lee Smith saw innovations like cable television (see p. 236) as a way of providing an 'electronic communications highway' for 'a wired nation' along which all kinds of services could be provided for home, office and factory.

During the 1960s the development of technologies to provide such services was still at an experimental laboratory stage, although theory was well advanced, and even during the 1980s, a critical decade, when their possible range began to be appreciated, there was still no certainty as to which technologies would be successful. It seemed likely, not certain, that digital technology would prevail in most, if not all, branches of communication. 'Going digital' had still not become the participle of a verb. It was only after 1993 that the term 'super-highway' or variants on it, like 'data highway' or what *Wired* magazine, an immediately best-selling periodical, called 'Infobahn' (February 1994), really took off – another verb derived from transportation. That was after the new American President and Vice-President, Bill Clinton and Al Gore, had introduced it into politics. Digitalization, a unifying process, soon began to be taken for granted, as was the global context in which it would operate. In the 1980s, however, public discussions of technology implied multiplicity.

Cornucopia, Choice and Crisis

Three other 'Cs' figured prominently: cornucopia, choice and crisis. A non-C, 'interactivity', quickly followed, to be used even more frequently than a fifth 'C', 'creativity'. 'Interactivity' was a word employed not only in relation to television, but also to a range of devices developed in shops, museums and classrooms. For an insider biographer of 'the architects of the Web', Robert H. Reid, interactive television was 'the ultimate big convergence ploy as late as the early 1990s. It would bring full-scale video on demand to millions', and its infrastructure would be 'integrated with a marketing and transactions system that would seize the mega-billion dollar catalog industry's jugular'.

Cornucopia – abundance – was a word traditionally applied to products and to resources, not to the electronic media which had been restrained in their early history by a scarcity of wavelengths. What Anthony Smith, a critical and creative scholar of all the media – from 1979 to 1988 he was Director-General of the British Film Institute – called 'the comfortable logic of scarcity', going back to the beginnings of broadcasting, now had at last to be abandoned. New technologies would make possible greater individual choice of what to see and hear – and of when to see and hear it.

Whether that choice would be 'real' or 'beneficial' were matters for argument as listeners and viewers alike came to be thought of as 'customers'. (So, too, did 'citizens'.) Would not more 'channels' provide more and more of 'the same'? 'Crisis', a word which was used so often that it lost some of its alarm, referred both to finance and, more generally, to authority; and it was one of the oldest of media institutions, one committed to universal service, the Post Office, that faced the most difficult financial problems in adjusting itself to change. In the United States, where it had never acquired the authority that it exercised in Britain and in continental Europe, a Presidential Commission reported in 1970 that:

> The United States Post Office faces a crisis. Each year it slips behind the rest of the economy in service, in efficiency and in meeting its responsibilities as an employer. Each year it operates at a huge financial loss.

After congressional compromises a new postal service was set up, but financial problems would not go away, and electronic alternatives – eventually to take the form of e-mail – were under consideration in the late 1970s. A paper on the subject by Henry Geller and Stuart Brotman covered computers, digital links, satellites, cable television, fibre optics and facsimile. Fax, originally a spin-off from telegraphy, they suggested correctly, might, at least in the short run, be 'the bridge to future all-electronic systems using digital input and output'.

In broadcasting, the institutional framework within which broadcast pro-grammes were produced and distributed, whether by public broadcasting agen-cies, which had to face up to new forms of competition, or in the United States by the big television networks (a fourth, Fox, was added in 1992), was under con-stant scrutiny. Cable, treated as a competitor, held out the 'promise of conve-nience, entertainment in abundance and many other remarkable uses of the cathode ray tube'; and Geller, influential behind the scenes in shaping attitudes towards communications in Washington, believed that the prospect of 'abun-dance' that it offered was an incentive to deregulation, another of the key words of the period. Competition, even if Darwinian, would usher in a new age of communications.

This scenario seemed promising to most commentators in the United States, including Neil Hickey, a frequent contributor to *TV Guide*, an invaluable source for historians. The thought of a *Götterdämmerung* for the networks appealed to him. 'It is certain that today's twenty-year-olds will enjoy a far saner, more mul-tifarious communications environment than anything we know today. . . . The public will be addressed, at last, in all its variety, potentiality and dignity rather than as an immense herd of dim-witted sheep to be delivered to the highest bidder.' Although this hope was misplaced, optimism was not confined to the United States. The London *Economist* in 1982 could describe a Cabinet decision to wire Britain with fibre optics as offering 'as much potential for Britain as it moves into the next century as laying the railway network did in the last'.

The first Thatcher government was then in power and as much committed to competition as Reagan's United States. Its thinking was strongly influenced by the report of an Information Technology Advisory Panel (none of its members had broadcasting experience) on 'Cable Systems' handed to it late in 1981 which saw no need for public funding of cable enterprise. Nevertheless, governments, however much they might be committed to deregulation – and some were reluc-tant converts – found it difficult to stay out of the scenario. In any discussion of 'futures', 'infrastructure' was another key word in the vocabulary, as 'heritage' was soon to be; and in Britain, where transportation was becoming a topical issue in Parliament, much of the domestic infrastructure was to remain Victo-rian, as the press was always quick to point out. There was scope for immediate disaster as well as for long-term crisis.

The press itself was often deemed to be in crisis – on both sides of the Atlantic. In this case, the computer ultimately came to the rescue, as Smith explained in 1980 in a book with the arresting title *Goodbye Gutenberg*, but this was only after resistance from printers and journalists, organized in strong trade unions. Meanwhile, suggestions in the United States that the press might go 'the same way as the railroad' relied more on 'logic' than on history. The press was no more on its way out there than it was in Britain, where the power of the tabloid press, fed by photographs which broke all sense of privacy, actually increased during the last decades of the twentieth century. Nor did most public service broadcasting institutions disappear in many parts of the world where they had been established by law. They were forced, however, to restate (often eloquently, if at first defensively) the case for public service broadcasting. The initials PSB were not enough in themselves.

The technological and cultural context continued to change and was the subject of many press articles, political pamphlets and books (with the book trade itself often being described as 'in crisis'). In 1983, when a new gallery of communications was opened in London's Science Museum, Eryl Davies wrote an informative brochure, *Telecommunications, A Technology for Change*, which began with telephones (and photographs of submarine repeaters, instruments of international communication stacked on board cable ships), and ended with radio towers and television dish aerials. He included sections on laser links as well as satellites, stressing the possibilities of 'far more capacity' or 'bandwidth'. 'When every source of information is reduced before transmission to a stream of digital information just like computer data', he concluded, 'there is no reason why all information should not share the same highways and exchanges.'

Similar points had been made in two revealing collections of papers, published in 1976 and 1979. The first of them was *New Perspectives in International Communications*, edited by Jim Richstad, and published by the East–West Communication Institute in Honolulu to which Tehranian was to move (via UNESCO) after the revolution in Iran in 1979, which was followed by an American hostage crisis vividly reported on television. The second was *Communications for Tomorrow*, published under Aspen auspices and edited by Glen O. Robinson. These were only two collections out of a huge assembly of writings on media themes, many of the best of which are to be found in topical pieces in *Intermedia*, which ran a series of special surveys, covering a very wide range of countries, on subjects like high-definition television, the frequency spectrum and teletext. It was particularly informative on the 'Arab world'.

The name of one contributor in particular stood out among those assembled by Richstad – Wilbur Schramm (1907–87), who wrote on 'Cross Cultural Communication: Suggestions for the Building of Bridges', just as important in the history of communications as highways. Schramm had been a speech-writer for Roosevelt, a concert musician and a minor league baseball player before turning to communications. He had published his *Communications in Modern Society* in 1948 and had gone on in 1961 to produce a joint study, *Television in the Lives of Our Children*, and, three years later, *Mass Media and National Development*. Through his own experience, including a spell of teaching in the Chinese University of Hong Kong, Schramm was as familiar with broadcasting in the East as in the West and indeed, in what were then identified as the 'North' and the 'South': he had written a chapter on Communist press theory in a book published in 1956. By the end of the twentieth century China had won the title 'workshop of the world' and was moving actively into a controlled world of communications, in the market not only as a customer but also as a player. India too was an active player.

The Robinson volume, *Communications for Tomorrow*, emphasized the plurality of different technologies rather than their convergence. As Robinson himself put it: 'the heart of communications policy issues is a scheme of social control of the structure and performance of communication industries: common carriers, specialized common carriers, value-added networks, satellite facilities and services, telecommunications equipment, television and radio broadcasting, cable TV, pay TV, citizens band mobile radio etc.' The 'etc.' was significant. Broadcasting was being put into a new technical context before digitalization became the key word. The stakes, Robinson added, were high. In 1977 the gross revenues of AT&T surpassed the gross national product of 118 of the 145 member nation-states of the UN.

As always, the economics of development involved the attempt to get in first with a patent, as was the case with the invention of the integrated circuit (see p. 223), and subsequent patent battles and deals. Yet securing initial and follow-through investment posed as many awkward questions as the technologies themselves. There was a high degree of risk, and there were more bankruptcies than break-ups. The biggest break-up, that of AT&T on 1 January 1984, followed the biggest anti-Trust case in history. For the historian of the media it was as important as the Microsoft case was to be almost twenty years later. And there were to be other Microsoft cases too outside the United States. By then, however, the scenario had completely changed, as had the actors in the communications game, some of whom were on the stage, by permission of Wall Street, for only a short time.

The communications scene changed – at the time it seemed dramatically – in one night, the last night of December 1983. Before its break-up, AT&T, having over the years been forced out of dealings in other markets by law or by policy, dominated the four major markets in telephony, including that for computerized switching manufacture, a bridge market, linking directly broadcast media and telecommunications agencies, but as early as November 1974 *Businessweek* complained that 'the regulating process was no longer able to contain AT&T's power'. That was the month when the law case *United States* v. *AT&T* (with AT&T, Western Electric and Bell Labs as defendants), which was to drag on for years, was filed in the District of Columbia federal district court. It was to be settled out of court in August 1982 through a voluntary divestiture just before it was due, at last, to end. Under the settlement, the 'Bell system', which under different names had evolved over more than a century, was broken up. The AT&T chairman described the reorganization of 1984 as 'the most complex restructuring job in any business anywhere'.

A detailed study of the case suggests that few people before the mid-1970s saw 'the extraordinary ways in which the technologies would soon converge'. It was their plurality that stood out then, as it did for Robinson, and because of the plurality a sense that a host of separate options would have to be considered and decided upon not only by the various players in the communications game – a few of them, young new entrants – but by thousands of users who would often find the choices bewildering. They now had available to them, however, a greatly extended range of sometimes highly specialized periodicals that offered them advice – their numbers were to increase, with *Wired* (noted above, p. 217) setting a new style twenty years later in 1994 – and some users became players themselves. As John Howkins, the then editor of *Intermedia*, put it in 1979: 'every few days a new publication appears, or an old one is relaunched, to report on the ever growing business of communications.' Meanwhile, the business pages of newspapers were increasingly devoted to commenting on it, and they were to change almost totally in character in all countries as new technology stocks were launched and business options increased. Communications supplements also became common, and with them a common language of discourse. Even in an Italian sports supplement you could read the words '*Futurshow di Bologna*' and '*computer*'.

There were some people who for occupational reasons felt it necessary to follow carefully events at a less media-dominated level. Thus, in 1985, John Black was examining what was happening to communications neither from a law court nor from a laboratory but from one of the oldest of communications centres: a library, that of the University of Guelf in Canada. He clumped existing new technologies under nine headings: satellites, laser-based transmission, fibre optics, microwave digital terminal systems, local area networks, other broadband links (CATV, community antenna television, for example), extended uses of existing telephone networks, cellular radio (initially for voice, in the future for data and much else as well), and new 'off-line' distribution devices. Black was among the best informed of those librarians who, like the most forward-looking of museum directors, were confronting the new technologies in a pioneering, if controversial, way. Like all other commentators, he recognized that it was developments in microelectronics and, in particular, 'vastly increased computer power' that had made possible most of the changes realized by that date.

In London, the annual report of the reorganized National Electronics Council described the year July 1984 to July 1985 as 'among the most active' in its brief fifteen-year-old history. During the course of it, emphasis had shifted to 'encouraging children to take courses at school which could lead to a career in electronics and information technology'. An accompanying article by Basil de Ferranti, Chairman of the Ferranti computer company, was called 'Electronics, Energy and Survival'. In 1950, Ferranti had built and sold the first computers to be marketed in the world, ten Manchester Mark Is. There was little intimation then, however, of the way in which computers would affect all the media, their structure and their programme production.

Computers

While the history of technology is not the only strand in the media history of the second half of the twentieth century, computers must come first in any historical survey, for once they had ceased to be generally thought of merely as calculating machines or as useful office adjuncts – and that was not until the early 1970s – they enabled all kinds of services, not only communications services, to take on new shapes. In order to do so, however, they had to become smaller and

Fig. 27 The Colossus electronic code-breaker was used at Bletchley Park, Buckinghamshire, to help Britain and its allies win the Second World War. It used 1,500 valves. Meanwhile, the University of Pennsylvania developed ENIAC (Electronic Numerator Integrator and Computer) between 1942 and 1946. The Soviet Union developed MLSM.

cheaper. And in the achievement of that task the United States, not Britain – or Europe – dominated the course of events.

The first operational electronic digital computers had been devised on both sides of the Atlantic for war and Cold War military purposes. As in earlier history, war not profit was the stimulus, although profits could be made. Colossus, ENIAC and UNIVAC (1953) were giant, some said monster, machines, dependent on thousands of not always reliable valves, called in America vacuum tubes. In 1950 they were correctly described by the brilliant British computer pioneer Alan Turing as 'universal machines', which rendered it 'unnecessary to design various new machines to do various computing processes', but their design changed radically after the replacement of valves by transistors. In the first phase of their development, transistors were even less reliable than valves, but in the long run they made possible a necessary revolution in scale.

The making of the first transistors depended on advances in semi-conductor physics following team experiments in the Bell Laboratories and elsewhere. In 1947, William Shockley (see p. 99), along with John Bardeen and Walter Brattain, who became Nobel Prize-winners three years later, devised solid state amplifying devices made out of germanium and looking like two cat's whisker detectors. It was not until 1959 that sales of transistors (the first customers for them were makers of hearing aids) exceeded those of valves. The unfamiliar name 'transistor', which their devisers gave to them, was initially adopted by the public to refer not to the devices themselves but to the small battery-driven portable radios incorporating them, which were first marketed seven years later (see p. 183). (Bardeen was appalled that the users' main fare was rock music.)

Naming is an interesting and often revealing subject, not least in the history of the media, which is littered with acronyms, or of the underlying technology. The imaginative choice of names sometimes triumphs over functional description of objects. In this particular case, however, it was less interesting than further developments in the technology, for which a number of different physicists and computer engineers were responsible. The first of them, Gordon Teal, replaced germanium with silicon in what was quickly called the 'chip'. He had moved from Bell Laboratories to a very different setting, that of an 'outsider' firm, Texas Instruments, which had started as an oil service supplier and which in October 1954 began selling tiny silicon chips, the size of a fingernail. After other technological advances at the Fairchild Semi-Conductor Company, which introduced photolithography into the process of chip production, miniaturization became cheaper and transistors more reliable, but, as had been the case when the transistor was invented, there was still inadequate demand to inspire business confidence. Government procurement mattered.

Nor did confidence grow at once after it became known that an engineer working for Texas Instruments, Jack Kilby, had applied for a patent in 1959 for the integrated circuit, 'a body of semi-conductor material . . . wherein all the components of the electronic circuit are completely integrated': he had written in his log book in July 1958 that 'extreme miniaturization of many electrical circuits could be achieved by making resistors, capacitors and transistors and diodes on a single slice of silicon'. A patent had already been granted to Robert Noyce, one of the founders of Fairchild and later (1968) of Intel, who wrote one of the best-known of early articles about the significance of microelectronics, using the word 'revolution' to describe it in a special issue of *Scientific American* in 1977. The first full-length feature on the subject had appeared in *Fortune* magazine two years earlier. This and other business magazines are good sources for the historian, although their forecasts have to be read critically and judged in the light of subsequent experience.

With the advent of the integrated circuit, a silicon chip one-sixth by one-eighth of an inch, containing 2,250 miniaturized transistors, now had the same power as ENIAC, which had taken up an entire room. With in-built logic circuits, the new chip made possible the development of computers for all kinds of purpose. Their minuscule central processing units would take instructions from specially written ROMS (read-only memories). Nonetheless, their first uses proved strictly limited. In 1963, only 10 per cent of circuits on sale were integrated circuits.

The idea of an integrated circuit had been thought of by an English physicist, G. W. A. Dummer, as early as 1952, but even after it was patented simultaneously, the computer industry's reaction on the supply side was 'ho hum' (Noyce's words): the device did not immediately appeal to established specialists. And when the microprocessor, which was subsequently to be described as the heart of the computer, was eventually devised by Marcian (Ted) Hoff in 1971, it was first applied, as an eighteenth-century French mechanical invention might have been, in a clock which could sound like a piano. Nevertheless, manufactured and marketed by Intel, it made possible not only an enormous increase in computer power but also a decentralization in its use. Intel's RAM (random-access memory) chip, introduced in 1970, substantially reduced the cost of the memory component, and from now on there were to be 'generations' of computers: the Japanese, in particular, warmed to this concept.

Noyce, who had a way with words as well as the ability to invent things, compared the minuscule microprocessor with the often large automobile: it was 'the simplest way to get from here to there'. Hundreds of thousands of components could be carried on a microprocessor, and as their versatility became recognized a stimulus was given to digital over analogue technology in all the media which were soon to become their main users – print, film, recording, radio and television and all forms of telecommunications, now being thought of increasingly as part of one complex. What was called 'digital compression' – eliminating data, including audio-data, from a file to save space – was of particular value in relation to radio and television.

As early as 1964, Gordon Moore, a chemist who was another co-founder of Intel and its first president, had formulated what came to be called Moore's Law, which has more or less held true ever since, that the number of transistors that could be placed on a single chip would double every eighteen months. Moore, like Shockley, Teal, Kilby, Hoff and bevies of other semi-conductor physicists, was working in what had recently been fruit groves in Silicon Valley, California, an area that was now beginning to stand out on a new global communications map as prominently as the Eiffel Tower, London's Broadcasting House and Television Centre, the Bell Laboratories or – closer to home – Hollywood, which had itself been built on orange groves.

It was of major significance in the history of communications that it was new businesses – more innovative, more informally structured, more 'bottom-up', and less hierarchical than established businesses – that pointed the way forward in financially risky computer development, slower on the demand than on the supply side. In the first phase of computer history, IBM, the International Business Machines Company, had a huge business advantage. The product of a 1924 merger, which included the successor to the digital punched-card Tabulating Machine Company, founded by Herman Hollerith in 1896, it had a distinctive corporate culture which served it well in dealing with governments and large-scale customers. Yet its products belonged to what one historian of the media, Brian Winston, looking back for comparison to the early years of printing, has called 'the incunabula period' in the history of the computer. This ended in 1952 with the demonstration, unclassified, of IBM's 701 computers, first called 'defence calculators', along with Ferranti's Mark Is. By 1961, IBM was marketing no fewer than seven separate lines of computers, but none of them pointed forward to what the microprocessor made possible – the personal computer.

There was by then a marked divergence between American and British computer history, with Japan playing an increasing part in the international scenario. The first computers in the world to be built and marketed in 1950 were British, as has been noted, but although their manufacturers, the Ferranti Company, went on to build a large Atlas computer which attracted great interest, the company and its British corporate successors, including ICL (1980), lacked the assurance offered by the scale of the American market to continue their development. Nor did they have access to the massive American military, naval and space establishment. Meanwhile, Japan, unburdened by such an expensive establishment, became not only a producer of microchips but a major player in the whole communications game.

An interesting survey of Japanese involvement appeared in a comprehensive study of microelectronics published in 1985 by the Japanese National Institute for Research Advancement (NIRA). It identified six periods after the imperial restoration of 1868, the fourth from 1955 to 1964, that of the post-Korean War economic boom and the setting-up of a governmental Science and Technology Agency in 1956. The sixth period, 'the last ten years', saw a further advance, with the country ready 'to counter US initiatives'. There was now more than a touch of pride. Tape recorders and VCRs (see p. 241) were 'almost a Japanese monopoly'.

'The Japanese entry into the field of computer research was not late by world standards', the survey went on modestly, 'and much [had] depended on the cooperation of American computer manufacturers, notably IBM.' The advent of transistors had led to the production in 1964 of a transistorized television set by Sony, a new company. (Naming mattered here, and how to spell the company's name, which became world-renowned, was decided by inspiration.) Sony also introduced the Walkman, a personal, portable stereo, which transformed the way of listening largely to recorded music. It was a mobile instrument, and personal mobility (walking on the street as well as riding in the automobile) was to influence the direction of much future technological development, notably the mobile phone (see p. 266). It was possible now to have easy personal access to 'pop music' wherever you went.

An American paper of 1977 entitled 'Communications for a Mobile Society' referred to 'long commutations between residence and work place within expanding metropolitan areas', 'a large amount of intercity travel using an advanced highway system' and 'a high degree of dependence on trucks to transport goods'. There were approximately 105 million automobiles and 25 million trucks and buses, most of them equipped with 'standard radio receiving units for entertainment services'. The paper referred to the 'cellular system' which increased mobile communication capacity, to FM cellular technology, and to the use of 'narrow band digitized voice systems'. 'Mobile phones' had not then begun to be promoted vigorously – although there were 100,000 of them in use – but Citizens' Band radio had proved so popular that nearly a million people had applied to the FCC for CB licences in January 1977. For the author of the paper, Raymond Bowers, 'the growing use of CB had implications that extended beyond the domain of the service itself'.

Among the 'social and cultural factors supporting technological development' in Japan, the Japanese survey concluded, were 'a society based on equality', 'specialized technology in small and medium-sized companies', 'a tradition of respect for human relations', and, not least, 'cultural respect for technology', evident in the late nineteenth century in the early introduction of the telephone (1890) and the telegraph (1893) – note the order – as government services expanded and 'cultural willingness to adopt new ideas' was evident. 'Skill at miniaturization' came last. These factors operated within a Pacific context which was now being favourably compared with that of Europe. A final factor was the development between 1965 and 1973 of a substantial Japanese automobile industry, rapidly global in scale.

It is evident from this brief summary that on the supply side the history of the evolution of the computer cannot be told simply chapter by chapter, step by step, or even 'page' by 'page', without gross over-simplification. Like the history of the evolution of the railway (see p. 100), it encompassed different features – design, memory, language, logic circuitry, software – and different new devices, like the modem (modulator/demodulator), necessary for transmitting computer data over telephone lines, and the mouse, an input device to control a pointer on a computer screen. Different people and places played their part in the story over different periods of time. It was a story of evolution, not of revolution, the word used by Noyce, but Noyce himself was right to stress that the history was not 'linear'. Design was always crucial, as everyone involved in any computing business, old or new, recognized.

The beginnings of 'memory' went back to the 1940s, even before MIT's Jay Forrester started working on project 'Whirlwind', concerned with the stability of aircraft. It was Forrester who secured the incorporation in computers of magnetic core memory in 1953. Programme languages had a shorter and more complex history; it was John Backus, working in IBM, who developed in 1957 a new 'internal program' computer language, FORTRAN (formula translating system). The first of many such languages, Plankalku had been devised by a German engineer, Konrad Zuse, who has largely been forgotten. Joseph Licklider, a psychologist at MIT, author of a seminal article of 1960 on 'Man-Computer Symbiosis', has not. He also wrote a book *Libraries of the Future* and pioneered ARPANET (see p. 244).

Licklider's vision of 'human brains and computer machines . . . coupled . . . tightly' was shared by a group of computer pioneers employed at the Xerox Palo Alto Laboratory, founded in 1970 by another psychologist, Bob Taylor, and led by Alan Kay. It was they who developed the mouse, originally called 'an X–Y position indicator for a display system'. Xerox, concerned in its daily operations exclusively with copying, did not choose to exploit their pioneering efforts commercially: their ideas were taken up by other companies, including Apple and Microsoft (see p. 230). Meanwhile, Douglas Engelbart, a wartime radar specialist, had invented the phrase 'intelligence amplification', and in 1962 he set out a 'conceptual framework' for networked computing. He used a 'tool kit', as he called it, to demonstrate his oNLine System (NLS) in San Francisco in 1968.

It is difficult to do justice to the many software providers whose numbers multiplied after the invention of the microprocessor, keenly aware that they represented the 'creative side' of the new technology. It was they who gave a new meaning to the word 'software' itself, a word already in use, the opposite of hardware. No computer could function without some kind of programming software. As Reed Hundt, Clinton's first Chairman of the FCC, was to put it, without software programmers computers would sit, 'like inert creatures, awaiting the Creator's life'.

To think in terms of precise chronological landmarks in the history of computing may be misleading. While in Cold War conditions, military, naval and space order books are often accountable for in terms of public events, continually changing market processes, in which academic or commercial users have to identify themselves or be identified, are scheduled and recorded differently. Even before great increases in sales, it was already beginning to be recognized before the end of the 1970s that communications history, into which media history was now being slotted, had entered a new age. Computers were now serving not only as business instruments but as 'the mainspring of a whole range of media activities', stimulating the imagination as locomotives had done. Sometimes they were affecting traditional media, not least print. The term 'electronic book' was coined by Andy Van Dam, who had founded a company in Rhode Island called Electronic Book Technology. Meanwhile, traditional books, magazines and newspapers were increasingly being edited, designed, printed and distributed according to computer routines. Sometimes they facilitated an entirely new activity. In 'multifarious data communications systems' they were 'setting the pace'. This was the title of a leader in *Intermedia* in 1978. The word 'intermedia' had earlier been used in 1966 by Richard Higgens with reference to what he called 'the art of mixed means'.

How fast the pace of development would be depended not only on advance in technological knowledge but also on entrepreneurial drive within an always changing economic climate. The greatest technological advance was the introduction of the personal computer. Yet in a collection of essays published in Britain in 1979 called *From Television to Home Computer* this was picked out as only one in a range of items in consumer electronics, with video cassette recorders (VCRs) being dealt with first. Many computerized gadgets were sometimes dismissed as 'vanilla' 'communications paraphernalia'. 'Smart', a very different adjective from 'vanilla', was soon to be applied to things more than to people, to everything from cards to houses.

Nonetheless, as far as Britain was concerned, the author of the chapter on the personal computer in the 1979 collection found it necessary to strike a reassuring rather than an excited note: a personal computer could cost as little as a cheap colour TV. In a section called 'a look at software', he explained that while such computers were 'fairly complex pieces of electronics', that did not 'mean that you have to know all about them to benefit from them'. A personal computer – and one of the first was called 'The Pet' – was as 'simple to set up as a hi-fi system, if not simpler'. 'Just as when you buy a hi-fi system it is worth looking for reputable manufacturers and dealers.' The industry was growing fast, and 'your knowledge as a user' would grow too. 'Your needs are bound to expand as you become more experienced.'

It is revealing to compare this view from the home with views from the laboratory or from the library or, above all, from the office, where 'word processing' became a major computerized activity and the typewriter, by that time a highly sophisticated object, quickly became obsolete. Yet word processing, with debatable effects on the content and style of writing, was often conceived of as part of the same complex as fax rather than as part of a computerized technological complex; and when the first personal computers appeared, they were, in Eli Noam's (retrospective) judgement, 'the most consumer unfriendly products ever built since the uni-cycle'.

A mini-computer, the PDP8, had been put on the market in 1963 by William Olsen, and that there was a demand for it was proven by a ninefold increase in the sales of Olsen's Digital Equipment Corporation between 1965 and 1970 – and a twentyfold increase in its profits. Yet the company, founded in 1957 and located not in the Silicon Valley but in Massachusetts, did not foresee how markets would change, while some other companies did. It looked to educational users as its most promising clients at a time when still newer companies had groups of computer enthusiasts in mind. They knew that their ranks would grow fast.

The first computer shop was opened in Los Angeles in July 1975, and the first home computing magazine, *Byte*, appeared a month later. 'Byte' and 'bits' went together, and in 1973 Anthony Smith was to publish a book called *From Books to Bytes*. The word 'bit', which was first 'concatenated' in 1946 by John Stukey, a Princeton statistician, had no literary connotations. It was an abbreviation of 'binary digit', the smallest units of digitalized information. (A digital system, as opposed to an analogue system of recording and transmitting words, pictures and music, only has to determine which bits are zeros (0s) and which are ones (1s).) Nevertheless, from the start technical talk was not the only attraction of a visit to a computer shop or of the copy of a computer magazine. One of the successes of the Internet was to be the selling by Amazon of millions of books, new and old. For several years its founder, Jeff Bezos, could do no wrong. His senior editor, James Marcus, moved from New York to Seattle to join him and has described his experiences in *Amazonia: Five Years at the Epicentre of the Dot.Com Juggernaut* (2004).

More important than books – or education – in the early history of personal computers was entertainment, directly in the line of vision of entrepreneurs such as Nicholas Bushnell, one of the developers of the video game, who in 1974 began selling a microprocessor-driven toy called Pong that could be attached to a television set. By 1980, his company, Atari, was retailing $100 million of video games and simple home computers. Adults as well as children were to become keen players of computer games, but there were marketing reasons for concentrating on children and young adults, as there were in the film industry.

It had been said a generation earlier that 'the child born at the same time as broadcasting takes it so much for granted that he cannot think of a previous age. He is apt to think of it as our days.' And the same was true of children born at the same time as the first computer game. Yet not all children were actively responsive to new technologies, and geniuses like a Dutch boy, Wouter Couzijn, reported in *The Times* in 1996, were exceptional. He constructed a walking, talking, self-locating robot, built from yellow Lego pieces but with a microcomputer system installed. At the age of thirteen he had built his own laptop computer with twelve parallel processors that could run simultaneously or share one task between them. The press and television like to publicize prodigies, including young computer hackers: they also came to devote critical attention to video games.

The relative 'prioritizing' (a new word) within the household of television sets and of personal computers took time to settle and economics (pricing) was as important as technology in settling it. In the early stages of development, however, it is plain in retrospect that on both sides of the Atlantic the play element in the popularization of a so-called new technology was as strong a point in the early history of the personal computer as it had been in the early history of the telephone (see p. 120). *Space War*, said to have been created by an MIT student of the 1960s, was one of the first games. In the early 1990s one of the first games to use 3-D was called *Doom*.

Games, however technically sophisticated – and by the 1990s they were only one item in computer advance – had been described in a BBC publication, *Television in the Eighties: The Total Equation* (1982), as 'the natural descendants of the electronic machines in the amusement arcades', which themselves had a long pedigree. But it was their role in the home, where they supplanted other games, that was to prove different. By 1983, video games were being played on the television screen in fifteen million American homes, only one in fifteen of which possessed a personal computer. Ball games with sound effects and on-screen scoring become immediately popular, and the microprocessor, making them cheaper and changeable, extended the genre. Violence was as familiar an ingredient as sport. Given the increasingly highly organized 'leisure market', in which the media were involved either directly or through mergers, it was inevitable that business should seek new opportunities. Bushnell sold out his Atari company to Warner Communications.

There was a characteristically bewildered argument, particularly in Britain, about the likely effects of video game-playing, particularly on children. *Video Fever* was the title of a paperback by C. Beamer, published in 1982, which had as its sub-title *Entertainment, Education, Addiction*. The book, both practical and speculative, is particularly interesting historically because of the contrast between its two brief appendices. The first, 'A Brief History of Video Games', was too brief and too lacking in chronological detail to be of much value. The second, 'How the Games Work', which dealt with the underlying technology, was written clearly and concisely, far more so than most early personal computer manuals. The chapter in the main text which summed up value questions was called 'Family Activities: A Fresh Look'.

Other and different notes might be struck in advertising or criticizing computer culture. *Radio Electronics* in July 1974 introduced a computer along with a manual under the heading 'Your Personal Minicomputer', while *Popular Electronics* in January 1975 advertised a new product of its own as 'The World's First Minicomputer Kit to Rival Commercial Models'. The first commercial model to succeed became available in July 1976 when Steve Wozniak, who had worked for Bushnell, and Steve Jobs, both natives of Silicon Valley, launched the factory-assembled Apple I, which sold initially to computer enthusiasts in local clubs. In the same year Apple II was launched with the capability to carry out a variety of tasks. One of its backers was Mike Markutta, formerly Intel's marketing manager, who had left Intel a millionaire at the age of thirty-two. Jobs was twenty-two.

Apple Macintosh became a public company, valued in 1980 at $1.2 billion, and in 1984 it launched one of the most remarkable advertisements of all time – a television commercial, '1984', which was, in fact, broadcast only once during the Superbowl game. Apple was reluctant to use it, but it had cost $500,000 to make, and it cost $600,000 to put on the screen. The viewer saw first a tubular tunnel in which minute human figures were marching. They were prisoners, wearing heavy, thick-soled boots. They had been 'mind-washed' by an Orwellian Big Brother. The viewer saw the process and, as part of it, a beautiful blonde girl who represented resistance. There were many layers of meaning in this advertisement, which placed it in the middle of a cultural context brilliantly examined by Asa Berger in *Manufacturing Desire* (1996). In commercial terms, Big Brother was IBM, and the prisoners were either IBM employees or the American public. The blonde image was that of Apple. The contrast was binary, and the presentation, directed by Ridley Scott, suggested an art form rather than a commercial.

There was one brief verbal 'announcement' to make: 'On January 24th, Apple Computers will introduce Macintosh and you will see why 1984 won't be like *1984*.' Was this 'reality'? Apple was to retain its mystique, but, ironically, it was the established firm, IBM, slow to develop personal computers, which had first applied the adjective 'virtual' to 'reality' during the late 1960s when it began to refer to non-physical links between processes and machines, and which in 1983 had announced a Virtual Universe Operation System, OS/VU, incorporating in its announcement the words 'planetary system' and 'galaxies'. Also in 1983, thirty-one-year-old Jaron Lanier had talked of virtual reality when working on new approaches to computer use, and in 1985 his company produced a range of virtual reality product accessories or 'tools', far removed from the range of IBM. Lanier had been in the video games business. One of his colleagues came from NASA. There was a close association, therefore, between the exploration of outer space and what came to be called inner space.

It was to a small firm, Microsoft, which IBM had turned in 1980 to provide an operating system. Within three years – back to the fateful 1984 – 40 per cent of all personal computers were running Microsoft programmes. When Microsoft became a public company two years later, Bill Gates, nineteen years old when he founded it, became an instant millionaire. It was obvious by then, when there were fewer than a million computers in use worldwide, many of them incompatible, all of them quickly becoming obsolete, that software was the key to increased use of all computers, personal and organizational, small and big, and Microsoft quickly became the biggest supplier as its Windows operating system was carried around the world. Yet while it dominated the market, there were early competitors, notably Netscape, whose initiator Marc Andreessen had developed 'Mosaic' browsing software while he was an undergraduate. When Gates announced on 7 December 1995, the anniversary of Pearl Harbor, that Microsoft was 'hard core about the Internet' and that it was introducing an Internet Information Server, Internet Explorer, Netscape's Navigator was already in production.

Three years before this announcement was made, after huge political and social changes had taken place in the world – and there had been many legal wrangles in the computer market – London's *Financial Times* produced a survey of 'Computers and Communications' in October 1992, which began by acclaiming 'the slow but inevitable convergence of computing and telecommunications' (note the adjectives used as well as the noun), added that the convergence would provide the 'motive force' for 'an implosion of new information processing practices and technologies'. Five Japanese businesses were then in the world's top ten producers of microchips, with Toshiba and Hitachi second and third. The European multiproduct firm Philips came tenth, and Korea had already entered the picture.

An earlier development was compact discs with memory (CD-Roms, read-only memory), which were capable of storing for home replay the content not only of newspaper files but of whole encyclopaedias. You could play games on them too. At first they had limited capacity for showing film, but they revolutionized the transmission and distribution of music, classical and pop. Soon DVDs (digital video versatile discs) were to be marketed with six times the amount of storage of a CD-Rom. Price was a key factor in marketing. So, too, was advertising.

In 1992, however, there was less optimism about the saleability of the whole range of computerized products than there was to be two years later. The computer industry was in flux, like many other industries, in a period of economic depression following a dramatic Wall Street crash in 1987: new technologies were cutting profit margins as well as costs; and while sales prices plummeted, structural unemployment reached peak figures. Nonetheless, optimism about the long-run seemed justified as talk moved to 'interactivity' and 'networking'. The change in mood was obvious ten years later when Peter Schwartz and Peter Leyden, in a brief 'history of the future, 1980–2020', published in *Wired* in 1997, could write breathlessly of a new 'long wave' (see p. 95), 'the biggest boom in the world's history'. What had started with the spread of personal computers and the break-up of the Bell system had acquired new thrust, and new 'Titans of industry' were eager and determined to push the wave forward with government backing. Inflation was now being kept in check, and all the time globalization was being forced forward. After the millennium, it was predicted, there would be further innovative breakthroughs, including alternative energy and a landing on Mars.

Satellites

The ability to get to Mars would depend on advances in space communications, and these already had their own history in 1960, a point to which we must now return. For a brief spell in world history, communications satellites, 'comsats', impossible to launch without computers, were attracting more attention than the computers themselves. Satellites were the most glamorous (some said 'sexy') expressions of technology after the launching of Sputnik by the Soviet Union in October 1957, the surprise 'happening' which led the American government to seek to respond as quickly as possible. It also led to a burst of popular American interest in space which television drew upon and magnified.

In what had already become a famous prediction made and published in 1945, Arthur C. Clarke, then treasurer of the British Interplanetary Society and a future writer of science fiction, had foreseen a chain of three manned geo-stationary radio satellites. Now in 1961, seven years before Clarke's science fiction novel *2001, A Space Odyssey* was turned into a Stanley Kubrick film, NASA, the new National Aeronautics and Space Agency, agreed to launch Telstar, which could circle the globe in less than 2.75 hours. It contained more than 2,500 transistors, but no integrated circuits. The British and French Post Offices, still looking secure, agreed to build related ground stations, one not far from the place where Marconi had sent out his transatlantic messages decades before.

A later ground station in Bahrain, to be built by the Marconi Company, was owned not by the government of Bahrain but by British-based Cable and Wireless, which gained in business strength when it became clear that satellites, for all their glamour – and a fall in cost as new systems were introduced – would not supplant cable in which Britain had had a long-term interest. Fibre optics guaranteed the continuation of cable, and the first optical cable link to carry commercial traffic, two colour-television channels, was installed in Sussex, England, in 1976. The first fibre optic cable television system in the United States was operating in Birmingham, Alabama, in 1984. Four years later, a fibre optic cable was laid across the Atlantic by AT&T and its partners, and thirty companies inaugurated a cable across the Pacific a year later. The oceans still mattered as well as the skies. There was to be a tenfold increase in transatlantic cable capacity between 1996 and 1999.

The first experimental telecasts using Telstar were exchanged on 11 July 1962, when there was a familiar initiating dialogue, this time overheard by millions. An American television announcer broke into a 'drama' to declare that the British were 'ready to bounce a program off Telstar'. The viewers went on to see as well as to hear the Britons sitting around a table across the Atlantic. 'On my right is that dour Scot, Robert White. On my left John Bray, who is in charge of our planning in the space field. It is half-past three in the morning. Good luck.' This was a less memorable programme, only twenty minutes long, than many later television-by-satellite programmes, among them Churchill's acceptance of honorary American citizenship.

Telstar was the first of many such moving satellites, costly to build, which served the pre-broadcasting functions of wireless as a substitute for cables as well as for the transmission of television. AT&T was in the lead in what was now familiar rivalry between companies and systems, but the Kennedy administration, committed to 'a man-in-the-moon' programme, was not anxious to depend entirely on AT&T; and while the Soviet Union was creating a planned twelve-hour orbit system (Orbita), other options were being explored in Washington. A control framework was set out in the first Communications Satellite Act of 1962, which led to the setting-up of a new company, the Communications Satellite Corporation, half its stock owned by AT&T and other communications carriers, the other half open to public purchase. It was neither a private monopoly nor a public agency, but there was a market for its stock which quickly rose in value.

Syncoms I and II were launched in 1963, as was Telstar II, and in the following year Syncom III transmitted the Tokyo Olympics (see pp. 194–5). The World Cup soccer matches in 1966 drew on six transatlantic television satellites for reporting the games. Television, however, was an intermittent, not a continuous, client: the 'instantaneous pictures' which viewers saw depended on journalistic – and financial – priorities. The press, too, had its own unprecedented opportunities, and it was possible for a new American daily newspaper, *USA Today*, to be launched in 1982, printed simultaneously via low-powered domestic satellites, in seventeen cities: it came to be divided into separately folded sections – media might be dealt with both in 'life' and in 'business' and, not least, in 'sports', as well as figuring intermittently in the news section. In every country the press turned 'the media' into a staple news item, with information about regular programmes being accompanied by gossip, increasingly about 'celebrities', and sometimes, rarer in the United States, serious criticism, comparable to literary criticism, often, particularly in the case of film criticism, relying heavily on theory. This was a new media world.

It had never been possible in the history of satellites to ignore international possibilities – and obstacles – and in August 1964, five years before the FCC announced a domestic 'open skies' policy, an International Telecommunications Satellite Organization (Intelsat) had been established under intergovernmental agreements, which became definitive in 1973. Ownership was initially determined by telephone usage: the United States through Comsat held 61 per cent in 1964, Britain 8.4 per cent. The Soviet Union did not participate – this was the height of the Cold War – and in 1968 it had created an alternative international body, Intersputnik, which, however, drew in only seven countries. Meanwhile, Intelsat attracted a large number of countries, many non-aligned, and by 1975 no fewer than eighty-nine countries, large and small, with varying telecommunications needs, were members. The first of its geo-stationary satellites, Intelsat I (1965), weighing only about ninety pounds, commissioned by NASA and made by the Hughes Corporation, was named Early Bird. It was successful enough to ensure further Hughes contracts for the next generation of Intelsat satellites launched in 1967.

The geo-stationary satellites were located in a precise and limited orbit above the equator, the only orbit that allowed a continuous contact between a satellite and a single ground station. Slots on the orbit were finite and were consequently bargained about, the bargaining carried out behind the scenes through the International Telecommunications Union and World Administrative Radio Conferences (WARCs). Each old slot had what were called terrestrial 'footprints', and these largely determined the price that they fetched. Another factor was the content that they might offer. There were sometimes surprises in their allocation. Thus, in 1985 WARC allotted seven orbital slots to Tonga, a 'port of call' in the Pacific which it then leased to profit-seeking corporate interests unassociated with government. Monroe Price in his *Media and Sovereignty* (2002) has looked far back in time and compared satellite routes through the air to the trade routes of the seventeenth and eighteenth centuries.

There were subsequent 'generations' of satellites, each generation offering greater capacity, reliability and power at lower service costs. International satellites were all required by contract to provide 'equitable access' to users, but there were few limitations on domestic satellites. When the first low-powered US domestic satellite was launched in 1974, it was owned not by Comsat but by Western Union. A year earlier, Canada had launched the world's first domestic satellite, Anik (Brother), an Inuit name, but it was built in the United States and was used there by RCA before the Western Union satellite was put into orbit.

This was a time of reassessment as well as of planning for the future. In a special number of August 1975, *Intermedia* reported problems as well as excitement, similar problems of an international kind (it did not use the word 'global') to those of 'environment, energy, disarmament and seabeds and oceans'.

'Analyses of the significance of satellite communications provide as many inter-pretations . . . as there are theories about the role, function and effect of com-munications upon society and individuals.' The number of topics *Intermedia* covered was wide. It was noted, for example, that Algeria was the first African country to use a satellite system for national purposes and that in Asia SITE (satellite instructional television experiment) proposals for educational broad-casting to six different regions in four languages were well advanced. Broad-casting, using a NASA satellite, was to start in 1975 and would cover health, hygiene and agriculture. SITE had a real but limited success, and subsequently figured prominently in all accounts of recent educational history. More recently in the history of satellite communication, India, where the pattern of broad-casting had been influenced by several countries, including Britain, figured in the 1990s as a country anxious to keep out international satellite transmissions of entertainment and news.

In the United States, it was only after a convergence of satellite and cable inter-ests, the latter fully deregulated under the Reagan administration, that effective use of a domestic satellite system began. Meanwhile, satellite television devel-opment in Europe, despite high costs, had moved ahead independently, making it impossible for an American-backed Coronet project to launch a communica-tions satellite and operate from a Luxembourg base. A Franco-German agree-ment of 1974 to construct a multi-purpose co-operative satellite system, Symphonie, to provide sound broadcasting and telephone circuits between Europe and regions of Africa and later of Latin America, initiated the process, which in 1988 culminated in the launchings, unsuccessful, of a German TV-Sat and a French TDF-1. Ten years earlier, a European Space Agency had been set up 'to probe space and to launch and operate satellites', and it launched its first satellite in 1983.

In 1982 the European Community declared that the projection of European culture through a European television policy offered the key to European integration:

> The sharing of pictures and information will be the most effective means of increasing mutual understanding among the peoples of Europe and will give them a greater sense of belonging to a common social and cultural unity.

In the same year, therefore, the first operational European satellite cable televi-sion delivery system, SATV, was set up, and the European Broadcasting Union started ambitiously an experimental European Service, Eurikon, later called Europa, employing the European Space Agency's orbital test satellite, OTS-2. The first evening's programmes included speeches, an hour and a half of 'high culture' (mainly Haydn), an episode from *Coronation Street*, a *World in Action* programme, and fifty minutes of pop music. For once, content was deemed as worthy of acclamation as technology.

It was unlikely that all the countries in an expanded European Community would fully accept the principle of integration through European television, which was restated in a landmark directive, *Television Without Frontiers*, adopted in 1989, the year when the German wall fell and communism collapsed (see p. 249), and applied in 1991, fundamental though the principle seemed to pan-

Europeans. Instead, the commercial market appeared to have triumphed by 1989, although there were significant differences, despite the word 'convergence', in what was happening in radio and television and what was happening in telecommunications. As far as telecommunications were concerned, the British government, which had appointed its first Minister for Information Technology in 1980, led the way, putting its trust in the business sector; and in 1984, having already sold its shares in Cable and Wireless, privatized British Telecom. For some politicians this was a matter of principle. For most, however, it was a matter of competitive efficiency. New Investment would be mobilized and competition stimulated. Related plans to develop direct satellite broadcasting through a risk-sharing consortium failed in 1988, however, even though the consortium included powerful players like British Telecom, British Aerospace, GEC/Marconi and the Rothschild Bank.

A new consortium, BSB (British Satellite Broadcasting), which included several television companies and Pearson, a conglomerate which included a newspaper business, the Westminster Press, the *Financial Times* and *The Economist*, as well as an established book business, Longman (which went back to 1724), succeeded in 1990 in launching a satellite, built by Hughes Communications. Yet it found the costs of operating it and supplying programmes so high that later in the year it was forced into a merger, BSkyB, with its competitor Sky Television, owned by Murdoch, who was by then as powerful a figure in television as he was in the press. He had been using Luxembourg's Astra satellite which the BBC, the first player in the game – before the consortium was set up – had been told would not be powerful enough. With multiple international media interests, including film (Fox) and newspapers, his News Corporation was then based in Australia. Murdoch had demonstrated that commercial satellite broadcasting could be a profitable enterprise which eventually would be able to outbid the BBC, particularly in sport, and to challenge it in the presentation of news. By 1993/4 three million British households, one in seven, were then subscribing to his services, and more than 30 per cent of television households in sixteen European countries were viewing BSkyB satellite television, the highest proportion (92 per cent) in the Netherlands, which like Belgium, Denmark, Sweden and Switzerland already had high cable penetration. (Half of Dutch homes had been wired for radio in 1939.)

The relationship between satellite use and cable numbers requires analysis as well as survey. In Finland, for example, which was taking pride in its whole-hearted adoption of new technologies, the satellite audience was as low as 1 per cent, but the cable audience was 40 per cent. The United Kingdom, where cable had been slow to develop, had a far smaller satellite audience in the early 1990s than the Netherlands, probably because the BBC and ITV were offering free a more generally acceptable service. The BBC had opposed wired radio before 1939 on the grounds that if uncontrolled 'it might be disruptive of the spirit and intentions of the BBC's Charter'. Now it objected strongly, but in vain, to cable television, whether terrestrial or based on satellites.

Differences in the national approaches to satellite and cable were as significant as earlier variations in broadcasting systems and the audience preferences that they reflected. The overall figures in each country, therefore, were interesting also, particularly when examined over time. The proportion of British households subscribing to satellite services accounted for nearly 6 per cent of viewers in 1993: three years later, it accounted for over 11 per cent. In Japan, where an experimental satellite, Yuri, launched in 1978, was said to be the first to be 'dedicated' to communications, NHK had taken the lead in new development in 1991 in scheduling cable and direct-to-home broadcasts, and this was followed later in the year by Japanese Satellite Broadcasting which began operating a 24-hour channel. In 1996 it had more than two million subscribers.

By 1997 Murdoch, then an American citizen, sold out his American satellite business, ASkyB, which he had set up in January 1996 when he promised Americans 200 channels. He and his company, News Corporation, had envisaged it as a major element in a global strategy. He had secured control of Star TV in Hong Kong in 1993 and in Japan had launched JSkyB in December 1996 as a joint venture with the Japanese company Soft Bank. Sony came in soon afterwards. When Murdoch abandoned ASkyB, therefore, a television executive described the satellite business as 'a theoretician's delight and a practitioner's nightmare'. But this was only partially true even after Murdoch sold out his controlling interest in Star IV. By the mid-1990s, there were eleven million Asian viewers linked together through Asia Sat-2 and in 1991 the BBC launched World Service Television which quickly claimed to have millions of viewers in Asia, Australasia, America and Africa. Significantly, China preferred Murdoch television to that offered by the BBC.

Cable

In lists of new technologies drawn up during the 1960s (see p. 219), 'other broadband links', CATV (Cable Television) had figured well below satellites. At first, cable television stations, wherever they operated, were local and one-way and offered viewers a selection of up to twelve programmes. The promise of better reception mattered then at least as much as greater choices. In many countries the history of cable went back as far as wired radio, which had improved reception without usually offering listeners a wide range of programmes. As it developed during the 1970s, however, there were enthusiasts who believed that it was the core of a revolution in telecommunications – and in broadcasting.

The first real excitement of cable television came with the recognition that it could offer a greater number of channels (at first usually twelve, eventually up to a hundred or more) than the air waves. One of the American enthusiasts for it was Ralph Lees Smith, who coined the slogan 'Wired Nation', which he used in a widely read article in *The Nation* in May 1970. Nevertheless, the first steps were faltering, and Smith's prediction was dismissed in some circles like a dubious weather forecast. In the not very long run it was the sceptics – those who talked of 'Cable Fable' – who were to be proved wrong or at least partially wrong, as cable spread from rural areas and small towns to big cities (see p. 238). In 1970 there were 2,639 cable systems in the United States, with 5.3 million subscribers, 8.7 per cent of American television households; in 1975 there were 3,506 systems, with 9.8 million subscribers, 14.3 per cent of households; and five years later the comparable figures were 4,300, 17.2 million and 23 per cent.

The development of cable raised major policy issues for the FCC which, without any guidance from Congress, did not care directly to confront cable interests. In 1959 the FCC had ruled that since cable was neither broadcasting nor common-carrier communication, the FCC had no jurisdiction over it. Later, after fears were expressed in network circles that cable growth could put 'free' network television out of business or siphon off from it popular outside events, particularly sporting events, it intervened directly in the cable business in 1968, going so far as to restrict cable stations from importing 'distant signals', that was all signals outside their own designated service areas. Such 'freezing' proved unpopular in a variety of circles, and in 1972, as an uneasy compromise, following discussions between different interests, the FCC decided that cable systems could import at least two distant signals. They were still to be subject to regulation, however, including the requirement to set aside some channels for education, local government and 'the general public'.

After another four years – and a number of law suits – many, but not all, of these restraints on cable were removed, but even this was not enough for the increasing number of believers in deregulation. In 1977, a three-judge panel of the Court of Appeals in the District of Columbia declared that all the protective restraints on cable were invalid, that there was no 'constitutional distinction between cable and newspapers', and that in First Amendment terms cable television was not broadcasting. Fears of a different kind were being expressed by then, in particular that with the increasing convergence of electronic and print media, print would become entangled in regulations similar to those applied by the FCC to broadcasting. In these circumstances, with Congress still unwilling or unable to intervene, there were constitutional lawyers who urged that spectrum scarcity should no longer be treated as a rationale for regulating broadcasting.

More important in practice than such legal argument was the growth in American cable use. Between the early 1960s and the end of the 1970s cable penetration of households increased from 2 to 20 per cent, with viewers in some parts of the United States being able to watch up to twenty and later thirty channels. Later, in city areas, they might be able to watch up to fifty. Genuine choice seemed to be opening up locally, as cable, while fragmenting the mass audience, permitted some channels to be used for more than entertainment. There was now a place, as in periodical and book publishing, for niche content channels, like the History or Discovery Channels, since limited local audiences could now be aggregated. Not all such channels were to prove successful or profitable. Nor did greater choice provide the variety that it might have done. For Brian Winston, writing in 1998, American cable channels had 'almost totally failed to alter the established genres and forms of television broadcasting in any significant way'. In financial terms, however, pay television had established itself and provided a lucrative source of income for cable owners. It had also opened up the opportunities for 'tele-shopping'.

The first major American shift in cable orientation and in profits came in 1976 when Home Box Office, linked with Time Inc., decided to hitch its future to RCA's Satcom I thereby acquiring national distribution capabilities comparable with those of the three big television networks at a fraction of the cost. Other companies quickly followed HBO's lead, some companies becoming multi-service operators specializing in 'movies' and sport. A familiar process of business concentration ensued, with some stations transformed into cable 'super stations', among them WOR-TV (New York) and WTBS (Atlanta). Cross-media ownership was common. So were deals with Hollywood. These offered more profits than most niches ever could. Some local programme channels were 'give-away', however, and many were not dependent on advertising.

In the most active city areas, cable subscribers were able to have access to a wide range of programme channels, however restricted their content, and appetite grew. In consequence, the National Citizens' Committee for Broadcasting, an organization blessed by consumer guru Ralph Nader, suggested that citizens should ask for twice as many local channels as a cable company was offering their community, and exact from it a high franchise fee. They should find out what was available for funding the finest cable companies already in existence – and then ask for more. Charges for customers varied, and in the beginning cable systems were often expensive to construct. That was part of the economics. It was estimated in the city of Dallas, for example, with 400,000 homes, that a take-off would cost $100 million. The financial prospects were attractive enough, however, for no fewer than six groups to bid for the franchise, and when the City Council granted it to Warner Amex, a local company asked for a referendum.

Already Dallas, the name of a city known through television throughout the world, had twice as many pay television companies as any city in the United States. It led the way. By the mid-1980s, nearly half of American homes had cable television. Some American cable companies had by then become billion-dollar enterprises, nationwide in scale. The top ten multiple-system operators then served nearly half the cable subscribers in the country. The comparative Canadian figure was 60 per cent.

The distribution of cable outside the United States in the mid-1980s was uneven. In Italy, where cable was thought of simply as a version of broadcasting, there had been one company, Tele Biella, as early as 1971. In the Netherlands municipalities owned more than half the cable systems. France did not adopt a comprehensive law relating to cable until 1982. Progress was slow in Germany and in Sweden. In Britain also cable was slow to develop even after the government, in the name of competition and choice, granted eleven pay cable franchises in 1983. Seven of them were operational by 1985. Thirteen were in operation, some part time, ten years later. Some of them formed transatlantic consortia with major American companies.

Both for programming and for business reasons there was often an international – as well as a local – dimension to cable development. Ted Turner's CNN, Cable News Network, based in Atlanta, was deliberately global in scope, and following its merger in 1995 with Time/Warner, itself international in outlook, the new conglomerate was capitalized at $36 billion. Time/Warner was itself the product of a merger in 1990. The unexpected new merger with CNN would have a bigger annual turnover than the Walt Disney Company, known throughout the world, which had recently bought Capital Cities/ABC, owner of what was then the largest American network. Time/Warner already held 18 per cent of CNN, and Turner is said to have made bids on more than one occasion to acquire CBS. Under the CNN banner in 1995, he was running two news channels and two movie channels, one of them the Cartoon Network. He also owned the film archive of Hollywood's MGM which could now be placed alongside the Warner archive. Murdoch had been mentioned in the press as one of Turner's suitors: in 1995 he had joined in an American 'gang of four' alliance with Brazil's Globo, Mexico's Televisa and the United States Telecommunications Inc. All this represented not technological, but business convergence. Globo and Televisa were huge Latin American concerns with tentacles everywhere.

Viewdata

Cable was obviously *big* business. Yet as Timothy Hollins wrote in his well-informed study *Beyond Broadcasting: Into the Cable Age* (1984), no more people in Britain than in Italy before 1982 'had any inkling that cable was more than just another name for a telegram or a piece of wire'. Now, many people on both sides of the Atlantic believed that it would be the 'vanguard of a technological revolution, the nervous system of an information-centred society'. Richard Hoggart, in a new role as chairman of a Broadcast Research Unit, wrote a preface to Hollins's study, noting that public discussion in Britain on such issues had not gone much beyond 'semi-utopian speculations' on the one hand and 'Cassandra-like prophecies of doom on the other'. In the United States, by contrast, Hollins added, there was 'a stock of superlatives' but little sense of proportion.

The comment had more general application in relation not only to cable itself but to a wide range of what was usually described as 'viewdata' – with 'teletext' being brought into what was then called a 'family' of 'new developments associated with the television receiver'. Teletext was a system for broadcasting pages of information (words and graphics) on a television screen, making use of spare lines not previously employed in regular broadcasting. Videotex, a more comprehensive term, was the delivery via telephone line or cable of computer-stored information to be displayed on a television screen or specialized videotex terminal.

Because of the access to computerized data that videotex made possible and the way that it was provided by information service agencies, much that was said about its advantages – and problems – anticipated what was to be said later about the Internet and the World Wide Web. So, too, did the questions it raised. Would viewdata become 'a mass medium or an individual medium or, as the Japanese say, a mass individual medium?' a writer in *Intermedia* asked in 1979. One of its slogans was 'the world of information is now at your fingertips', but the technology on which it rested was analogue, not digital, 'today's technology, not tomorrow's'. Interest in videotex centred, in the writer's view, largely on its likely 'evolution of identity'. As different electronic services grew, he and some other observers hoped that they would 'edge towards equilibrium'.

There was to be no such equilibrium. Instead, there was a further rush of new technologies, not all of which were to take off in what had been called as early as 1970 'a data-based society'. Some stayed at uncompleted points of development, even at the prototype stage. One, in particular, high-definition television (HDTV), which offered better colour and clarity of picture through 1,125 lines (instead of 525 and 625) and a wider screen, more like a cinema screen, was successfully demonstrated in the United States and elsewhere, but to the chagrin of the Japanese, who worked hard and long to develop it, for a variety of reasons there was no breakthrough. Nor had there been in 'cinorama', 'sensorama' or 'holography', although Denis Gabor, using lasers, had produced a 47-second movie in Moscow in 1976, showing a full-size woman carrying a bouquet of flowers.

The fact that HDTV was capable of delivering video images carrying five times as much information as conventional images could do did not count. There were more compelling facts. A shift of system would have involved not only heavy investment but a new spectrum allocation. Technical standards in different countries were different; and, most important of all, as noted, the technology was analogue, not digital. Digitalization, or digitization, as some people continued to describe it, was already considered to be the likely basis of much new technology during the 1980s, but the process of switching to it was slow. A turning point came in 1997 when the British government, in its plans for digital broadcasting, chose to go ahead with the provision of more channels rather than with the introduction of high-definition television.

Before that turning point it was a fragmented telecommunications system, with telecommunications and broadcasting having radically different cultures, that reared the Viewdata family. And in Europe, in particular, Post Offices, sometimes in co-operation with private business, were the ambitious parents. In the words of the British Post Office, the family they were rearing was sprawling and under constant scrutiny in the press. It was the British Post Office, soon to lose the telephone side of its business, which placed on offer in 1979 the world's first operational Viewdata system, Prestel, following an experimental period, common to other new technological developments. This was 'the year of Videotex', when observers could describe the new services as 'one of the first manifestations of the much heralded convergence of computer and communications technologies'. They were discussed in London in March of that year at what was described as 'the first ever international forum on video data'.

Prestel would have been called 'Viewdata' had the Post Office been able to copyright the name, but it was not the only Viewdata system then being developed. The IBA in Britain had Oracle, the French Teletel, Finland Telset, CBS in America Teletext, and Canada Telidon. In all these cases, the hallmark of the systems was 'not technological wizardry but social utility'; and Prestel, 'the pioneer', which did not incorporate microprocessors in its terminals, was never alone in not exploiting new technology.

The subsequent chronology of viewdata development is not easy to sort out, for there were delays between demonstrations and installations, and gaps between rhetoric and performance. Ambitious announcements were often made and reported while planning was at an early stage. Sets were expensive, and modes of charging were complicated and controversial to calculate and implement. In France, there was to be cross-subsidization, but in Britain there was none. In the United States, popular interest was difficult to arouse. A local experiment, like that of the *Los Angeles Mirror*, which started in California in 1984, was halted after several years of loss-making.

There were two types of viewdata systems: telephone-based, like Prestel and Telidon, and broadcast-based, like the BBC's Ceefax and IBA's Oracle; and it was ITU's consultative committees that chose videotex as the generic name for them all. The former type of system, claiming simplicity, relied for the data which it offered on information providers who acquired 'pages': there was no central editor or coordinator of content. The Post Office's role was similar to that of a common carrier, therefore, and in this and other respects there were anticipations of the Internet both in the language used and in the procedures.

'The first problem the Prestel method poses for the Information Provider', one of its managers noted, 'is how to direct the user to the information as quickly as possible.' The manager of an Internet software company might have said the same. At the time, however, information providers, wooed by the Post Office, drew old parallels. Prestel, potentially 'a mass medium', was much closer to printing and publishing, it was argued, than it was to radio and television. This was given as one of the reasons why newspaper interests, among them the *Financial Times* and *The Economist*, decided sometimes defensively, to become information providers. Some were opposed. In particular, the German press was bitterly hostile to the system introduced by the German Post Office in 1984.

Two points were emphasized by an early British information provider, one of 160, who was not on the defensive and who saw new business opportunities in the venture. First, there was no 'tyranny of peak hour transmission time', 'prime time', either for an information provider or for a user. Second, the user had to be active. Unless he made decisions and pressed buttons on a control page the same page would sit on the screen for ever. The number of data pages was strictly limited, however, and it required enterprise on the part of the information provider to introduce 'simple graphics' as well as text. In Canada, Telidon, developed by specialists attached to the Research Centre of the Canadian Department of Communications, displayed public enterprise when it attached great importance to offering visual as well as verbal information.

A different range of videocommunications devices, owing nothing to Post Offices or governments, had been the videocassette recorder (VCR) and the videodisc, to be followed by CD-Roms. The technologies were different, with VCRs soon to be laser-based, but their use raised issues of copyright and of piracy, particularly in relation to music, that had been aired in a very different social and economic context in the eighteenth and nineteenth centuries. All the devices permitted individuals to 'time shift', that is, to record television programmes that could be seen on the home screen later than they had been broadcast. In practice, however, their main use was to be the playing of pre-recorded commercial films, bought or hired, a source of profit for cinema interests, particularly Hollywood. Home-produced video developed later and eventually made its way as a form of public entertainment onto network and cable channels.

The statistics were striking. By 1985 there were more videocassette stores in the United States than there were cinemas. Between 1980 and 1995, the number of VCRs in the United States increased from 1.8 million to 86 million, the most impressive of all the media statistics of those years. Seventy per cent of American homes possessed a VCR by 1990. Outside the United States, British demand had risen even faster than demand in the United States; and outside Europe, 85 per cent of all homes in Saudi Arabia had a VCR by 1985.

Home VCRs had been first put on sale in 1972 after years of experiment both with cassettes and discs, as American, Dutch, Swedish and Japanese companies engaged in a race to capture a new consumer market. Sony introduced a magnetic tape into its cassettes in 1969, while RCA, fully familiar with the use of tape, persisted with discs until 1984. Philips in the Netherlands demonstrated laser videodisc technology in 1978. In America, the first laser disc was on sale in time for Christmas 1980.

The social effects of the diffusion of VCRs have received less attention than the technology – there was a battle of standards – and the economics which involved heavy investment in research. Because in many countries tapes could be hired as well as bought, video shops became a more prominent and ubiquitous feature in townscapes than bookshops. Many shops sold both. Newsagents were in the hiring business, too. Ethnic groups, some of them far away from their place of birth, now had separate access to video in their own language. Family watching could give new life to the home. In *From Television to Home Computer*, published in 1979, Adrian Hope envisaged a day when 'the well-heeled home of the future' would 'boast' both a videocassette recorder and a videodisc player. He added that those people lucky enough to own either should hold on to them even after they had become obsolete. They would become 'valuable antiques in their own lifetime like an original Edison phonograph'.

Hollywood, initially resistant to video-recording as it had been to television, boomed through video sales. So, too, did the musical industries in audio as well as in video when music could be heard and recorded. The long-playing record, itself hailed as a major invention when it superseded '78s', became as obsolete as the typewriter. Video cameras became part of the family kit also. The most successful of what have been called 'the spin-offs of the video cassette', was Sony's video camera of 1984, the small camcorder, 'the TV version of the Polaroid'. And the day of the digital camera was still to come.

There was one feasible invention which did not take off – the videophone – much 'flashier' than a voice-alone phone, although AT&T began to market an analogue-based Picturephone in the 1960s, projecting a market of up to 1 per cent of all domestic phones by the 1980s. Well before then, however, it decided to drop manufacture of the phone in 1973. The idea never lost its attractions, however, and was taken up again in the 1990s, when according to an eighteen-month European survey of 1992/3, which covered Britain, France, Germany, the Netherlands and Norway, videophone calls, lavishly advertised, were longer than telephone calls and often required ten times as much bandwidth.

Videophones were far more expensive than cellular mobile phones and their quality was unreliable, but there was clearly a limited market for them as there was for video-conferencing. In January 1994, ImagiNation, a joint venture of AT&T and Sierra On-Line, recorded 40,000 households paying monthly subscriptions in excess of £400,000. 'Telephonoscopique kiosks' were predicted, although they would clearly need a different name if they were to make their way onto the streets, as Internet bars and cafés were about to do.

Given the great future for the mobile phone, which was to acquire uses not at first anticipated, including digital cameras as part of its repertoire (see below, p. 266), in retrospect it was those communications experts who focused on mobility who were the most prescient. Citizens' Band Radio had led the way, with yachtsmen and hunters following in the wake of truck drivers. The first mobile telephone system was licensed in the United States in 1983, ten years after the installation of Citizens' Band in the wake of the oil crisis and a consequent reduction of the speed limit on American roads. By 1989 there were a million American cellular phone users, but the great mobile telephone boom came later, despite often poor reception and lack of privacy (some users were unconcerned about this or openly exhibitionist in making calls). In Europe and Asia, as much as in the United States, numbers continued to grow. Thus, by 1996 there were more than six million mobile phone users in Britain and, four years later, between April and June 2000, no fewer than three-and-a-half million phones were sold, 'one every two seconds'. This was a distribution-led phenomenon that inspired a front-page heading in *The Times*, 'Half the country is mobile mad'.

A different *Times* commentator preferred to describe what was happening as a 'mobile love affair'. Britain was by now ahead of the United States, where there had always been far more home phones, and in Europe, Finland and Italy were ahead of Britain. In Japan, where there was a huge increase in the diffusion of cellular phones after 1996, the main group of purchasers were between twenty and twenty-four years old, and they used their phones mainly to keep in touch with a small group of friends, described in Japanese as 'cellular mates'. The market, expanded with the aid of massive advertising, was built up on the basis of a single service – voice communication – but there was an implicit promise that this would soon change. Wireless applications protocol (WAP) would turn mobile data and multimedia into major revenue providers for the companies.

Already there were new services, like the provision of short service messages which were deemed 'transitional', an old word in the history of radio technology. Soon they became something different. In what was treated as a 'fad', just as old a word in the history of technology, teenagers became 'hooked' on sending text messages. Around 400 messages were transmitted in Britain alone by March 2000. In March 2001, the *Sunday Times* described (with photographs) a teenage girl who was sending more than a thousand text messages each month. Such messages, which could not be more than 160 characters long, include a variety of 'smiley faces' and symbols. Grammar and spelling were totally irrelevant.

When the phenomenon was described in the press, it was finance that stole most of the headlines, but some of them (and broadcasts) raised the possible side-effects of the new technology. Was there a health risk in radio waves near the ear? Should children use mobile phones? Should mobile phone companies be able to erect transmitter masts without planning permission? Should mobile phone users be controlled in railway carriages as they were in aeroplanes? In every country non-users complained. The correspondence columns of newspapers provided a regular location for the complaints. So, too, did phone-in radio programmes, now a major constituent in the programming of the media. The fact that 'experts' differed gave zest to the questioners and, perhaps less often, to some of the questioned.

The Internet

As late as 1991, a book written by leading figures in computing, *Technology 2001: The Future of Computing and Communications*, published by MIT, made no references to the Internet. Nor did the words 'World Wide Web' or 'cyberspace' figure in the index. Yet in that same year David Gelernter published a book for technologists, *Mirror Worlds*, a fascinating extended research paper in which, without using the word, he forecast the Web; and by the end of the 1990s, E. M. Noam, then Director of Columbia University's Institute for Tele-Information, could make the judgement that 'when the media history of the 20th century will be written, the Internet will be seen as its major contribution'.

The breakthrough came between September 1993 and March 1994 when a network hitherto dedicated to academic research became a network of networks open to all. The network was loose and under no single ownership, although it depended on telecommunications agencies. In this same period public access to browsing software (Mosaic), described in the business sections of the *New York Times* in December 1993 as 'the first window into cyberspace', made it possible to attract users, at that time called adaptors, and providers, software pioneers whose origins have already been described.

In a period of accelerating communications technology, the Internet defied prediction and brought with it many surprises. 'More phenomenon than fact', it was said, as it was of mobile phones. It was also said that this was 'the wild west frontier' of communications. Quickly leaving physics behind, it developed its distinctive psychology, as the frontier had done, and along with it what came to be called its 'ecology'. More portentously, by 1997 it began to be treated as a paradigm (see p. 211). Its origins, however, lay in physics and in the politics of defence during the Cold War period a generation before. It was set up initially in 1968/9, with indispensable financial support from government, through ARPA, the United States Department of Defense's Advanced Research Projects Administration, which had been founded in 1957 as part of the governmental response to Sputnik.

At first, it was a limited network (ARPANET), sharing information between 'hi-tech' (another new word) universities and other research institutions – by 1975 there were 2,000 users – and because of the nature of the information which was being shared it was an essential element in its rationale that the network could survive the removal or destruction of any computer within it and, indeed, the nuclear destruction of all communications 'infrastructures'. That was the view from the Pentagon. The view from the universities was that the Net offered 'free access' to academic and research users, and that it was they who were the communicators.

Whatever the vantage point, from above or from below, it was of crucial importance both immediately and in the long run that the 'architecture of the system' (the term often employed) differed from that of the telephone network. Any computer could tap into the Net anywhere, with the information being exchanged 'sliced' at once into 'packets'. The sending system broke information into encoded pieces: the receiving system put them together again after they had travelled to their destination. This was the first packet data system in history.

The idea of breaking up messages into 'packets of information', 'message blocks', had been in the mind of computer researchers since the mid-1960s, among them Donald Watt Davies of Britain's National Physical Laboratory, who used the term 'packet switching'. He appreciated also that in order to network computers with different 'faces' and with different computer languages, the use of micro-computers to act as 'interfaces', known in the United States as IMPs, interface message processors, would be necessary. The first of them arrived at the Los Angeles campus of the University of California in January 1969 when Professor Leonard Kleinrock installed and used them in his laboratory; within two years ARPANET was fully operational. E-mail messages were its staple mode of communication. Not all of them dealt with defence matters. Already by then many of the conventions of the later Internet had been established. Thus, the @ in the address became routine and in 1986 the further abbreviations 'com' for commercial, 'mil' for military and 'e' for educational were introduced.

The value of the Net outside military units and universities depended on a broader awareness of its commercial possibilities, and the first on-line commercial service provider, CompuServe, at first catering for what has been called 'a private club', partly owned by Time/Warner (see p. 238), started operating in 1979. A formidable rival, American Online, linked to German and French groups, followed. There was also a third, 'Prodigy'. The three of them, keen rivals, had a combined subscriber base in 1993 that had doubled in two years to 3.5 million. Given their strength, it is possible, at least in retrospect, to trace what looks like a logical phasing in the complex history of the Internet, as there was in most branches of communications history, with a new phase opening when the Net attracted business interests and its uses were extended.

The ecology of a World Wide Web (www) had been transformed, not from a United States base, but from CERN, a European particle physics research institute, nestling under mountains in Switzerland, where an Englishman, Tim Berners-Lee, devised what he called the 'world wide web' in 1989. 'Suppose I could programme my computer to create a space in which anything could be linked to anything', he speculated. 'Suppose all the information stored on computers everywhere were linked.' Berners-Lee did not then know that Vannevar Bush of MIT, who had been intimately involved in the early history of the computer and who had headed the US Office of Scientific Research Development during the Second World War, had pondered on similar lines in an article in the *Atlantic Monthly* in 1945 when he projected a photo-mechanical machine called 'the Memex'.

For Berners-Lee, 'weaving' the Web – Thomas Hardy's verb and noun (see p. 215) – was primarily neither a high-security nor a profit-making task, but a means of widening opportunity. He sought to keep the Web non-proprietary, open and free. Yet, like those American entrepreneurs who developed the

Internet for profit – and in his autobiography he referred briefly to Vint Cerf and Bob Kahn – he was driven by a fervent belief in its potential global use: it could and should be 'world wide'. His development of hyper-links, highlighting words or symbols within documents by 'clicking in', was the key to all future progress. *Time* magazine, which hailed him as the Web's sole parent, called his achievement 'almost Gutenbergian'. He had taken a 'powerful communications system that only the elite could use and turned it into a mass medium'.

Not everyone wanted it to be converted in this way. To some of the pioneer users of ARPANET, the adjective 'mass' carried with it the same connotations as it did when attached to broadcasting. The more Internet users there were, the more a waste land would lie ahead. Such critics were in the minority, however, and there were far more signs of euphoria than of alarm. Most of the pioneer software providers considered that the Internet liberated and empowered individuals and offered unprecedented advantages to society. So, too, did enthusiasts for an uncontrolled Internet. William Winston in his *Twilight of Sovereignty* (1995) argued confidently that through technological convergence we would journey towards 'more human freedom', 'more power to the people' and more international co-operation. Nevertheless, there were others, including some communications scholars in the United States and in Japan, who claimed that the Internet was a 'polluter of the human spirit', and some who forecast that ultimately – and that time was not far away – there would be a further concentration of power. Neil Postman in the United States coined the word 'technopoly' to cover what he called 'the surrender of culture to technology'.

There were sharply contrasting approaches, therefore, to the future of the Internet. Like the railway, it would bring strangers together: you never knew whom you would meet on it. Like the media – and through the media – it would offer information, entertainment and education. Unlike all of these, however, it would grow from below, undirected by government. This was an attraction even to its critics. Yet could the Internet remain so? For Benjamin Parker, an American writer with a self-declared 'passion for democracy', new Titans of telecommunication were emerging, eager to exercise 'monopoly control not just over material goods like coal, oil, steel and the railroads, but over the essential instruments of power in an information-based civilization'.

One of the main uses of the Internet, as it had been for ARPANET, was the sending of e-mail messages in 'real' language, many of them person-to-person. This was a subject for an issue of the *New Yorker*, 'The Digital Age', in December 1999, which also included an article entitled 'Smart Cars, Technology in Motion'. There was fancy, not fantasy, in the approach taken in the article, not so much because the writer described e-mail as 'the return of the word' after a long visual age, but because of the suggestion that reactionary e-mail did not just look back. It looked 'way back' to Swift and Pope and Lord Chesterfield, each of whom it endowed with a Web page. Cutting out the fancy, e-mail had an obvious person-to-person importance inside the families, particularly scattered families, which it helped to bring together far more than the Post Office had done. And it did this at a time when complaints were being made about the impact on the family of Internet addiction, 'a real mental illness', from which its younger members, in particular, would be prone to suffer.

The 'meteoric' growth of the Web overshadows most other aspects of media history, and in March 1996 there was a great symbolic event for President Clinton and Vice-President Gore when they joined others, including the Chairman of the FCC – Newt Gingrich's Republicans had wanted to abolish the Commission – in installing telephone wires linking California's schoolrooms with the Internet. The President promised that all American classrooms would be so connected by the next century through the National Information Infrastructure (NII). This was at a time when Clinton's Secretary of Education could describe the Internet as 'the blackboard of the future'. Entertainment was not mentioned on this occasion. Nor television. Nor politics, although it required intricate political skills and the threat of a presidential veto to ensure the passing in compromise form of the Telecommunications Reform Act of the same year. Earlier attempts to bring up to date the last Act of 1934 had always failed, and the new Act had the dual purpose through deregulation of further opening up competition and of stimulating new investment. In fact, the new Act added to the tangle of regulation without broadening competition.

The linking of schoolrooms with the Internet was a symbolic occasion, and the metaphors employed were still bright, not least the metaphor of the highway favoured by Clinton and Gore, but it was a metaphor that was employed less often in the press during the late 1990s than it had been earlier in the decade. E-words, like e-commerce, now became more fashionable, most of them more concerned with business than with education. E-commerce was now often seen as the culmination of the consumer revolution, a shoppers' heaven which, in the words of Bill Gates in his book *The Way Ahead* (1995), would enable 'all the goods in the world [to be] available for you to examine, compare, and often customize', but what Gates himself was saying about technology – and doing with it – could also be seen as the culmination of an older revolution in production. In historical perspective we would have to go back, as the previous chapters in this book have done, to Boulton and Watt.

Gates himself spoke a different language, regarding machines as liberators, freeing his fellow men for creative tasks. He used a substantial part of the huge personal fortune that he had acquired to endow educational projects. Meanwhile, Microsoft – and its patents – were seldom out of the news before and after the millennium. Nor was the Internet which in fewer than ten years went through exceptional boom and dramatic crash. An early collapse was the Swedish concern Boo.com during the summer of 2000, followed by a remarkable fall in the value of shares in Amazon, one of the best-known Internet companies, dealing in books: they lost a fifth of their value on Wall Street in one day. 'Dealers await Amazon waves' was one newspaper headline. By contrast, a headline of July 2001 read: 'Amazon beats expectations, closing in on profitability.' It had just worked out a deal with AOL, Time/Warner. In a 'thinkers' guide to the e-conomy', *The Economist* in April 2000 referred not to its fluctuations, a recurring word in the history of capitalism, but to its 'gyrations'.

The fates of cyber millionaires, 'a dotcom plutocracy', were daily in view along with other 'celebrities' when, during the sharp swings in share prices on Wall Street and the stock exchanges of the world, they were exposed more dramatically to the ups-and-downs of the high-tech NASDAQ shares which had begun to be listed as a distinct group in the United States in 1993.

Yet the economics behind the technology of the Internet was only one dimension of current debate. The politics of sleaze often captured attention as did the manoeuvres and scandals of politicians. Thus, in his book *Communication and Control* (1991), Geoffrey Mulgan, having examined what he called 'a lattice of world networks', went on to consider 'techniques of swamping, spin control, the unattributable leak and the unanswerable lie, all part of the mediating process', all of which, he suggested, developed 'in tandem with the technologies which carry them'. Significantly, the role of the press in these processes received more critical attention during the 1990s on both sides of the Atlantic than the role of other media and the new technologies on which they rested; more, indeed, than the impact of the Internet on journalists and journalism. For this reason alone, leaving out all questions of 'hype', the most recent period in the social history of the media cannot deal with the Internet as the climax. It was a period when, as always, there were diverse strands. For this reason the next and last chapter of this book, which covers the period from 2000 to 2004, is called 'Multimedia'.

In a multimedia society, what was proving most alarming to most contemporaries was not 'technopoly' but the rise of what the American critic David Halberstam called 'a culture of allegation and assertion at the expense of an older culture of verification'. He was writing in the introduction to a study, *Warp Speed* (1999), which included among its chapter headings 'The Rise of Anonymous Sourcing', 'There Are No Gatekeepers Here' and 'The Argument Culture'. Its authors Bill Kovach and Tom Rosenstiel quoted a Lippmann comment of 1920: 'Public as well as private reason depends on [the importance of having an accurate, reliable account of "events"]. Not what somebody says, not what somebody wishes were true, but what is so, constitutes the touchstone of sanity.' Habermas would concur.

Conclusions

Such judgements, like condemnation of the press for relying on anonymous political sources or of television producers for failing to present 'hard news' or of the Internet for turning out 'garbage', including pornography, rather than facilitating exchange of opinions or ideas, require to be placed in historical context. It is valuable, therefore, to return in conclusion to the fate in the last years of the twentieth century of the by then familiar trinity of information, education and entertainment.

Information raised the same issues as before, with continuing argument about particular events as well as about the 'information economy' and 'information society', although one new book of 2000, *The Social Life of Information*, gained in interest in that one of its two authors, John Seely Brown, had been Chief Scientist at the Xerox Corporation. His argument that the gap between 'hype' about communications technology and 'end-user gloom' was largely due to the 'tunnel vision' that 'information-driven technologies' breed.

The particular events, some of them dramatic, included the tearing down of 'the Wall' in Germany in 1989 and the collapse of the Soviet Union; Tiananman Square; the toppling of Ceausescu in Romania; 'Irangate'; the Gulf War; the United States' bombing of Libya; the break-up of Yugoslavia, Bosnia, and the NATO attack on Serbia; and the fall of Milosević, subsequently tried in the Hague as a war criminal. These have all been subsequently chronicled and interpreted, in diverse fashion, by historians, most of them drawing on the description of the events at the time by journalists. Then and since, independently of technology, which made possible the bringing of words – and even more important, images – into the home, veracity as a necessary value behind both press and television 'stories' seemed in jeopardy. Both events and issues were sometimes turned confidently into drama too, with fictional elements being introduced. The dividing lines between information, entertainment and education were consequently more blurred than ever before.

In the decade after the American withdrawal from Vietnam, with the development of satellite and computer communication (a technological factor), news travelled faster than before, and the handling of the Gulf War by Ted Turner's 'global' CNN captured world attention. When Saddam Hussein invaded Kuwait in 1990, CNN had fewer than a million viewers. By the time that Allied planes were bombing Baghdad each night in 1991, it had nearly seven million. The Pentagon sought to manage the supply of news, using videotape as well as briefings – and to a considerable extent succeeded in doing so – but its coverage was watched by Margaret Thatcher, Boris Yeltsin and Colonel Gaddafi as well as by the first President George Bush and Saddam Hussein. There was a sense of immediacy, but with the help of videocassettes viewers could pick up what was happening when they wanted – out of 'real time'. There was feedback too. CNN got 'hate mail': Peter Arnett, reporting from 'enemy territory in Baghdad', was for many viewers a villain. Victory against Saddam was to be described as 'hollow', but the media had had a victory of their own. In a repeat performance in 2003 (see below, p. 259) the role of the media was to be quite different.

Given the record of information presented, sometimes misrepresented, sometimes by-passed during the last decade of the twentieth century, what can be said of education and entertainment in these multimedia years, when the ownership of both print and electronic media was often in the same hands? Education was usually under scrutiny; entertainment dominated the strategies of planning. At all times, entertainment was the staple of the visual media, although the supply of news always figured prominently in the planning strategies of the BBC in the United Kingdom, and CNN did not include entertainment as such in its remit.

There always seemed to be unique educational opportunities in digital convergence, despite fears in all societies and cultures of 'digital gaps', domestic and international, gaps between those who were literate in the new technology and those who were not and, probably, never would be. Yet the same critics who attacked debased entertainment could also complain that computer literacy might be a substitute for, not a complement to, verbal and visual literacy. Not everyone discussing the gap related it directly, as it must be, to economic inequalities.

When the state had chosen to intervene directly during the 1950s and 1960s to widen access to higher education in the interest, as its leaders saw it, not only of individuals but of societies, its intervention had coincided with the emergence of television, and the word 'convergence' had been used then in a spirit of hope, the same kind of hope that had been evident in the early years of radio. There had also been a related and encouraging shift in language at the same time, and the word 'learning' began to be more generally used, sometimes, but never universally, in place of the word 'teaching' (or, indeed, the word 'knowledge'). As part of the shift, phrases like 'learning how to learn' and with it 'lifelong learning' began to be taken seriously. There was even talk of a 'learning society', a phrase used by the second Rector of the new United Nations University, the Indonesian Soejatmoko, who invited Edi Ploman (see p. 207) to Tokyo to join his staff as a Vice-Rector to head a new 'knowledge division'. The words 'learning society' were subsequently to be used in the title of an official paper produced by the European Community in 1995.

The British Open University, planned meticulously but imaginatively during the 1960s, led the way in recruiting distance-learning students, in the first instance on the political initiative of Britain's Prime Minister Harold Wilson, who was determined both to widen access to higher education and to employ new technologies: he talked, the first British politician to do so, of a white-hot technological revolution, fully aware that it was largely taking place outside Britain. No formal qualifications at entry were demanded by the Open University. In

(a)

Fig. 28 Education finds an ally in communications technology: a. Pupils from Wembley School listening to a radio broadcast in 1933.

(b)

Fig. 28 *b*. Walter Perry (left), first Vice-Chancellor of the Open University, at the opening of its first (BBC) television studio at Alexandra Palace, 1970.

the words of its first Chancellor, Geoffrey Crowther, a former editor of *The Economist*, who welcomed Wilson's initiative, it was open to students, open to ideas and open to methods. The University enrolled its first degree students in 1971, and its hundred-thousandth student graduated in 1989. It greatly extended its non-degree work during the 1980s and its area of operations during the 1990s, setting up a United States branch in 1999.

Distance learning had been launched earlier than 1971 in Canada, Australia and New Zealand, and in 1989 a 'Commonwealth of Learning' was created, with its head office in Vancouver, to foster 'the channelling of resources to projects and programmes in distance education in Commonwealth countries'. The report leading to its establishment was called for by a Caribbean Secretary-General of the Commonwealth, 'Sonny' Ramphal, and its first executive head, James Maraj, was a Caribbean also. Financial resources were restricted, but the enterprise was global in scale. By then, other open universities had come into existence, among them the Indira Gandhi National Open University, established in India in 1985, and the Israeli Open University, along with so-called 'mega' open universities in Thailand and China, with huge numbers of students enrolled. In Japan, a University of the Air, founded in 1984 and modelled on the Open University, used NHK's second educational channel. More than institutionalization had been involved: there were significant changes in perception. 'Traditional' universities themselves came to take up distance learning in the name of 'outreach'. Some of them also changed their ways of teaching within their own campuses in response to an increased number of students, a general phenomenon.

With the arrival of the Internet, there were extended possibilities of learning throughout life, formally and informally, whenever experience or expectation called for it, and there were claims that the World Wide Web, if access were open, would serve for many as a 'university without walls', even that it would eliminate the classroom. Yet in the European Community's 1995 publication, distributed on the eve of a European 'Year of Lifelong Learning' – and in member governments, particularly Britain – the technologies of the information society were considered more for their effects on the workplace than for their effects on classroom or university. Meanwhile, Cisco Systems, one of the most effective of the Internet companies, founded in 1984 by a group of computer scientists from Stanford University, deeply involved in education and dealing in hardware, software and services, was seeking, it said, with the same emphasis, to help change 'the way we work, live, play, and learn'. John Chambers, in charge of its strategies, also appreciated the necessity of working through and not against other educational institutions.

One scholar of the Internet, not directly involved in business as Chambers was, used different and deliberately provocative language. When David Gelernter published *Mirror Worlds*, forecasting the Web, in 1991 (see p. 244), a picture of him appeared on the front page of the business section of the Sunday *New York Times* in 1992. Sadly, in June 1993 he was critically injured by a terrorist nail bomb. *The Second Coming* was a fitting title therefore, to his manifesto published in 2000, although it referred to the computer and not to himself. He argued that while in the first age of computers the main themes had been rising power, falling prices, computers for everybody, the theme of the second age, now approaching, would be 'computing transcends computers'. In this second age, 'your whole electronic life' would be shared in a 'cyberbody'. A 'lifestream' would replace the desktop.

The languages of advertising and of education might converge – the last version of 'convergence', the title of this chapter – as they did in a press release announcing the publication by Eurydice, the European Commission's 'information network on education', of *Two Decades of Reform in Higher Education in Europe* (2000). The press release was entitled: 'Convergence across European Higher Education Systems viewed in the Light of the Facts'. In contrast, Gelernter seemed more interested in metaphors than in facts. For him, 'desktop' was the wrong image, based on a false analogy between computers and filing cabinets – on or below the desk. Computers were 'fundamentally unlike filing cabinets' because they could lead to 'action' at any level. They created a 'lifestream' in a 'landscape' that you could 'navigate' or fly over at any level.

'Flying over', a metaphor derived from the aeroplane, was a very different aerial metaphor from 'take off'. And the landscape you flew over (or descended into) was 'cyberspace', a word used for the first time by the *avant-garde* science fiction writer William Gibson, who envisaged a 'cyberworld' where the world's telephones had been superseded by the 'Matrix', the interconnected sum of all the world's computer networks.

Describing the sky above the port over which he was then flying in his New Age Science Fiction Special *Neuromancer*, published in 1984, he introduced the potent image of the sky being of 'the color of television tuned to a dead channel'. Television did not die in the early twenty-first century, however, and there were to be few dead channels. Indeed, television remained a strong and persistent popular medium, as did the printed press, in a multimedia environment. And Gibson himself, looking back twenty years to his early writings, fully appreciated this. In 2002 he wrote the foreword to Randall Packer and Ken Jordan's collection of historic texts, *Multimedia: From Wagner to Virtual Reality*, in which he described the 'unevenly emergent cyberstuff' of the 1980s and his 'artboy' role in helping to create it. His twenty-first-century enthusiasm for 'multimedia' rested on a belief that it was not 'an invention but an ongoing discovery of how the mind and the universes it imagines – fit together and interact'.

8 Multimedia

The last three chapters, ranging, briefly and selectively, through territory as yet often unmapped, have suggested that the newness of recent developments in communications, particularly technological, can be greatly exaggerated, and that, whatever the coincidences and convergences, there has been no one single line of development. Revealing and useful as it may be to affix labels like the 'Age of Television' or the 'Digital Age' to past and present phenomena, as it was to write of an 'Age of Broadcasting' in the 1920s and 1930s (see p. 173), at best the labels tell us more about perception than they do about fact. Above all, there seemed in the 1980s and 1990s to be increased 'complexity', another key word beginning with 'c'. 'Cold War' retained its capital 'C'.

It was difficult not only to understand the political, economic and social implications of 'new technologies', but also to determine how to escape from 'moral mazes' associated with their development. Old problems centring on freedom and obligation were accompanied by new problems associated with human rights. Questions multiplied, many of them relating to the role of parents. Should children, for example, be prevented from watching 'harmful' media programmes? Technology to deal with technologies did not necessarily help. Nor did the law necessarily back up technology. The Communications Decency Act, seeking to bring the 'V-chip' into use, the law was declared unconstitutional by the Supreme Court (see p. 254). That was one manifestation of the dilemmas posed by television in the home, not a new phenomenon. But the Internet made matters more complex during the late 1990s. Should different rules be applied to the Internet from those applied to older media? Should, for example, 'pornography' be banned by law? It might be more difficult to control it, but doubtless new technological devices would be discovered to 'control' new technologies. In 2000 the US Congress enacted legislation requiring libraries to install 'filtering systems' as a condition for obtaining favourable 'e-rates' for connections to the Internet. That was regulation in an age of deregulation.

More frequently, however, in the USA and several other countries, although not in India, China or Singapore, 'self-regulation', a controversial term, was applied to new media as it had been in Britain to the press. Thus, when in 1999 Australia passed an Online Services Act, referring not only to 'prohibited' but also to 'unsuitable' and 'offensive' material, it was left to the Australian Broadcasting Authority to negotiate an industry code of conduct for home-produced material.

The 1990s was a decade when the shifting boundaries between media, old and new, and within each medium between the experimental and the established were blurred, as were the boundaries between national media strategies and global problems and opportunities. National decisions had global implications and vice versa. The widely used term 'digital gap' was a gap not only between but also within countries. In culture the boundaries had been breaking down for decades between 'high' and 'low', the comic strip and the illustrated history. So also had the boundaries between disciplines – history, sociology, anthropology, psychology, economics, law, for example – and between literary and film criticism and fiction, particularly science fiction. In behaviour, habit and addiction had become confused. And so, within the 'drug cultures' of many parts of the world – a term which remained in use in the twenty-first century – did hallucination and psychosis. For Timothy Leary, drug guru of the 1960s, writing twenty years later, computers were 'more addictive than heroin'. Twenty years after that, 'computer crime', some but not all of it highly sophisticated, was as much publicized as older forms of crime.

The American novelist William Burroughs, whom Gibson acknowledged as one of his predecessors, had applied the word 'virus' to the media – it had already been a theme in the cinema – before it began to be used by technologists and journalists in relation to computers in particular. There were also cross-media references. When a 'real-life computer virus' was described in the press in 'real time' in 1988, both the *New York Times* and *Time* magazine used comic strips to illustrate what was meant by 'viral infection', with *Time* adding an older historical gloss in its title, 'Invasion of the Data Snatchers'.

Each virus had its own 'signature', and while protection against some of them could be provided by anti-virus software, there was no complete guarantee of non-infection. Health parallels seemed pertinent, If only because there was an increasing concern during these years in the media and among politicians for both private and public health, the latter being redefined to cover bans on smoking and defences against obesity, but 'the soul' might provide images as well as the body. A so-called 'love bug' was widely publicized not least because it seemed to have originated not in the United States but in the Philippines. It was truly global, as were the so-called millennial bugs, the fear of which had by then dissipated, at a great expense.

The New Millennium

There had been much writing about the end of an old millennium and the beginning of a new since the 1960s, when a number of commentators, including self-styled 'futurologists', looked forward in their analyses and predictions to the year 2000. Yet ironically, perhaps, when it came – amid celebrations – there was less talk about the future than there had been in the 1960s and 1970s. It was the immediate present that loomed largest, and the year ended with fireworks and lavish displays of entertainment in the world's capital cities, the scale and impact of which claimed press headlines. There were fewer published balance sheets of social gains and losses than there had been at the end of the previous century. Relatively little attention was paid in most countries to a Millennial Summit held at the United Nations in New York in September 2000, and attended by 150 heads of state, when a number of millennial goals were set. Jonathan Sacks,

Britain's Chief Rabbi, who was present, noted that large crowds in downtown Manhattan had gathered not to watch political or religious leaders on their way to the United Nations building but to catch sight of celebrities gathered for the MTV Video Awards. The television corporation MTV dealt entirely in entertainment.

For American journalists, there in large numbers, the year 2000 was the year too of a presidential campaign and both they and politicians rated low when the election was over. For one journalist, Elizabeth Weise, the campaigners themselves were not yet ready for the Internet: the technology, itself open to criticism, was 'clunky', the databases failed to cover crucial information, and the websites were 'tedious'.

In Britain the Millennium Dome erected in London's East End was a matter of continuing media controversy before and after the new millennium began, although the project had been backed by Conservative and Labour governments in turn. It attracted fewer visitors than had been anticipated, although those who bought tickets were impressed by the sophisticated acrobatic entertainment and the sections of the Dome devoted to education and transportation. The most lasting of a wide range of millennial projects, a large number of them local, was a chain of new underground stations between Westminster and Greenwich. The BBC had attempted to broaden the millennial agenda. It opened a BBC History 2000 website providing a guide to British history with audio and visual material including 3D models, run in conjunction with an ambitious oral history, the first time that this had been possible, *The Century Speaks*.

Religion played a less prominent part in the celebrations than it had done in the centennial celebrations of 1900; in the Dome, a 'spiritual zone', a noun derived from the Internet, one of fourteen zones, was difficult to finance. Nevertheless, during the years that immediately followed 2000 there was ample evidence in Britain and elsewhere both of the strength of religious 'fundamentalism', Christian and Islamic, and of 'new age' spirituality. The Internet was widely used by supporters of both groups, as it was in 2003 and 2004 by Anglican supporters and opponents of gay priests and gay marriages. There were sharp and bitter regional divisions on this issue between Africa and the United States, with dissenting minorities, particularly in the latter. 'Globalization', now a buzz-word, did not imply either religious or cultural uniformities.

The main theme of the still prestigious British 1999 Reith Lectures *Runaway World* had been 'globalization', with more stress then on what unified than on what divided. The object of the lecturer, Anthony Giddens, then Director of the London School of Economics, was to 'initiate an electronic global conversation about globalization', which in his view was less explicable in terms of economics – integration – than 'political, technological and cultural' development. As he himself recognized, it was a subject not only for conversation, but also for debate. He had little to say himself about the role of the media in Europe, but there was as much media comment on 'globalization' as there was on the Eurocurrency, with little consensus either in Europe or in Third World countries.

In some parts of the world the lectures provoked not only a fundamentalist recoil or reassertion, a religious response with political ramifications, but also a wave of more general criticism in very diverse intellectual circles, where global-ization was often identified with Americanization. In London, Michael Gove, reviewing recent Hollywood films that were as usual designed for a world market, many of them now endowed with impressive and expensive 'special effects' which could not have been achieved before, feared that to halt globalization might be 'mission impossible'. (That was the title of one of the best-directed and best-acted of recent Hollywood films.) Gove added that 'globalization might be inevitable but we don't have to like it'. 'Globalization may make it easier for peoples to encounter new cultures, but it makes the journey less worthwhile as individual cultures become more like each other.'

The desire to curb, if not to halt, globalization in order to protect national 'cul-tures', an object capable of being very broadly perceived, had played a big part in the politics – and even more in the rhetoric – of the media and of media politi-cians during the 1990s; and it continued to do so after the millennium. Canada, confronted with its powerful neighbour the United States, continued its previ-ous policy of encouraging the development of Canadian media content that could 'compete with the best the world has to offer', including cultural, enter-tainment and educational products. This was the pledge of the Canadian media administrator Paul Racine. He was speaking in Finland, another country with a powerful neighbour: Russia. Finland (see p. 235) had announced that its goal was to become 'the leading country' in the world of communications. Its other neigh-bours, former states of the Soviet Union, in 'reconstructing' national media systems after the collapse of communism, were not so ambitious, but were equally determined to assert their cultural identities. So, too, were countries outside Europe with a colonial heritage, notably Malaysia and neighbouring Singapore. Mohammed Maharthir, Malaysia's prime minister until 2004, em-phasized 'Asian Values'; and in 1996 in Singapore the Singapore Broadcasting Authority required all Internet service providers to be registered and made subject to general media laws such as a Defamation Act, a Sedition Act, a Main-tenance of Religious Harmony Act, and a new category, broadest of all categories, 'undesirable content'.

Attitudes towards globalization changed further between 2000 and 2004, but they remained enthusiastic, hostile or ambivalent according to place and to intellectual and social positioning. The Select Committee on Economic Affairs of Britain's House of Lords produced a report on the subject in 2003 which covered most of the relevant issues, ranging from law – Geoffrey Howe, a former foreign secretary, talked of the globalization of law – to technology. This was the first official report in Britain to be published (along with evidence submitted to it) on CD-Rom. The Chairman of the Committee, Lord Peston, a professional economist, noted how protests against globalization had brought together an 'extraordinary array of concerns', some of them 'mutually contradictory'. On the positive side, he quoted another like-minded economist – and there were many such – who claimed that all 'the success stories' in the recent history of economic development were countries that had 'got into the world economy'.

India and China were singled out by many speakers. Indians were now pro-cessing a flow of information and messages transferred there by European organizations, including banks and corporate businesses. China, which joined the World Trade Organization in 2001, had taken pains to introduce tighter regulations for controlling 'piracy', including piracy in software. Almost all the speakers focused on the activities of the World Bank and the International Monetary Fund as they confronted what one of them called 'shameful' world poverty. One argued that globalization 'effectively meant' communications: 'physical, electrical and electronic'. It was they that had produced 'an interchangeable world in which trade, culture, language and social advances became rapidly interchangeable'.

Peston himself quoted the American economist Joseph Stiglitz, who took a somewhat different line from most of the participants in the debate. In a newspaper review (*Financial Times*, 25 February 2004) of the report of a Commission on the Social Dimensions of Globalization, set up by the International Labour Organization in 2002, he noted that some of the Commission's 'messages', such as the need for restructuring debt, might have seemed controversial 'a short while ago', but they were now 'mainstream'. So was the agreement that the state had a part to play in 'cushioning' individuals and societies from 'the impact of rapid economic change'. His review was headed 'The Social Costs of Globalization'. An American newspaper headline put it succinctly: 'Globalization Just Is: Is It Just?'.

9/11 and its Aftermath

Whatever was said about the advantages and costs of globalization in 2002, 2003 or 2004 or of the role of the media in explaining them, there was a general recognition that the planet had not been the same place since 11 September 2001 when suicide bombers in a terrifying attack had destroyed the great towers of the World Trade Centre in New York and on the same day part of the Pentagon buildings in Washington. 'Tragedy is history's pivot', wrote Michael Wines, Moscow correspondent for the *New York Times*. For other journalists – and historians – this was the 'real' beginning of the new millennium.

There was a sense of world shock, not diminished by the fact that many other countries, including Britain, had experienced terrorist attacks long before. The American response, characteristically American, included the passing of the so-called 'Patriot Act', designed to 'unite and strengthen' America by 'providing appropriate tools to obstruct terrorism'. The tools included the authorization of intelligence wiretap orders that did not need to specify the place to be tapped or require that only the suspect's conversations could be 'eavesdropped upon'. Internationally a 'war on terrorism' was ordained, a war to mobilize 'hearts and minds'.

A coalition, led by the United States, was built up to wage war in Afghanistan, the remote country, recently invaded by and abandoned by the Soviet Union, where Osama Bin Laden, a Saudi-born terrorist, responsible for organizing an international terrorist network, al-Quaeda, had his headquarters. Bin Laden was not captured, but the Afghan war was won more quickly than the media or the public expected, and the Taliban regime overthrown. Extravagantly repressive, it had once built bonfires of television sets. Now, in the course of waging war, the United States and its allies bombed Taliban radio transmitters.

There were so many complexities in the Afghan situation, however, that it was difficult to broadcast reliable information during and after the war, not least about Bin Laden. He was to appear again on world television, care of the Arab television station, al-Jazeera, towards the end of the American presidential election of 2004, threatening continued terrorist action. Afghan elections were then on the agenda. Little was known about Bin Laden in 2001, except that he had once been backed by the United States when he was rebelling against the Soviet Union. During the successful war of 2001 all the information about the Afghans came from the geographical periphery, some of it collected by women reporters. Women had been among the main victims of the Taliban, which had also banned the Internet. Much of the information, then and earlier and later, was propaganda. It was difficult to draw a line between the two. There were no illuminating photographs. Images had to be cobbled together.

In 2003 the second military response of the United States to terrorism, war in Iraq against Saddam Hussein, with more troops but with fewer allies, had sharply divided public opinion, at first more in Britain, the Americans' closest ally, than in the United States. Within the United Nations, which had imposed sanctions on Saddam, France and Germany refused support to President George W. Bush and Prime Minister Tony Blair in what was from the start a controversial venture, opposed by both Russia, which had its own problems of terrorism, and China. It was a far more controversial venture than an earlier American-led attack on Saddam, the first Gulf War, after his invasion of Kuwait in 1991. This stopped short of the overthrow of Saddam (on the first President Bush's orders, which took account of the views of Saudi Arabia on which the United States depended for oil).

The American sense in 2003 and 2004 that their country had not retained the support of 'world opinion' that had been almost unanimously in their favour in September 2001 was evident in Iraq itself, where attempts were being made by a nominated government to hold elections, and in the US presidential election of 2004, where both candidates were aware of it. Bush took advantage of his experience as a leader in the battle against terrorism. In Iraq, however, there was no experience of democracy, and terror attacks were regular items in the news before and after the elections that took place in January 2005. In Michael Moore's anti-Bush film, *Fahrenheit 9/11*, based on 9/11, which was a winner at the Cannes Film Festival, where the European left was well represented, fact and fiction mingled in a way that showed that Bush faced some of his most hostile opponents inside the United States itself. A question posed by Congressman Harry Hyde in 2003 had not lost its relevance. How could it be that 'the country that invented Hollywood and Madison Avenue has so much trouble promoting a positive image of itself overseas'?

The controversy in 2004 both in the United States and in Britain pivoted on one central issue, although there were many sub-themes, like the role of the United Nations. Had the decision in 2003 to destroy Saddam Hussein, which was justified officially in the light of military intelligence, been a wise or a just one? Had there been an adequate case for war? Bush and Blair were in no doubt. Both of them, too, refused to see the war against terrorism as a war between 'the Christian world' and an Islamic *jihad*. Substantial sections of Islamic opinion thoughout the world saw it in that way.

There was a media dimension – a war of words – to the argument in Britain, in particular, at every stage of the conflict and its aftermath, with the government submitting the BBC in particular to a barrage of criticisms but with none of the media taking the blatantly propagandist line of some of the American press and television companies, notably Fox News, controlled by Rupert Murdoch, which showed the American flag flying on the corner of the screen and played martial music as American troops advanced. By contrast, in Britain critics of the BBC, some of whom had totally different grounds for criticism, accused it of taking an anti-war stance even before the claim was made on air that Downing Street had 'sexed up' a dossier suggesting that Saddam could use 'weapons of mass destruction', which it was believed he then held, within 45 minutes.

No weapons of mass destruction were ever discovered in Iraq after Saddam's fall, but Andrew Gilligan, the journalist responsible for making the claim, followed journalistic practice in consistently refusing to disclose the source for his claims, Dr David Kelly, a weapons inspector, not a member of the intelligence community, whose name had been leaked from within the Ministry of Defence. Hounded by the press, Kelly committed suicide, a personal tragedy which made it necessary for the government to appoint a committee, presided over by a senior judge, Lord Hutton, to investigate not the accuracy of the intelligence information but the circumstances of Kelly's death. Before Hutton's report appeared, sharply criticizing the BBC, most of the newspaper media – and the BBC itself – seem to have expected it to concentrate on the activities of government and of Alastair Campbell, Blair's highly political director of communications, not a civil servant, who had been responsible for a barrage of e-mail criticisms sent to Broadcasting House.

The Report did not do so. Press journalists, who had harassed Kelly, might have been more sharply criticized in a report that concentrated on the BBC, which had been reluctant at first to apologize for Gilligan – and its self-confident Director of News since 2001, Richard Sambrook, responsible for 2,000 BBC journalists throughout the world. The Corporation was hit so hard that its Chairman, Gavyn Davies, resigned and its Governors went on to accept the resignation of its pugnacious Director-General, Greg Dyke, who had moved over to the BBC from commercial television when Birt retired in 1999. Speaking in a House of Lords debate on the Hutton Report after Dyke had left the BBC, Birt, who had himself moved to the BBC from commercial television and was now an adviser on transport to Blair, asserted that the BBC had been damaged most in 2003 by 'its failure to respond properly after the [Gilligan] story was broadcast'. There were other speakers in the debate who agreed with Birt, but strong support was expressed for the continued existence of the BBC, 'warts and all', which was hailed by one speaker as 'an international jewel in the crown'. Its staff supported Dyke.

Even stronger support was offered in April 2004 in a House of Lords debate on the BBC's Charter, which was due for renewal in 2007. Many of the same speakers took part who had spoken during the debate on the Hutton Committee, one of whom, Lord Sheldon, observed that 'when one looks at the inaccuracies of Fleet Street journalism, one is impressed by the standards of the BBC which has the highest standards of all the media'. Nevertheless, the matter was not closed and a further inquiry was held under the chairmanship of Lord Butler, former Head of the Civil Service. In January 2005 a government panel headed by a Labour peer, Lord Burns, a former civil servant, claimed that the BBC system whereby the Governors acted as both regulators and champions of the BBC was 'unsustainable'.

Public Service Broadcasting in a Changing Political and Technological Context

Burns made his claim in a letter to Tessa Jowell, Secretary of State, Department for Culture, Media and Sport, a new designation for a department which under Blair now had a wide remit. She had confirmed earlier that the Hutton debate would not influence the government's decisions on BBC Charter renewal. The process had already begun, with the BBC, she affirmed, holding a 'special place in the heart of the nation'. She had instituted a research inquiry in December 2003 to discover what people did and did not like about the BBC. By 31 March 2004 more than 5,000 written responses had been received and 25,000 people had visited a Charter Review website. Not everyone – but certainly a large majority, 75 per cent – had good things to say about the BBC. 'Lack of advertising' was placed in the top three qualities of the BBC that were most praised: it came after 'high-quality programmes' and 'high-quality news programmes'.

That, if true, was not necessarily true of public service broadcasting institutions in most countries, most of which, with a less established institutional identity – and fewer funds at their disposal – went through a crisis in the years between 2000 and 2004. Moreover, with a sizeable proportion of its funds not derived from licence fees, the BBC itself was proposing to cut 2,900 of its staff in December 2004. Few other public broadcasting organizations had as strong a sense of their global role as the BBC; some of them, indeed, had managers who did not think in global terms. The BBC's radio World Service, however, had long established its reputation, not least in Arab countries, and its television service was capable wherever it could be received of confronting CNN or any other global rival. A communiqué of May 2004 referred to its expression of 'British values of openness, fairness [and] diversity of view'. It built bridges 'in an insecure world'.

Particular attention was paid to Islam. In Iraq itself, where Sunni and Shiite passions had now been unleashed, audience research in June 2004 suggested that more than a fifth of the adult population (3.2 million people) were listening to the Arabic Service at least once a week. A further 1 per cent were listening to the World Service's English language programming, although it was only available in two cities on FM and elsewhere only on short wave. The achievement was recognized abroad, even in the United States, where a brightly written and researched number of *Time* magazine concentrating on the BBC (13 October 2003) showed on its cover a BBC microphone and a title 'The Beeb Takes on the World'.

As far as domestic broadcasting was concerned – and *Time* was concerned with that too – three issues were raised repeatedly in the many discussions of the future of public service broadcasting that took place both informally and in organized forums, many of the latter part of the Charter renewal process. They were programme content, institutional management and governance, and finance. On the first of these, which necessarily raised the question of the quality of other providers' output, there was wide consensus: there had been 'dumbing down' in BBC entertainment programmes despite some brilliant new 'sitcoms' such as *The Office*. Channel 4, which celebrated its twenty-second anniversary in 2004, was equally subject to criticism. One of the main supporters of a fourth channel from before its inception, Anthony Smith, complained in 2004 not so much of 'tasteless' programmes – and there were many of these – but of the lack of genuinely 'innovatory' programmes, like Film Four, which Channel 4 had abandoned.

One new category of entertainment programme was particularly under attack whoever produced them – so-called 'reality TV' shows such as *Castaway 2000*, *Big Brother* and *I'm a Celebrity, Get Me Out of Here*, which exploited melodramatic settings, and which critics considered morally repugnant. Yet they attracted huge audiences, and the revelations (edited exposures) of the people taking part in them, some of whom were said to have been left emotionally distressed, fascinated psychologists. The programmes gave a new connotation to the word 'reality' at a time when 'virtual reality', once so creatively explored, was losing out.

Whether the BBC could set standards in entertainment was a matter of argument, although the Voice of the Listener and Viewer, a voluntary organization, celebrating its own twenty-first anniversary in 2004, believed that it must. It focused, however, not only on standard setting by public service broadcasters in face of commercial competition, much of it from abroad, but also on enlightened and imaginative management and governance. Strongly supporting the system of radio and television finance by licence fee for the BBC, deemed to be a basic feature of British broadcasting both in opinion polls and in parliamentary debate, it noted with concern that there were individuals and groups not so much querying its level as advocating its abolition or gradual withdrawal and replacement by advertising or more usually by pay television. A report for the Broadcasting Policy Group of the Conservative Party in 2003 recommended the latter, with the support of economist Alan Peacock, who had first pointed in this direction almost twenty years earlier in 1986. A compulsory subscription rate would cover core BBC public service radio and television channels, but access to other channels would have to be paid for separately.

By 2003 BBC finance had come to depend increasingly on commercial revenues. BBC Worldwide ran a cluster of consumer businesses on both sides of the Atlantic. BBC Ventures carried out tasks on contract to non-BBC organizations, and published books, magazines, videos and multimedia products. It also sold sports series to mobile phone users. All organizations demand a 'critical mass' to be effective, and BBC Worldwide and BBC Ventures and their subsidiaries were soon large enough to challenge bigger organizations than themselves and above all to penetrate difficult markets. For example, a new advertising-funded general entertainment television channel – BBC Japan, within the orbit of BBC World-wide – was announced in October 2004 to start broadcasting later in the year. It was the second BBC channel available there. BBC World was already available in more than a million and a half homes. A similar general entertainment channel, BBC Prime, was on offer in Europe, India, the Middle East and Africa.

Together, the two main commercial 'arms' of the BBC, carefully kept separate from other BBC operations, employed more than 5,000 people, dependent for their success or failure on competitive media markets. Their revenues in 2002 were 35 per cent higher than in 2000. Meanwhile, competing interests claimed that several of the operations from which they derived their profits should not be carried out by the BBC at all. They also protested against the BBC's online presence and the power of what had proved to be Europe's most attractive website.

In all countries with public service broadcasting as part of their multimedia systems there were similar criticisms in the first decade of the new millennium. The public service institutions, it was argued, were going beyond their mandate and in the process distorting unsubsidized competition. Their role should be restricted to providing a universal service in the public interest. Yet such a restriction implied keeping public service institutions locked in a time warp, unable to adapt to new technologies or to convert public service into public enterprise. Commercial pressures in some countries succeeded in enforcing their own economic and political philosophy. Thus, in the spring of 2002 in Portugal it was announced that public service television (RTP) would be left with only one channel and that a new 'civic' channel, run by a consortium of partners, would have access to RTP's production facilities; and in the same year Spain announced proposals to privatize the news department of Channel 9 in Valencia. In the following year the Netherlands cut the budget of its public service broadcasting and Denmark planned to privatize TV2.

The fate of underfinanced PBS in the United States, which also faced political problems, offered a warning rather than a model to public service broadcasters elsewhere, and from quite a different direction in Western Europe the determination of the European Union to widen competition disturbed some public service broadcasting institutions. So did judgements in a number of communication law cases brought before the European Court, not all of which, however, went in favour of new commercial entrants.

In most Western European countries and in some countries outside, including some in Asia, there were now national regulators, like Ofcom in Britain, CSA in France, RegTP in Germany and ASCOM in Italy, with both licensing and coordinating functions, including oversight – or more – of the whole 'communications sector'. There was little significant Ofcom pressure in Britain in 2004 to limit the BBC's independence, and Ofcom's Chairman went out of his way to praise it. Nevertheless, the first annual report of Ofcom, covering the period from its inception, revealed the wide range of its preoccupations and responsibilities, including organizing spectrum sharing, bought and distributed through licences, 'protecting audiences' and the public, promoting greater competition in broadcasting, telecoms and in spectrum allocation, and providing 'enforcement' and 'monitoring'. This was a wide enough remit to keep Ofcom far busier than its predecessor with limited powers, Oftel, which had taken shape within the Department of Trade and Communications, the name of which had itself changed in 1982. It also absorbed other bodies, such as the Broadcasting Complaints Commission.

Whatever the problems of public service broadcasting institutions in the new millennium, corporate businesses within the communications sector had ample problems of their own in all countries. The businesses were larger, however, than most of the non-profit-making institutions, and those that were global in scale were placed high in Forbes's invaluable annual list of the world's top 2,000 companies. Microsoft came second in 2002, IBM ninth, Vodafone twelfth, Intel thirteenth, and Cisco Systems eighteenth. Conglomerates like Pearson (operating from Britain) and Bertelsmann (operating from Germany) were large enough to shift strategies, dispensing with as well as adding to their constituents, with Bertelsmann buying in 2000 the American online music retailer CDNow, and in 2001 teaming up with RealNetworks Inc. to create MusicNet to license music technology to other online music services.

The chief executive officers were written about (and gossiped about) at length in the business pages of the press, some switching from one large organization to another, a few disappearing from view. Among the former in Britain was Dawn Airey whose move from Channel 5 to BSkyB in September 2002 was hailed as a 'coup'. She had been widely expected to move to ITV, most of which was owned by Granada and Carlton, whose merger in 2002 led to the ousting of Michael Green as Chairman. The power behind Channel 5 was Gerhard Zeller, an Austrian, little known in Britain, although as CEO of the sizeable European RTL group he had ambitions to acquire a stake in Channel 4. On a world scale Michael Eisner, the man who ran Disney – and had earlier revitalized it – was often under the spotlight on both sides of the Atlantic, largely because of the pushing out of his erstwhile friend, Michael Ovitz, from the presidency in 1996 after only fourteen months. Contrasts in 'corporate cultures' were blamed. And there was an element of the absurd in the story.

A few young entrepreneurs were capable of receiving celebrity attention even when there were no corporate cultures to praise or blame. The two most publicized of them in August 2004 were Sergey Brin and Larry Page, 'whizz kid' founders (in a San Francisco garage) of an Internet service, Google, in 1998. Brin was then 24 and Page 25. The reason for the publicity in 2004 was that their company had just embarked on a public flotation through an unconventional auction and that they had introduced themselves to the public through an article in *Playboy*. Comparisons were drawn with their youthful and only slightly older rivals, Jerry Yang and David Filo, who had founded Yahoo! in 1994, but there seems to have been no reference in the European press to the fact that Eric Schmidt had moved over from Novell (see p. 100) in 2000.

Youth was the theme, too, in a British *Sunday Times* 'Tech Track' supplement of October 2004 giving details of a hundred of Britain's fastest growing technology companies, headed by Cambridge Broadband, which attracted from a laboratory with ties to Cambridge University an international panel of investors. China was one of the targeted markets. All hundred companies had their own financial as well as technological histories, yet one of the few articles in the sup-

Fig. 29 The founders of Yahoo!, the Internet search engine. Jerry Yang and David Filo were typically young Internet pioneers. Without the ability to search, an expanding Internet would lose its power. In 2001, their main rivals were the young pioneers of Google, Sergey Brits and Larry Page, who carried out an imaginative public flotation in 2004.

plement was written by an executive of Microsoft, Natalie Ayres, who urged British innovators to join 'the US software giant's partnership programme'.

Google and Yahoo! were search engines, assisting web-surfing on the Internet – Google was said to have been inspired by the computer on the television programme *Star Trek* which could answer (almost) any question; but the Internet was now so taken for granted that less popular attention was paid in the press to search techniques than to advertising revenues, the timetable for creating a digital society and the changing technology of mobile communications. Thus, when Tessa Jowell instituted her inquiry into what people did or did not like about the BBC, she asked a second question: what did they think about its role in 'the multi-channel digital [she did not add multimedia] age'.

There was, in fact, less public interest in digitalization in Britain than the government hoped for, although it was a governmental and BBC priority. In his last address to BBC staff in 1999 Birt had made 'the digital revolution' one of his main topics. Digital technology, he explained, had not one but many characteristics.

It would 'move us from the world of scarcity', 'enable us to call up programmes and services on demand at a moment of our choosing', and offer interactivity. Moreover, it would increase access, and publishers would multiply. None of this was new, but it was left to Ofcom in September 2004, to announce that the switchover from analogue could begin in 2007, setting out details of ITV and Channels 4 and 5 licences before the government set a firm date.

Birt's successor as Director-General of the BBC, Dyke, had taken up the same cause months earlier. *The Times* in December 2003 wrote of his being willing 'to pour millions' into completing a national transmitter system that would bring digital radio and television to the entire UK population. Its continued unavailability in certain areas had created a sense of frustration, even of disillusionment. Dyke argued in an Edinburgh Television Festival Lecture in 2003 that in a multi-channel world of fragmenting audiences the BBC would be more important, not less.

A list of 'risks' and 'dangers', which Birt had incorporated in his own lecture, was as pertinent in 2003 and 2004 as it had been in 2000, and they were spelt out again in a very different context at a World Summit on the Information Society held at Geneva in December 2003. The language of those speakers who concentrated on the dangers – and said little about the advantages – of digitalization or, indeed, globalization, had not changed much since UNESCO debates thirty years before; and in an article in *Intermedia* (April 2004) Guy Gough Berger, Head of the Department of Journalism and Media Studies at Rhodes University in South Africa, with the title 'Interrogate the Information Society', could still ask the question 'Is the "Information Society" something we already see and know or something yet to be decided and determined?', wisely adding a subsidiary question, 'Could it be both things simultaneously – something here and now and something still to be?' Unconsciously, it echoed William Gibson's comment, not original, that the future is already here.

Berger made no reference to mobile communications, yet it was in this branch – and it was far more than a branch – of media development that there had been significant expansion between 2000 and 2004 in the developing world as well as in Europe and the United States, even when economic conditions were unfavourable. In 2000 there were five million mobile phones in the United Kingdom; in 2004 there were nearly fifty million. Their modes of use remained controversial. So, too, did the concomitant increase in mobile phone masts. (This provoked the formation of a new pressure group, Mast Sanity (www.mastsanity.org) which focused on contentious health hazards.)

There was continuing uncertainty about the future of third- and fourth-generation mobile phones, whose operators needed governmental licences. The likely demand for cellular mobile phones that in combination could incorporate multimedia features such as digital cameras (and there was certainly an increasing demand on their own for these), digital music players and hand-held devices for playing games (another still expanding market between 2000 and 2004) was difficult to calculate. Nevertheless, competition in producing cellular mobile phones was sharp, with Philips, Ericcson, Sony and Nokia among the manufacturers offering marketing deals. Vodafone too was seldom out of the advertisement pages – or the news. Arun Sarin, who took over as CEO in July 2002, laid all the stress on implementation. Having failed in a bid to acquire the wireless division of AT&T, he did not abandon his hope of turning Vodafone into a generic name for mobile communications, a global counterpart to Coca Cola and Kleenex. He knew well, as did his competitors, that there was no shortage of 'hype', but there were different patterns of demand, as there were of licensing arrangements, in different countries.

There was, however, one factor in common – speed: 3 Gs had a far greater capacity to send and receive data at high speeds. South Korea and Japan were leaders in the process of change both in manufacturing and distributing, evidence that the North East Asian economy, which had suffered during the economic turmoils of the 1990s, had recovered. The South-East Asian economy, however, was dramatically unbalanced by the 'tsunami' of December 2004, the earthquake under the sea which carried giant waves as far as Somalia in Africa. The aid of technology was to be invoked in the future, but when the waves struck, the horror of the present revealed the limits of communication in an age when entertainment counted for more than information and an ugly new word 'edutainment' had been coined. Only disaster on an unprecedented scale could influence priorities. Meanwhile, the choice of underlying technologies was still a matter of disagreement. Not everyone sounded optimistic about broadband use or the creation of a 'new' satellite wireless world (Sirius and XM), and in 2004 Intel warned that the Internet could no longer cope with the huge volume of traffic passing through it, including 'spam'. This consisted of unsolicited messages which were said to account for four-fifths of e-mail. In September 2004, Vint Cerf, sometimes described as the father of the Internet, told a San Francisco audience that the world was still in the stone age as far as networking was concerned. It was a metaphor that Gutenberg would never have used.

Envoi

It has been rare for pioneers of new media to concern themselves with long-term perspectives. Historians more than futurologists must now supply it. There were some curious historical twists to the short period covered in this last chapter. In 2002 Winston Churchill stormed US television awards in the aftermath of 9/11 when the British actor Albert Finney won the Best Actor Award for his impeccable and deeply moving portrayal of Churchill in *The Gathering Storm*. In the autumn of 2004 a German film about Hitler, *Der Untergang*, was on display in Berlin, the first German film focused on him since 1945 and the first to treat him as a human being. At the same time German television presented a documentary on the making of the film to underline its national importance. In a changing global context Churchill and Hitler now stand out differently from the way that they did at the time. So, too, do Stalin and Franklin D. Roosevelt.

So do old films. Yet Metro Goldwyn Mayer's sales of old films, introduced by the snarling lion, a cinema icon, increased nearly three times between 2001 and 2004 when Sony set about acquiring them in face of initial competition from America's Time Warner. MGM's DVD sales of old films had increased nearly three times since 2001. The films included *Ben Hur*, *The Wizard of Oz*, *Dr Zhivago*, *The Pink Panther*, *West Side Story* and the James Bond films, a twentieth-century constellation. In 1989, when Sony had acquired Columbia Pictures and the Loews cinema chain, the event had been compared to Pearl Harbor. Now Pearl Harbor was ancient history.

There was another event in 2004 with ancient echoes – the Athens Olympics, 'Olympian Olympics', globally reported and televised in the United States alone on seven different networks. They evoked not only 1896, the first of the modern Olympics, but also the ancient Olympics, about which several new books were now written. Recent history was turned aside as China, chosen to host the next Olympics (2008), rose high in the medals table. Sport, with its own records and its own codes, must now figure prominently in any long-term account of global media history – economic, political or even diplomatic. And in multimedia circumstances it is now figuring more prominently in television and the press than in film or in the Internet. The psychology is fascinating. The *Financial Times* in September 2004 headed its weekend supplement: 'The year sport became an obsession'. 'It used to be a distraction from war and politics', Simon Kruger observed, but 'after a summer in which the Olympics, Euro 2004 and Wimbledon grabbed the attention of huge television audiences it is more difficult to distract us from sport.'

The word 'historic' is now used more in relation to sporting events than to economic, political or diplomatic issues, for on the latter the media concentrate on the day (today and tomorrow) and on the week, often suggesting what will happen next rather than reporting what has happened. Much is ephemeral. The authors of this book, living in a society and a culture with a long history, cannot treat time as the media do, and they will leave it to their readers, as was stated in the Introduction, to prepare their own chronologies and frame their own judgements. For the future there is no set agenda.

Chronology

*c.*5000 BCE	Invention of writing
*c.*2000 BCE	Invention of the alphabet
*c.*764	Earliest known example of woodblock printing (Japan)
868	First known printed book (China)
*c.*1040	Invention of movable type (China)
*c.*1390	First pictorial woodcuts
1390	First Renaissance medal
1403	Movable type cast in bronze in Korea
*c.*1456	Gutenberg prints Bible
1460	Antwerp Bourse founded
1467	First press established in Rome
1468	First press established in Paris
1476	First press established at Westminster
1492	Columbus lands in America
1492	Oldest surviving globe (Behaim)
*c.*1500	First etchings
1506	First printed map to include information about America
1517	Luther's 95 theses printed
1522	Luther, *New Testament*
1525	Twelve Articles of German peasants printed
1526	Tyndale, *New Testament*, published (in Worms)
1529	Luther, Small Catechism
1534	'Affair of the Placards' in France
1544	First *Index of Prohibited Books* published in Paris
1554	London Exchange founded
1557	Charter granted to Stationers' Company of London
1562–94	Religious wars in France
1563	First printed timetable of postal service in Habsburg Empire
1564	First general *Index of Prohibited Books*
1564	First press established in Moscow
1566	Iconoclasm in France and the Netherlands
1568–1648	Eighty Years War between Spain and the Netherlands
1570	Ortelius, *Theatrum Orbis Terrarum*
1576	First London theatre
1579–94	'Kralice Bible' published, Bohemia
1585	Teatro Olimpico opened at Vicenza
1594	First opera performed in Florence
1598	Globe Theatre, London

1605	Cervantes, *Don Quixote*
1609	First news-sheets (in Germany)
1611	Authorized Version of the Bible published
1617	First logarithmic tables
1618–48	Thirty Years War
1620	*The Corrant out of Italy* published
1626	Ben Jonson, *The Staple of News*
1631	*Gazette* began publication in Paris
1637	First public theatre opened in Venice
1638	First theatre opened in Amsterdam
1640	Bicentenary of printing celebrated
1640	Root and Branch Petition, London
1641	Grand Remonstrance, London
1642–60	English Civil War
1642	First mezzotint
1644	Milton, *Areopagitica*
1648–52	Fronde in France
1662	*Gazette d'Amsterdam* began publication
1663	First Turnpike Act
1668	*Giornale de' letterati* began publication in Rome
1665	*Philosophical Transactions of the Royal Society of London* began
1672	*Mercure Galant* began
1679–81	Exclusion Crisis in England
1683	Louis XIV moved into Versailles
1684	*Nouvelles de la République des Lettres* began
1688	'Glorious Revolution' in England
1689	Procope's Café founded, Paris
1695	English Licensing Act lapsed
1695	*Flying Post, Post Boy,* founded in London
1704	*Boston Newsletter* founded
1709	British 'Copyright Act'
1710	Sacheverell's sermon
1711–12, 1714	*The Spectator* published
1711	First press established in St Petersburg
1712	Stamp duty imposed
1719	Defoe, *Robinson Crusoe*
1726	First press established in Istanbul
1731	*Gentleman's Magazine*
1740	Tercentenary of printing celebrated
1740	Richardson, *Pamela*
1749	Fielding, *Tom Jones*
1751–65	*Encyclopédie* published
1755	Johnson's *Dictionary*
1761	First aquatints
1764	*Il Caffè* published in Milan
1765	Repeal of the Stamp Act
1766	Lunar Society of Birmingham founded

1768	Royal Academy founded
1771	First edition of *Encyclopaedia Britannica*
1775	Steam engine perfected by Watt and Boulton
1776	American Declaration of Independence
1779	First Derby horse race
1780	First British Sunday newspaper
1787	Constitution of the USA
1788	First Amendment to it
1788	John Walter founded *The Times*
1789	French Revolution
1790	First steam rolling mill in Britain
1790	First patent law in the USA
1792	Cable-making machine invented
1794	Boulton and Watt partnership
1794	Chappe's long-distance signalling system in France
1796	Senefelder invented lithography
1798	Paper-making machine
1798	Stamp tax on newspapers raised in Britain; imports of foreign newspapers prohibited
1800	Stanhope's iron press
1802	Cobbett's *Weekly Political Register*
1802	*Edinburgh Review* launched
1803	Fulton propelled a boat by steam power
1804	Trevithick's steam engine ran on rails
1805	Completion of Britain's Grand Union Canal
1807	'Clermont' plied on the River Hudson
1809	*Quarterly Review* launched
1811	Koenig's steam press began operation
1812	Luddite riots
1814	*The Times* printed by steam
1815	Increase in stamp duty
1816	Isolation of selenium, the moon element
1816	Cobbett's cheap (twopenny) *Political Register*
1819	Carlsbad decrees abolished freedom of the press
1819	Six Acts: new stamp duties
1820	Ampère's laws of electrodynamics
1820	First iron steamship
1821	St Simon, *Système Industriel*
1821	*Manchester Guardian* founded
1823	Babbage began building his mechanical computer
1827	Chromolithography – Niepce produces permanent photographic image on a pewter plate
1829	First typewriter
1830	Liverpool and Manchester Railway
1831	Ottoman *Gazette*
1832	British Reform Act
1834	Hansom cabs introduced in London

1834	Lloyd's *Register of Shipping*
1835	New York *Herald*
1836	First railroad in Canada
1837	First French passenger railway
1837	Electric telegraph
1837	Pitman's shorthand
1838	Brunel's 'Great Western'; crossing of the Atlantic
1839	Daguerreotypes and collotypes demonstrated
1839	Opening of telegraph line between Paddington and West Drayton (13 miles)
1840	Britain introduced penny post
1840	Wood pulp used in Germany to make paper
1840	First unofficial newspaper in Turkish
1841	*Punch*
1841	New York *Tribune*
1841	Bradshaw's first *Railway Guide*
1842	British Copyright Act
1842	Mudie's circulating library
1842	*Illustrated London News*
1843	Morse's first telegraph message transmitted using Morse code
1844	Britain's first Railway Act
1844	Cooke and Wheatstone formed Electric Telegraph Company
1846	Rotating cylinder press
1846	Siemens insulated electric wiring
1846	Smithsonian Institute, Washington
1846	*The Economist*
1846	*News of the World*
1848	Year of revolutions
1849	Berlin and Frankfurt linked by telegraph
1850	*Harper's New Monthly*
1850	First British Public Libraries Act
1850	Patent for first typewriter with continuous paper feed
1850	First submarine cable between Britain and France
1851	Great Exhibition in London's Crystal Palace
1851	Wet plate photography
1854	Boole's *Laws of Thought*
1854–6	Crimean War
1857	First transatlantic cable (failed)
1858	Phonautograph
1861–5	American Civil War
1861	*Harper's Weekly*
1862	London Exhibition; peak of stereoscopy
1864	Maxwell expounded electromagnetic wave theory
1864	London's Metropolitan Railway
1865	British Red Flag Act limiting speed on roads
1865	First successful transatlantic cable
1865	International Telegraphic Convention

1867	Michaux started manufacturing bicycles
1868	N. W. Ayer and Son, first multi-service advertising agency, founded in Philadelphia
1868	First American newspaper to use woodpulp paper
1868	First British Telegraph Act
1869	First postcards
1869	Transcontinental meeting of railroad lines in USA; Golden Spike celebration
1869	Opening of Suez Canal
1870	Velocipede
1870	Britain's first national Education Act
1872	Muybridge demonstrated moving pictures of animals
1873	Recognition of the photo-sensitive properties of selenium
1873	Globe Telegraph and Trust Company
1874	Universal Postal Union founded
1876	US Centennial Exhibition
1876	Bell's telephone: first transmission from Boston to Cambridge (2 miles)
1877	Prototype of Remington typewriter
1877	Dry plate photography
1877	Edison's phonograph
1878	First American telephone exchange in New Haven
1878	Hughes's microphone
1879	Siemens's electric tram in Berlin
1880	Hertz described radio waves
1880	Half-tone black used in New York *Daily Graphic*
1883	Sydney–Melbourne railway opened
1883	Hoe's newspaper folding machine
1884	Nipkow's rotating disc
1885	Gottlieb Daimler developed lightweight petrol engine in Germany
1886	William Friese-Greene employed motion picture camera
1886	Berne Convention on Copyright
1886	Eastman's hand camera (Kodak)
1886	Canadian Pacific Railway opened
1886	Daimler's four-wheeled automobile
1888	Use of celluloid in photography
1888	*Financial Times*
1889	American Copyright Act
1889	Edison's motion picture camera
1890	First electric underground trains in London
1892	First automatic telephone switchboard
1892	Pulitzer buys the New York *World*
1892	British Post Office acquires control of all telephone trunk lines
1893	Telefon Hirmondo, Budapest
1893	*McClure's Magazine*: 'muckraking'
1893	Spanish–American War (the 'correspondents' war')

1893	Kinetoscope
1894	Expiry of Bell's patents
1894	First railway over the Andes
1895	Discovery of X-rays
1895	Skladanowsky brothers exhibited films in Berlin
1896	Athens Olympic Games
1896	Marconi arrived in London with wireless devices
1896	Harmsworth's *Daily Mail*
1896	Lumière's cinema show in London
1896	Hollerith formed Tabulating Machine Company to make punch cards
1896	London–Brighton automobile rally
1896	Langley's flying machine
1897	Marconi founded Wireless Telegraph and Signal Company
1897	Type-setting machine (Monotype)
1898	Airship (Zeppelin)
1898	Poulson's magnetic recording telegraphone
1899	British Telegraph Act
1899	Magnetic recording of sound
1899–1902	Anglo-Boer War
1900	Paris Exhibition
1900	Fessenden broadcast voice messages
1901	Marconi transmitted messages from Cornwall to Newfoundland
1901	Mercedes-Simplex automobile model
1901	First motor bicycle
1901	Trans-Siberian railway reached Port Arthur
1902	Fleming's thermionic valve (vacuum tube)
1903	First world congress on wireless telegraphy
1903	Wright brothers flew a petrol-driven aeroplane
1903	Detroit, called the automobile capital of the world
1903	First motor taxis in London
1904	First work on Panama Canal
1904	Harmsworth's *Daily Mirror*
1904	Fleming's thermionic diode valve
1904	First New York subway
1904	British Wireless Telegraphy Act
1905	First motor buses in London
1905	Neon signs
1906	British Patents Act
1906	Fessenden broadcasted words and music
1907	De Forest's audion valve patented
1908	Harmsworth acquired *The Times*
1909	Ford's 'Model T'
1909	Blériot crossed the Channel by aeroplane
1909	Cinematograph Licensing Act in Britain
1909	Imperial Press Conference in London
1911	British Copyright Act

1911	First Hollywood studio
1912	Post Office took over British telephone companies
1912	First American Radio Act
1912	Loss of *Titanic*
1912	*Daily Herald*
1912	First diesel locomotive in Germany
1913	Ford introduced moving conveyor belt
1913	London Wireless Club
1913	First Eiffel Tower wireless signals
1914–18	First World War
1915	Griffiths, *Birth of a Nation*
1917	UFA company formed In Berlin
1919	Alcock and Brown flew across Atlantic
1919	Ross Smith flew from Britain to Australia
1919	First successful helicopter flight
1919	First motor scooter
1919	Radio Corporation of America founded
1920	Dame Nellie Melba broadcast in Britain
1920	Marconi Company opened Writtle broadcasting station
1920	KDKA station opened in Pittsburgh
1920	British Board of Film Censors
1922	British Broadcasting Company founded
1923	*Radio Times*
1923	*Time Magazine*
1923	First transatlantic radio conversation
1924	First stretch of Italian motorway completed
1925	*New Yorker*
1925	Greenwich time signal
1925	BBC's long-wave transmitter opened at Daventry
1925	First general assembly of International Broadcasting Union
1926	Geneva plan for international distribution of wavelengths
1926	First broadcast on NBC Red Network (formerly WEAF/AT&T)
1926	Hugo Gernsback's *Amazing Stories*
1927	British Broadcasting Corporation
1927	CBS (Columbia Broadcasting System) purchased by William Paley
1927	Federal Radio Commission
1927	First transatlantic wire and wireless telephone service
1927	H. S. Black employed negative feedback
1927	Cable and Wireless merger
1927	London acquired automatic telephone system
1927	First Oscars awarded
1928	Baird demonstrated television
1928	Mickey Mouse created
1929	Wall Street Crash
1929	Kodak 17mm colour film
1929	Warner Brothers announced end of black and white films

1929	*Graf Zeppelin* flight around the world
1929	*The Listener*
1930	Picture telegraph service between Britain and Germany
1930	Photo-flash bulb
1930	First television play (Baird system)
1930	Hays cinema code in Hollywood
1932	F. D. Roosevelt's presidential election victory
1932	Opening of Broadcasting House, London
1932	BBC short-wave Empire Service inaugurated
1932	International Telecommunications Union
1933	Hitler appointed German Chancellor
1933	London Passenger Transport Board
1933	British Film Institute founded
1934	Mutual Broadcasting System
1934	International wavelengths agreement signed
1934	Nuremberg Rally
1934	Regular airmail from Britain to Australia
1934	Federal Communications Commission
1935	Radar
1935	35mm Kodachrome film
1936	Ford Foundation founded
1936	*Life* magazine
1936	BBC television inaugurated
1936	Berlin Olympic Games
1936	Chaplin, *Modern Times*
1937	Alec Reeves proposed pulse code (binary) modulation
1938	First BBC broadcasts in a foreign language (Arabic)
1938	Germany produced first Volkswagen Beetle
1938	PEP report on the British press
1938	Orson Welles's Martian invasion broadcast
1939	Frequency Modulation (Armstrong)
1939–45	Second World War
1941	Welles's *Citizen Kane*
1943	Contract signed for ENIAC (Electronic Numerical Integrator and Computer)
1943	Colossus put into action at Bletchley
1945	Vannevar Bush, 'As We May Think'
1945	Arthur C. Clarke forecast satellites
1946	Television service restarted in London
1947	Royal Commission on the Press in Britain (reported 1949)
1947	Transistor devised by Bardeen, Brattain and Shockley
1948	First long-playing record
1948	Norbert Wiener's *Cybernetics*
1948	Claude Shannon pioneers information theory
1950–3	Korean War
1950	European Broadcasting Union formed
1950	Copenhagen plan for frequency distribution

1950	First cable systems
1952	First IBM computers
1952	Last London tram
1952	Universal Copyright Convention
1953	Press Council set up in Britain
1954–75	Vietnam War
1954	Texas Instruments started selling 'chips'
1954	Television Act established 'independent television' and a controlling Authority in Britain
1955	End of wartime newsprint controls
1955	First commercial television programme in England
1955	Ultrahigh frequency waves (UHF) generated at MIT (Massachusetts Institute of Technology)
1955	Beginnings of rock music
1955	First British subscriber trunk dialling exchange, Bristol
1956	First transatlantic telephone cable laid
1956	Suez and Hungarian crises
1957	Russia launched Sputnik (first man-made satellite)
1958	Income from television advertising exceeded that of press advertising in Britain
1958	Stereophonic gramophone records
1958	First live television from Africa via Eurovision
1948	USA launched Explorer I
1958	USA established ARPA (Advanced Research Projects Agency)
1959	*Manchester Guardian* became *Guardian,* printed in London
1959	British hovercraft crossed Channel in two hours
1959	First stretch of motorway in Britain
1959	Sales of transistors exceeded sales of valves
1959	Advent of the integrated circuit
1960	Pilkington Committee on Broadcasting
1961	Yuri Gagarin first man in space
1961	Breaking of genetic code
1961	*Sunday Times* colour supplement
1961	*Private Eye*
1962	First live television from the USA via Telstar satellite
1962	Anglo-French agreement to develop Concorde
1962	Packet-switching opened way to networking
1963	Assassination of President Kennedy
1963	Lay members joined Press Council
1963	William Olsen's mini-computer on sale
1964	Tokyo Olympic Games
1964	Japan introduced 'bullet' trains
1964	Start of pirate radio (Radio Caroline)
1964	First American space walk
1965	Early Bird commercial communications satellite
1965	First 'action replays' on American television
1965	Ban on television tobacco advertising in Britain

1966	*The Times* printed news on its front page
1966	Television of football World Cup (world audience *c.*400 million)
1966	Optical fibre announced
1966	Roman Catholic World Communications Day
1967	Pirate radio banned in Britain
1967	BBC local radio
1967	USA created Commission for Public Broadcasting
1968	Russian invasion of Czechoslovakia
1968	Assassination of Martin Luther King
1968	Student riots in Europe
1968	Demonstration of oNLine System (NLS) in San Francisco
1969	Neil Armstrong landed on moon
1969	BBC and ITV started regular colour television
1969	Rupert Murdoch acquired *Sun*
1969	Sony launched videotape cassettes
1969	Woodstock rock festival
1970	OPEC threatened rise in oil prices
1971	Microprocessors launched
1971	First independent local radio in Britain
1972	E-mail developed within ARPA
1972	Home video cassette recorders on sale
1973	Oil crisis
1973	Britain joined European Economic Community
1974	Resignation of President Nixon
1974	Annan Committee on Broadcasting (reported 1979)
1974	Two general elections in Britain
1974	Royal Commission on the Press (reported 1979)
1975	Fibre optics
1975	Prestel Viewdata system in Britain and teletext
1975	First computer shop (in Los Angeles)
1975	Liberalization of Radio Televisione Italiana (RAI)
1975	Helsinki Final Act
1976	Apple Corporation founded; first portable computers
1976	United States Copyright Act
1977	End of South African ban on television
1977	First optical fibre cable installed in California
1977	Cellular telephone
1978	Apple II personal computer
1979	European Space Agency set up
1979	Commercialization of Internet began
1980	American Computer Software Act
1980	First mass-produced car with four-wheel drive (USA)
1980	Voyager I: first signals from Saturn
1981	Murdoch acquired *The Times*
1981	American ruling that home taping of broadcast signals did not breach copyright
1982	Falklands War

1982	*USA Today*
1983	Laser videodiscs marketed
1984	William Gibson, *Neuromancer*
1984	Compact discs marketed in the USA
1984	Camcorders
1984	First Congress statute deregulating cable TV
1984	Break-up of AT&T
1984	British Cable and Broadcasting Act
1985	British Copyright (Computer Software) Amendment Act
1986	*The Times* moved to Wapping
1986	Chernobyl disaster
1986	Microsoft became a public company
1987	Intifada
1988	International Services Digital Network (ISDN) launched in Japan
1988	British Copyright Act
1989	First mass-produced car with four-wheel steering (Japan)
1989	First transatlantic optical fibre cable
1989	Fall of Berlin Wall
1989	Tiananmen Square
1989	Fall of Ceausescu
1989	Merger of Time Inc. and Warner Brothers
1989	European Union: Television Without Frontiers Directive
1990	New British Broadcasting Act
1990	Rise of Berlusconi Empire in Italy
1990	BSkyB formed by merger of BSB and Sky
1991	CAVE (Cave Automatic Virtual Environment)
1991	Gulf War
1991	Channel Tunnel completed (first railway train 1994)
1991	ISDN in Britain
1992	Clinton elected President of USA
1993	FCC authorized to auction unused portions of spectrum
1993	Separate listing of NASDAQ shares
1993	Proclamation of the 'super-highway'
1993	Privatization of British Rail announced
1994	Russian troops entered Chechnya
1994	Netscape founded
1994	GATT Conference (Uruguay) removes audiovisual sector from agreement
1995	Merger of CNN and Time/Warner
1995	National Science Foundation handed over Internet to commercial interests
1995	Java programming language
1995	Dayton Peace accord for Bosnia-Herzegovina
1996	Russian Telecommunications Act
1996	United States Telecommunications Act
1996	European Year of Lifelong Learning

1996	British Broadcasting Act
1996	Al-Jazeera television station opened
1996	Internet Content Task Force set up in Germany
1996	European Commission: Communication on Illegal and Harmful Information on the Internet
1997	WARC Conference
1998	European Human Rights Act
1998	American Copyright Extension Act
1998	Internet Corporation for Assignment of Names and Numbers (ICANN) founded
1999	Disruption of World Trade Organization, Seattle
1999	Australian Online Services Act: Internet code of practice
2000	Year of the millennium
2000	America On-Line merged with Time/Warner
2000	Microsoft battled against anti-Trust break-up
2000	Television showed Belgrade crowds ousting Milosević
2000	British Terrorism Act
2001	Merger of Disney and Fox
2001	Afghan war
2001	Disruption of G8 Summit, Genoa
2001	Council of Europe: Convention on Cyber Crime
2001	Singapore Broadcasting Authority Act
2001	Terrorist air attacks on New York and Washington (9/11)
2001	USA 'Patriot Act'
2003	War in Iraq
2003	British Communications Act: setting up of Ofcom
2003	World Electric Media Forum
2004	Hutton and Butler Reports in Britain
2004	Presidential election in United States: Bush vs Kerry
2005	*Fahrenheit 9/11*
2005	Tsunami in Asia
2005	Labour returned to power in Britain for third consecutive term

Further Reading

The list which follows is highly selective, our choice from what, in the time-honoured metaphor, we might call the 'ocean' of studies in these fields. To pursue further the topics discussed in the Introduction, we recommend the books discussed in the text itself.

Periodicals, including specialized periodicals, are indispensable, among them *The Economist, Publishing History, Fortune, The Author, Variety, Popular Music and Society*, the *American Sociological Review*, the *Journal of Communication, Media, Culture and Society, Intermedia, Media Studies Journal, New Media and Society* and the *Historical Journal of Film, Radio and Television*. Sadly, the *Melody Maker*, also on this list, ceased to be published in 2001.

The four-volume *International Encyclopedia of Communications* (New York, Oxford, 1989) is an invaluable, though now dated, scholarly work of reference. Erik Barnouw was Editor-in-Chief and George Gerbner the Chairman of its Editorial Board. It was published jointly by the Oxford University Press and the Annenberg School of Communications at the University of Pennsylvania. Wilbur Schramm was consulting editor.

2 The Print Revolution in Context

On the print revolution, see J. Moran, *Printing Presses, History and Development from the Fifteenth Century to Modern Times* (Berkeley, 1973); E. Eisenstein, *The Printing Press as an Agent of Change*, 2 vols (Cambridge, 1979); G. Marker, 'Russia and the "Printing Revolution"', *Slavic Review* 41 (1982); H.-J. Martin, *The French Book* (Baltimore, 1996); M. Giesecke, *Der Buchdruck in den frühen Neuzeit: Eine historische Fallstudie über die Durchsetzung neuer Informations- und Kommunikationstechnologien* (Frankfurt, 1991); and D. McKitterick, *Print, Manuscript and the Search for Order, 1450–1830* (Cambridge, 2003).

On newspapers, see C. J. Sommerville, *The News Revolution in England* (New York, 1996); J. D. Popkin, *News and Politics in the Age of Revolution* (Ithaca, 1989); B. Dooley, *The Social History of Scepticism: Experience and Doubt in Early Modern Culture* (Baltimore, 1999) – despite the title; E. Fischer, W. Haefs and Y.-G. Mix (eds), *Von Almanach bis Zeitung: Ein Handbuch der Medien in Deutschland, 1700–1800* (Munich, 1999); and H. Barker, *Newspapers, Politics and English Society, 1695–1855* (London, 2000).

On physical communication, see F. Braudel's famous *The Mediterranean and the Mediterranean World in the Age of Philip II* (originally published in French in 1949; English translation, 2 vols, London 1972–3); I. K. Steele, *The English Atlantic 1675–1740* (New York, 1986); and D. Cressy, *Coming Over: Migration and Communication between England and New England in the Seventeenth Century* (Cambridge, 1987).

On oral communication, see G. Lefebvre's classic *The Great Fear* (London, 1973; first French edn, 1932); A. Lord's report on his fieldwork with M. Parry, *The Singer of Tales* (Cambridge, MA, 1960); J. Goody, *The Domestication of the Savage Mind* (Cambridge, 1977); W. Ong, *Technology and Literacy* (London, 1982); and P. Burke, *The Art of Conversation* (Cambridge, 1993), and 'Oral Culture and Print Culture in Renaissance Italy', in *ARV: Nordic Yearbook of Folklore* (1998).

On images, see R. Barthes, *Image, Music, Text* (New York, 1977); D. Freedberg, *The Power of Images* (Chicago, 1989); P. Wagner, *Reading Iconotexts, from Swift to the French Revolution* (London, 1995). On printed images, see W. Benjamin's famous and controversial essay 'The Work of Art in the Age of Mechanical Reproduction' (1936; English translation in his *Illuminations,* 1968); W. M. Ivins, *Prints and Visual Communication* (1953); M. D. George, *English Political Caricature: A Study of Opinion and Propaganda,* 2 vols (Oxford 1959); A. H. Major, *Prints and People: A Social History of Printed Pictures* (Princeton, 1971); D. Kunzle, *The Early Comic Strip* (Berkeley, 1973), about strips rather than comics; R. W. Scribner, *For the Sake of Simple Folk* (1981; 2nd edn, Oxford 1994), on polemic in the German Reformation; and D. Landau and P. Parshall, *The Renaissance Print 1470–1550* (New Haven, 1994).

On the spectacle, compare G. Debord, *The Society of the Spectacle* (1967; English translation, Detroit 1970); R. G. Schwartzenberg, *L'Etat-Spectacle* (Paris, 1977); and J. M. Taylor, *Evita Perón: The Myths of a Woman* (Oxford, 1979); with F. Yates, *Astraea* (London, 1975); and P. Burke, *The Fabrication of Louis XIV* (New Haven, 1992).

On manuscripts, censorship and clandestine communication, see A. M. Marotti, *Manuscript, Print and the English Renaissance Lyric* (Ithaca, 1995); P. Grendler, *The Roman Inquisition and the Venetian Press* (Princeton, 1977); D. Kahn, *The Codebreakers* (New York, 1967); I. Wade, *The Clandestine Organisation and Diffusion of Philosophic Ideas* (Baltimore, 1938); F. Moureau (ed.) *Les Presses grises* (Paris, 1988); R. Darnton, *The Forbidden Best-Sellers of Pre-Revolutionary France* (New York, 1995); G. Minois, *Censure et culture sous l'ancien régime* (Paris, 1995); B. Dooley and S. Baron (eds), *The Politics of Information in Early Modern Europe* (London, 2001); M. Infelise, *I libri proibiti da Gutenberg all'Encyclopédie* (Rome and Bari, 1999); and M. Infelise, *Prima dei giornali* (Rome and Bari, 2002).

On intellectual property, see M. Woodmansee, 'The Genius and the Copyright: Economic and Legal Conditions for the Emergence of the Author', *Eighteenth-Century Studies* 17 (1984); R. Iliffe, 'In the Warehouse: Privacy, Property and Priority in the Early Royal Society', *History of Science* 30 (1992); and M. Rose, *Authors and Owners* (Cambridge, MA, 1993).

On the commercialization of leisure, see N. McKendrick, J. Brewer and J. H. Plumb, *The Birth of a Consumer Society: The Commercialisation of Eighteenth-Century England* (London, 1982); R. Sandgruber, *Die Anfänge der Konsumgesellschaft: Konsumgutverbrauch, Lebenstandard und Alltagskultur in Österreich im 18. und 19 Jht* (Vienna, 1982); C. Campbell, *The Romantic Ethic and the Spirit of Modern Consumerism* (Oxford, 1987); J. Brewer and R. Porter (eds), *The Consumption of Culture 1600–1800* (London, 1995); and D. Roche, *A History of Everyday Things: The Birth of Consumption in France* (Cambridge, 2000).

On literacy and the history of books and reading, approaches informed by theory include L. Lowenthal, *Literature, Popular Culture and Society* (Englewood Cliffs, 1961); R. Chartier, *The Cultural Uses of Print* (Princeton, 1987); and D. R. Olson, *The World on Paper: The Conceptual and Cognitive Implications of Writing and Reading* (Cambridge, 1994). Lucid syntheses include C. M. Cipolla, *Literacy and Development in the West* (Harmondsworth, 1969); H. Graff (ed.), *Literacy and Social Development in the West* (Cambridge, 1981) and *The Legacies of Literacy* (Indianapolis, 1987); R. A. Houston, *Literacy in Early Modern Europe* (London, 1988); and G. Cavallo and R. Chartier (eds), *A History of Reading in the West* (Cambridge, 1999).

Important monographs include J. Raven, H. Small and N. Tadmor (eds), *The Practice and Representation of Reading in England* (Cambridge, 1996); A. Johns, *The Nature of the Book: Print and Knowledge in the Making* (Chicago, 1998); J. Pearson, *Women's Reading in Britain 1750–1835: a Dangerous Recreation* (Cambridge, 1999); and W. St Clair, *The Reading Nation in the Romantic Period* (Cambridge, 2004).

On the Habermas debate and its background, see J. Habermas, *The Structural Transformation of the Public Sphere* (1962; English translation, Cambridge, MA, 1989); C. Calhoun (ed.), *Habermas and the Public Sphere* (Cambridge, MA, 1992); P. Dahlgren, *Television and the Public Sphere: Citizenship, Democracy and the Media* (London, 1995); W. Lippman, *Public Opinion* (New York, 1922); G. Boas, *Vox Populi, Essays In the History of an Idea* (Baltimore, 1969); J. Raymond, 'The Newspaper, Public Opinion and the Public Sphere in the Seventeenth Century', *Prose Studies* 21, no. 2 (1998); E. Noelle-Neumann, *The Spiral of Silence: Public Opinion, Our Social Skin* (Chicago, 1984, translation from the German of 1980); D. F. Eickelman and J. W.

Anderson (eds), *New Media in the Muslim World: The Emerging Public Sphere* (Bloomington, 1999); D. Zaret, *Origins of Democratic Culture: Printing, Petitions and the Public Sphere in Early-Modern England* (Princeton, 2000); and J. Van Horn Melton, *The Rise of the Public in Enlightenment Europe* (Cambridge, 2001).

3 The Media and the Public Sphere in Early Modern Europe

On Italian city-states, see J. K. Hyde, *Society and Politics in Medieval Italy: The Evolution of the Civil Life, 1000–1350* (London, 1973). On the Reformation, see G. Strauss, *Luther's House of Learning: Indoctrination of the Young in the German Reformation* (Baltimore, 1978); Scribner, *Simple Folk* (cited in chapter 2); M. Aston, *England's Iconoclasts* (Oxford, 1988); C. Eire, *War Against the Idols* (Cambridge, 1989); and J.-F. Gilmont (ed.), *La réforme et le livre* (Paris, 1990).

On the revolt of the Netherlands, see C. Harline, *Pamphlets, Printing and Political Culture in the Early Dutch Republic* (Dordrecht, 1987). On France from the Religious Wars to the Fronde, see D. R. Kelley, *The Beginning of Ideology. Consciousness and Society in the French Reformation* (Cambridge, 1981); C. Jouhaud, *Mazarinades: la fronde des mots* (Paris, 1985); and J. K. Sawyer, *Printed Poison: Pamphlet Propaganda, Faction Politics and the Public Sphere in Early Seventeenth Century France* (Berkeley and Los Angeles, 1990).

On English 'news culture' in the seventeenth century, see A. Bellany, *The Politics of Court Scandal in Early Modern England* (Cambridge, 2002); and D. Zaret, *Origins of Democratic Culture: Printing, Petitions and the Public Sphere in Early-Modern England* (Princeton, 2000). On the English Civil Wars, see N. Smith, *Literature and Revolution in England, 1640–1660* (New Haven, 1994); J. Raymond, *The Invention of the Newspaper: English Newsbooks 1641–1649* (Oxford, 1996); the special issue of *Prose Studies* (vol. 21, no. 2, 1998) on 'News, Newspapers and Society in Early Modern Britain'; K. Lindley, *Popular Politics and Religion in Civil War London* (Aldershot, 1997); and D. Norbrook, *Writing the English Republic* (Cambridge, 1999).

On media and events leading up to 1688, see J. Kenyon, *The Popish Plot* (London, 1972); L. Schwoerer, 'Propaganda in the Revolution of 1688–9', *American Historical Review* 82 (1977); M. Knights, *Politics and Opinion in Crisis, 1678–81* (Cambridge, 1994); and H. Weber, *Paper Bullets: Print and Kingship under Charles II* (Lexington, 1996). On eighteenth-century England and especially John Wilkes, see J. Brewer, *Party Ideology and Popular Politics at the Accession of George III* (Cambridge, 1976). On coffee-houses as part of the public sphere, see B. Cowan, 'The Rise of the Coffeehouse Reconsidered', *Historical Journal* 47 (2004).

On the Enlightenment, see Wade, *Clandestine Organisation* (cited in chapter 2); N. Hampson, *The Enlightenment* (Harmondsworth, 1968); D. Goodman, *The Republic of Letters: A Cultural History of the French Enlightenment* (Ithaca, 1994); Darnton, *Forbidden Best-Sellers* (cited in chapter 2); D. Outram, *The Enlightenment* (Cambridge, 1995); and for a spirited case-study on the interaction between oral and written media and their political consequences, see R. Darnton, 'An Early Information Society: News and the Media in Eighteenth-Century Paris', *American Historical Review* 105 (2000).

The shift towards a cultural interpretation of the French Revolution was led by F. Furet in his *Interpreting the French Revolution* (1978; English translation, Cambridge, 1981); see also L. Hunt, *Politics, Culture and Class in the French Revolution* (Berkeley, 1984); and K. Baker, *Inventing the French Revolution* (Cambridge, 1990). On the role of the media, see J. A. Leith, *The Idea of Art as Propaganda in France, 1750–1799* (Toronto, 1965); M. Ozouf, *Festivals and the French Revolution* (1976; English translation, Cambridge, MA, 1988); J. Landes, *Women and the Public Sphere in the Age of the French Revolution* (Ithaca, 1988); R. Darnton and D. Roche (eds), *Revolution in Print: The Press in France, 1775–1800* (Berkeley, 1989); and J. D. Popkin, *Revolutionary News: the Press in France 1789–99* (Durham, NC, 1990).

For developments in China and Japan, see S. Cherniack, 'Book Culture and Textual Transmission in Sung China', *Harvard Journal of Asiatic Studies* 54 (1994); J.-P. Drège, 'Des effets de l'imprimerie en Chine sous la dynastie des Song', *Journal Asiatique* 282 (1994); H. D. Smith III (1994), 'The History of the Book in Edo and Paris', in J. McClain, J. Merriman and U. Kaoru (eds),

Edo and Paris (Ithaca, 1994); P. Kornicki, *The Book in Japan: A Cultural History from the Beginnings to the Nineteenth Century* (Leiden, 1998).

4 From Steam to Electricity

A. Briggs, *The Power of Steam* (London, 1982) is a lead into the subject. D. Lardner, *The Steam Engine Explained and Illustrated* (London, 1824), is an illuminating contemporary source. The best general account of the comparative history of industrialization is D. S. Landes, *The Unbound Prometheus* (Cambridge, 1969); its sub-title is 'technological change and industrial development in Western Europe from 1750 to the present'. See also C. M. Cipolla (ed.), *The Industrial Revolution* (London and Glasgow, 1973); P. K. O'Brien (ed.), *The Industrial Revolution in Europe* (Oxford, 1994); J. Mokyr, *Twenty-Five Centuries of Technological Change* (London, Paris, New York, 1990); and M. Berg, *The Age of Manufactures: Industry, Innovation and Work in Britain, 1700–1820* (Oxford, 1985). See also M. Berg and K. Bruland (eds), *British Technological Revolutions in Europe, 1760–1860. Historical Perspectives* (Cheltenham, 1998). For the United States, T. C. Cochran, *Frontiers of Change: Early Industrialisation in America* (New York, 1981), and N. Rosenberg, *Perspectives on Technology* (Cambridge, 1976), are stimulating.

See also G. N. von Tunzelmann, *Steam Power and British India to 1860* (Oxford, 1978) and *Technology and Industrial Progress* (Aldershot, 1995); I. Spiegel-Rösing and D. de Solla Price (eds), *Science, Technology and Society* (Beverly Hills, 1977); A. Pacey, *Technology in World Civilization* (Oxford, 1990); M. Daumas (ed.), *Histoire général des techniques*, 5 vols (Paris, 1962–); D. R. Headrick, *The Tools of Empire: Technology and European Imperialism in the Nineteenth Century* (New York, 1981); and CNRSS, *Innovation technologique et civilisation, xix–xxe siècles* (Paris, 1989).

For Boulton and Watt, see E. Robinson and A. E. Musson, *James Watt and the Steam Revolution* (London, 1969). H. W. Dickinson wrote biographies of Watt (Cambridge, 1939) and Boulton (Cambridge, 1937). Their social and cultural background is well covered in W. Bowden, *Industrial Society in England towards the End of the Eighteenth Century* (New York, 1925); and R. E. Schofield, *The Lunar Society of Birmingham* (Oxford, 1963). For patents, see C. MacLeod, *Inventing the Industrial Revolution: The English Patent System* (Cambridge, 1988); H. I. Dutton, *The Patent System and Inventive Activity During the Industrial Revolution, 1750–1852* (Manchester, 1984); W. and M. Ray, *The Art of Invention: Patent Models and their Makers* (Princeton, 1974); and US Department of Commerce, *The Story of the United States Patent and Trademark Office* (Washington, 1981).

The factory system, 'scientific management' and mass production are examined in J. Tann, *The Development of the Factory* (London, 1970); S. Pollard, *The Genesis of Modern Management* (London, 1963); S. B. Saul (ed.), *Technological Change – The United States and Britain in the Nineteenth Century* (London, 1978); and D. A. Hounshell, *From the American System to Mass Production* (Baltimore, 1984). See also A. D. Chandler's important and influential study, *The Visible Hand: The Managerial Revolution in American Business* (Cambridge, MA, 1977), and his *Scale and Scope: The Dynamics of Industrial Capitalism* (Cambridge, MA, 1990); A. D. Chandler, F. Amatori and T. Hikino (eds), *Big Business and the Wealth of Nations* (Cambridge, 1997); J. Diebold, *Automation, The Advent of the Automatic Factory* (New York, 1952); and L. Hannah, *The Rise of the Corporation* (London, 1987).

For electricity, see T. P. Hughes, *Networks of Power: Electrification in Western Society, 1880–1930* (Baltimore, 1983); M. MacLaren, *The Rise of the Electrical Industry during the Nineteenth Century* (Princeton, 1943); P. Dunheath, *A History of Electrical Engineering* (London, 1962); F. Cardot (ed.), *Histoire de l'Electricité, 1880–1980* (Paris, 1987); and D. E. Nye, *Electrifying America: Social Meanings of a New Technology* (New York, 1990).

For the greatest of all inventors, see, pending the completion of what can also be described as a great project to publish all his papers, R. V. Jenkins et al., *The Papers of Thomas A. Edison* (Baltimore, 1989–); M. Josephson, *Edison* (New York, 1959); and W. Wackhorst, *Thomas Alva Edison: An American Myth* (Cambridge, MA, 1981). See also M. Chancy, *Tesla: Man Out of Time*

(Englewood Cliffs, NJ, 1981), and, for a contemporary view of a new technology, P. Benjamin, *The Age of Electricity* (New York, 1987).

For more general works relevant to this chapter, several of which have stimulated academic argument, see L. Mumford, *Technics and Civilisation* (New York, 1934); S. Giedion, *Mechanisation Takes Command* (New York, 1948); L. Marx, *The Machine in the Garden* (New York, 1964); H. G. Gutman, *Work, Culture and Society in Industrialising America* (New York, 1976); J. Kasson, *Civilising the Machine: Technology and Republican Values in America, 1776–1900* (New York, 1976); T. S. Ashton, *The Industrial Revolution, 1760–1830* (Oxford, 1948); J. Makyr (ed.), *The British Industrial Revolution: An Economic Perspective* (Boulder, 1993); J. Hoppit and C. A. Wrigley (eds), *The Industrial Revolution in Britain* (Oxford, 1994); J. Jewkes, D. Sawers and R. Stilleman, *The Sources of Invention* (London, 1958); B. Hindle, *Emulation and Invention* (Washington, 1981); T. Veblen, *Theory of the Leisure Class* (New York, 1899); A. Briggs, *Victorian Things* (London, 1988); V. W. Ruttan, *Technology, Growth and Development* (New York, 2001); D. F. Nye, *American Technological Sublime* (Cambridge, MA, 1994); J. Ellul, *The Technological Society* (American translation, New York, 1964); and M. Heidegger, *The Question Concerning Technology and Other Essays* (American translation, New York, 1977).

For literature, including publishing, see I. Watt, *The Rise of the Novel* (London, 1957); C. N. Davidson, *Revolution and the Word: the Rise of the Novel in America* (New York, 1986); G. Day, *From Fiction to the Novel* (London, 1987); J. P. Hunter, *Before Novels* (New York, 1990); R. D. Altick, *The English Common Reader* (London, 1963); J. A. Secord, *Victorian Sensation* (Chicago, 2000); J. O. Jordan and R. L. Patten (eds), *Literature in the Market Place: Nineteenth-Century British Publishing and Reading Practices* (Cambridge, 1995); and D. Vincent, *Literature and Popular Culture, England, 1750–1944* (Cambridge, 1989).

For literacy, see H. J. Graff, *The Legacies of Literacy* (Bloomington and Indianapolis, 1987); and P. Brantlinger, *The Reading Lesson: The Threat of Mass Literacy in Nineteenth-Century British Fiction* (Bloomington and Indianapolis, 1998). For readers and readership, see A. Manguel, *A History of Reading* (London, 1996); W. Iser, *The Act of Reading, A Theory of Aesthetic Response* (Baltimore, 1978); S. R. Suleiman and I. Crossman (eds), *The Reader in the Text: Essays on Audience and Interpretation* (Princeton, 1980); J. Raven, H. Small and N. Tadmor (eds), *The Practice and Representation of Reading in England* (Cambridge, 1996); and M. Woodmansee, *The Author, Art and the Market* (New York, 1994).

For the role of the visual imagination, see F. D. Klingender, *Art and the Industrial Revolution* (London, 1947); A. Briggs, *From Ironbridge to Crystal Palace: Impact and Images of the Industrial Revolution* (London, 1979); P. Anderson, *The Printed Image and the Transformation of Popular Culture* (Oxford, 1991); W. Ivins, *Prints and Visual Communication* (London, 1953); C. T. Christ and J. O. Jordan (eds), *Victorian Literature and the Victorian Visual Imagination* (Berkeley and Los Angeles, 1995); and K. Flint, *The Victorians and the Visual Imagination* (Cambridge, 2000).

5 Processes and Patterns

There is a dauntingly large literature on the history of the railway in almost all its aspects. For Britain, see M. Robbins, *The Railway Age* (London, 1962); G. R. Hawke, *Railways and Economic Growth in England and Wales, 1840–1870* (Oxford, 1970); T. R. Gourvish, *Railways and the British Economy, 1830–1916* (London, 1980); P. J. G. Ransom, *The Victorian Railway, How it Evolved* (London, 1990); and J. Simmons, *The Victorian Railway* (London, 1991). For the United States, see G. R. Taylor and I. D. New, *The American Railroad Network, 1801–1890* (New York, 1956); E. G. Kirkland, *Men, Cities and Transport*, 2 vols (Cambridge, MA, 1948); A. Martin, *Railroads Triumphant: The Growth, Rejection and Rebirth of a Vital American Force* (New York, 1992); and B. A. Borthein and A. F. Harlow, *A Treasury of Railroad Folklore* (New York, 1956). For Canada, see R. F. Leggett, *Railways of Canada* (Vancouver, 1973), and for India, see M. A. Rao, *Indian Railways* (New Delhi, 1973). D. Thorner, *Investment in Empire: British Railway and Steam Shipping Enterprise in India, 1825–49* (Philadelphia, 1950) was a pioneering study. See also

D. R. Headrick, *The Tentacles of Progress: Technology Transfer in the Age of Imperialism, 1850–1940* (New York, 1988); P. O'Brien, *Railways and the Economic Development of Western Europe, 1830–1914* (London, 1983); P. J. Hugill, *Global Communications since 1844: Geopolitics and Technology* (Baltimore, 1999); and C. A. Schwantes, *Going Places, Transportation Redefines the Twentieth Century* (Bloomington, 2000).

For shipping see A. McGowan, *The Century Before Steam, The Development of the Sailing Ship, 1700–1820* (London, 1980); S. Polland, *The British Shipping Industry, 1870–1914* (London, 1979); and C. E. McDowell and H. M. Gibbs, *Ocean Transportation* (New York, 1952).

For the mail and the role of the Post Office, see K. Ellis, *The History of the Post Office in the Eighteenth Century* (London, 1958); H. Robinson, *Britain's Post Office* (London, 1953); M. J. Daunton, *Royal Mail, The Post Office since 1840* (London, 1985); C. R. Perry, *The Victorian Post Office* (Rochester, 1992); W. E. Fuller, *The American Mail, Enlarger of the Common Life* (New York, 1972); and R. John, *Spreading the News* (Cambridge, MA, 1995).

The literature of the electric telegraph seems almost as large as the literature of the railway. The best lead-in is J. Kieve, *The Electric Telegraph: A Social and Economic History* (Newton Abbot, 1973). Compare R. L. Thompson, *Wiring a Continent: The History of the Telegraph Industry in the United States, 1832–66* (Princeton, 1947); and A. Moyal, *Clear Across Australia, a History of Telecommunications* (Melbourne, 1984). For what seemed – and seems – to be a distinctive Antipodean situation, see G. Blainey, *The Tyranny of Distance* (Melbourne, 1966), a brilliant study. See also F. Gabler, *The American Telegraph, 1860–1900: A Social History* (Rutgers, 1988) and, with a different time dimension, T. Standage, *The Victorian Internet* (New York, 1998).

For the telephone in its media setting, see P. J. Povey, *The Telephone and the Exchange* (London, 1979); J. Brooks, *Telephone, the First Hundred Years* (New York, 1975); A. Harlow, *Old Wires, New Waves: The History of the Telegraph, Telephone and Wireless* (New York, 1935); J. Martin, *The Wired Society* (Englewood Cliffs, NJ, 1978); R. V. Bruce, *Bell: Alexander Graham Bell and the Conquest of Solitude* (Boston, 1973); I. De Sola Pool (ed.), *The Social Impact of the Telephone* (MIT, 1977); F. G. C. Baldwin, *The History of the Telephone in the United Kingdom* (London, 1925); and A. Stone, *How America Got On-Line* (Armonk, New York, 1997).

Early wireless, always described in the United States as 'radio' before the 1990s, has been studied in detail. See from a long list of books, H. J. Aitken, *Syntony and Spark: The Origins of Radio* (Princeton, 1976) and *The Continuous Wave: Technology and American Radio 1900–1932* (Princeton, 1985); R. N. Vyvyan, *Marconi and Wireless* (London, 1974); W. J. Baker, *History of the Marconi Company* (London, 1974); S. J. Douglas, *Inventing American Broadcasting, 1899–1922* (Baltimore, 1987); G. H. Douglas, *The Early Days of Radio Broadcasting* (New York, 1987); E. Barnouw, *The Golden Web* (New York, 1968); and A. Briggs, *The Birth of Broadcasting* (Oxford, 1961).

The story of the camera, which leads on into the story of the film, is covered in B. Coe, *Camera from Daguerreotypes to Instant Pictures* (London, 1978); J. Lewinski, *The Camera at War: A History of Photography from 1848 to the Present Day* (New York, 1978); A. Thomas, *The Expanding Eye* (London, 1978); H. and A. Gernsheim, *The History of Photography* (London, 1969); H. Gernsheim, *The Origins of Photography* (New York, 1982); and J. Tagg, *The Burden of Representation: Essays on Photographies and Histories* (London, 1988). See also N. Lyons (ed.), *Photographers on Photography* (London, 1966); and V. Goldberg, *The Power of Photography: How Photographs Change Our Lives* (New York, 1991). For an interesting contemporary essay, see S. Sontag, *On Photography* (New York, 1979).

For a contemporary survey of the early cinema, see E. Barnouw, *The Magician and the Cinema* (Oxford, 1981); B. Hodsden, *The Dawn of the Cinema, 1894–1915* (Sydney, 1996); R. Abel, *The Ciné Goes to Town: French Cinema, 1896–1914* (Berkeley, CA, 1994); and I. Christie, *The Last Machine: Early Cinema and the Birth of the Modern World* (London, 1994). For the longer story, see E. Bowser, *The Transformation of Cinema, 1907–1915* (New York, 1990); H. Sklar, *Movies Made America* (New York, 1975); H. Powdermaker, *Hollywood, The Dream Factory* (Boston, 1950); D. M. White and R. Averson (eds), *Sight, Sound and Society: Motion Pictures and Television in America* (Boston, 1968); O. Friedrich, *City of Nets, a Portrait of Hollywood in the 1940s*

(New York, 1986); E. Rhode, *A History of the Cinema from its Origins to 1970* (Harmondsworth, 1978); S. Kindem (ed.), *The American Movie Industry: The Business of Motion Pictures* (Carbondale, 1982); G. Jowett, *Film: The Democratic Art* (Boston, 1976); T. Balio (ed.), *The American Film Industry* (rev. edn, Madison, 1985), a useful collection of historical and contemporary judgements; J. Richards and A. Aldgate, *Best of British, Cinema and Society, 1930–1970* (Oxford, 1983); R. Taylor and I. Christie (eds), *The Film Factory: Russian and Soviet Cinema in Documents, 1896–1939* (Cambridge, MA, 1988); P. Kenez, *Cinema and Soviet Society, 1917–1953* (Cambridge, 1992); and R. Taylor, *Film Propaganda: Soviet Russia and Nazi Germany* (London, 1979).

Different electronic technologies were learnedly pulled together by C. Marvin, *When Old Technologies Were New* (New York, 1988). See also B. Winston, *Technologies of Seeing: Photography, Cinema and Television* (London, 1996); I. Udelson, *The Great Television Race: A History of the American Television Industry, 1925–1941* (Tuscalosa, Alabama, 1982); J. F. MacDonald, *One Nation under Television: The Rise and Decline of Network TV* (New York, 1990); M. Winship, *Television* (New York, 1988); and S. W. Head and C. H. Sterling, *Broadcasting: A Survey of Television, Radio and New Technologies* (5th edn, Boston, 1990).

Far less has been written about gramophones than about films or radio, but see R. Gelatt, *The Fabulous Phonograph, 1877–1977* (rev. edn, New York, 1977); and M. Chanan, *Repeated Takes: A Short History of Recording and its Effects on Music* (London, 1995). For aspects of the more recent story, see R. S. Denisoff, *Solid Gold: The Popular Record Industry* (New Brunswick, 1975); R. Burnett, *Concentration and Diversity in the International Phonogram Industry* (Gothenburg, 1990); P. Gronow, 'The Record Industry: The Growth of a Mass Medium', *Popular Music* 3 (1983), pp. 53–75; and J. Sterne, *The Audible Past: Cultural Origins of Sound Reproduction* (Durhain NC, 2003).

For the media generally, see H. Tunstall, *The Media are American: Anglo-American Media in the World* (New York, 1977; rev. edn, London, 1994); D. J. Czitrom, *Media and the American Mind* (Chapel Hill, 1992); D. Morley, *Television, Audiences and Cultural Studies* (London, 1992); and M. Skovmand and K. C. Schroder (eds), *Media Cultures: Reappraising Transnational Media* (New York, 1992). Changes in perception of time as well as space are the subject of D. S. Landes, *Revolution in Time* (Cambridge, MA, 1983); S. Kern, *The Culture of Time and Space, 1880–1918* (London, 1983); R. Levine, *A Geography of Time* (New York, 1999); W. R. Taylor, *Inventing Time Square: Commerce and Culture at the Grassroots of the World* (New York, 1991); G. Cross, *Time and Money: The Making of Consumer Culture* (London, 1993); and S. Lash and J. Urry, *Economics of Signs and Space* (London, 1994).

For changes in transportation, see P. S. Bagwell, *The Transport Revolution from 1770* (London, 1974); L. H. Adams, *Cycles and Cycling* (London, 1965); H. Perkin, *The Age of the Automobile* (London, 1976); S. O'Connell, *The Car in British Society* (Manchester, 1998); J. B. Rae, *The American Automobile* (Chicago, 1965); J. J. Flink, *The Automobile Age* (Cambridge, MA, 1988); M. Wachs and M. Crawford (eds), *The Car and the City* (Ann Arbor, 1992); M. S. Foster, *From Streetcar to Superhighway* (Philadelphia, 1981); T. C. Barker and M. Robbins, *History of London Transport*, 2 vols (London, 1963, 1974); C. H. Gibbs Smith, *Aviation: An Historical Study from its Origins to the End of World War II* (London, 1970); and D. Edgerton, *England and the Aeroplane* (Manchester, 1991).

6 Information, Education, Entertainment

A critical approach to the history of 'knowledge' and of 'information' and to the term 'information society' is followed in J. R. Schement and T. Curtis, *Tendencies and Tensions of the Information Age* (New Brunswick, 1995), although it deals only with the United States. See also the volume which Schement edited with L. Lievrouw, *Competing Visions, Complex Realities: Social Aspects of the Information Society* (Norwood, 1988); A. G. Smith (ed.), *Communication and Culture* (New York, 1972); and P. Drucker, *The Age of Discontinuity* (New York, 1969).

For the development of the term 'information society' and related terms, see C. Clark, *The Conditions of Economic Progress* (London, 1940); M. Porat, *The Information Economy: Definition and Measurement* (Washington, 1977); F. Machlup, *The Production of Knowledge in the United States* (Princeton, 1962); D. Bell, *The Coming of Post-Industrial Society* (New York, 1976); A. Toffler, *Future Shock* (New York, 1970) and *The Third Wave* (New York, 1980); Y. Masuda, *The Information Society as Post-Industrial Society* (Bethesda, 1981); W. Dizard, *The Coming Information Age: An Overview of Technology, Economics and Politics* (New York, 1984); and J. Salvaggio (ed.), *Telecommunications: Issues and Choices for Society* (New York, 1989). See also M. Castells, *The Information Age: Economics, Society and Culture*, 3 vols (Oxford, 1996, 1997, 1998).

J. Beniger, *The Control Revolution* (Cambridge, MA, 1986), explained clearly how the information society concept emerged from within the processes of industrialization, and the Marxist H. I. Schiller, in a number of books, particularly *Who Knows: Information in the Age of the Fortune 500* (Norwood, 1981), related it to capitalism and imperialism. For an opposing view see Chin-Chuan Lee, *Media Imperialism Reconsidered: The Homogenisation of Television Conflict* (Beverly Hills, London, 1980). The key book in France was S. Nora and A. Minc, *L'informatisation de la société* (Paris, 1978).

See also A. S. Edelstein, J. F. Bowes and S. M. Harsel, *Information Societies: Comparing the Japanese and American Experiences* (Seattle, 1978); The European Commission, *An Action Plan: Europe's Way to the Information Society* (Brussels, 1994); A. Gore and R. Brown, *Global Information Infrastructure: Agenda for Cooperation* (Washington, DC, 1995); and H. Kubicek, W. H. Dutton and R. Williams (eds), *The Social Shaping of the Superinformation Highway: European and American Roads to the Information Society* (Frankfurt, 1997). See also J. S. Brown and P. Duguid, *The Social Life of Information* (Boston, 2000).

The American press is dealt with in detail in the standard American textbook by E. and M. Emery, *The Press and America* (latest edn, 2000), and figures prominently in D. Sloan, J. G. Stovell and J. D. Startt, *The Media in America* (Scottsdale, AZ, 1989). See also G. J. Baldasty, *The Commercialisation of News in the Nineteenth Century* (Madison, 1992). There are stimulating biographies both of particular journalists and proprietors. See also M. Schudson, *Discovering the News* (New York, 1978). For the development of American photojournalism, see R. Taft, *Photography and the American Scene, 1839–1889, A Social History* (New York, 1938). Useful reading lists can be found in E. E. Dennis and J. C. Merrill, *Debates in Mass Communication* (New York, 1991; 2nd edn, 1996), which is related to but departs from standard journalism texts. For journalism viewed from the British angle, see T. Crook, *International Radio Journalism* (London, 1998). See also T. Hopkinson (ed.), *Picture Post, 1938–50* (London, 1970).

For the British press, see F. Knight Hunt, *The Fourth Estate* (London, 1850); S. Koss, *The Rise and Fall of the Political Press in England*, 2 vols (London, 1981–4); L. Brown, *Victorian News and Newspapers* (Oxford, 1985); A. J. Lee, *The Origins of the Popular Press* (London, 1976); and L. Brake, A. Jones and L. Madden (eds), *Investigating Victorian Journalism* (Basingstoke, 1990). One of the most comprehensive and illuminating detailed biographical studies is R. Pound and G. Harmsworth, *Northcliffe* (London, 1959). O. Woods and J. Bishop, *The Story of The Times* (London, 1983), make selective use of the five volumes of the *History of The Times* (1935–52).

For the French press, see R. Mazedier, *Histoire de la presse parisienne* (Paris, 1945) and J.-M. Charon, *La Presse en France de 1945 à nos jours* (Paris, 1991). See also J. Sandford, *The Mass Media of the German-speaking Countries* (London, 1976).

For broadcasting, see A. Briggs, *The Birth of Broadcasting* (Oxford, 1961) and *The Golden Age of Wireless* (Oxford, 1995); P. Scannell and D. Cardiff, *A Social History of British Broadcasting, 1922–1939* (London, 1991); S. Briggs, *Those Radio Times* (London, 1985); and M. Pegg, *Broadcasting and Society, 1918–1939* (London, 1983). The important contemporary text is J. C. W. Reith, *Broadcast Over Britain* (London, 1924). See for the United States, E. Barnouw, *The Golden Web* (New York, 1968) and for the American who should be compared with Reith, E. Lyons, *Sarnoff* (New York, 1966). See also J. S. Waller, *Radio, the Fifth Estate* (Boston, 1950); E. S. Foster, *Understanding Broadcasting* (Reading, MA, 1978); P. Collins, *Radio: The Golden Age* (New York, 1988); I. Kerjan and R. Dickason, *La consommation culturelle dans le monde anglophone* (Rennes, 1999); G. Wedell, *Broadcasting and Public Policy* (London, 1978); and R. W.

McChesney, *Telecommunication, Mass Media and Democracy* (New York, 1993). For the defence of public broadcasting see W. Stevenson and the Carnegie Commission, *A Public Trust* (Washington, 1967).

There was a valuable survey of American broadcasting, with some international comparisons, in *The Annals of the American Academy of Political and Social Science*, 117 (1935). For the role of the FCC, see M. D. Paglia (ed.), *A Legislative History of the Communications Act of 1934* (New York, 1989); and E. G. Krasnov, L. D. Longley and H. A. Terry, *The Politics of Broadcast Regulation* (3rd edn, New York, 1982). See also B. M. Owen, *Economics and Freedom of Expression: Media Structure and the First Amendment* (Cambridge, MA, 1975).

For other countries, see, out of a huge list, R. Collins, *Culture, Communication and National Identity* (Toronto, 1990); V. Porter and S. Hasselbach, *Pluralism, Politics and the Marketplace: The Regulation of German Broadcasting* (New York, 1991); A. Papa, *Storia politica della radio in Italia*, 2 vols (Milan, 1978); E. W. Ploman, *Broadcasting in Sweden* (London, 1976); E. Katz and G. Wedell, *Broadcasting in the Third World: Promise and Performance* (Cambridge, MA, 1977); S. Head, *Broadcasting in Africa* (1972); B. McNair, *Glasnost, Perestroika and the Soviet Media* (New York, 1991); S. W. Head, *World Broadcasting Systems* (Belmont, CA, 1985); and B. Paulu, *Radio and Television Broadcasting in Eastern Europe* (Minneapolis, 1974). For two other relevant general studies see K. Deutsch, *Nationalism and Social Communication* (Cambridge, MA, 1953); and E. U. Heidt, *Mass Media, Cultural Tradition and National Identity* (Fort Lauderdale, 1987). See also R. Negrine and S. Papathanassopoulos, *The Internationalisation of Television* (New York, 1990); and R. Kubey and M. Csikszentmihalyi, *Television and the Quality of Life* (Hillsdale, NJ, 1990).

For changing technology in its business context, see A. F. Inglis, *Behind the Tube: A History of Broadcasting Technology and Business* (Boston, 1990); R. E. Davis, *Response to Innovation: A Study of Popular Argument about New Media* (New York, 1976); and J. M. Utterhack, *Mastering the Dynamics of Innovation* (Boston, MA, 1993). Because of the interaction of radio, television and film, there are many stories which both converge and diverge. Thus, 'The March of Time', which began as a ten-minute radio programme in 1928, consisting of items taken from *Time* magazine, became a newsreel in 1935. For the history of newsreels, see R. Fielding, *The American Newsreel* (Norman, OK, 1972), and *The March of Time, 1935–1951* (New York, 1978). For British newsreels, see A. Aldgate, *Cinema and History: British News Reels of the Spanish Civil War* (London, 1979). See also D. Dayan and E. Katz, *Media Events: The Live Broadcasting of History* (Cambridge, MA, 1991); and J. L. Baugnison, *Henry R. Luce and the Rise of the American News Media* (Boston, 1987) and *The Republic of Mass Culture* (2nd edn, Baltimore and London, 1992).

Probably the first book to refer to an age of television was I. Bogart, *The Age of Television* (New York, 1956). Likewise, J. J. Klapper, *The Effects of Mass Communication* (New York, 1960), first distributed in mimeographed form in 1949, was probably the first book of its kind. H. J. Skornia's book *Television and Society* (New York, 1965) was published before communications technology introduced radical changes in the media. See also, for a slightly later period, J. Green, *The Universal Eye* (London, 1972).

For early television in the United States and Britain, compare E. Barnouw, *Tube of Plenty* (New York, 1975), and A. Briggs, *Sound and Vision* (Oxford, 1979). For television in Europe, see E. Noam, *Television in Europe* (New York, 1991), and, for its role as a world force, R. Moorfoot, *Television in the Eighties, the Total Equation* (London, 1982); A. Smith (ed.), *Television, an International History* (Oxford, 1995); and F. Wheen, *Television* (London, 1985). See also R. Adler (ed.), *Television as a Social Force: New Approaches to TV Criticism* (New York, 1975); G. A. Steiner, *The People Look at Television: A Study of Audience Attitudes* (New York, 1963); H. Newcombe, *Television: The Critical View* (New York, 1976); J. Fiske, *Television Culture* (London, 1987); T. Gitlin, *The Whole World is Watching* (Berkeley and Los Angeles, 1980); E. Taylor, *Prime-time Families: Television Culture in Post War America* (Berkeley and Los Angeles, 1989); L. Spigel, *Make Room for TV: Television and the Family Ideal in Post-War America* (Chicago, 1992); A. A. Berger, *The TV-Guided American* (New York, 1976); R. Silverstone, *Television and Everyday Life* (London, 1994); and R. Powers, *Supertube, The Rise of Television Sports* (New York, 1984).

For television and the news, see D. J. Levey and C. H. Sterling (eds), *Mass News: Practices, Controversies and Alternatives* (Englewood Cliffs, NJ, 1973); S. Mickelson, *The Electric Mirror: Politics in the Age of Television* (New York, 1972); and M. Fishman, *Manipulating the News* (Austin, Texas, 1980). See also R. MacNeill, *The People Machine: The Influence of Television on American Politics* (New York, 1968); M. Schudson, *The Power of News* (Cambridge, MA, 1995); and J. Newman, *Lights, Camera, War* (New York, 1996). There is a detailed study by H. S. Gans, *Deciding What's News: A Study of CBS Evening News, NBC Nightly News, Newsweek and Time* (New York, 1979). See also S. Herman and N. Chomsky, *Manufacturing Consent: The Political Economy of the Mass Media* (New York, 1988), and, for a major international news agency, D. Read, *The Power of News: The Story of Reuters* (Oxford, 1992).

For advertising, considered from different angles, see S. Ewen, *Captains of Consciousness: Advertising and the Social Roots of the Consumer Culture* (New York, 1976); F. S. Turner, *The Shocking History of Advertising* (London, 1953); V. Packard, *The Hidden Persuaders* (New York, 1980); T. R. Nevett, *Advertising in Britain, a History* (London, 1982); D. Pope, *The Making of Modern Advertising* (New York, 1983); and R. M. Hoyer, *The History of an Advertising Agency: N. W. Ayer and Sons, 1869–1939* (Cambridge, MA, 1939). For the social, economic and cultural setting, see D. M. Potter, *People of Plenty* (2nd edn, Chicago, 1969); S. Strasser, *Satisfaction Guaranteed: The Rise of the American Mass Market* (New York, 1989); and compare M. Schudson, *Advertising: The Uneasy Persuasion* (New York, 1984); R. Marchand, *Advertising, the American Dream* (Berkeley, 1985); T. Richards, *The Commodity Culture of Victorian England: Advertising and Spectacle, 1851–1914* (London, 1991); and B. Henry (ed.), *British Television Advertising: The First Thirty Years* (London, 1986).

The history of comment and research on and analysis of the media has never been fully charted. In 1959 Bernard Berelson, researcher into media content, and Wilbur Schramm commented on the state of research in the *Public Opinion Quarterly*, vol. 23. For the period after 1959 see a special issue of the *Journal of Communication* (1983). For the approach of the Frankfurt School, see T. W. Adorno, *The Culture Industry: Selected Essays on Mass Culture* (London, 1991), and M. Horkheimer and T. W. Adorno, *Aspects of Sociology* (Frankfurt, 1972). See also J. Corner, P. Schlesinger and A. Silverstone, *International Media Research: A Critical Survey* (London, 1997). For a critical survey of key texts, see E. Katz, J. D. Peters, T. Liebes and A. Orloff (eds), *Canonic Texts In Media Research* (Oxford, 2003). Their footnotes constitute a bibliography.

Marshall McLuhan published his *Gutenberg Galaxy: The Making of Typographic Man* (Toronto, 1962) as 'a mosaic image' with a 'field approach', but many of his ideas had already been set out in the Toronto 'little magazine' *Explorations*, which ran from 1953 to 1954. An anthology of articles from it, which he edited with E. Carpenter, appeared in 1960. See also his *Understanding Media: The Extensions of Man* (New York, 1964) and (with Q. Fiore) *The Medium is the Message* (New York, 1967). Some of the controversies surrounding him are covered in E. Steyn (ed.), *McLuhan: Hot and Cool* (New York, 1967) and R. Rosenthal (ed.), *McLuhan: Pro and Con* (New York, 1968). For Britain, R. Williams's brief paperback *Communications* (London, 1976) has had as much influence as his many longer books, including *Television: Technology and Cultural Form* (London, 1974). See also his 'Base and Superstructure in Marxist Theory' in *Problems in Materialism and Culture* (London, 1980); A. O'Connor (ed.), *Raymond Williams on Television* (1989). Compare D. McQuail (ed.), *Sociology of Mass Communications* (Harmondsworth, 1972); and D. McQuail, *Mass Communications Theory* (London, 1987).

The pre-eminently quotable historian D. Boorstin's *The Image* (Harmondsworth, 1962) should be compared with an interesting but neglected book with the same title by K. Boulding (Ann Arbor, 1956). See also B. Berelson and M. Janowitz (eds), *Reader in Public Opinion and Communication* (New York, 1969), and compare it with B. Rosenberg and D. M. White (eds), *Mass Culture: The Popular Arts in America* (Glencoe, 1957). Among later Readers, see D. Cater, and M. J. Nyhan (eds), *The Future of Public Broadcasting* (New York, 1976); M. Gurevitch et al. (eds), *Culture, Society and the Media* (London, 1982); P. Golding, G. Murdock and P. Schlesinger (eds), *Communicating Politics: Mass Communications as a Political Process* (New York, 1986); J. Curran, A. Smith and P. Wingate (eds), *Impacts and Influences: Essays on Media Power in the*

Twentieth Century (New York, 1989); D. Crowley and P. Heyer (eds), *Communication in History: Technology, Culture, Society* (New York, 1991); J. Blumler, J. M. McLeod and K. E. Rosengren (eds), *Comparatively Speaking: Communication and Culture Across Space and Time* (London, 1992); and B. P. Bloomfield, R. Coombs, D. Knights and D. Littler, *Information Technology and Organizations: Strategies, Networks and Integration* (Oxford, 1997).

Monographs include H. Gans, *Popular Culture and High Culture* (New York, 1974); N. Stevenson, *Understanding Media Cultures: Social Theory and Mass Communication* (London, 1995); and C. W. E. Bigsby (ed.), *Approaches to Popular Culture* (London, 1976). For an influential contribution to the study and teaching of media studies, see J. W. Carey, *Communication as Culture: Essays on Media and Society* (Boston, 1989).

Writers on the media in French include in translation G. Debord, *Society of the Spectacle*, cited above; J.-F. Lyotard, *The Post-Modern Condition: A Report on Knowledge* (1979: English translation, Minneapolis, 1984) and *The Lyotard Reader* (Oxford, 1989); and J. Baudrillard, whose *Mythologies* appeared in Paris in 1962. Later works of his, translated into American, include *Simulations* (New York, 1983). See D. Kellner, *Jean Baudrillard: From Marxism to Postmodernism and Beyond* (Stanford, 1989). For the approach of Pierre Bourdieu, see his *Distinction: A Social Critique of the Judgement of Taste* (Paris, 1979; Cambridge, MA, 1984), *On Television* (English translation, New York, 1988) and *In Other Words: Essays Towards a Reflexive Sociology* (English translation, Stanford, 1990). A special issue of *Media, Culture and Society* was devoted to him in 1980. See also for an English approach to old and new media themes A. Smith, *The Shadow in the Cave* (London, 1976).

For education, see J. Robinson, *Learning Over the Air: 60 Years of Partnership in Adult Learning* (London, 1983); W. Perry, *The Open University* (Milton Keynes, 1976); J. Langham, *Teachers and Television* (London, 1990); T. Bates and J. Robinson, *Evaluating Educational Television and Radio* (Milton Keynes, 1977); R. J. Blakely, *To Serve the Public Interest: Educational Broadcasting in the United States* (Syracuse, 1979); H. E. Hill, *The National Association of Educational Broadcasters, a History* (Urbana, 1954); and the British White Paper, *Teaching and Learning: Towards the Learning Society* (1996).

The history of media entertainment, which increasingly came to incorporate the history of sport, has been less well covered than that of education except in a huge number and range of autobiographies, biographies and accounts of particular programmes, but see R. C. Toll, *The Entertainment Machine: American Show Business in the Twentieth Century* (New York, 1982), and H. Vogel, *Entertainment Industry Economics: A Guide for Financial Analysis* (2nd edn, Cambridge, 1990). One British pioneer of cybernetics, G. Pask, argued in *An Outline Theory of Media: Education is Entertainment* (Richmond, Surrey, 1976) that educating and entertaining were the same, but he left out show business. For aspects and phases of the history, see R. W. Malcolmson, *Popular Recreations in English Society, 1700–1850* (Cambridge, 1973); G. Seldes, *The Great Audience* (New York, 1950); A. Briggs, 'Mass Entertainment: The Origins of a Modern Industry', in *Collected Essays*, vol. 3 (London, 1991); R. C. Allen, *Speaking of Soap Opera* (Chapel Hill, NC, 1985) and *To Be Continued: Soap Opera Around the World* (New York, 1995); H. O'Donnell, *Good Times, Bad Times: Soap Operas and Society in Western Europe* (Leicester, 1999); J. Corner (ed.), *Popular Television in Britain* (London, 1991); H. Newcomb, *TV, the Most Popular Art* (New York, 1974); N. Harris, *The Art of P. T. Barnum* (Boston, 1973); A. F. McLean, *American Vaudeville and Ritual* (Lexington, 1965); B. Sobel, *A Pictorial History of Vaudeville* (New York, 1961); W. C. de Mille, *Hollywood Saga* (New York, 1939); and R. Silverstone, *The Message of Television: Myth and Narrative in Contemporary Culture* (London, 1981).

For pop music and sport, see D. Ewen, *The Life and Death of Tin Pan Alley, The Golden Age of American Popular Music* (New York, 1964); S. Cohen, *Rock Culture in Liverpool, Popular Music in the Making* (Oxford, 1919); P. Farmer, *Ragtime and Blues* (London, 1979); S. Frith, *Performing Rites: On the Value of Popular Music* (Cambridge, MA, 1996); D. Rowe, *Popular Cultures: Rock Music, Sport and the Politics of Pleasure* (London, 1995); S. Barnett, *Games and Sets: The Changing Face of Sport on Television* (London, 1990); and G. Shanel, *Fields in Vision: Television Sport and Cultural Translation* (London, 1993). See also R. Stites, *Russian Popular Culture: Entertainment and Society since 1900* (Cambridge, 1997), which includes a discography as well as a bibliography. L. Braudy, *The Frenzy of Renown, Fame and its History* (New York, 1997) charts the shift from 'fame' to 'celebrity'.

7 Convergence

Given that the word 'convergence' has had a long history, it is necessary to relate it to a far shorter period of time in order to understand how it was eventually brought into regular use. See, therefore, T. F. Baldwin, D. S. McVoy and C. Steinfeld, *Convergence: Integrating Media, Information and Communication* (Thousand Oaks, CA, 1996). E. M. Rogers, *Communication Technology: The New Media in Society* (New York, 1986) provides an initial vantage point. Two useful books are concerned with a more recent context: W. H. Dutton and M. Pelto (eds), *Information and Communication Technologies: Visions and Realities* (Oxford, 1996), and W. H. Dutton, *Society on the Line: Information Politics in the Digital Age* (Oxford, 1999). They include useful references to further reading. See also M. Castells, *The Information Age, Economy, Society and Culture*, 3 vols (Oxford, 1996–8).

For landmark changes see T. Forester (ed.), *The Microelectronic Revolution* (Oxford, 1980); E. Brown and S. Macdonald, *Revolution in Miniature: The History and Impact of Semiconductor Electronics Re-explored* (2nd edn, Cambridge MA, 1982); H. Gierech (ed.), *Emerging Technologies* (Tubingen, 1982); S. Brand, *The Media Lab: Inventing the Future at MIT* (New York, 1987); E. M. Noam (ed.), *Technologies without Boundaries: On Telecommunication in a Global Age* (1990); N. Garnham, *Capitalism and Communication: Global Culture and the Economics of Information* (London, 1990); C. Freeman, M. Sharp and W. Walker (eds), *Technology and the Future of Europe* (London, 1991); and R. Mansell and U. Wehn, *Knowledge Societies: Information Technology for Sustainable Development* (New York, 1998).

For Japanese contributions to technology, see G. Gregory, *Japanese Electronics Technology: Enterprise and Innovation* (Tokyo, 1986); M. Fransman, *The Market and Beyond: Cooperation and Competition in Information Technology in the Development of the Japanese System* (Cambridge, 1990) and *Japan's Computer and Communications Industry. The Evolution of Industrial Giants and Global Competitiveness* (Oxford, 1995); and H. Anchordoguy, *Computers Inc: Japan's Challenge to IBM* (Cambridge, MA, 1989).

For computers and computerization, see H. H. Goldstone, *The Computer from Pascal to von Neumann* (Princeton, 1972); G. I. Rochlin, *Trapped in the Net: The Unanticipated Consequences of Computerization* (Princeton, 1997); S. Augarten, *Bit by Bit: An Illustrated History of Computers* (New York, 1984); M. R. Williams, *A History of Computer Technology* (Englewood Cliffs, NJ, 1985); N. Metropolis, J. Howlett and G.-C. Rota (eds), *A History of Computing in the Twentieth Century* (New York, 1980); and M. Hally, *Electronic Brains: Stories from the Dawn of the Computer Age* (London, 2005), the last of these a book with a broadcast origin.

For some of the implications of computerization, see J. Preece et al., *Human Computer Integration* (London, 1994); S. Johnson, *Interface Culture: How New Technology Transforms the Way We Create and Communicate* (San Francisco, 1999); H. R. Pagels, *The Dream of Reason: The Computer and the Rise of the Society of Complexity* (New York, 1989); R. M. Friedhold, *Computer Revolution: Visualisation* (New York, 1989); S. Turkle, *The Second Self: Computers and the Human Spirit* (New York, 1984). A useful reader is R. Mansell and R. Silverstone (eds), *Communication by Design: the Politics of Information and Communication Techniques* (Oxford, 1996). Effects on domestic life, often contrasted with public life, are recorded in A. Robertson (ed.), *From Television to Home Computer* (Poole, Dorset, 1979); and J. Miles, *Home Informatics: Information Technology and the Transformation of Everyday Life* (London, 1988).

For the variety of new technologies and their social and cultural significance, see N. Rosenberg, *Exploring the Black Box: Technology, Economics and History* (Cambridge, 1994); I. De Sola Pool, *Technologies of Freedom* (Cambridge, MA, 1983); H. Inose and J. R. Pierce, *Information Technology and Civilisation* (San Francisco, 1984); G. Gilder, *Life after Television: The Coming Transformation of Media and American Life* (New York, 1990); M. Derthick and P. J. Quirk,

The Politics of Deregulation (Washington, 1985); E. G. Krasnow, L. D. Longley and H. A. Terry, *The Politics of Broadcast Regulation* (3rd edn, New York, 1982); G. J. Mulgan, *Communication and Control* (Cambridge, 1991); R. Mansell, *The New Telecommunications* (London, 1993); N. Negroponte, *Being Digital* (London, 1995); and M. Riordan and I. Hoddesdon, *Crystal Fire* (New York, 1988). See also D. R. Browne, *International Radio Broadcasting, The Limits of the Limitless Medium* (New York, 1982).

For other media see A. Smith, *Goodbye Gutenberg* (London, 1980); H. Bagdikian, *The Media Monopoly* (3rd edn, Boston, 1990); W. R. Neuman, *The Future of the Mass Audience* (New York, 1991); L. B. Becker and K. Schoenbach (eds), *Responses to Media Diversification, Coping with Plenty* (Hillsdale, NJ, 1989); K. Auletta, *Three Blind Mice: How the TV Networks Lost Their Way* (New York, 1991); K. Washburn and I. Thornton, *Dumbing Down: The Stripmining of American Culture* (New York, 1998); N. Maynard, *Mega Media* (New York, 2000); A. Jones, *Power of the Press* (Aldershot, 1996); R. Negrine, *Politics and the Mass Media in Britain* (2nd edn, London, 1994); B. Bovach and T. Rosenstiel, *Warp Speed* (New York, 1999); M. Greenberger (ed.), *Electronic Publishing Plus* (White Plains, 1985) and (ed.), *Multimedia in Review, Technologies for the 21st Century* (Santa Monica, 1992).

For cable, see R. L. Smith, *The Wired Nation: Cable TV: The Electronic Communications Highway* (New York, 1972); J. G. Blumler and K. I. Kreems (eds), *Wired Cities, Shaping the Future of Communication* (New York, 1987); R. M. Negrine (ed.), *Cable Television and the Future of Broadcasting* (London, 1985); S. Doheny-Farina, *The Wired Neighbourhood* (New Haven, 1996); T. Hollins, *Beyond Broadcasting into the Cable Age* (London, 1984); D. LeDuc, *Cable Television and the FCC: A Crisis in Media Control* (Philadelphia, 1973); J. L. Baughman, *Television's Guardians: the Federal Communications Commission and the Politics of Programming* (Knoxville, 1985); J. Aumenti, *New Electronic Pathways: Videotext, Teletext and Online Data Bases* (London, 1982). See also A. Nununguun, *Videorecording Technology: The Impact on Media and Home Entertainment* (Hillside, 1989). An interesting account of distrust and fear of an innovation is offered in C. Beamer, *Video Fever, Entertainment? Education? Addiction?* (Nashville, 1982). See also P. M. Greenfield, *Mind and Media, The Effects of Television, Video Games and Computers* (Cambridge, MA, 1980).

For satellites, see R. Collins, *Satellite Television in Western Europe* (rev. edn, London, 1992); and International Telecommunications Union, *From Semaphore to Satellite* (Geneva, 1965).

For some of the international implications of convergence, see A. Smith, *The Geopolitics of Information* (London, 1980). T. L. McPhail, *Electronic Colonialism* (Newbury Park, Beverly Hills, London, New Delhi, 1987) is a valuable lead-up to Sean McBride et al., *Many Voices One World* (Paris, 1980). For a very different aftermath from that envisaged by McBride, see A. Gore and R. Brown, *Global Information Infrastructure: Agenda for Cooperation* (Washington, DC, 1995).

For the Internet, with which the name of Gore has often been bracketed, and the World Wide Web, see K. Hafner and M. Lyon, *Where Wizards Stay Up Late: The Origins of the Internet* (New York, 1996); J. Abbate, *Inventing the Internet* (Cambridge, MA, 1999); R. H. Reid, *Architects of the Web* (New York, 1997); T. Berners-Lee, *Weaving the Web* (San Francisco, 1999); Bill Gates (with N. Myhrvoid and P. Rinearson), *The Road Ahead* (London, 1985, accompanied by CD-Rom); and J. Nielsen, *Multimedia and Hypertext: The Internet and Beyond* (London, 1999).

8 Multimedia

Virtual reality is discussed in R. Ralawsky, *The Science of Virtual Reality and Virtual Environments* (London, 1993); K. Pimentel and K. Teixeira, *Virtual Reality, Through the New Looking Glass* (New York, 1992); S. R. Ellis, *Nature and Origins of Virtual Environments: A Bibliographical Essay* (Oxford, 1991); M. Rheingold, *The Virtual Community: Homesteading on the Electronic Frontier* (Reading, MA, 1993); L. MacDonald and J. Vince (eds), *Interacting with Virtual Envi-*

ronments (New York, 1994); M. Benedikt (ed.), *Cyberspace: First Steps* (Cambridge, MA, 1991); B. Danet, *Cyberpl@y: Communicating on Line* (Oxford, 2001); B. Wellman and C. Hathornthwaite, *The Internet In Everyday Life* (Oxford, 2002).

On computer culture, considered from very different angles, see D. Porter (ed.), *Internet Culture* (London, New York, 1997); B. Laurel, *Computers as Theatre* (New York, 1993); J. Palfreman and D. Suede, *The Dream Machine: Exploring the Computer Age* (London, 1991); R. M. Friedhold, *Computer Revolution: Visualisation* (New York, 1989); S. G. Jones, *Virtual Culture: Identity and Communication in Cyber Society* (Thousand Oaks, CA, 1997); R. Shields (ed.), *Culture of the Internet: Virtual Spaces, Real History, Living Bodies* (Thousand Oaks, CA, 1996); S. Turkle, *The Second Self: Computers and the Human Spirit* (New York, 1984) and *Life on the Screen: Identity in the Age of the Internet* (New York, 1995); D. de Kerekhove, *The Skin of Culture: Investigating the New Electronic Reality* (Toronto, 1995); W. A. McDougall, *The Heavens and the Earth: A Political History of the Space Age* (New York, 1985); and S. Bukatman, *Terminal Identity* (Durham, NC, 1993).

For other questions concerning cyberculture – and there is no consensus about the answers to them (or even the questions) – see W. Gibson's novel *Neuromancer* (New York, 1984); H. Foster (ed.), *Post-Modern Culture* (London, 1985); F. Jameson, *Postmodernism or the Cultural Logic of Late Capitalism* (Durham, NC, 1991); B. Nicolls, *Blurred Boundaries: Questions of Meaning in Contemporary Culture* (Bloomington, 1994); G. Himmelfarb, *On Looking into the Abyss: Untimely Thoughts on Culture and Society* (New York, 1994); A. Kroker and D. Cook, *The Postmodern Scene* (New York, 1986); B. Mazlish, *The Final Discontinuity: The Co-evolution of Humans and Machines* (New Haven, 1993); J. A. Barry, *Technobabble* (Cambridge, MA, 1992); G. Stock, *Metamorphosis: The Merging of Humans and Machines into a Global Superorganism* (New York, 1993); and M. Featherstone, *Undoing Culture: Globalization, Postmodernism and Identity* (London, 1995). There is limited consolation in V. Sobchak, *The Persistence of History* (New York, London, 1996) and in A. Smith, *Culture and the Self* (Oxford, 1996). Smith is not struck dumb by or overwhelmed by technological visions. For two highly critical considerations of the subject by N. Postman, see his *Technopoly, The Surrender of Culture to Technology* (New York, 1993) and *Amusing Ourselves to Death: Public Discourse in the Age of Show Business* (New York, 1985).

A. Giddens, author of *The Consequences of Modernity* (Cambridge, 1990), concentrated not on simulation but on globalization in his Reith lectures, *Runaway World* (London, 1999). For politics, see W. Rash, *Politics on the Net: Wiring the Political Process* (New York, 1997); R. Davis, *The Web of Politics: The Internet's Impact on the American Political System* (Oxford, 1999); M. D. Ayer, *Cyberactivism* (New York, London, 2003); and M. E. Price, *Television, the Public Sphere and National Identity* (Oxford, 1995) and *Media and Sovereignty: The Global Information Revolution and Its Challenge to State Power* (Boston, MA, 2002). See also I. Lessing, 'The Law of the Horse: What Cyber Law Might Teach', *Harvard Law Review*, 113 (1999).

For 9/11, see B. Zelizer and S. Allan (eds), *Journalism After September 11* (London, 2002); and T. Friedman, *The Lexus and the Olive Tree* (New York, 1999) and *Longitudes and Attitudes. Explaining the World After September 11* (New York, 2002). Book publishers, while they faced new difficulties more because of changing corporate structures than because of changes in technology, continued to produce books. See, L. A. Coser, C. Kadushin and W. P. Powell, *Books: The Culture and of Publishing* (New York 1983); F. Kobtak and B. L. Lucy (eds), *The Structure of International Publishing in the 1990s* (New Brunswick and London, 1994); P. G. Altbach and E. Shapiro, *International Book Publishing: An Encyclopaedia*; G. Nunberg (ed.), *The Future of the Book* (Berkeley, 1996); and J. Epstein, *Publishing, Past, Present and Future* (New York, 2001).

Index

ABC, 189–90
access programmes, 202
Acton, Lord, 16
Adams, Henry, 150
Addison, Joseph, 26, 59
Adler, Richard, 202
Adorno, Theodor, 200
advertising, 46, 130, 172, 180, 185–6, 196, 229–30, 253, 261
Afghanistan, 258–9
AFP, 233
Africa, 10–11, 194–5, 234
Agency, 11, 19
Agnew, Spiro, 202
Alexandria, 6
Algeria, 234
Al-Jazeera, 259
American Revolution, 81, 88
Ampère, André Marie, 111
Anderson, Benedict, 1, 26, 85
Andreesen, Marc, 229
Annan, Noel, 196
Apple Macintosh, 229
Archer, Frederick Scott, 134
Aretino, Pietro, 43
Ariosto, Ludovico, 51
Arkwright, Richard, 86
Armstrong, Edwin, 186
Arnett, Peter, 249
Arnold, Frank, 131
Arnold, Matthew, 159–60, 179
ARPANET, 226, 244–6
ASCOM, (Italy), 263
Associated Press, 111
Associated Television, 171
Assyria, 5
AT&T, 123, 130, 220, 232, 242, 267
Atatürk, Kemal, 11
Athens, 6, 153
Attlee, Clement, 170
Aubrey, John, 54
'aura', 32–3
Australia, 109–10, 115, 118, 158, 199, 254
automobiles, 148–9

Babbage, Charles, 94, 109
Backus, John, 226
Bacon, Francis, 14, 35, 45, 96
Baedeker, Karl, 102
Bagehot, Walter, 151, 161
Baily, Kenneth, 172
Baines, Edward, 155
Baird, John Logie, 142–3
Baldwin, Stanley, 169
ballads, 24, 38–9
Bandello, Matteo, 51
Bardeen, John, 222
Barlaeus, Caspar, 48
Barnes, George, 190
Barnes, Thomas, 163
Barthes, Roland, 31, 199
Bartholdi, Frédéric Auguste, 104
Basil of Caesarea, 7
Baudrillard, Jean, 201–2
Bauman, Zygmunt, 23
Bayeux Tapestry, 7
Bayle, Pierre, 48
BBC, 130, 132, 143–4, 169, 173, 176–7, 182–3, 186, 190–3, 206, 235, 256, 260–3, 266
Beaumarchais, Pierre-Augustin, 80
Beaverbrook, Lord, 168–70
Behaim, Martin, 33
Belgium, 113
Bell, Alexander Graham, 117–19, 145–6
Bell, Daniel, 210–12
Bell Laboratories, 123, 220, 223
Bell Telephone Company, 118
Bellarmino, Roberto, 41
Benjamin, Walter, 32–3
Benn, Tony, 193
Bennett, James Gordon, junior, 126, 155
Bennett, James Gordon, senior, 155
Bentham, Jeremy, 161
Berelson, Bernard, 201
Bergman, Ingmar, 138
Berle, Milton, 185, 190
Berliner, Emile, 146

Berlusconi, Silvio, 196
Berners-Lee, Tim, 245–6
Bertelsmann, 264
Bible, 31, 50, 63, 69
Bibliothèque Bleue, 17, 54
bicycles, 148–9
Bidwell, Shelford, 141
Biggelow, Erastus Brigham, 88
Bin Laden, Osama, 258–9
bioscope, 137
Birkinshaw, D. C., 144
Birt, John, 260, 265
'bit', 228
Black, John, 221
Blaeu, Joan, 49
Blaeu, Willem, 19
Blainey, Geoffrey, 23, 109
Blériot, Louis, 168
Blumlein, Alan, 143
Boccaccio, Giovanni, 9, 41–2, 51, 64
Bonifacio, Giovanni, 31
book reviews, 16, 58
Boorstin, Daniel, 57, 200, 216
Borromeo, St Carlo, 2–3, 50
Borthwick, Algernon, 168
Bossuet, Jacques, 24
Boston, 23
Boswell, James, 25
Botticelli, Sandro, 31
Boulton, Matthew, 87–8
Bourdieu, Pierre, 201–02
Bowers, Raymond, 225
Boyle, Robert, 32
Brando, Marlon, 190
Branley, Edouard, 124
Brassey, Thomas, 103
Braudel, Fernand, 21–2
Brazil, 39, 198, 239
Bright, Charles, 110
Brissot, Jacques-Pierre, 81
'broadcasting', 129
Brotman, Stuart, 218
Brunel, Isambard Kingdom, 103, 105
Bryce, James, 96
BSB, 235
BSkyB, 235, 264
BT, 235
Bulwer, John, 31
Bunyan, John, 73, 102, 167
Burnet, Gilbert, 78
Burritt, Elihu, 108
Burrows, Arthur, 129
Burton, Robert, 16–17
Bushnell, Nicholas, 228

cable, 132, 218, 232, 236–9
Cadbury, George, 168
Calvin, Jean, 15
camera, 134–6
Cameron, Julia Margaret, 135
Campbell, Alastair, 260
Campbell, Colin, 45
Campbell Swinton, A. C., 129, 141
Canada, 5, 10, 180, 197, 233, 241
canals, 90
Canning, George, 162
Carey, James W., 165, 201
Carter, Charles, 206
Caruso, Enrico, 129
Castiglione, Baldassare, 38–9, 52
Catherine de'Medici, 72
Catherine the Great, 22, 80
CATV, 236
CBS, 131, 174, 185, 188–90, 194
CD-Roms, 223, 231, 257
cellular phones, see mobile telephones
censorship, 40–2, 48, 78, 81, 138, 140, 157–8, 198
Centre for Cultural Studies (Birmingham), 199
Cerf, Vint, 246, 267
CERN, 245
Cervantes, Miguel, 46
Chamberlain, Joseph, 168
Chandler, A.D., 115
chap-books, 17–18, 39
Chaplin, Charles, 136–8
Chapman, Sydney, 151
Chappe, Claude, 84
Charles I of England, 24, 74, 103
Charles II of England, 77–8
Charles IX of France, 35
Charles V, emperor, 21, 35–6, 83
Chartism, 157
Chaucer, Geoffrey, 9
Chénier, Marie-Joseph, 81
Chesterfield, Lord, 39
Chevalier, Michel, 94
Children's Hour, 186
China, 13, 85–6, 219, 236, 258
Churchill, Winston, 169–70, 267
cinema, 133, 135–40, 187, 189–90, 267
ciphers, 43
Cipolla, Carlo, 4
Cisco, 252, 264
Citizens' Band radio, 225, 243
Clark, Colin, 212
Clarke, Arthur C., 231
Clayre, Alasdair, 186

Clinton, Bill, 203, 217, 247
CNN, 171, 238–9, 249
Cobbett, William, 162
Cobden, Richard, 157
coffee-houses, 25–6, 73, 79
Colbert, Jean-Baptiste, 72
Coleridge, Samuel Taylor, 88
Collins, Norman, 191
Collins, Wilkie, 159
communicative events, 31, 200
computer games, 228–9
computers, 94, 221–31, 252, 255
Condorcet, Marquis de, 15
Conrad, Frank, 130–1
'conservative dilemma', 68, 76
Contemporary Review, 166
conversation, 39
Cook, Thomas, 102, 106
Cooke, William Fothergill, 111–12
copyright, 46
coronation of Elizabeth II, 8, 191
Cranach, Lukas, 65
Crawford Committee, 179
Crimean War, 92, 112
Cronkite, Walter, 192, 204
Crookes, William, 126
Crowther, Geoffrey, 250
Cunard, Samuel, 105
cybernetics, 152
'cyberspace', 253

Daguerre, Louis, 133–4
Dahrendorf, Ralf, 200
D'Alembert, 80
Dalhousie, Marquis of, 103–4, 109
Dallas, 204
Dante, 9, 31, 41
Darnton, Robert, 80
Darwin, Charles, 95
Darwin, Erasmus, 90–1
David, Jacques-Louis, 82–3
Davies, Donald Watt, 245
Davies, Gavyn, 260
Dawson, Geoffrey, 169
De Lesseps, Ferdinand, 105
Debord, Guy, 34, 201
Defoe, Daniel, 53, 86, 93
Delane, John Thaddeus, 165
Della Casa, Giovanni, 39
Der Untergang, 267
Desmoulins, Camille, 83
Deutsch, Karl, 21, 75
Dickens, Charles, 102, 105, 156, 161
Diderot, Denis, 30, 46, 80

digitalization, 240, 246, 255, 265–6
Dimbleby, Richard, 191
Disney, Walt, 138, 190, 238
Disraeli, Benjamin, 163
Dizard, Wilson, 194, 203
Donne, John, 24, 37
Donneau de Visé, Jean, 58
Drucker, Peter, 212
Dr Who, 192
Dryden, John, 77–8
Du Bellay, Joachim, 31
Dunton, John, 59
Dutch Republic, 20, 48, 72–3
DVDs, 231, 267
Dyke, Greg, 260, 266

Eastlake, Lady, 134
Eastman, George, 134, 136
e-books, 227
Eckersley, Peter, 128
Edison, Thomas, 115–17, 135–6, 145–6
education, 151–2, 159–60, 187, 204–6, 249–53
Egypt, 5–6
Eiffel tower, 106, 144–5
Eisenstein, Elizabeth, 18–19, 47, 72
Eisenstein, Sergei, 138
electricity, 111, 120–1, 125, 150
Elizabeth I, 24, 34, 45
Elizabeth II, 8, 191
Elzevir family, 48, 54
e-mail, 245–6, 267
EMI, 143–4
Encyclopédie, 80, 91
Engels, Friedrich, 92, 115
ENIAC, 222
entertainment, 54–5, 151, 154, 160, 187, 204,
    228–9, 249, 256
Erasmus, 42, 63
Ericsson company, 145
Estienne, Henri, 19
etching, 31
European Broadcasting Union, 234
Eurydice, 253
Evans, Harold, 167
Evelyn, John, 27

Fairbanks, Douglas, 138
Falwell, Jerry, 202
fax, 218
FCC, 156, 179, 185–7, 189, 197–8, 206, 225–6,
    233, 237, 247
Federal Radio Commission, 179
Felix, Edgar, 131
Fenno, John, 162

Ferranti, Basil de, 222
Fessenden, Reginald, 128
festivals, *see* spectacle
fibre optics, 232
Fielding, Henry, 93
film, *see* cinema
Finland, 27–8, 235, 257
Fitch, John, 104
Fleming, Ambrose, 128
Florence, 35, 41–2, 47, 61, 75
Ford, Henry, 138, 149
Forest, Lee de, 128–9
forms, official, 58
Forrester, Jay, 226
FORTRAN, 226
fourth estate, 154
Fox News, 218, 260
Fox Talbot, William Henry, 133–4
Foxe, John, 63
France, 34, 38, 42–3, 54, 57–8, 70, 81–4, 90,
    113, 122, 124, 145, 156, 180, 195, 263, 280
Frankfurt Book Fair, 45
Frankfurt School, 200–1
Franklin, Benjamin, 94
Frederick the Great, 80
freedom of the press, 74, 81, 155–7, 210
French Revolution, 80–3
Friendly, Fred, 189
Fulton, Robert, 104

Gadaffi, President, 249
Galileo, 37
'gatekeepers', 54
Gates, Bill, 230, 247
Gaumont, 137, 140
Gay, John, 37
Gelernter, David, 244, 252–3
Geller, Henry, 218
gender, *see* women
Geneva, 43, 70, 132
Gengenbach, Pamphilus, 66
Germany, 13, 23–4, 35, 45, 62–8, 127, 136,
    138, 141–4, 149, 153, 174, 181, 195, 241,
    263
gesture, 31
Gibson, William, 253
Giddens, Anthony, 256
Gilligan, Andrew, 260
Gillray, James, 32
Gingrich, Newt, 247
Ginzburg, Carlo, 53
Giolito, Gabriel, 47
Giotto, 9
Gissing, George, 140

Giulio Romano, 43
Gladstone, William, 113–14
'global village', 1, 197
globalization, 213, 256–8
Goebbels, Josef, 174
Goethe, Johann Wolfgang von, 53, 80
Goody, Jack, 1, 10–11
Google, 264–5
Gore, Al, 217, 247
Gorki, Maxim, 136
Gove, Michael, 257
graffiti, 62, 74
gramophones, 145–7
Gramsci, Antonio, 92
'graphic revolution', 57
Gray, Elisha, 118
Greece, 6–8, 153
Greeley, Horace, 155
Greene, Sir Hugh, 192
Gregory the Great, 7
Griffiths, D. W., 138
Grub Street, 49
Guazzo, Stefano, 39
Gutenberg, Johann, 5, 13, 15

Habermas, Jürgen, 1, 60, 62, 83–5, 99, 164,
    187, 201
hack writers, 47, 49, 94
Halberstam, David, 248
Haley, Sir William, 177, 190
Hall, Stuart, 200
'hams', 126–7, 131–2, 162
Hancock, Tony, 192
Hand, Learned, 155
Hardy, Thomas, 215, 245
Harmsworth, Alfred, Lord Northcliffe, 148–9,
    154, 158, 165–9
Hartlib, Samuel, 14
Havas Agency, 110
Havelock, Eric, 6
Hays, Will, 138
Hayward, Sir John, 45
Hazlitt, William, 163
HDTV, 240
Hearst, William Randolph, 158
Henri II, 35
Henri III, 36, 69
Henry, William, 104
Herald Tribune, 172
Hertz, Heinrich, 124
Hickey, Neil, 218
'highway', 96, 111, 217
Hill, Rowland, 107
Himmelweit, Hilde, 198

Hirohito, Emperor, 181
Hitler, Adolf, 174–5, 267
Hobbes, Thomas, 54
Hobhouse, L. T., 168
Hofstadter, Richard, 167
Hogarth, William, 25, 37, 46
Hoggart, Richard, 199, 239
Hollerith, Herman, 224
Hollins, Timothy, 239
Hollywood, 136–9, 189, 241
Holmes, Oliver Wendell, 155
Home Service, 177, 183
Hoover, Herbert, 131, 188
Hopkinson, Tom, 171
'hot' media, 10, 197
Hudson, George, 103
Hugo, Victor, 7
Hulton, Edward, 171
Hume, David, 49–50
Hungary, 120–1
Hunt, Leigh, 158
Hus, Jan, 63
Huskisson, William, 102
Hussein, Saddam, 259
Hutton Report, 260
Huygens, Christiaan, 43

IBM, 224–6
iconoclasm, 7, 49, 68–71, 82
iconography, 7, 68
'iconotext', 37
Ignatius Loyola, St, 39
images, 7, 31–3, 41, 65–7, 69–70, 77, 79, 82
Index of Prohibited Books, 41–2, 57–8, 70, 77
India, 103–4, 111, 158, 203, 252, 258
information society, 210–13, 266
information, 15, 151, 188, 206–7, 249; *see also* monopolies of information
Innis, Harold, 1, 5–6, 10–11, 56
integrated circuit, 99
Intel, 223–4, 229, 264, 267
intellectual property, 46
'interactivity', 59, 217
Internet, 51, 214, 230, 244–8
IPC, 170
Iran, 11, 208
Iraq, 249, 259, 261
Islam, 7, 11, 14, 16, 68, 256, 258–61
ITA, 192–3
Italy, 124, 181, 195–6, 238, 263
ITU, 209, 241
ITV, 193, 264
Ivins, William M., 33

James II, 77–8
James, Henry, 159
Japan, 13, 85–6, 138, 145, 149, 153, 158, 172, 180–1, 194–5, 203, 205, 212–13, 224–6, 230–1, 236, 252, 267
Jobs, Steve, 229
Johnson, Samuel, 25, 49, 93, 94
Jonson, Ben, 35, 45
journalism, journalists, 164–5; *see also* newspapers
Jowell, Tessa, 261, 265

Karlstadt, Andreas von, 70
Katz, Elihu, 65, 200
KDKA, 130
Keillor, Garrison, 179–80
Kelly, David, 260
Kelvin, Lord, 117
Kempis, Thomas, 45
Khomeini, Ayatollah, 208
kinetoscope, 135
King, Cecil, 170
Knight, Charles, 86, 97, 161
Kodak camera, 134
Koenig press, 19, 91–2
Kondratieff, Nikolai, 95
Korea, 13, 231, 267
Kovach, Bill, 248
Kovacs, Ernie, 197
Kuhn, Thomas, 211
Kurosawa, Akira, 138
Kuwait, 249

Lafayette, Madame de, 51
Lafontaine, Jean de, 45
Lambert, R. S., 173
Landes, David, 89
Lang, Fritz, 138
Lardner, Dionysius, 88
Lasswell, Harold, 4–5, 203
Latin, 24, 30, 63
Latin America, 208, 194, 203, 239
Laud, William, 74–5
Lazarsfeld, Paul, 65
Le Bon, Gustave, 96
Lecky, W. E. A., 159
Lee, Robert, E., 163
Lefebvre, Georges, 24–5, 82
leisure, *see* entertainment
LeMahieu, D. L., 267
Lenin, Vladimir Illych, 174
Lerner, Daniel, 53, 183, 207–8
Lesseps, Ferdinand de, 105
L'Estoile, Pierre, 70

L'Estrange, Sir Roger, 15, 76
letters, 21, 27, 33, 39, 59, 106–7, 157, 177
Lévi-Strauss, Claude, 1
libraries, 6, 15, 187
Licklider, Joseph, 226
Light Programme, 177
Lippmann, Walter, 164
literacy, 9–11, 26–31
lithograph, 31, 166
Lloyd, Edward, 161
London, 29, 35, 41, 44, 49, 74, 108, 112, 136, 156, 161
Longmans, 50, 235
Lord, Albert, 6, 24–5, 40
Lotter, Melchior, 63
Louis XIII, 72
Louis XIV, 34, 38, 54, 57–8, 87, 96, 99
Louis XVI, 80, 82
Lowenthal, Leo, 51
Luce, Henry, 171
Ludendorff, Erich von, 75
Lufft, Hans, 63
Luhmann, Niklas, 1
Lumière, Louis, 136
Luther, Martin, 23–4, 35, 37, 62–8, 71
Lytton, Edward Bulwer, 162

Macaulay, Thomas Babington, 95, 154
McCarthy, Joe, 54, 76, 189
Machiavelli, Niccolò, 41–2
Machlup, Fritz, 211–12
MacLeish, Archibald, 171, 174
McLuhan, Marshall, 2, 1, 10, 16, 18, 149, 186, 197, 205, 209–10
Madrid, 21, 109
Maine, Henry, 159
Mâle, Emile, 7
Malraux, André, 140
Manchester, 92, 95, 157
Mandeville, Sir John, 53
Manuel, Nikolas, 66
manuscripts, 37, 68, 158
Manuzio, Aldo, 47, 54
maps, 19, 33, 48
Maraj, James, 250
Marconi, Guglielmo, 124–7, 132
Marey, Etienne, 135
Marie-Antoinette, 80, 82
market, 31, 39, 45–50, 93, 97, 110, 112, 115, 155, 159
Marvell, Andrew, 15
Marx, Karl, 91–2, 155
Massacre of St Bartholomew, 21, 70–1

'mass market', 97
'mass media', 23, 64, 96, 246
'mass politics', 73, 96
'masses', 4, 97, 108
Masuda, Yoneji, 212–13
Mather, Increase, 23
Maxim, Hiram, 149
Maxwell, James Clerk, 111, 124, 133
Mazarin, Jules, 73
medals, 57, 79
media events, 57, 200
media system, 19, 64, 82
Mee, Arthur, 120
Melba, Nellie, 168
Méliès, Georges, 136
Menocchio, 53
Mexico, 22–3, 27, 203, 239
mezzotint, 31
Michelangelo, 41
Microsoft, 230, 247, 265
Mill, James, 163
Mill, John Stuart, 163
Millar, Andrew, 50
Miller, Arthur, 45
Milosević, President, 249
Milton, John, 31, 74, 81
Minow, Newton, 197
Mirabeau, comte de, 81
Mitterrand, François, 196
mobile telephones, 242–3, 266
modernization, 4, 183, 207–8
monopolies of information, 6, 63, 92, 143, 160, 178, 246
Montaigne, Michel de, 14, 18, 42
Moore, Gordon, 224
Moore, Michael, 259
More, Thomas, 52
Morley, John, 166
Morse, Samuel, 111, 116, 133
Mosley, Sir Oswald, 169
'muck-raking', 3, 167
Mulgan, Geoff, 248
Murad III, 14
Murdoch, Rupert, 167, 170, 202, 235–6, 239, 260
Murrow, Ed, 173–4, 189
Muybridge, Eadweard, 135

Nadar, Félix, 145
Nagai, Michio, 209
Napoleon, 84, 90
Napoleon III, 94, 110
National Information Infrastructure, 247
NBC, 131, 185, 188, 190

Netherlands, the, 132, 144, 183–4, 235, 263;
    see also Dutch Republic
Netscape, 230
'network', 5, 215
New York, 81, 121–3, 155–6, 164
New Zealand, 108, 132, 250
Newman, John Henry, 102
Newman, Sydney, 192
Newnes, George, 158, 167
newspapers, 14, 27, 31, 45, 48, 72–4, 78–9,
    81–2, 91–2, 154–73, 200
newsreel, 171
Newton, Isaac, 25, 31
NHK, 180–1, 194–5, 205, 236, 252
Nicholas I, 113
Niepce, Joseph Nicéphore, 133
Nipkow, Paul, 141
Nixon, Richard, 202–3, 206
Noam, E. M., 244
Nokia, 266
Nora, Simon, 211
Nordenstreng, Karle, 208
Northcliffe, Lord, 148–9, 154, 158, 165–9
Norway, 172, 244
novels, 46, 51, 93, 159
Noyce, Robert, 223–4, 226
Nuffield, Lord, 148

O'Connor, Feargus, 157
Odhams, 170
Oersted, Hans Christian, 111
Ofcom, 263
Ogilby, John, 19
Oldenburg, Henry, 14
Olsen, William, 287
Olson, David, 19, 33
Ong, Walter, 10, 16, 21, 25, 38
Open Universities, 250, 252
Opitz, Martin, 31
orality, 6, 8, 10, 12, 23–6, 38–40, 79, 82
Ortelius, Abraham, 33
ORTF, 195
Orton, William, 118
Orwell, George, 211
Oscars, 187
Ottoman Empire, 14–15
outside broadcasting, 181

Page, C. G., 117
Paine, Thomas, 81
Paley, William, 131, 189
Palladio, Andrea, 19
pamphlets, 63–5, 72–4, 81
Panorama, 191

Paracelsus, 31
Paris, 21, 27, 35–6, 37–8, 41, 70, 72, 97, 106,
    109–10, 122, 133, 136, 144–5, 168, 195,
    201
Park, Robert Ezra, 164
Parry, Milman, 6, 24–5, 40
Pascal, Blaise, 44
PBS, 206, 263
PCs (personal computers), 227–8
Pearson, 264
Pearson, C. A., 168
Peel, Sir Robert, 163
Pepys, Samuel, 43
periodicals, 26, 46, 58–9, 79, 93, 161, 167,
    170, 181
Peru, 22
Peter the Great, 13
petitions, 28, 74
Petrarch, 9, 31, 41
Philadelphia, 134
Philip II, 21–2, 34, 72
Philips company, 144
phonograph, 145
photography, 69, 133–5
Pickford, Mary, 138
Pilkington Committee, 239, 247, 254
'piracy', 49, 68, 183, 241
plagiarism, 6, 46, 56–7
plays, 35, 41, 45, 66, 75, 80, 192
Ploman, Edi, 207, 250
Poland, 37
Pool, Ithiel de Sola, 210, 216
Pope, Alexander, 49
Popish Plot, 76–7
Popoff, A. S., 124
Porat, Marc, 210
pornography, 43–4, 96, 254
Portugal, 73, 263
Possevino, Antonio, 41
postal services, 21, 106–09, 240
posters, 57–8, 75
Postman, Neil, 198
Post Office, 113, 124, 128–9, 143
Prague, 132
preaching, 23–4, 64, 73, 78
Preece, Sir William, 117–18, 125–6
Preminger, Otto, 190
Prestel, 240–01
'print culture', 16, 55
prints, 31–3, 38, 65, 70, 75, 79, 82, 101
privacy, 54, 149, 167
'programme', 183
propaganda, 1, 57–8, 68, 72, 83, 174, 180
'pseudo-events', 57, 200

public opinion, 60, 62, 164
'public sphere', 3, 60–87, 187
'publish', 95
Pulitzer, Joseph, 164
Puskas, Theodore, 120
Putney Debates, 75

Rabelais, François, 41
radio, 3, 9–10, 49, 65, 88, 124–32, 140, 172–88,
    233, 243, 264
Radio Act, 1912, 127
Radio Caroline, 183
Radio 2, 183
Radio 4, 183
Radishchev, Aleksandr, 44
RAI (Italy), 181, 196
railways, 98, 100–4, 159
Raimondi, Marcantonio, 43
RAM, 224
Ramphal, Sonny, 250
ratings, 182–3
Raymond, Henry, 155
RCA, 127, 129, 142, 189
reading, 50–4, 187
recording, 181
Reith, John, 132, 169, 177–9, 188
Rejlander, Oscar, 135
Renan, Ernest, 88
repeatability, 33
Reuters, 110–12
Reynolds, G. W. M., 160
rhetoric, 1, 24, 30, 68
Richardson, Samuel, 93
Richelieu, Cardinal, 72
Richstad, Jim, 219
Riddell, Lord, 172–3
Righi, Augusto, 124
ritual, 8, 34, 66; see also spectacle
roads, 19–20
Robertson, William, 49
Robinson, Henry, 135
Robson, W. A., 178
ROMS, 223, 231, 257
Roosevelt, Franklin D., 176, 188, 219
Rosenstiel, Tom, 248
Rosing, Boris, 141
Rothermere, Viscount, 140, 169
Round, H. J., 128
Rousseau, Jean-Jacques, 53, 80
RTP (Portugal), 263
rumour, 24, 77, 82, 91
Rumsey, James, 104
Russia, 13–14, 26, 37, 44, 53, 113, 122, 132,
    138, 141–2, 174, 177, 233

11 September 2001, 258–9
Sacheverell, Henry, 78
Sade, marquis de, 43
Saint-Simon, 94
Sala, G. A., 156
Salutati, Coluccio, 62, 75
samizdat, 37–8
Sarnoff, David, 127, 129–31, 142, 186
Sarpi, Paolo, 44
satellite communications, 231–6
satire, 53, 65–6, 79, 192
Saudi Arabia, 242
scepticism, 59–60
Schiller, Herbert, 208, 212
Schilling, Pawel, 111, 113
Schramm, Wilbur, 219
Schumpeter, Josef A., 95, 99
Schwartzenberg, Roger-Gérard, 34
Scott, C. P., 156
Scripps, E. W., 158
Scudamore, Frank, 113
Seldes, Gilbert, 137, 177, 190
Selim I, 13
semaphore, 84, 109, 112
Senefelder, Aloys, 31
Sennett, Mack, 137
sensationalism, 55, 166–7
serials, 3, 185, 194, 198
sermons, 23–4, 64, 73, 78
Sesame Street, 198–9
Shaftesbury, Earl of, 77
Shakespeare, William, 45
Shibutani, Tamotsu, 77
ships, 21–2, 104–6, 117, 125
Shockley, William, 99, 222
Shoenberg, Isaac, 143
Shulman, Milton, 197
Sidney, Sir Philip, 37
silicon chips, 223
Silicon Valley, 100, 224
Singapore, 257
Sismondi, 163
sitcoms, 192
Skornia, Harry J., 204
Sky Television, 235
Smiles, Samuel, 152
Smith, Anthony, 172, 217
Smith, Ralph Lees, 236
Smith, W. H., 102
Smith, Willoughby, 141
'soap opera', 185, 194, 198
Soejatmoko, 250
Sony, 225, 236, 266, 268
sorcerer's apprentice model, 62, 73, 102

SOS, 125
Soviet Union, 37, 152, 174, 177, 180
Spain, 21–2, 34, 72, 195, 263
spam, 267
spectacle, 8, 34–5, 41, 82–3, 201
speech balloons, 3
Spencer, Herbert, 96, 99
Spinoza, Baruch, 50
sport, 120, 152–3, 160, 182, 194, 268
Springer, Axel, 181
Stalin, Josef, 174, 177
standardization, 18, 39, 56, 64
Stanhope iron hand-press, 19
Star Trek, 192
Stead, W. T., 166–7
steam power, 19, 91
Steele, Joseph, 26, 59
Steffens, Lincoln, 167
Stephenson, Rowland M., 103
Stevens, John, 104
Street, Brian, 11
Strowger, A. B., 119
'super-highway', 217
Sweden, 26–7, 122, 138, 144–5, 153, 172
Swift, Jonathan, 53
Switzerland, 106–7, 109, 112, 133, 182

Taliban, the, 259
Tanzania, 195
Tarde, Gabriel, 97
Tassis family, 21
Tauschnitz, 102
taverns, 65
Taylor, Bob, 226
'technology', 91
Tehranian, Majid, 208, 219
Telefon Hirmondo, 120
telegraph, 84, 109–17
telenovela, 194
telephones, 117–24, 242–3, 266
teletext, 239
televangelism, 202
television, 2, 8, 10, 34, 45, 92, 141–5, 170–2,
    182, 185, 188–97, 201–06, 218–20, 234–6,
    240, 314
Telstar, 232
Teresa, St, 51
Tesla, Nikola, 120
text messages, 243
Thackeray, William Makepeace, 102
Thailand, 196–7
theatre, 36, 49, 54–5, 81, 90, 96, 100
'themes', 6, 24, 40
Third Programme, 177, 183, 190

Thomason, George, 74
Thomson, Roy, 170
Time/Warner, 238, 245
Tintoretto, Jacopo, 2–3
Tocqueville, Alexis de, 97
Toynbee, Arnold, 99
trams, 135
Transactions of the Royal Society, 58, 79
transistors, 99, 183–5, 223
Trevelyan, George Macaulay, 159
Trollope, Anthony, 163
Turing, Alan, 222
Turkey, 11, 14, 109
Turner, J. W. M., 102
Turner, Ted, 239
Tyndale, William, 31, 69

UNESCO, 4, 207
United Nations, 109, 207
USA, 100–1, 108, 111–13, 115, 117–19, 122–3,
    126, 129–31, 136–9, 152–6, 158, 162, 164,
    167, 171, 176, 178–82, 185–6, 194, 217–18,
    219–20, 237–9, 241–5
USSR, 37, 152, 174, 177, 180

Vail, Theodore, 118, 123
Valentino, Rudolf, 138
VCRs, 225, 227, 241–2
Veblen, Thorstein, 97
Venice, 13, 35, 41, 42–3, 47, 51, 58
Veronese, Paolo, 41
Victoria, Queen, 112, 117, 125, 134
video cameras, 242
video games, 228–9
videophones, 242
Videotex, 240
Vietnam War, 204
Viewdata, 239–44
virtual reality, 230
Vodafone, 264, 266–7
Voltaire, 26, 80–1

Walkman, 225
Walter, John (I and II), 91
WARC, 233
Warner Brothers, 139, 190
Watergate, 206
Watson, Thomas, 117
Watt, James, 26, 88, 90
weather forecasts, 182
'web', 5, 215, 244–5
Weber, Max, 28
Wedgwood, Josiah, 90
Welles, Orson, 158, 174

Wells, H. G., 122, 143
Western Electric, 123, 130
Western Union, 113, 115, 117–18, 123
Westinghouse, 130–1
Wheatstone, Charles, 111–12
Wheldon, Huw, 182
Whitehouse, Mary, 193
Whitman, Walt, 101
Wiener, Norbert, 152
Wilkes, John, 79
William of Orange (William III), 78
William the Silent, 72
Williams, Raymond, 18, 199–200
Wilson, Harold, 170
Wilson, Woodrow, 129, 138
wireless, *see* radio
Wireless Telegraphy Act (1904), 128
women, 27, 51, 70, 73, 166, 186
Wordsworth, William, 91
World, 104, 164

World Congress on Wireless Telegraphy, 125
World Trade Center, 258
World War, Second, 123–4, 145, 168–70,
    173–4, 176–7, 183, 188–9, 222
World Wide Web, 245
Wozniak, Steve, 289
Wright, Frank Lloyd, 197
Wright, Thomas, 160

Xerox, 226

Yahoo, 264–5
Young, Brian, 194
Yugoslavia, 6, 25, 48, 206

Zhdanov, Andrei, 132
Zukor, Adolph, 138–9
Zuse, Konrad, 286
Zwingli, Ulrich, 64, 70
Zworkykin, Vladimir, 142